The Organization of Transport

Over the past ten years, the study of mobility has demonstrated groundbreaking approaches and new research patterns. Those investigations criticize the concept of mobility itself, suggesting the need to merge transport and communication research, and to approach the topic with novel instruments and new methodologies. Following the debates on the role of users in shaping transport technology, new mobility research includes debates from sociology, planning, economy, geography, history, and anthropology.

This edited volume examines how users, policy-makers, and industrial managers have organized and continue to organize mobility, with a particularly attention to Europe, North America, and Asia. Taking a long-term and comparative perspective, the volume brings together thirteen chapters from the fields of urban studies, history, cultural studies, and geography. Covering a variety of countries and regions, these chapters investigate how various actors have shaped transport systems, creating models of mobility that differ along a number of dimensions, including public versus private ownership and operation as well as individual versus collective forms of transportation. The contributions also examine the extent to which initial models have created path dependencies in terms of technology, physical infrastructure, urban development, and cultural and behavioral preferences that limit subsequent choices.

Christopher Kopper is Professor of Modern German History at the University of Bielefield, Germany.

Massimo Moraglio is a Senior researcher at the Technische Universitaet Berlin, Germany.

Routledge International Studies in Business History

Series editors: Ray Stokes and Matthias Kipping

For a full list of titles in this series, please visit www.routledge.com

1 **Management, Education and Competitiveness**
Europe, Japan and the United States
Edited by Rolv Petter Amdam

2 **The Development of Accounting in an International Context**
A Festschrift in Honour of R. H. Parker
T. E. Cooke and C. W. Nobes

3 **The Dynamics of the Modern Brewing Industry**
Edited by R.G. Wilson and T.R. Gourvish

4 **Religion, Business and Wealth in Modern Britain**
Edited by David Jeremy

5 **The Multinational Traders**
Geoffrey Jones

6 **The Americanisation of European Business**
Edited by Matthias Kipping and Ove Bjarnar

7 **Region and Strategy**
Business in Lancashire and Kansai 1890–1990
Douglas A. Farnie, David J. Jeremy, John F. Wilson, Nakaoka Tetsuro and Abe Takeshi

8 **Foreign Multinationals in the United States**
Management and Performance
Edited by Geoffrey Jones and Lina Galvez-Munoz

9 **Co-Operative Structures in Global Business**
A new approach to networks, technology transfer agreements, strategic alliances and agency relationships
Gordon H. Boyce

10 **German and Japanese Business in the Boom Years**
Transforming American management and technology models
edited by Akira Kudo, Matthias Kipping and Harm G. Schröter

11 **Dutch Enterprise in the 20th Century**
Business Strategies in small open country
Keetie E. Sluyterman

12 **The Formative Period of American Capitalism**
A materialist interpretation
Daniel Gaido

13 **International Business and National War Interests**
Unilever Between Reich and Empire, 1939–45
Ben Wubs

14 **Narrating the Rise of Big Business in the USA**
How Economists Explain Standard Oil and Wal-Mart
Anne Mayhew

15 **Women and their money 1700–1950**
Essays on women and finance
Edited by Anne Laurence, Josephine Maltby and Janette Rutterford

16 **The Origins of Globalization**
Karl Moore and David Lewis

17 **The Foundations of Female Entrupreneurship**
Enterprise, Home and Household in London, c. 1800–1870
Alison C. Kay

18 **Innovation and Entrepreneurial Networks in Europe**
Edited by Paloma Fernández Pérez and Mary Rose

19 **Trademarks, Brands, and Competitiveness**
Edited by Teresa da Silva Lopes and Paul Duguid

20 **Technological Innovation in Retail Finance**
International Historical Perspectives
Edited by Bernardo Bátiz-Lazo, J. Carles Maixé-Altés and Paul Thomes

21 **Reappraising State-Owned Enterprise**
A Comparison of the UK and Italy
Edited by Franco Amatori, Robert Millward, and Pierangelo Toninelli

22 **The Dynamics of Big Business**
Structure, Strategy and Impact in Italy and Spain
Veronica Binda

23 **Family Multinationals**
Entrepreneurship, Governance, and Pathways to Internationalization
Edited by Christina Lubinski, Jeffrey Fear, and Paloma Fernández Pérez

24 **Organizing Global Technology Flows**
Institutions, Actors, and Processes
Edited by Pierre-Yves Donzé and Shigehiro Nishimura

25 **Tin and Global Capitalism**
A History of the Devil's Metal, 1850–2000
Edited by Mats Ingulstad, Andrew Perchard, and Espen Storli

26 **The Power of Corporate Networks**
A Comparative and Historical Perspective
Edited by Thomas David and Gerarda Westerhuis

27 **The Organization of Transport**
A History of Users, Industry, and Public Policy
Edited by Christopher Kopper and Massimo Moraglio

The Organization of Transport
A History of Users, Industry, and Public Policy

Edited by Christopher Kopper and Massimo Moraglio

NEW YORK AND LONDON

First published 2015
by Routledge
711 Third Avenue, New York, NY 10017

and by Routledge
2 Park Square, Milton Park, Abingdon, Oxon OX14 4RN

First issued in paperback 2018

Routledge is an imprint of the Taylor & Francis Group, an informa business

© 2015 Taylor & Francis

The right of the editor to be identified as the author of the editorial material, and of the authors for their individual chapters, has been asserted in accordance with sections 77 and 78 of the Copyright, Designs and Patents Act 1988.

All rights reserved. No part of this book may be reprinted or reproduced or utilised in any form or by any electronic, mechanical, or other means, now known or hereafter invented, including photocopying and recording, or in any information storage or retrieval system, without permission in writing from the publishers.

Trademark Notice: Product or corporate names may be trademarks or registered trademarks, and are used only for identification and explanation without intent to infringe.

Library of Congress Cataloging-in-Publication Data

The organization of transport : a history of users, industry, and public policy /
    edited by Massimo Moraglio, Christopher Kopper.
        pages cm. — (Routledge international studies in business history ; 27)
    Includes bibliographical references and index.
    1. Urban transportation. 2. Transportation and state. I. Moraglio,
Massimo. II. Kopper, Christopher.
    HE305.O74 2014
    388—dc23
    2014028363

ISBN 13: 978-1-138-34071-8 (pbk)
ISBN 13: 978-0-415-74420-1 (hbk)

Typeset in Sabon
by Apex CoVantage, LLC

Contents

List of Figures	ix
List of Tables	xi

1 Introduction 1
CHRISTOPHER KOPPER AND MASSIMO MORAGLIO

PART I
Framing the issue: Manifestations of mobility over time and space

2 Clashes of Cultures: Road vs. Rail in the North Atlantic World during the Interwar Coordination Crisis 8
GIJS MOM

3 Half-Holiday Excursions and Rambling Clubs: How Did Leisure Shape the Mobilities of the Early Twentieth Century? 32
JILL EBREY

4 Towards a Better Understanding of Bicycles as Transport 49
PETER COX

5 Mobile Worths: Disputes over Streets 68
JIM CONLEY

PART II
Coming together: Urban mobilities in comparison

6 Urbanization and Transport Restructuring before World War II: A Comparison between London and Osaka 86
TAKESHI YUZAWA

viii *Contents*

7 Why the "Los Angelization" of German Cities Did Not
   Happen: The German Perception of U.S. Traffic Planning
   and the Preservation of the German City 106
   CHRISTOPHER KOPPER

8 Automobility, Utopia, and the Contradictions of Modern
   Urbanism, Concerning Karel Teige 118
   STEVEN LOGAN

9 The Conquest of Urban Mobility: The Spanish Case,
   1843–2012 135
   ALBERTE MARTÍNEZ AND JESÚS MIRÁS

10 Shifting Transport Regimes: The Strange Case of Light
    Rail Revival 155
    MASSIMO MORAGLIO

PART III
Moving forward: Present challenges and future perspectives

11 The Creation and Perpetuation of an Automobile-Oriented
    Urban Form: Dispersed Suburbanism in North America 173
    PIERRE FILION

12 Transportation Planning as Infrastructural Fix: Regulating
    Traffic Congestion in the Greater Toronto and Hamilton Area 195
    JOHN SAUNDERS

13 Move and Maintain: Mapping Multilocal Lifestyles
    in Hyderabad, India 216
    ANGELA JAIN AND GOWKANAPALLI LAKSHMI NARASIMHA REDDY

14 Dwelling in between? Multilocation between History and
    New Sociotechnical Systems 231
    HANS-LIUDGER DIENEL AND MASSIMO MORAGLIO

   Contributors 245
   Index 247

Figures

2.1	Gross capital creation in Dutch mobility infrastructure, 1921–1940, in constant guilders (× 1,000) of 1913 (from top to bottom in 1922: waterways, roads, railroads)	10
2.2	Buses and coaches and goods vehicles in the U.K., 1904–1939	12
2.3	Modal split in France, 1830–1970	20
2.4	Modal split in freight mobility in Germany, 1928–1938	24
6.1	Numbers of buses driven by horses and motors in London	88
6.2	Organization of UERL group	90
9.1	Total length (km) of tramlines in operation, according to their type of traction, 1892–1934	138
9.2	Current fare and fare in 1913 pesetas for A Coruña, 1903–1966	139
9.3	Tickets and journeys per inhabitant of A Coruña, 1903–1966	140
9.4	Travelers transported by tram, 1901–1930	140
9.5	Urban transport in Spain, 1948–2012, in millions of passengers	144
9.6	Inhabitants per car in Spain, 1972–2012	146
9.7	Wholesale real prices of electricity and petrol in Spain, in index numbers, 1935–1973	146
11.1	Circumstances and decisions associated with dispersed suburbanism (DS)	185
12.1	Map of proposed rapid transit network	201
12.2	Toronto's Transit City plan	203

Tables

6.1	Passenger journeys in Greater London (millions of passengers carried)	88
6.2	Comparison of UERL group and Metropolitan Railway in 1910	91
6.3	Tramways in the Greater London area controlled by LCC and UERL	91
6.4	Revenue and expenditure of tramways and omnibuses in 1923 (£000)	92
6.5	Traffic receipts and net revenues of principal undertakings, 1931 (£000)	92
6.6	Transport in Tokyo and Osaka in 1925	99
9.1	Length of tramlines (km) in Europe in 1895, according to the type of traction employed	137
9.2	Length of electric tramlines in Europe (in km), January 1, 1934	137
13.1	Growth trend of motor vehicles in Hyderabad	221

1 Introduction

Christopher Kopper and
Massimo Moraglio

Much like debates over technology, transport debates in academia and policy-making circles have largely been focused on innovation, production, and incremental trends. The ingenuity of inventors, the novelty of technologies, the organization of mass production, and the "progressive" impact of higher standards of mobility have been the focus of both researchers and political discussions. The history of transport was born, not by chance, as a subfield of economic history in which the main role was occupied by product innovations and producers' successes, all embedded in a progressive story tracing development from "poor" and "inefficient" preconditions to "smart" and "proficient" outcomes (Edgerton 2010).

In the past two decades, transport studies have been a part of a broader "cultural turn" that has witnessed not only different approaches to the topic, but even a shift from *transport* research to *mobility* studies, a conceptual reorientation that highlights an agenda shift. This has led to a corpus of texts (Kaufmann 2002; Mom 2003; Divall and Revill 2005; Sheller and Urry 2006; Cresswell 2006; Urry 2007; Merriman 2012, just to mention a few) driving the field to groundbreaking approaches and research methods. Those investigations criticized and historicized the concept of mobility itself, and suggested that transport and communication research should be merged and the topic should be approached through novel instruments and new methodologies. Following, to some degree, the debate during the 1990s on the role of users in shaping transport technology, different perspectives from sociology, planning, economics, geography, history, and anthropology are begging to be integrated into the field. Such a development has not only affected academia. Planners, policy-makers, and students of transport economy are facing a paradigmatic shift, too. The classical view of transport as a demand-driven process is crumbling under pressure from a new wave of studies that underline the complexity of the relationship between transport supply and demand (Mees 2010; Metz 2008; Bergmann and Sager 2008).

Following the outcome of the debate on user agency in the history of technology (Van der Vleuten 2006), the transport field is also recognizing the relevance of users in forming, shaping, and changing the mobility landscape, well beyond the classical concept of transport as a pure consequence

2 Christopher Kopper and Massimo Moraglio

of individuals' need to move from point A to B. Slowly, transport and mobility are becoming less and less dominated by engineers, planners, and research agendas related to large infrastructure projects. The role of users as full actors in the transport game is widely recognized not just in social science, but also by the industry (with respect to user involvement) and by policy-makers (with respect to public participation). Still, mobility remains a gendered space (Spain 1992) in which transport is too often misconstrued as a playground for enthusiastic "boys" and their "toys" (e.g., locomotives, big planes, or sports cars).

Users' tastes, culture, and background can play a role in how transport systems develop (or fail to develop). And, even more radically, users can organize their own mobility by shifting away from large industrial apparatuses, big infrastructural investments, and omnipresent industrial organizations. In other words, the research agenda is shifting from mobility apparatuses to user choices (Oudshoorn and Pinch 2003).

These issues were the focus of a workshop organized jointly by the German Historical Institute Washington (GHI), the Canadian Centre for German and European Studies (CCGES), and the Schulich School of Business, York University, Toronto, held in March 2012 in Toronto, Canada. The workshop, entitled "Models of Mobility: Systemic Differences, Path Dependencies, Economic, Social and Environmental Impact (1900 to tomorrow)," was convened by Matthias Kipping (Schulich), Christina Kraenzle (CCGES), and Christina Lubinski (GHI). This volume, which aims to examine the role of users, industry, and policy-makers in mobility development, not as separate agents with disparate outcomes, but rather as overlapping players with intersecting agendas and results, was one of its key outcomes.

It makes perfect sense to develop this topic in Routledge's "International Studies in Business History" book series. Transport history emerged as a branch of economic history, and studies of industry and business have dominated this field for a long time. Their overrepresentation in the literature led—following the "cultural turn"—to a backlash, the result of which was that industry and economic issues are today largely underrepresented in the field. Not only has industry and other institutional and business operators' role been under-researched, the entire sector of freight mobility seems to have been deserted by scholars, despite its potential and appeal for innovative scholarly investigations. We face the risk of throwing the baby (namely the role of economic factors) away with the bathwater (namely an obsession with industrial production).

In this vein, the title of this book, *The Organization of Transport*, should be read as part of a trend towards reintegrating forces that are currently marginalized in the transport debate. In other words, mobility studies has to avoid the epistemological pitfalls inherent to traditional approaches and to the field of new mobility studies. Traditional approaches to mobility held an essentialist view of transport systems and took for granted that they were used in a rational manner based on rational preferences. New Studies of Mobility invigorated the field of transport studies by taking cultural patterns and the agency of users into account. However, users' opportunity structures proved to be too complex to be reduced to simplistic supply and demand models. Mobility researchers agree that information deficits and "irrational" behavioral patterns affect the individual choices of transport users. But the cultural turn in mobility studies confronts researchers with similar epistemological challenges as the cultural turn in history and the social sciences. Culturally oriented choices and lifestyles must be analyzed *together* with "hard" socioeconomic factors and material infrastructures of transport.

This leads us to another overarching question: What role should history play in a volume about mobility? Transport, traffic, and mobility require—often, but not always—expensive infrastructures that have been planned and completed over long periods of time. Transport infrastructures grow slowly, are physically durable, and can only be altered over the long term. Infrastructures create path dependencies with long-term effects lasting more than a generation. Recent research on mobility has demonstrated that socially and culturally determined patterns of mobility also change slowly and show unexpected degrees of persistence (Geels et al. 2012). The same *long durée* trends also play a role in institutional regulations of transport and traffic, such as domestic market regulations, freedom (or lack of) in international exchanges, and even mundane and seemingly self-evident regimes such as official—and unofficial—traffic rules (Seiler 2008). Understanding these conditions is thus essential for understanding the present situation, whether scholars are historians by profession and familiar with the methods of historiography or not.

We feel that this volume offers a significant contribution to these studies by providing a long-term and comparative analysis of models of mobility that addresses the transportation of both passengers and freight over long, as well as short, distances. The volume, finally, examines how these models were shaped by consumer choices, market structures, political preferences, and policy decisions. The chapters in this volume demonstrate how initial choices and decisions led to long-term path dependencies that limited subsequent options. We are not alone in our quest. In recent years, there have been a number of similar studies, but these have tended to be more limited in their geographic and temporal scope (Badenoch and Fickers 2010), have focused on a single means of transportation (Norton 2008), or have dealt with single rather than multiple actors (Schiefelbusch and Dienel 2009).

This volume, therefore, focuses on how users, policy-makers, and entrepreneurs have organized, and continue to organize, mobility, with a particularly attention to Europe, North America, and Asia. Taking a long-term and comparative perspective, the volume brings together thirteen chapters from the fields of urban studies, history, cultural studies, and geography. Covering a variety of countries and regions, these chapters investigate how various actors have shaped transport systems, creating models of mobility that differ along a number of dimensions, such as ownership (public vs. private), operation (individual vs. collective), technical mode (motorized vs. nonmotorized), availability (affluence vs. scarcity), and hegemony (dominance vs. fringe position). The chapters also examine the extent to which initial models created path dependencies in terms of technological progress, evolution of physical infrastructures, varieties of urban development, and cultural and behavioral preferences in the use of transport that limited subsequent choices.

Researchers from disciplines such as sociology, political science, transport engineering, economics, history, and cultural studies have turned mobility into a field of interdisciplinary research par excellence. The multitude of methodological approaches in this volume and the diverse backgrounds of its contributors mirrors the interdisciplinarity of mobility studies. Because true interdisciplinarity would exceed the intellectual capabilities of a single contributor, the challenge of interdisciplinarity is mastered by the collaborative effort of a group of authors.

By covering a wide range of regions, including North America, Europe, and Asia, and by combining a historical framework with an analysis of current and future trends, the volume therefore fills an important gap within the mobility studies literature. This volume is one example of the growing tendency to overcome the former national parochialism of transport studies through a comparative perspective. The international diversity of paths in transport policies and patterns in the use of transport, as well as the manifold forms of transnational transfers of infrastructural models, varieties of ownership, and regulatory regimes, is striking. Transnational transfers and translations of foreign role models into different preferential orders often shaped national infrastructure policies and influenced national patterns of mobility. International comparisons are created by the compilation of national case studies that often enclose implicit and explicit references to foreign role models, parallel developments, adaptations, variations, and modifications in other parts of the world. This volume also contributes to the ongoing renewal of transportation studies in business and economic history, where the role of regulatory policies, the transport industry, and technological achievements had long dominated the research agenda. More recent studies (Fava 2012; Puffert 2009) have taken a broader approach by including consumers of mobility—an approach also espoused by this volume.

With respect to its specific themes and objectives, in geographic terms, the volume covers both developed economies, which struggle to modernize and integrate their aging infrastructures and reduce the environmental, social, and economic costs of mobility, and emerging economies, which often have to build new transportation systems to accommodate rapid urban growth and changing user preferences. In terms of the temporal dimension, the volume offers comparisons between constraints of the past, such as population growth, increased urbanization, and growing trade flows, and current environmental challenges in the transport field. In this respect, many of the contributions show that progress sometimes does not follow a linear path, but often takes a cyclical evolutionary course contrary to the expectations of contemporary actors. The book will therefore not only contribute to a better understanding of the various consequences of different historical models of mobility, but will also offer important insights for ongoing policy debates about the most appropriate models for the future.

The contributions to the volume are subdivided into three parts: The first part, entitled "Framing the Issue: Manifestations of Mobility over Time and Space," covers the evolution of general trends in mobility from a transatlantic prospective. It also touches on hidden histories and new trends in the transport field and in mobility behaviors. In his chapter, Gijs Mom gives new insights regarding the evolution of two divergent paths of mobility in the western world: the European and the American track. Mom demonstrates that major path decisions took place in the 1930s and should be primarily understood as representing cultural processes. Although Mom, like most transportation researchers, focuses on motorized road and rail traffic, the following two chapters by Jill Ebrey and Peter Cox highlight the importance and the potential of nonmotorized modes of transportation, namely walking and biking. Cox examines the long-term evolution of biking that began in the era before mass motorization. In his contribution, James R. Conley takes a novel approach, looking at mobility not based on the various modes of transportation, but from a spatial perspective by examining previously neglected conflicts between pedestrians and other users of urban street space. He shows, in particular, that, contrary to perceived wisdom, these conflicts existed prior to the rise of motorization.

The second part of the volume is entitled "Coming Together: Urban Mobilities in Comparison" and examines the influence of different modes of transportation on the evolution and use of urban spaces. Contributors adopt long-term perspectives and deal with parallel developments, knowledge transfers, and adaptations of transit modes. Comparing the origins of urban transport in London and Osaka, the chapter by Takeshi Yuzawa highlights how regional transport planning and the construction of mass transport systems were influenced by the international transfer of managerial knowledge and concepts. Based on the example of post–World War II Germany, Christopher Kopper demonstrates that mobility patterns and infrastructure concepts from the leading nation in individual motorization, the United States, were not implemented unchanged, but carefully and critically assessed and adapted to national conditions and preferences in West Germany. Steven Logan also looks at the role of ideas in shaping urban spaces by analyzing utopian concepts of mobility and urbanism developed by Czech intellectual Karel Teige and his contemporaries—a topic thus far overlooked by scholars of architecture and city planning. Taking a long-term perspective from the late nineteenth century to the present, Alberte Martínez and Jesús Mirás analyze the social construction of mobility technologies in a case study of

6 *Christopher Kopper and Massimo Moraglio*

urban transportation in Spanish cities. Examining changing perceptions of technological progress, Massimo Moraglio confirms the value of historical analysis by showing how a seemingly outdated mode of urban transport, the tram, underwent an unexpected revival due to its compatibility with the idea of pedestrian-friendly cities and the concept of shared street space.

The third part, "Moving Forward: Present Challenges and Future Perspectives," focuses on the current challenges of urban sprawl and how these are being addressed in different contexts. It also draws attention to emerging models of mobility, in which people do not simply live in one space and travel to another but rather dwell in between defined spaces. In their contributions, city planners Pierre Filion and John Saunders offer their perspective on current trends in transportation and mobility policies in North American metropolitan areas, the latter using Greater Toronto as a case study. The chapter by Angela Jain and G. L. N. Reddy also looks at a specific case, the city of Hyderabad in India. Focusing on the day-to-day living practices of rural migrants, they go beyond conventional migration studies that analyze the movement of people from one place to another, instead arguing that many people are simultaneously part of the city in which they reside and part of their place of origin. In a similar vein, Hans-Liudger Dienel and Massimo Moraglio investigate the recent phenomenon of hypermobility and multilocality resulting from changes in the temporal and spatial organization of work and shifts in work–life balance—a phenomenon that has yet to be researched by scholars in the fields of transportation and mobility.

THANKS

As editors, we would like to thanks all the participants in the "Models of Mobility: Systemic Differences, Path Dependencies, Economic, Social and Environmental Impact (1900 to tomorrow)" workshop held in March 2012 in Toronto, Canada. Above all, we are grateful to the workshop conveners—Matthias Kipping, Christina Kraenzle, and Christina Lubinski—who conceived and organized the meeting. We are also indebted to the German Historical Institute Washington, which provided a subvention for copyediting this volume.

WORKS CITED

Badenoch, A., and A. Fickers. *Materializing Europe: Transnational Infrastructures and the Project of Europe.* Houndmills, Palgrave Macmillan, 2010.

Bergmann, S., and T. Sager. *Ethics of Mobilities: Rethinking Place, Exclusion, Freedom and Environment.* Farnham, Ashgate, 2008.

Cresswell, T. *On the Move: Mobility in the Modern Western World.* London, Routledge, 2006.

Divall, Colin, and G. Revill. "Cultures of Transport: Representation, Practice and Technology." *Journal of Transport History* 26 (2005), p. 99–111.

Edgerton, David. "Innovation, Technology, or History What Is the Historiography of Technology About?" *Technology and Culture* 51 (2010), p. 680–697.

Fava, Valentine. *The Socialist People's Car*. Amsterdam, Amsterdam University Press, 2012.

Geels, F. W., R. Kemp, R., G. Dudley, and G. Lyons. *Automobility in Transition? A Socio-Technical Analysis of Sustainable Transport*. London, Routledge, 2012.

Kaufmann, V. *Re-thinking Mobility: Contemporary Sociology*. Aldershot, Ashgate, 2002.

Mees, Paul. *Transport for Suburbia. Beyond the Automobile Age*. London/Washington DC, Earthscan, 2010.

Merriman, Peter. *Mobility, Space, and Culture*. London, Routledge, 2012.

Metz, D. "The Myth of Travel Time Saving." *Transport Reviews* 28 (2008), p. 321–336.

Mom, Gijs. "What Kind of Transport History Did We Get? Half a Century of JTH and the Future of the Field." *Journal of Transport History* 24 (2003), p. 121–138.

Norton, Peter D. *Fighting Traffic: The Dawn of the Motor Age in the American City*. Cambridge MA, MIT Press, 2008.

Oudshoorn, N., and T. Pinch. *How Users Matters: The Co-construction of Users and Technologies*. Cambridge MA, MIT Press, 2003.

Puffert, D. *Tracks across Continents, Paths through History*. Chicago, University of Chicago Press, 2009.

Schiefelbusch, Martin, and Hans-Liudger Dienel (eds.). *Public Transport and Its Users. The Passenger's Perspective in Planning and Customer Care*. Farnham, Ashgate, 2009.

Seiler, C. *Republic of Drivers: A Cultural History of Automobility in America*. Chicago, The University of Chicago Press, 2008.

Sheller, M., and John Urry. "The New Mobilities Paradigm." *Environment and Planning A* 38 (2006), p. 207–226.

Spain, D. *Gendered Spaces*. Chapel Hill, University of North Carolina Press, 1992.

Urry, John. *Mobilities*. Cambridge, Polity, 2007.

Van der Vleuten, E. "Understanding Network Societies. Two Decades of Large Technical System Studies." In: E. Van der Vleuten and A. Kaijser (eds.), *Transnational Infrastructures and the Shaping of Europe,1850–2000*. Sagamore Beach MA, Science History publication, 2006, p. 279–314.

2 Clashes of Cultures
Road vs. Rail in the North Atlantic World during the Interwar Coordination Crisis

Gijs Mom

INTRODUCTION

In 1931 the International Chamber of Commerce (ICC), which was located in Paris but held its annual congress in Washington, D.C., adopted a resolution launching an investigation "to determine the effects of the development of motor traffic upon railroad traffic in its various classes" and "to consider the nature of the resulting modifications which may be desirable in the fundamental principles governing the railroad rate schedules." Two years later, a committee of independent experts finished an introductory report, followed in 1935 by an overview publication entitled *Road and Rail in Forty Countries.*

Although the resolution restricted the proposed measures to railroads, a Dutch commentator from the bus and truck sector lamented that the ICC introductory report was "pro railroad." This conflict over the role of road mobility can be seen as symptomatic for what has been called the "coordination debate" or the "coordination crisis" during the interwar years, a "struggle of the systems" that in a way is still ongoing. Equally symptomatic was the ICC's failure to synthesize or analyze this very complicated struggle: The end report was a long parade of regulatory measures and legislation in thirty-seven countries that had responded to the survey. The ICC was hardly exceptional in this respect. When the League of Nations published its *Enquiry Addressed to Governments* in 1938 as an overview of the international coordination crisis, it could not do any better. The report contained a large table listing all measures per country without any synthesis or analysis of the data.

Despite the highly technical nature of both overviews, which must have discouraged generations of historians from trying to get a grip on this elusive topic, the ICC's report reveals two interesting aspects. First, the brief introduction to the report contained terms and concepts that hitherto had been mostly absent in "railway language," such as "consumer," and the authors of the report resolved to look upon "the road and rail question (not) merely as a transport problem, but . . . from the standpoint of the general economic welfare." Second, the ICC report (just like the League's report) displayed a willingness to analyze the coordination crisis as a fundamentally international problem.

The international "credit crisis," which started in 2008 and has since taken the form of a global crisis of neoliberalism, seems to make the questions addressed in this chapter very timely indeed. As this chapter will show, the coordination crisis was nothing less than a dichotomy between two different societies with two different mobility systems. The central (and centralizing) state saw this struggle as a justification for intervention, which was invited by some of the actors themselves. Others promoted the "freedom of the road," advocating the beneficial effects of the market rather than state intervention. After the Second World War, the debate raged on, now under the guise of regulation versus liberalism. Since liberalism as a concept is once again under scrutiny, the principle question will be whether we will see a new phase of regulation in the context of the road–rail controversy in the twenty-first century.

Historians have analyzed the "coordination debate" before,[1] but thus far their works are national in scope (in great contrast to the debate itself) and are dominated by economic discourse. Only very recently, two studies promise to break open this narrow national perspective (Sjöblom 2007; Schlimm 2011). This chapter, which takes the Dutch motorbus industry, and especially the truck industry, as a case study, is another effort to overcome both drawbacks in the historiography. At the same time, its aim is to provide a model of transnational history writing not limited to supranational flows and institutions, but based on local evidence (Mom 2009).

TWO SYSTEMS COLLIDING

The Dutch mobility infrastructure illustrates how, despite political and technical bias towards older systems, road building during the 1920s emerged gradually as an infrastructural element (Figure 2.1).

A similar situation is seen with motorbuses, whose numbers increased dramatically during the 1920s. Until 1926 these "wild" (unregulated) buses operated in a pure *laissez-faire* market environment. Dutch road censuses during the 1920s indicate that the increase in "intensity of use" (expressed as the number of vehicles passing road census counting points) was by far the highest for buses, higher even than that for bicycles. At their zenith in 1939, buses constituted one-third of general passenger road mobility. When compared to the United States (where only 3% of total passenger kilometers were "produced" by the motorbus, despite more frequent and longer personal trips), this performance is all the more impressive (de Graaff 1948).

In 1926, the government tried to protect its investment in railways (and those of the regional and local governments in their tramway systems) by prohibiting outright competition between buses and tramway companies, forcing bus operators to acquire a license if they wanted to start a scheduled

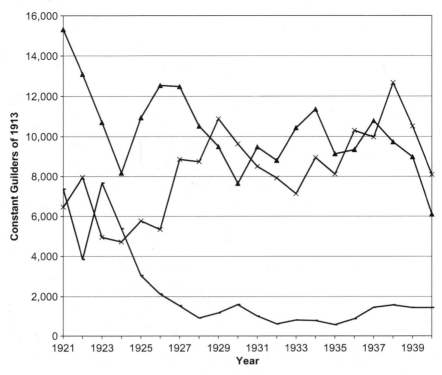

Figure 2.1 Gross capital creation in Dutch mobility infrastructure, 1921–1940, in constant guilders (× 1,000) of 1913 (from top to bottom in 1922: waterways, roads, railroads)

service. However, because provinces issued the licenses, the interests of the national railways and the municipal tramways were often bypassed, so much so that hundreds of bus routes mushroomed, especially in the less dense northern provinces (Stieltjes 1933).

The regulation of 1926 could not stem the tide of "wild buses" for two reasons. First, illegal regular services survived because bus riders were willing to support operators and drivers in unexpected ways. For instance, passengers on illegal bus lines were willing to sign a document declaring that they were enjoying "excursions," which were exempted from the 1926 regulation. Most bus travel was local; the first long-distance regular bus service began in 1935 between Amsterdam and Rotterdam, a distance of sixty kilometers. Although the total number of trips in the Dutch public transport sector remained more or less constant in the 1930s, the share of motorbus trips increased from 5% to 31%, indicating a direct substitution for tramway use. Because of the capacity increase in the bus system, the growth in the number of bus passengers was even more spectacular, from 10 million in 1924 to 154 million in 1939 (P.H. 1940; Stieltjes 1933). In other words, buses helped lure tramway riders towards a "road experience," expanding the societal base of the road lobby considerably.

Secondly, and ironically, the 1926 regulation forced outlaw bus operators to offer irregular, long-range, tourist trips. To this end, a Dutch auto body manufacturing industry emerged, first copying the American touring car concept and then developing native designs. One of the larger operators, VIOS in the small town of Wateringen, had a fleet of seventy touring cars that were only used during the summer months. The fleet "produced" annual mileages of 15,000 to 19,000 kilometers per vehicle (A.C.Q. 1939). Beginning in the 1930s, an international bus tourism industry developed, laying the basis for a special relationship between Dutch travelers and motorbuses after World War II, when the Netherlands—until it was overtaken by France in the early 1950s—had one of the largest fleets of motorbuses per capita in the world, after the U.K. and the United States. (Rocholl 1962).

Inhabitants of Amsterdam were the dominant users of tour buses, and, in general, tour bus companies were located in the big cities, whereas regular, short-range bus firms tended to be found in the smaller cities and villages. Women made up the majority of customers. To counteract ruinous competition among themselves, operators founded a Central Office for the Promotion of Touring Car Travel (CEBUTO) in 1933, which organized "merry evenings" during the winter months, during which "songs at the piano" were played, "a chorus of cooperating drivers" sang, and movies were shown about distant countries.[2]

No doubt, similar situations can be found in other countries, but, like the truck, the motorbus does not enjoy much favor among mobility historians (Sjöblom 2007). In Belgium, for instance, "dozens of improvised buses" from the Netherlands invaded the nation's densely populated northern provinces, which were badly covered by the steam tram, provoking legislation in 1923 requiring licenses for operators, followed by a second law a year later that protected the interests of the national railroads much more effectively than in the Netherlands. As in the Netherlands, however, only during the second half of the 1930s was a true "coordination regulation" reached, which put about 40% of all licensed bus lines in the hands of the regional railway company (Weber 2008).

The U.K. appears to be the European nation in which regulations on buses were most effective, as Figure 2.2 suggests. Although the number of British truck expanded continually during the entire period, the number of buses and coaches declined drastically in 1925, and then stabilized during the remainder of the period. This decline took place well before the British Road Traffic Act of 1930, which introduced a rigorous licensing system resulting in "a controlled monopoly" that lasted until the 1980s (Sjöblom 2007; Hibbs 1968; Mulley 1983).

By contrast, German passenger transport coordination did not develop as abruptly as in the U.K. The Road Transport Services Act of 1928 exempted the *Reichspost* from licensing. But here, as in the U.K., the trend favored

12 Gijs Mom

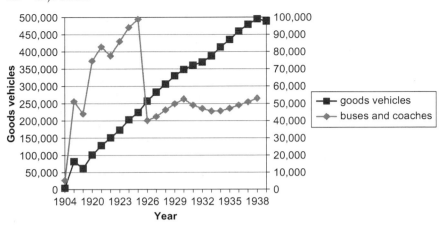

Figure 2.2 Buses and coaches and goods vehicles in the U.K., 1904–1939
Source: Savage, 144–145, Tables V and VI

road mobility that was "more similar to railway traffic." *Autobahnen* were given regular bus services as soon as stretches were complete, but the Nazi holiday organization, *Kraft durch Freude*, mainly employed trains for its cheap collective excursion programs (Sjöblom 2007; Vahrenkamp 2007).

Little is known about how many people used buses for tourism in the United States. Incidental evidence suggests that there, too, transcontinental bus tours became an important part of the road tourism movement. In 1934, one-third of the 25,000 buses, which were owned by 3,500 operators and carried about half as many passengers as railways over a network of 350,000 miles, operated on interstate routes. These were hardly affected by the Motor Bus Industry Code of self-regulation introduced during the New Deal by the Interstate Commerce Commission. By the end of the 1920s, it took five-and-a-half days to cross the country by bus. Trip lengths for passengers (which averaged 71 miles) fell between those of Class I railroads (about 50 miles) and Pullman trains (340 miles).[3]

Motorbuses added a crucial "mode" to the "modal split" (the division over four modes—rail, road, water, and pipelines—of all freight and passengers transported) of road mobility, strengthening the road lobby against the rail lobby considerably, although the real threat to railways was not so much the bus but the passenger car (Mom and Filarski 2008; Sjöblom 2007). This became clear when a new type of driver joined the growing ranks of road users: the businessman with a clear trip destination who decisively began to reject using trains for reaching his destination. If a correlation ever existed between the number of cars and the quality and expanse of the road network (which clearly was *not* the case before the 1930s) (Mom 2004), then it was in this period that business interests discovered the straight, unhampered road as an alternative to the railroad. This can not only be substantiated by national (and often nationalized) railroad companies' loss of many first-class and subscription passengers, but also by sporadic road censuses indicating a dramatic increase in annual mileage per car. This has been revealed most convincingly for the Netherlands, where, from the early 1930s, average mileage started to rise dramatically, indicating that business-people had discovered the car. This anomaly lasted until the 1950s, when pleasure use regained dominance (Mom and Filarski 2008). In other words, only when the road/car system gained a railway-like character did trains start to lose customers (Mom 2005).

For the Netherlands, then, the resulting "automobile system" was fully developed on the eve of the Second World War. This was facilitated through a careful strategy employed by the national government that encouraged automobile and touring clubs as well as other "traffic associations" to cooperate and left the bulk of the railroad system largely intact. Similar conclusions may be drawn from other North Atlantic countries, including the United States (here, though, auto clubs played a much more modest role and car manufacturers played a much greater role). On the other side of its mobility spectrum, however, the Dutch mobile culture was largely characterized by its slowness: as late as 1939, in terms of passenger-kilometers, bicycling still dominated the nation's mobility culture. In France, too, users favored bicycles over motorbuses, but cars had overtaken bicycles in popularity (Orselli 2009). Comparable high figures of cycle use are also reported for the U.K. based on analyses of road censuses (Sjöblom 2007).

THE EMERGENCE OF THE TRUCK

Just like its counterparts in the passenger mobility sector, the highly atomized, fledgling post-World War I truck sector was considered to be "wild" and "anarchistic" by existing transport interests. Among the state's civil servants, trucks equipped with solid-rubber or even iron tires acquired a bad reputation as destroyers of roads (Trischler 1997). As in other European countries, trucks experienced a spectacular increase in popularity in the Netherlands. Truck usage increased fifteenfold between 1923 and 1935, from 52 to 750 million ton-kilometers, spurred during the 1920s by an increase in truck numbers and during the subsequent decade by growth in loading capacity and speed (Jongma 1992). The expansion of the truck fleet was such that in 1932 the Netherlands (together with Belgium and Japan) had the highest share of trucks (37%) amongst road vehicles in all motorizing countries, about 10% more than most other European countries (and three times the share of American trucks with respect to all motor vehicles) (Weber 2008). Road censuses in 1923 and 1929 on the primary road network revealed that their use had increased by a factor of ten (against a factor of six for passenger cars) (Tiepen 1936).

Many of the truckers were recruited from horse-drawn, urban courier and haulage services as well as intercity delivery services (*bodediensten*).

14 *Gijs Mom*

The prominent role of the Dutch inland navigation system in the "modal split" not only lowered the volume of freight hauled by domestic railroads, but also made it easier for trucks to enter the transport market, aided in part because inland shippers during these years suffered from a permanent state of crisis. More than a few of the single-owner truckers were impoverished barge skippers who bought a cheap truck as a means to make additional income on the side.

This new, "wild" segment of the motorized road freight sector thus started to become a real threat to the production and trade companies that hitherto had used horse traction and were starting to motorize themselves. And although such firms soon dominated the sector (70% of the Dutch truck fleet and 60% of its loading capacity—were on "own account" [*eigenvervoer*]), this share decreased to 63% in 1939 (and 50% in terms of loading capacity). By then half of all ton-kilometers were generated by commercial truckers, because they made longer trips with fewer empty returns. More than half of the eight thousand Dutch road transport companies were one-man businesses, making average delivery trips of only twenty-three kilometers, whereas one-third of all trips were intercity hauls with an average trip length of sixty kilometers. Urban delivery trucks, most of them on their own account, generated most of these trips by far.[4] Measured by weight in tons, the truck overtook both inland navigation and railways during the first half of the 1930s, but rail had never outpaced waterborne haulage in the Netherlands in terms of tons of freight transported.

The most important reason for the low share (in comparison with other European countries) of trucking on "own account" was the fully unregulated road transport market (the only regulation regarded maximum axle weights), so much so "that any company that could hire commercial transport, would do so, because competition had diminished transport costs to a ridiculous level." Whereas production and trading companies bought their trucks from the European truck manufacturers who kept to the letter of the Dutch law in their axle configuration, small commercial truckers often bought their trucks from the blossoming rebuilding industry (Greebe 1949; Mom 2014). This conclusion is supported by developments in Germany, where trucking for own account was also untouched, but where commercial trucking was curtailed from its very start shortly after the war.

Unlike to the bus sector, the Dutch truck fleet continued to grow (albeit in smaller numbers) during the Depression years. This was not only true for the highly atomized commercial truck fleet, but also for some large fleet owners on own account, such as the Dutch post authorities and the road hauler *Van Gend en Loos* (with a history reaching back into the *diligence* era), which was taken over in 1928 by the Dutch National Railways.[5]

In all other industrializing countries, too, truck use exploded after the First World War, fuelled initially by surplus wartime trucks, but soon supported by considerably expanded manufacturing facilities. Trucking introduced new transport functions, such as door-to-door transport (without much transshipment) and agricultural transport of perishable commodities (Bureau of Public Roads 1927). The latter transport function seems to have been particularly important in the emergence of American trucking, where, in addition to perishable goods, cotton also formed an important truck load. In Ohio in 1926, more than a quarter of all hauls were for agricultural purposes, the largest share after the 56% of hauls for "products of manufacture." With nearly one million trucks in 1930, American farmers formed the largest group of truck owners, followed by owners of wholesale distribution trucks and retailers. By 1932, two-thirds of the American truck fleet belonged to one-man firms. At the time, 2.2 million Americans drove their *single* truck, most of them as "private carriers" (Childs 1985; Moulton 1933). In 1936 farmers bought a quarter of trucks produced in the United States. Due to a largely unregulated road freight sector, "wildcat" truckers were everywhere. "Farm boys and young men from country villages," male "southern whites" in particular, prepared to work long hours for very low wages, nurturing "an intense individualism . . . that challenged the labor and regulatory structures of New Deal economic liberalism," including the powerful labor unions. The 1935 Motor Carrier Act tried to protect the interests of the large haulers and the unions, with little success, as we will see later (Hamilton 2008).

In Germany, quite the opposite was the case. Right after the war, the trucking sector was highly regulated, the result of the state transport structure during the war. State-owned trucking companies (*Kraftverkehrsgesellschaften*, [KVG], "nothing more than war companies"), supported by *Länder* and provinces, helped Germany through a series of crises in the railroad sector, including strikes, coal shortages, the conflict over the Ruhr area, and strains on railroad finances due to reparations required under the Versailles Treaty. With nearly three thousand trucks in 1920 (most of them war surplus) and one thousand trailers, divided over fourteen *Kraftverkehrsämter* (Road Traffic Offices), the KVGs were not subject to taxation and were considered to be an adjunct to the railroads. From its onset, intercity trucking was dependent on licensing and effectively contributed to the development of an "automobile system by encouraging a network of cooperating companies to spread impressively across the country.[6]

Germany's independent truck fleet was much larger than the independent fleet in the Netherlands (80% in 1930, most of them delivering no further than fifty kilometers). Statistics about delivery truck ownership (under two thousand kilograms) reveal that this fleet grew tenfold during the 1920s to 89,000 light trucks. Only in 1931 did an emergency measure (*Notverordnung*) distinguish between professional and independent hauling. The former group set up cooperative express associations (such as the *Gemeinschaft deutscher Kraftwagenspediteure* [Gedekra], in 1929 and the *Reichsverband Deutscher Auto-Ferntransport-Unternehmer* [RDF]), to protect themselves against the one-man-one-truck wildcatters, whose activities increased during the Depression. Only the Nazi regime managed to establish "order"

16   *Gijs Mom*

by creating, through a law on long-range truck transport (*Gesetz über den Güterfernverkehr mit Kraftfahrzeugen,* 1935), a so-called *Zwangsverband* (coercive association) of the *Reichs-Kraftwagen-Betriebsverband* (RKB) (Vahrenkamp 2010). A recent comparison between the German and the British coordination practices revealed that the structure of the truck fleets in both countries differed substantially, reflecting the differences between these "societies" in both sociocultural and economic respects. Whereas it took longer in Germany to replace the horse, light trucks (mostly used for retail delivery tasks) were underrepresented in the German fleet compared to the U.K., while the number of heavy trucks did not differ very much between both countries. Most of these differences were wiped out after 1933, when Germans' use of trucks exploded again (Sjöblom 2007). Originally, representatives of the "old" transport systems were not alarmed by the rapid expansion of the trucking sector. They saw the truck as a potential extension to their geographical coverage (as feeders and distributors) and counted on national governments to protect them from any competition that might jeopardize their monopoly.

Railroad officials' self-confidence seemed well-founded, because most national railroad companies came out of the war with significant prestige. Often belonging to a select group of the largest companies in the country (if not *the* largest, such as in Germany, with one million employees), the railroads' special tariff structure had enabled them to construct networks covering entire nations, such that the most remote customer could count on "fair" transport costs that depended upon the value of the freight alone. An elaborate system of exceptional (discount) tariffs, developed during the previous decades, softened this so-called *ad valorem* system and supported a social and economic state policy of industrialization and spatial development. Social, spatial, and industrial politics became both personally and theoretically intertwined with national transport policy. For instance the principle of *Gemeinwirtschaft* (common or public economy) in Germany assumed that certain state functions intrinsically belonged to the "public sphere." Whether state owned or not, railways, at least in continental Europe, were considered to belong in the public sphere, implying that they had a legal duty to offer transport to all customers and that their tariffs had to be published and widely disseminated. Regional and local networks of lighter railways, built since the 1880s, completed these national systems. However, it was at this level that the first indications of serious problems came to the fore. During and shortly after the war, railway companies began to run deficits because they had to adapt to extensive social changes related to the eight-hour day and the forty-hour week. They were prevented from increasing their tariffs to cover these financial burdens, although, which, in turn, perpetuated a tradition of underinvesting in innovative technologies (such as electrification).

That may have spurred state officials to rethink the role of railroads in a changing society. The emergence of the truck helped to catalyze this process, both because it began to undermine the seemingly solid system of state regulation and also because it represented a different system of transportation for a new type of society. Two phenomena were at the root of the pending crisis. First, the synchronized growth of both industrial production and railroad traffic during the second half of the nineteenth century became decoupled during the interwar years, partly because of productivity gains in the industrial sector and partly because demand for coal as a source of energy declined and its replacement, oil, could be transported by pipeline (Lippert 1999). Second, the productive sector underwent a deep structural change. In most Western European countries, industrial employment numbers passed those of agricultural employment during the 1920s (except for the Netherlands where the service sector was more important, which made the country comparable to the United States), whereas heavy industry's share of the gross national product declined relative to light industry. As a herald of a new mobility system, if not an entirely different society, the truck represented the decentralization of industry, the increasing need to transport small volumes of commodities rather than large carloads of bulk goods ("less-than-carloads" [LTC] in railway managers' jargon) and a productivity increase in the agricultural rather than the heavy industry sector (Rohde 1999; Fischer 1987; Sjöblom 2007). In short, the truck represented a society in which liberalism and marginal cost calculations were more important than central-state regulation and spatial policy based on an *ad valorem* transport system. From this perspective it should not surprise us that the International Chamber of Commerce in its 1935 report oscillated between the two systems (Vahrenkamp 2008). In an era in which *laissez-faire* liberalism was under severe criticism, even the *Reichsverband der Deutschen Industrie* "did not advocate free enterprise in transportation" (Kopper 2009).

This is all the more surprising if one realizes that transport expertise, at least in Europe, was dominated by a railway bias. Inspired by an economist's rationale, expert analyses often neglected road transport, because this did not substantially add to national wealth. A good example is the work of the British Institute of Transport, founded in 1919. Similarly, in the Netherlands, the leading transport professor, F. de Vries, neglected the role of road mobility in his findings. The bias was also caused by the completely different ways that experts approached the respective modalities. As a British journal concluded in 1921, "there is no means of correlating the views and knowledge of railway, motor, tramway, electric vehicle, and other engineers engaged on special phases of the one great problem of efficient movement" (Schlimm 2011: 93, 106; Mom and Filarski 2008: 168).

COORDINATION MEASURES IN THE 1920S AND THE DESIRE FOR "ORDER"

Although the emergence of the truck followed similar patterns in most industrializing countries, the solutions to the perceived crisis differed considerably

18   *Gijs Mom*

between these countries. Because the truck transported high-value goods in small quantities, it ran counter to the time-honored railway principle of internally subsidizing cheap bulk goods, which were often transported over long distances for low tariffs, with more expensive smaller units, which were transported over shorter distances for high tariffs. There seems to be a consensus in the coordination historiography that the truck, to a large extent, created new modalities for transporting goods, but it cannot be denied that the truck did hurt railroads' monopolies. For instance, in France trucks took nearly half of the medium-range coal and sand traffic from trains, but for distances less than 150 kilometers transportation of these bulk goods was left entirely to the railroads (Renouard 1960).

One obvious answer to the threat posed by trucks was to incorporate them into the railroad's network by replacing horse- and human-drawn, short-distance feeder and distribution functions with motorized means, at least as far as railroads were allowed to do so. It seems that this strategy was more successful, at least in some countries, for the passenger transport market. Railroads' most effective strategy was to start their own bus and truck divisions. This failed in the Netherlands largely because of the liberal coordination policy, but the strategy was highly successful in Switzerland, Germany (both with their protected mail bus systems), and the U.K. Despite trying to beat "the enemy" with its own means, the situation for most national railroad companies worsened in the 1930s, and they intensified lobbying campaigns for protectionism. This is why historiography often puts the start of coordination in the 1930s, while in reality the battle of the systems started in earnest at the beginning of the 1920s. In many countries the conflict led to some form of state regulation only during the 1930s, after initial, often futile, passenger transport regulations had been imposed in the 1920s. However, a recent study of Germany and the U.K. concludes that a "thorough reform was never seriously on the agenda" (Shrapnell-Smith 1946: 222). Judging coordination policy a "failure" on the basis of such conclusions would, however, put too much emphasis on the historical actors' expectations, and would narrow historical analysis down to a policy perspective based on transport economics. On top of that, it seems that in one country this policy *was* effective. Germany, through its constantly hostile *Reichsverkehrsministerium* (with its responsibility for the railways), "marginalized" the trucking sector, and the number of licensed trucks only rose to 10,600 vehicles in 1938 (accounting for 2.8 billion ton-kilometers, against 76 billion by the railways) (Vahrenkamp 2010). Therefore, the German interwar trucking sector deserves much more international scholarly interest, especially in relation to its authoritarian and National Socialist context.

Despite Great Britain's reputation for *laissez-faire* policies and the "strange paralysis of British law-makers" seen during an earlier period, coordination also appeared there. When the Select Committee on Transport began to study transport competition in 1918, its judgment was crystal clear: "In this country it is unquestionable that all other forms of internal transport are subordinate and ancillary to the railroad system." Government circles no doubt were largely on the side of the railroads, and trucks were more heavily taxed per horsepower than passenger cars, so much so that by the end of the 1920s some horse transport reappeared in the streets. One of the factors that weakened the cause of railroads was that they were simply unable to calculate what exactly they had lost to road transport. When the railroads appealed to the government for protection, the latter first followed the strategy of inviting the sector to organize its own coordination by establishing Area Transport Authorities. When the fragmentation of the road transport sector did not seem to diminish, two consecutive commissions were asked to study the road–rail controversy, including the questions of how large the threat was of long-range road transport and how fierce the competition was from small teamsters and from own-account transport. The Royal Commission on Transport (1928–1931) issued two reports, which not only strongly opposed the construction of motorways, but also formed the basis for the formulation of the Road Traffic Act of 1930. These regulations limited trucks to twenty miles per hour, a direct blow to long-range road traffic. When the third and final report (1931) left the whole controversy unresolved, however, a second commission, the Road and Rail Committee (better known as the Salter Conference, after the chair of its 1932 meeting), again put the emphasis on self-coordination.

The British coordination of freight mobility revealed what may be true for most national coordination debates: The "small man" was excluded from the deliberations, and the same was true for the "user." The Salter Conference's recommendations were adopted in the Road and Rail Traffic Act in 1933, which authorized the creation of regional Licensing Authorities for Goods Vehicles, whereas the Finance Act of the same year had introduced higher vehicle duties. The coordination regulation was the result of a coalition of railroad and trucking interests working to combat the "anarchy" and "cut-throat competition" of the 1920s. The parties envisioned that railroads and large trucking companies, through the licensing authorities, could check the further expansion of road haulage by small truckers. By introducing A, B, and C licenses, trucking for own account could effectively be separated from commercial trucking and excluded from the licensing regime (Gibson 2001; Bureau of Public Roads 1927; Savage 1966).

These regional authorities also formed the pivotal institution in the French coordination system as "merchants of kilometers" (Wolkowitz 1976), experts who could decide which sector was allowed which quota of the total freight hauling performance. Here, too, the state sector initially encouraged the industry to set up its own intrasectorial coordination, with a very intricate system of departmental cooperation in *Conseils généraux* (led by the *préfet*, a direct representative of the central state). This resulted in massive closures of the Freycinet network of regional railroads for passenger transport and very effective restrictions on long-distance trucking, so much so that the growth of the trucking fleet in France virtually stopped during the period of the *Front Populaire*. Some historians, echoing the trucking interests of the period, even claimed that Frances' stunted trucking fleet was responsible for the French Army's rapid defeat at the beginning of the Second World War (Neiertz 1999). Contemporary commentators spoke of a "corporatist phase" and an "authoritarian phase" of coordination policy, the turning point being 1937, when the railroads were "consolidated" into one state-owned system (SNCF) and the "policy by decree" reached its zenith. At no point had the coordination debate been brought into parliament (Pirou 1942; Wolkowitz 1960). Nevertheless, regulations for completely coordinating all modes of transport in France did not materialize, largely because of opposition from the *Sénat*, which at the time was dominated by state level agricultural interests (Neiertz 1999; Jones 1984). In France it became quite clear that the coordination crisis as a battle of the systems was also a battle between urban and agricultural interests. Just like in the United States, the French transport scene was further complicated by the revival of inland navigation (Figure 2.3).

Railroads' appeals for restrictions on competition were part of a general societal trend toward regulation, antiliberalism, and corporatism. Raoul Dautry, an advocate for central coordination in France for many years, looked in envy to the British "public trust" as an instrument for coordinating transport in London. Historically, large projects such as highway networks have been prone to this kind of management, implying that western parliaments often granted power to public authorities that they could not control (Tenenbaum 1991).

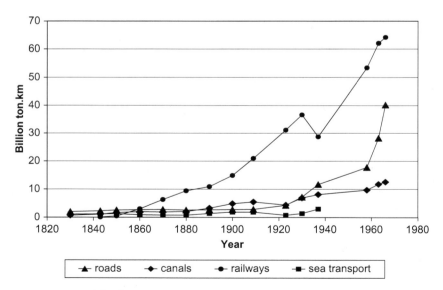

Figure 2.3 Modal split in France, 1830–1970
Source: Toutain

Apart from the politico-organizational aspect of this type of planning, theoretical and ideological repercussions also occurred that in recent years have been termed "social engineering." This type of "planned progress" and its accompanying desire for "order" and fear of "chaos," "fragmentation," and "congestion" saw its first heyday in the systemic gigantomania of New Deal, Fascist, and Stalinist planning in which the individual disappeared and the community of the "people" (the *Volk*) replaced the nation as a unifying concept. Not coincidentally, this type of central planning had its roots in the First World War with its unprecedented episodes of state intervention and central, as well as wartime military, planning (including logistics, in the sense of "materials handling," which blossomed for the first time in this war, too), while the desire for "order" was crucially strengthened by postwar, middle-class fears of political revolution. In the United States it was "republicanism," a fragile amalgam of individualism and community that provided the middle-class values for a vision of a friction-free, efficient society in which the topos of the "flow" was already a crucial element as far back as the early 1900s. In the United States, too, after the war and its subsequent social unrest, there was not only an eagerness to centralize, but also a certain willingness among the middle classes to be centralized. Planners had a mission as (male-dominated) experts with a "cool head," to create "harmony" and spatial "balance," seeing space from an aerial or bird's-eye perspective.[7] A technocratic version, the civil engineers' efforts to create unhampered traffic flows were part of an effort "to win the wilderness over to order," a practice for which American planners and engineers alike favored the metaphor of "taming" (Tichi 1987; Sutter 2002; Zelinsky 1990).

A well-documented example of this urge for order in the United States is the Interstate Commerce Commission (ICC). Founded as far back as 1887 and modeled on the British Railway and Canal Traffic Act of 1854, the ICC became a federal instrument for control of the five hundred or so fully independent railroad systems with their 230,000 miles of tracks and their one million employees after state-level control had been proven powerless in the case of interstate traffic. As the first regulated industry in the country, railroads' rates were reviewed by five commissioners appointed by the president to protect shippers, a highly political activity. The Supreme Court's case-by-case rulings formed an important element in this practical, ad hoc form of intramodal coordination. Congress extended the power of the commission in 1906, 1910, and 1912, with the "net result," as a recent study concluded, that the railroads were both regulated and isolated from other modes, making it more difficult to design intermodal regulations at a later point. The First World War had a major impact on transport regulations in the United States, just as in other countries, and by 1917, when the Wilson administration bypassed the ICC to directly control war transport through its War Industries Board (WIB), there was a consensus in U.S. government circles as to the expansion of federal control towards other transport modes.

22 Gijs Mom

The Transportation Act of 1920 returned the railroads to their private owners and exempted their mergers from the antitrust laws, provided they were approved by the ICC (Hoogenboom and Hoogenboom1976; Walker 1947).

The ICC "discovered" road transport as a potential threat to the railways through its survey in 1926 (the report was released in April 1928), but only the outbreak of the Depression and the combined threat to railways *and* large road haulers posed by wildcatters enabled the commission to formulate rules for a "Coordination of Motor Transportation" (as the title of the report of ICC examiner Leo J. Flynn ran) (Childs 1985).

THE 1930S AND THE CORPORATIST SOLUTION

As in other countries, American historians point to factors other than the Depression alone to explain the demise of the railroads. Next to the explosion of car, bus, and truck traffic on the many thousands of miles of newly paved highways, inland navigation also recovered from its weak nineteenth-century position, whereas coastal shipping and pipelines for the transport of gasoline and crude oil supported the decentralization of industry, making high transport costs and dependence on coal less necessary. Although America's railroads in 1932 still transported three-quarters of total ton-miles (excluding truck traffic, which by then transported half as much by weight as the railroads), inland waterways and transport through the Great Lakes took more than 17% and wet bulk transport through pipelines nearly 10% (Walker 1947).

Ideologically, the ICC's deliberations were based on former secretary of commerce and later president Herbert Hoover's concept of the "associative state," which led the ICC to include "practices that were normally antithetical to American beliefs—discrimination in favor of one group over others and the sanctioning of monopoly." In fact, by 1932, when the railroads had already lost their monopoly on freight transport and the government had started to subsidize road, bridge, and airport construction on a massive scale to fight the Depression, trucking interests strove for no less than state supported "cartelization." This happened through the American Trucking Association (ATA) and its president, Ted Rodgers, mostly during the years 1933 through 1935. Just like in other countries, forced association filled the organizational void at the federal level (Childs 1985; Hoogenboom and Hoogenboom 1976).

Hoover preferred self-government by trade association committees, a practice his successor and former governor of New York, Franklin Roosevelt, imitated at first. As soon as Roosevelt was installed as president in 1933, the National Industrial Recovery Act (NIRA) delegated authority to industrial trade associations that were supposed to formulate "codes of fair business practice" supervised by a National Recovery Administration (NRA). In February 1934, Roosevelt (the first president "who sought to mold transportation policy in detail") signed the Code of Fair Competition for the Trucking Industry. Its ten articles were intended to cartelize the trucking sector by setting salary levels, working hours, and tariffs (Trischler 1997; Rose, Seely, and Barrett 2006).

One of the NRA's strategies was to "freeze" the existing industrial structure. In 1933 Congress passed an Emergency Railroad Transportation Act (ERTA) on the same day as the NIRA. This led to voluntary reorganization of the railroads under state supervision, overseen by a federal coordinator of transportation, Joseph Bartlett Eastman, who had worked for the ICC since 1919. Eastman was a believer in the progressive ideal of independent "authorities," and became instrumental in implementing Hoover's associationalism. He managed to apply this concept successfully to the governance of the railroads, and saw the elimination of the "wildcatters" as a mission in the public interest. Yet, one-quarter of the firms that signed Roosevelt's code did not follow its rules, and rural truckers managed to get exempted from the 1935 Motor Carrier Act. When the NIRA was declared unconstitutional in 1935 by the Supreme Court, the railroads and their unions managed to "free" themselves from "the Coordinator" in order to be "sheltered from competition by the Interstate Commerce Commission." That same year, Congress extended the coordination powers of the ICC to interstate trucking and inland navigation (which would be regulated only in 1940) through the Motor Carrier Act. Influenced by the British experience, trucking regulation necessitated decentralization of coordination power into Motor Freight Bureaus and Conferences, which "represented the first time in U.S. history that federal authority was vested in state officials" (Childs 1985: 122–123, 174; Hamilton 2008: 52, 56; Hart 1998: 429). We see here the same governance mechanism as in road building: a concentration of executive power at the intermediate level sanctioned by an ever more powerful central state, often to the exclusion of legislative oversight and control (Mom 2005; Mom 2007; Mom, 2014).

Although the ICC, overburdened by the myriad of ad hoc cases, did not manage to introduce a sector-wide tariff system, let alone an intermodal one, the rhetoric of regulation in the very bastion of liberalism impressed many international commentators. No wonder that the "Roosevelt Codes" and the transfer of power from parliament to "authorities" such as the ICC formed the basis of far-reaching comparisons with corporatist projects in European countries (Walker 1947; Childs 1985; Trischler 1997). Nevertheless, the railways remained the largest player in the United States during the entire interwar era.

In this corporatist phase, the most extreme version of corporatism took place in Germany, where in 1931 an emergency decree (*Notverordnung*) subjected all trucking greater than fifty kilometers (as well as trucking on own account) to licensing and introduced a "tariff parity" with the railroads, plus an increase of 10%. When the trucking sector widely ignored the measure, the Nazi regime allowed the railroads to set up a compulsory truck cartel in 1935 (the *Reichs-Kraftwagen-Betriebsverband* [RKB]; Reich Truck Operating Association), although Hitler personally (supported by *Autobahn* builder Fritz Todt) prevented railroad director Dorpmüller from setting up a national truck monopoly fully controlled by his company. Nonetheless it is remarkable that Hitler did not show much interest in trucking until, in the second half of the 1930s, the military started to emphasize the importance of trucks for warfare. Coordination therefore remained in the hands of the transport ministry, whereas the construction of the *Autobahnen* network had largely been removed from its authority. For a quarter century thereafter, trucking tariffs would be coupled to those of the railroads. Nonetheless, the railroads themselves performed half of the regulated truck service (in net ton-kilometers, excluding trucks on own account and trips under fifty kilometers, so-called *Nah-und Werkverkehr*), a fact that is often used to explain the low number of trucks on German roads (Mierzejewski 2000; Klenke 1995; Borscheid 1995; Kopper 2002). Surprisingly, as Figure 2.4 shows, the German Nazi government was the only western government that managed to protect the railways effectively and only allowed the truck a very modest role in the modal split, until it started to concentrate on war preparation during the second half of the 1930s. This also reflects the dominant role of heavy industry's reliance on rail transport.

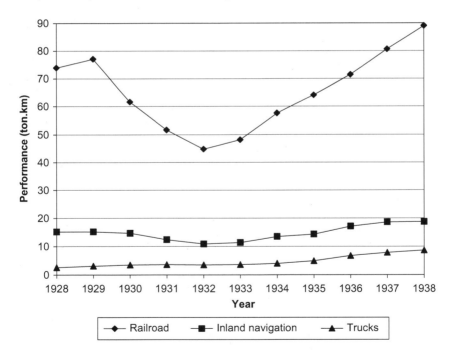

Figure 2.4 Modal split in freight mobility in Germany, 1928–1938
Source: Rohde, 37

CONCLUSION

As the analysis in this chapter has shown, the coordination crisis was nothing less than a polarization between two different societies with two different mobility systems and two different mobility cultures. This was not a class issue but an issue of two types of citizens, so it seems: those who saw mobility as "transport," as a serious but mundane utilitarian function that had to be managed as a service, just as education or mail, and those who saw mobility as an individual adventure, an experience that had as much to do with pleasure as with spatial displacement. Within this tension, the central (and centralizing) state saw this struggle as a justification for increasing its interventionism, invited by some of the actors themselves.

Although several national studies concluded that coordination did not bring the railroads any economic advantage, it cannot be denied that the coordination crisis can be seen as a giant operation against the single owner-driver and his "anarchistic" behavior (Wolkowitz 1951). Apart from a clash between two industrial sectors within capitalism (heavy industry and its railroads; light industry and its trucks), it was also a struggle of ideas about the necessity of societal order. Studies based on diffusion and substitution theories cannot cope with this complex phenomenon, which was much more than a "modal shift." Although the train was gradually abandoned, people started to do new things (much more intensely) with cars and trucks.

Why did all the societies under investigation invest in alternative transport modes that seemed to directly undermine the very protection they wanted to provide to the railways? It belongs to the salient ironies of mobility history that the state itself provided a train-like road system that allowed both the businessman in his passenger car and the small trucker to gradually increase trip lengths (Mom 2005). In hindsight, the state appeared capable, for a short turbulent period, of allowing two different types of society to coexist in its very bosom.

NOTES

1. The most recent publication for the United States: Mark H. Rose, Bruce Seely, and Paul F. Barrett, *The Best Transportation System in the World: Railroads, Trucks, Airlines, and American Public Policy in the Twentieth Century* (Columbus: Ohio State University Press, 2006); for the U.K.: Peter Scott, "British Railways and the Challenge from Road Haulage: 1919–39," *Twentieth Century British History* 13 (2002), no. 2, 101–120; for France: Nicolas Neiertz, *La coordination des transports en France; De 1918 à nos jours* (Paris: Ministère de l'Économie, des Finances et de l'Industrie, Comité pour l'histoire économique et financière, 1999); for Germany: Richard Vahrenkamp, "Lastkraftwagen und Logistik in Deutschland 1900 bis 1955: Neue Geschäftsfelder, neue Kooperationsformen und neue Konfliktlinien," *Vierteljahresschrift für Sozial-und Wirtschaftsgeschichte* 95 (2008), no. 4, 430–455, lately followed by his *Die logistische Revolution; Der Aufstieg der Logistik in*

26   *Gijs Mom*

der Massenkonsumgesellschaft (Frankfurt/New York: Campus Verlag, 2011); for the Netherlands: Jac. Verheij, *Wetten Voor Weg en Water (1923–1998); Het experiment van de Wet Autovervoer Goederen en de Wet Goederenvervoer Binnenscheepvaart en de jaren erna* (Delft: Eburon, 2001) and Gijs Mom and Ruud Filarski, *Van transport naar mobiliteit; De mobiliteitsexplosie (1895–2005)* (Zutphen: Walburg Pers, 2008), ch. 9 (203–235).

2. H.T., "Autobussen, Touringcars, en het Wetsontwerp Vergunningstelsel," *Bedrijfsauto* 13 (1933), 454–456; J. W. Kwak, "Is het einde van het touringcarwezen nabij?" *Bedrijfsauto* 16 (1936), 143–144; Autobusondernemer, "Feest in de schaduwen van morgen," *Bedrijfsauto*, 16 (March 26, 1936), no. 13, 192–194; "Cebuto," *Autobusdienst* 6 (July 1, 1933), no. 1, p. 9; H.T., "Ontwikkeling van het touringcar-wezen," *Bedrijfsauto* 15 (October 31, 1935), no. 44, 687, 691; quotation: M., "Groot-toerisme van den kleinen man," *Autokampioen* 36 (1942), 617–618, here: 618; P. Kuin and H. J. Keuning, *Het vervoerswezen* (De Nederlandse volkshuishouding tussen twee wereldoorlogen, III) (Utrecht/Brussel: Uitgeverij Het Spectrum, 1952), 133. Margaret Walsh also found a female dominance of long-range bus use in the United States: Walsh, *Making Connections*, 11.

3. *American Motorist* (February 1929) 35; *SAE Journal* (January 1929) 64; R. E. Plimpton, "Long-Distance Passenger Services," *SAE Journal* (September 1929), 285–297; *Hours, Wages, and Working Conditions in the Intercity Motor Transport Industries, Part I: Motor-Bus Transportation* (Washington DC: Federal Coordinator of Transportation, Section of Research, Section of Labor Relations, 1936), xv, 8 (n. 1); Code: Walsh, *Making Connections*, 25. On motorbus use in the United States (including the school bus, dominant in numbers) also see: Jakle and Sculle, *Motoring*, ch. 10 (183–203).

4. Figures on delivery trucks have not been found. In 1928 about 11,000 of the 25,000 Dutch trucks had a closed body. "Opkomst van vrachtauto en bus," *Bedrijfsauto* 22 (January 2, 1942), no. 1, 16–18, here: 16. Counting delivery trucks is extra difficult, because many passenger car owners in the big cities changed their vehicle into a delivery "van." Stieltjes, "III. Het verkeer te land; C. De exploitatie van het railloos verkeer," 545–565 (quoted on 561). In the U.K., the terms "own account traffic" and "ancillary traffic" have been used variously, according to Sjöblom, "The Political Economy of Railway and Road Transport in Britain and Germany, 1918–1933," 54 (n. 84).

5. "Postvervoer in Nederland . . . vóór den oorlog en thans," *Bedrijfsauto* 21 (April 17, 1941), no. 16, 269–272; H. Molhuysen, "Het moderne landbouwbedrijf is zonder autovervoer niet denkbaar," *Bedrijfsauto* 20 (January 4, 1940), no. 1, 17–18; Joost Dankers and Jaap Verheul, *Twee eeuwen op weg; Van Gend & Loos 1796–1996* (Den Haag, 1996), 75–77, 85.

6. Peter Missbach, "Die Verkehrspolitk im Deutschen Reich von 1919 bis 1929 unter besonderer Berücksichtigung der Tätigkeit des Reichsverkehrsministeriums" (unpubl. diss., Hochschule für Verkehrswesen "Friedrich List," Fakultät für Gesellschaftswissenschaften, Dresden n.y. [1990]), 56–58 (quotation: 57), 83–86; Vahrenkamp, "Lastkraftwagen und Logistik," 453; Frank Lippert, "Oekonomische Dimensionen des Lkw-Verkehrs in der Weimarer Republik; Zur Interdependenz von industrieller Rationalisierung und logistischer Flexibilisierung in den 1920er Jahren," *Zeitschrift für Unternehmensgeschichte* 42 (1997), no. 2, 185–216, here: 190; Peter Borscheid, "Lkw kontra Bahn; Die Modernisierung des Transports durch den Lastkraftwagen in Deutschland bis 1939," in: Harry Niemann and Armin Hermann (eds.), *Die Entwicklung der Motorisierung im Deutschen Reich und den Nachfolgestaaten; Stuttgarter Tage zur Automobil-und Unternehmensgeschichte; Eine Veranstaltung von Mercedes-Benz Archiv* (Stuttgart: Franz Steiner Verlag, 1995), 23–38, here: 24–25.

Clashes of Cultures 27

7. Anselm Doering-Manteuffel, "Konturen von 'Ordnung' in den Zeitschichten des 20. Jahrhunderts," in: Etzemüller (ed.), *Die Ordnung der Moderne*, 41–64, here: 20 (cool); Michael Hochgeschwender, "*The Nobles Philosophy and Its Most Efficient Use*: Zur Geschichte des *social engineering* in den USA, 1910–1965," in: *Die Ordnung der Moderne*, 171–197, here: 183 (WWI), 186 (fear), 190 (male); Nadine Klopfer, "'Clean Up'; Stadtplanung und Stadtvisionen in New Orleans, 1880er–1920er Jahre," in: *Die Ordnung der Moderne*, 153–169, here: 161 (flow), 167 (republicanism); Leendertz, "Ordnung, Ausgleich. Harmonie," 131 (bird's-eye); John S. Gilkeson, Jr., *Middle-Class providence, 1820–1940* (Princeton, NJ: Princeton University Press, 1986), 263 (fragmentation), 270 (centralized). Logistics: Monika Dommann, "Material manövrieren: Eine Begriffsgeschichte der Logistik," *Wege und Geschichte* 2/2009 (February 2009), 13–17. On the New Deal and liberalism see, for instance: H. W. Brands, *The Strange Death of American Liberalism* (New Haven: Yale University Press, 2001), 19–26; on the comparison between New Deal and Fascism/Stalinism, see: Wolfgang Schivelbusch, *Entfernte Verwandtschaft; Faschismus, Nationalsozialismus, New Deal 1933–1939* (München/Wien: Carl Hanser Verlag, 2005).

WORKS CITED

A.C.Q. "Een praatje met den toerwagenondernemer Lipman in Wateringen." *Bedrijfsauto* 19 (1939), no. 20, p. 12–13.
American Motorist. (1929), p. 35.
Autobusondernemer. "Cebuto." *Autobusdienst* 6 (1933), no. 1, p. 9.
———. "Feest in de schaduwen van morgen." *Bedrijfsauto*, 16 (1936), no. 13, p. 19, 192.
Borscheid, Peter. "Lkw kontra Bahn; Die Modernisierung des Transports durch den Lastkraftwagen in Deutschland bis 1939." In: Harry Niemann and Armin Hermann (eds.), *Die Entwicklung der Motorisierung im Deutschen Reich und den Nachfolgestaaten; Stuttgarter Tage zur Automobil- und Unternehmensgeschichte; Eine Veranstaltung von Mercedes-Benz Archiv.* Stuttgart, Franz Steiner Verlag, 1995, p. 23–38.
The Bureau of Public Roads, U.S. Department of Agriculture/The Ohio Department of Highways and Public Works. *Report of a Survey of Transportation on the State Highway System of Ohio* (n.p., 1927).
Brands, H. W. *The Strange Death of American Liberalism.* New Haven, Yale University Press, 2001.
Childs, William R. *Trucking and the Public Interest: The Emergence of Federal Regulation 1914–1940.* Knoxville, University of Tennessee Press, 1985, p. 12–171.
Dankers, Joost, and Jaap Verheul. *Twee eeuwen op weg: Van Gend & Loos 1796–1996.* Den Haag, 1996, p. 75–77, 85.
de Graaff, W.J. "Groei van het verkeer en zijn problemen." *De Ingenieur 60* (1948) nr. 10: V.21-V.36.
Doering-Manteuffel, Anselm. "Konturen von 'Ordnung' in den Zeitschichten des 20. Jahrhunderts." In: Thomas Etzemüller (ed.), *Die Ordnung der Moderne.* Bielefeld, Transcript Histoire, 2009, p. 41–64.
Dommann, Monika. "Material manövrieren: Eine Begriffsgeschichte der Logistik." *Wege und Geschichte* 2 (2009), p. 13–17.
Fischer, Wolfram. "Wirtschaft, Gesellschaft und Staat in Europa 1914–1980." In: Wolfram Fischer (ed.), *Europäische Wirtschafts-und Sozialgeschichte vom Ersten Weltkrieg bis zur Gegenwart.* Stuttgart, Klett-Cotta, 1987.
Gibson, Thomas. *Road Haulage by Motor in Britain.* Farnham, Ashgate, 2001.

28 *Gijs Mom*

Gilkeson, John S. Jr. *Middle-Class Providence, 1820–1940*. Princeton, NJ, Princeton University Press, 1968.

Greebe, A. "De toename van het eigen vervoer." *Bedrijfsvervoer* 28 (1949), no. 9, p. 259–260.

Hamilton, Shane. *Trucking Country; The Road to America's Wal-Mart Economy*. Princeton/Oxford, Princeton University Press, 2008, p. 47–56.

Hart, David M. "Herbert Hoover's Last Laugh: The Enduring Significance of the 'Associative State' in the U.S.A." *Journal of Policy History* 10 (1998), no. 3, p. 419–444.

Hibbs, John. *The History of British Bus Services*. Newton Abbot, David & Charles, 1968.

Hoogenboom, Ari, and Olive Hoogenboom. *A History of the ICC: From Panacea to Palliative*. New York, W.W. Norton & Company, 1976.

H.T. "Autobussen, Touringcars, en het Wetsontwerp Vergunningstelsel." *Bedrijfsauto* 13 (1933), p. 454–456.

———. "Ontwikkeling van het touringcar-wezen." *Bedrijfsauto* 15 (1935), no. 44, p. 687–691.

Hochgeschwender, Michael. "The Nobles Philosophy and Its Most Efficient Use: Zur Geschichte des social engineering in den USA, 1910–1965." In: Thomas Etzemüller (ed.), *Die Ordnung der Moderne*. Bielefeld, Transcript Histore, 2009, p. 171–197.

Jakle, John, and Keith Sculle. *Motoring: The Highway Experience in America*. Athens, GA, University of Georgia Press, 1999, p. 183–203.

Jones, Joseph. *The Politics of Transport in Twentieth-Century France*. Kingston/Montreal, McGill-Queen's University Press, 1984.

Jongma, Johan W. D. *Geschiedenis van het Nederlandse wegvervoer*. Drachten/Leeuwarden, FPB Uitgevers, 1992.

Klenke, Dietmar. *"Freie Stau für freie Bürger": Die Geschichte der bundesdeutschen Verkehrspolitik 1949–1994*. Darmstadt, Wissenschaftliche Buchgesellschaft, 1995, p. 11.

Klopfer, Nadine "'Clean Up': Stadtplanung und Stadtvisionen in New Orleans, 1880er–1920er Jahre." In: Thomas Etzemüller (ed.), *Die Ordnung der Moderne*, Bielefeld, Transcript Histore, 2009, p. 153–169.

Kopper, Christopher. *Handel und Verkehr im 20. Jahrhundert*. München, Oldenbourg, 2002, p. 94.

———. "Passenger Transportation in Inter War Germany." Paper presented at the workshop "Transport Coordination—Passenger and Freight Transport," Utrecht, March 26–27, 2009, p. 9.

Kuin, P., and Keuning, H. J. *Het vervoerswezen (De Nederlandse volkshuishouding tussen twee wereldoorlogen*, III. Utrecht/Brussel, Uitgeverij Het Spectrum, 1952, p. 133.

Leendertz, Ariane. "Ordnung. Ausgleich. Harmonie." In: Thomas Etzemüller (ed.), *Die Ordnung der Moderne. Social Engineering im 20. Jahrhundert*. Bielefeld, Transcript, 2009, p. 129–150.

Lippert, Frank. "Oekonomische Dimensionen des Lkw-Verkehrs in der Weimarer Republik." In: *Zeitschrift für Unternehmensgeschichte* 42 (1997), p. 185–216.

———. *"Lastkraftwagenverkehr und Rationalisierung in der Weimarer Republik": Technische und ökonomische Aspekte fertigungsstruktureller und logistischer Wandlungen in den 1920er Jahren*. Frankfurt am Main: Peter Lang, 1999, p. 89.

Mierzejewski, Alfred C. *Hitler's Trains: The German National Railways and the Third Reich*. Stroud: Tempus, 2000, p. 54–61.

Missbach, Peter. "Die Verkehrspolitik im Deutschen Reich von 1919 bis 1929 unter besonderer Berücksichtigung der Tätigkeit des Reichsverkehrsministeriums" (unpubl. diss., Hochschule für Verkehrswesen "Friedrich List," Fakultät für Gesellschaftswissenschaften, Dresden n.y. [1990]).

Molhuysen, H. "Het moderne landbouwbedrijf is zonder autovervoer niet denkbaar." *Bedrijfsauto* 20 (1940), no. 1, p. 17–18.

Mom, Gijs. "The Electric Vehicle: Technology and Expectations in the Automobile Age." In: *Business History Review* 78 (2004), p. 291–293.

———. "Roads without Rails; European Highway-Network Building and the Desire for Long-Range Motorized Mobility." *Technology and Culture* 46 (2005), p. 745–772.

———. "Constructing Multifunctional Networks: Road Building in the Netherlands, 1810–1980." In: Gijs Mom and Laurent Tissot (eds.), *Road History: Planning, Building, and Use*, Neuchâtel, Alphil, 2007.

———. "Writing 'Europe': The Dutch Case." In: Ralf Roth and Karl Schlögel (eds.), *Neue Wege in ein neues Europa: Geschichte und Verkehr im 20. Jahrhundert.* Frankfurt/New York, Campus, 2009, p. 85–102.

———. "Struggle of the Systems: Freight Mobility in a Transatlantic Perspective, 1920–2000." In: Gérard Duc, Olivier Perroux, Hans-Ulrich Schiedt, and François Walter (eds.), *Histoire des transports et de la mobilité. Entre concurrence modale et coordination (1918 à nos jours)/Transport and Mobility History. Between Modal Competition and Coordination (1918 to our days).* Neuchâtel, Alphil, 2014 (forthcoming).

———. *Atlantic Automobilism; Emergence and Persistence of the Car in Europe and the USA, 1895–1940.* New York, Berghahn Books, 2014 (forthcoming).

Mom, Gijs, and Filarski, Ruud. *Van transport naar mobiliteit; De mobiliteitsexplosie 1895–2005.* Zutphen, Walburg Pers, 2008, p. 203–235.

Moulton, Harold G. *The American Transportation Problem (Prepared for the National Transportation Committee).* Washington DC, The Brookings Institution, 1933, p. 575–578.

Mulley, Corinne. "The Background to Bus Regulation in the 1930 Road Traffic Act: Economic, Political and Personal Influences in the 1920s." *The Journal of Transport History*, Third Series, 4 (1983), no. 2, p. 1–19.

Neiertz, Nicolas. *La coordination des transports en France; De 1918 à nos jours.* Paris, Ministère de l'Économie, des Finances et de l'Industrie, Comité pour l'histoire économique et financière, 1999.

Orselli, Jean. *Usages et usagers de la route; Pour une histoire de moyenne durée, 1860–2008* (unpubl. doct. diss., Université de Paris I, 2009, p. 76).

P.H. 1940. "Autobus-Reminiscenties." *Bedrijfsauto* 20 (1940), no. 29, p. 592–594.

Pirou, Gaëtan. *Les cadres de la vie économique: Les transports.* Vol. 1 of Gaëtan Pirou and Maurice Byé, *Traité d'économie politique.* Bordeaux, Recueil Sirey, 1942.

Plimpton, R. E. "Long-Distance Passenger Services." *SAE Journal*, 1929, p. 285–297.

Renouard, Dominique. *Les transports de marchandises par fer, route et eau depuis 1850.* Paris, Librairie Armand Colin, 1960.

Rocholl, Peter. *Vergleichende Analyse der Entwicklung des Personenkraftverkehrs im westeuropäischen Wirtschaftsraum.* Düsseldorf, Droste, 1962, p. 129.

Rohde, Heidi. *Transportmodernisierung contra Verkehrsbewirtschaftung; Zur staatlichen Verkehrspolitik gegenüber dem Lkw in den 30er Jahren.* Frankfurt, Peter Lang, 1999.

Rose, Mark H., Bruce E. Seely, and Paul F. Barrett. *The Best Transportation System in the World: Railroads, Trucks, Airlines, and American Public Policy in the Twentieth Century.* Columbus, The Ohio State University Press, 2006.

SAE Journal. January 1929, p. 64.

Schlimm, Anette. *Ordnungen des Verkehrs; Arbeit an der Moderne—deutsche und britische Verkehrsexpertise im 20. Jahrhundert.* Bielefeld, transcript, 2011.

30   Gijs Mom

Savage, Christopher I. *An Economic History of Transport*. London, Hutchinson University, 1966, p. 140–175, 267.

Scott, Peter. "British Railways and the Challenge from Road Haulage: 1919–39." *Twentieth Century British History* 13 (2002), p. 101–120.

Schivelbusch, Wolfgang. *Entfernte Verwandtschaft; Faschismus, Nationalsozialismus, New Deal 1933–1939*. München/Wien, Carl Hanser, 2005.

Shrapnell-Smith, E. S. "Five Decades of Commercial Road Transport with Inferences about Its Future." *Journal of the Institute of Transport*, February–March (1946), p. 214–229.

Sjöblom, Gustav. *The Political Economy of Railway and Road Transport in Britain and Germany, 1918–1933* (unpubl. diss., Darwin College, University of Cambridge, 2007).

Stieltjes, J. J. III. "Het verkeer in Nederland in de XXe eeuw," *Tijdschrift van het Koninklijk Nederlandsch Aardrijkskundig Genootschap*, Tweede serie, 50 (1933) 331–662

Sutter, Paul S. *Driven Wild: How the Fight against Automobiles Launched the Modern Wilderness Movement*. Washington DC, Weyerhaeuser Environmental Books, 2002.

Tenenbaum, Susan. "The Progressive Legacy and the Public Corporation: Entrepreneurship and Public Virtue." *Journal of Policy History* 3 (1991), no. 3. p. 309–330.

Tichi, Cecilia. *Shifting Gears; Technology, Literature, Culture in Modernist America*. Chapel Hill/London, University of North Carolina Press, 1987, p. 123, 151–162, 325.

Tiepen, Jacq. Harms. "Wagon economischer dan vrachtauto?" *Bedrijfsauto* 16 (1936), no. 14, p. 210–212.

Toutain, J.-C. *Les transports en France de 1830 à 1965*. Paris: Presse Universitaires de France, Septembre–Octobre 1967.

Trischler, Helmuth. "Der epische Konflikt zwischen Schiene und Strasse: Der Güterverkehr der USA seit dem Ende des 19. Jahrhunderts." In: Harry Niemann and Armin Hermann (eds.), *100 Jahre LKW; Geschichte und Zukunft des Nutzfahrzeuges*. Stuttgart, Franz Steiner, 1997, p. 243–262.

Vahrenkamp, Richard. "Autobahnbau in Hessen bis 1943." n.p. [Darmstadt], Hessisches Wirtschaftsarchiv, 2007, p. 86–88.

———. "Lastkraftwagen und Logistik in Deutschland 1900 bis 1955: Neue Geschäftsfelder, neue Kooperationsformen und neue Konfliktlinien." *Vierteljahresschrift für Sozial-und Wirtschaftsgeschichte* 95 (2008), pp. 430–455, lately followed by his *Die logistische Revolution; Der Aufstieg der Logistik in der Massenkonsumgesellschaft*, Frankfurt, Campus, 2011.

———. "Die Entwicklung der Speditionen in Deutschland 1880 bis 1938." In: Hans-Liudger Dienel and Hans Ulrich Schiedt (eds.), *Die moderne Strasse*, Frankfurt, Campus Verlag, 2010, p. 309–337.

Verheij, Jac. *Wetten Voor Weg en Water (1923–1998): Het experiment van de Wet Autovervoer Goederen en de Wet Goederenvervoer Binnenscheepvaart en de jaren erna*. Delft, Eburon, 2001.

Walker, Gilbert. *Road and Rail: An Enquiry into the Economics of Competition and State Control*. London, George Allen and Unwin, 1947.

Walsh, *Margaret. Making Connections: The Long-Distance Bus Industry in the USA*. USA/Singapore/Sydney, Ashgate, 2000.

Weber, Donald. "Automobilisering en de overheid in België." (unpubl. doct. diss., Gent, 2008).

Wolkowitz, Maurice. "La bourgeoisie française devant l'évolution des techniques de transport." *La pensée; revue du rationalisme moderne* 39 (November 1951), p. 76–86

———. *L'économie régionale des transports dans le Centre et le Centre-Ouest de la France*. Paris, SEDES, 1960, p. 201.

———. "La décadence de la notion de service public pour les transports de voyageurs en milieu rural." *Transports* 1976, p. 52–55.

Zelinsky, Wilbur. "The Imprint of Central Authority." In: Michael P. Conzen (ed.), *The Making of the American landscape*. Boston, Unwin Hyman Ltd, 1990.

3 Half-Holiday Excursions and Rambling Clubs
How Did Leisure Shape the Mobilities of the Early Twentieth Century?

Jill Ebrey

INTRODUCTION

Using the city of Manchester (U.K.) as a case study, this chapter will consider how new ways of organizing time and space in the early twentieth century shaped new mobilities. Common sense might tell us, for instance, that particular technologies produce mobilities; that railways and buses, for example, made moving people and things through space easier. This chapter will introduce a new perspective: how newly created times and spaces may have produced new forms of mobility (Buscher et al. 2011; Urry 2000). The emergent "weekend," for example, inaugurated in Manchester (U.K.) in 1843 with an agreement among employers to close on Saturday afternoons, meant the beginning of the Saturday half-holiday and, later, the two-day break we now know as the weekend. The creation of this new leisure space produced almost immediately a "literature of mobility" orientated towards suggesting weekend itineraries, where the newly "emancipated" city and suburb dwellers could take their leisure. The practice of leisure walking was later formalized in such institutions as the Ramblers Association (1931), an organization that encouraged a collective rather than individual approach to activities.

This chapter will discuss the trajectory of these early "mobilities of modernity" and consider what factors shaped their emergence and development. It will discuss how forms of mobility produced in the late nineteenth and early twentieth centuries seemed to embody a commitment to a shared experience of everyday life, whether on buses and trains or through walking and cycling. To some extent, it was expedient for both the national and local state to make funds available to subsidize public transportation, as more "private" modes such as the car were not yet widely available.

HISTORIES OF THE WEEKEND RETOLD: THE WEEKEND, MOBILITIES, AND RESISTANCE

Urry (2000: 105) has argued that "indicators of the passage of time . . . have imposed very different temporal divisions upon human history . . . which often engender enormously powerful emotional sentiments." The weekend is one such temporal "indicator" that has particular resonances, often in the realm of activities unassociated with paid work. Saturdays and Sundays have come to mean so much more than merely two days at the end of the working week. They represent an autonomous time/space, a repository of dreams and hopes that the monotony and "grind" of work does not often provide. The weekend is contradictory: On the one hand it is a construct of capitalism, inaugurated to provide spaces and times for consumption, the "motor" of capitalist growth. On the other hand, it becomes a space of possibilities, when the hegemonic tick of the clock becomes less dominant and the emancipatory possibilities of life become evident. In the 170 years since its beginnings, from the Saturday half-holiday to the weekend, it has come to function both as a utopian imaginary for social actors and as a commodified and marketized time and space that uses this imaginary as a means of stimulating consumption.

This chapter considers the early symbiotic relationship between weekends and mobilities. It begins with a brief history of the nascent weekend and its origins in the Saturday half-holiday, arguably first inaugurated in Manchester, England, during 1843. It goes on to discuss this "reorganization" of time, and considers how it was contingent upon a similar "reorganization" and commodification of space. Indeed, one could not have worked without the other. Without "the weekend," this chapter argues, mobilities such as traveling by train and bicycling for pleasure would have developed very differently. The weekend allowed networks of mobility to develop that were not solely connected with work. At the end of the nineteenth century, as Slater (1997) argues, capitalism needed to encourage consumption as well as production—the weekend being produced as a space of leisure and consumption through emergent mobilities of pleasure. Early examples of a Manchester walking guide (1843)[1] will be cited to demonstrate how the division of time into "work time" and "leisure time" immediately produced a commodity that suggested the most suitable walks to take on a Saturday afternoon. The creation of "leisure time" expanded mobilities, whether through walking, cycling, or journeys by rail. A tremendous increase in the number of organizations organizing the time of leisure was evident. In some instances this was combined with political activism. The socialist "Clarion Clubs," which began in the late nineteenth century, created new political and recreational spaces and exemplified mobility both in their activities and their graphic representations. This organization will be discussed, paying particular attention to the way in which it mobilized the weekend, both for leisure and political purposes. As well as drawing on the new temporalities associated with industrial capitalism, the Clarion Clubs produced new spaces and new forms of human association in their appeal to "fellowship." This chapter will consider the relationship between the time of the weekend and those spaces created through the mobilities of the Clarion Cycling Club and associated clubhouses, cafes, and guesthouses.

34 Jill Ebrey

THE WEEKEND, TECHNOLOGIES, AND MOBILITIES: TIME AND SPACE

New Ways of Organizing Time and Space: The Saturday Half-Holiday in Manchester

Cross has asserted that "Part of the struggle for industrialization is the demand for space and time free from the market" (Cross in Silverstone 1997: 113). In mid-nineteenth century Manchester, against a background of industrial and class struggle around enfranchisement, working conditions, and hours, a group of bourgeois young men formed themselves into a committee. Chaired by 23-year-old William Marsden and other members of the Manchester Athenaeum (full name: "Club for the Advancement and Diffusion of Knowledge"). This was an institution for middle-class Mancunians, dedicated to "intellectual cultivation" and "rational recreation." Facilities included a library and reading rooms as well as a program of educational lectures for the general public (Rose 1985: 111). Committee members, including Robert Lowes, set about building support for the idea of a Saturday half-holiday, arguably the first secular "break" of industrial modernity and the precursor to the modern "weekend." The objective of the "Committee for the Establishment of the Saturday Half Holiday" was to establish an agreement on the need for a half-holiday. The work of this committee helped broker a citywide agreement by warehouse owners, secured and signed successfully in November 1843, and subsequently amended to include other Manchester employers. The Saturday half-holiday, and the contributions of Marsden and Lowes to the campaign, were deemed so significant that both men were honored posthumously through publicly subscribed memorial stones.

The idea provoked much debate in both local and national newspapers, highlighting the considerable anxiety felt by both the bourgeoisie and religious groups about what the working classes might get up to in their "time off" on Saturday afternoons. The bourgeois belief in "improving" and "rational" recreation "endeavored to reestablish through leisure a moral and codified framework which would stabilize and transform society." The Mechanics Institute and Athenaeum in Manchester provided a context for such debates, and academic instruction was practiced "on a mutuality basis or by the new working men's clubs, institutes and a wide variety of Friendly Societies" (Clarke 1996). These kinds of activities were seen as a more "respectable" means of using the new times and spaces, an alternative to the hedonism of drunken Saturday nights. Clarke and Critcher (1985: 5) in their analysis of early forms of leisure invoked the description "protestant leisure ethic" to describe this attitude.

Gary Cross (in Silverstone 1997: 108) has articulated how the weekend emerged from the temporal and spatial reordering of the Industrial Revolution and has argued that it "is a central construct of industrial society.

It is the logical culmination of the spatial division of market, work, and residence." Indeed, the precursor of the weekend, the Saturday half-day holiday in Manchester (inaugurated in 1843) was heralded by J. T. Slugg, a Mancunian businessman of literary tastes (1971 [1881]) as one of the most significant achievements of nineteenth-century Manchester, alongside the railway, free trade, and the cathedral. One could argue that the listing of these achievements in written form constructed what it meant to be living in "modern times." Slugg was a canny observer of the institutions of "modern life" and he recognized the importance of the Saturday half-holiday. Without the nascent "weekend," it could be argued that the modern social world would not have developed in the way that it has.

The emergence of the weekend (a temporal construct) can be considered as important as the development of, for example, the railways (a spatial construct). There are a number of possible reasons for the inception of the weekend at this particular historical moment. Firstly, because capitalists considered it necessary to rationalize and synchronize preindustrial working times and spaces of labor, the power and influence of the state and capital combined, meaning the gradual abolition of the traditional local "fairs" and "wakes." There was, as Malcolmson (1973, reprinted in Waites, Bennett, and Martin, 1982: 20) has pointed out, "an increasing willingness among people of authority to intervene against the customary practices of popular recreation. He reiterates this later (35: *Ibid.*), mentioning also the primacy of the economic motives:

> We can see then, that gatherings which were largely plebian and unabashedly devoted to pleasure, enjoyed considerably less security than those in which substantial economic interests were involved—and with time most of these popular events disappeared.

Secondly, there was anxiety among the middle classes about conditions of work and mortality rates in the new factories, as evidenced in the Kay Shuttleworth (1832) report about health in Manchester, which added to demands for "rational recreation" (Kidd 2002: 50) as a solution to "moral degeneracy." Thirdly, church authorities realized that realigning the times, and therefore the activities, of the lower orders, (reorienting "leisure" around Saturdays) might mean greater church attendance on Sundays. Fourthly, the years leading up to 1843 were those when Chartism was an active movement in Manchester and the U.K. more generally, although on the European mainland such activity had resulted in considerable political and social upheaval. It may have been thought that such temporal concessions would hinder the growth of radical politics in Manchester. Finally, the Saturday half-holiday, it could be argued, was essential as a time for the development and establishment of new practices and spaces of consumption, such as the opening of football grounds (e.g., the precursor of Manchester United F.C., Newton Heath, Lancashire, and Yorkshire railway F.C. was inaugurated in

36　*Jill Ebrey*

1878 and the Football League in 1888) and department stores (e.g., Kendal Milne [1862] and Lewis's [1880]).

As Harvey (1989: 232) puts it, "innovations dedicated to the removal of spatial barriers . . . have been of immense significance in the history of capitalism, turning that history into a very geographical affair—the railroad and the telegraph, the automobile, radio and telephone, the jet aircraft and television, and the recent telecommunications revolution are cases in point." He goes on to suggest (1990: 264) that these developments "all changed the sense of time and space in a number of different ways." Mobilities could regularly be extended beyond the local in the nineteenth century with the move from rural to urban centers, the separation of home and work, and the subsequent development of the bicycle, the barge, and the railway network. The new "leisure" time of Saturday afternoons facilitated journeys on trains, bikes, boats, and even on foot, which could be undertaken purely for pleasure. This chapter proposes, therefore, that the relationship between the new leisure time of the nascent weekend and that of, for example, the railways and the bicycle manufacturers, was symbiotic. It might be argued that without the weekend, popular culture would not have developed in the same way, if at all. Conversely, the railways and other forms of transport would not have been as commercially successful and featured so vividly in the popular imagination. A central feature, then, of the industrial reorganization of time and space was the inauguration of the emergent weekend, the Saturday half-holiday, firstly in Manchester and then throughout the U.K.

New Forms of Mobility and Consequent Sociability

The railway compressed time and space, making journeys relatively affordable in terms of both time and money. A combination of an emergent railway network and a Saturday half-holiday offered the possibility of physical mobility over longer distances for greater numbers of people. Flanders (2006: 32–33) details the expansion of the nineteenth century railway and the different purposes for which journeys were made. The train companies organized trips to see "notable feats of engineering," for instance, thus extending both the idea of the "sightseer" and the kinds of sights they might travel to see. This development of the tourist "gaze" amongst new class constituencies, including schoolchildren on school trips and day trippers and holiday makers to seaside resorts, was made possible by the creation of new train lines such as that to Blackpool in 1846, three years after the first Saturday half-holiday in Manchester.

These initial observations lead to some key considerations and questions. How did the conjuncture that we know as the Industrial Revolution produce the railway, the weekend, and leisure mobilities? Goldstone (1998) suggests that:

> Cheap coal made possible cheaper iron and steel. Cheap coal plus cheap iron made possible the construction of railways and ships built of iron,

fueled by coal, and powered by engines producing steam. Railways and ships made possible mass national and international distribution of metal tools, textiles, and other products that could be more cheaply made with steam-powered metal-reinforced machinery.

(275)

Goldstone considers that revolutionary changes, such as the Industrial Revolution, grew out of steam power—a contingent breakpoint that grew out of a highly improbable concurrence of events (1998). Following the contingent event, he asserts, come others that may be predictable and follow on from one another. The inauguration of the Saturday half-holiday was a similarly contingent event out of which was produced a weekly temporal rhythm that allowed the participation in, and production of, spaces of popular culture. The combination of time (Saturday half-holiday) and space (railways) to produce the culture of the weekend is intriguing. Could any of these institutions or processes separately have been independently "effective" or "successful?" How did they "articulate" to produce a particular form of capitalism, which involved an emergent "weekend?"

Harvey (2009: 136) suggests that "processes produce their own space and time. . . ." Industrial capitalism, as we have discussed, produced new organizations of space and time. The means of compressing such "spatial divisions" was imperative for capital accumulation, if nothing else, and was achieved through emergent transport systems such as the railways. For these to be profitable, trains had to run every day, and so the "reorganization of space" had to be matched by a similar "reorganization of time." As Harvey (2009: 137) points out, "It is impossible to disentangle space from time. They fuse into spacetime." So "the weekend" and "the railways" had, and indeed have, a symbiotic relationship. Had "the weekend" not happened, it is hard to see how the railways would have developed in the way that they did. Although their primary purpose might have been understood as the transport of commodities and people in the circulation of capital, the (possibly) unintended consequence of the railway was to extend the mobilities of even the less-well-off for purposes other than only work. Without weekends and holidays, the railways may not have developed in the way that they did. As De Sapio suggests, the train journey could encompass leisure, work, private contemplation, the train as a meeting-ground, and even the search for nostalgia and romance (2012: 4).

De Sapio (2012) has written of the "community of travelers" that was generated as part of the experience of travelling on the railways. This facilitated "meetings" between friends, relatives, and strangers, which fundamentally changed the "modern" social world. He has spoken of the variety of meeting places that the processes of modernity produced—museums, theatres, and ballrooms amongst them. These new spaces of leisure were meeting places for new classes of people. Public space was contradictory, being more regulated, yet at the same time democratized, through the production of new spaces of association. Forms of mobility such as the omnibus,

38   *Jill Ebrey*

the bicycle, and organized walking or rambling promoted different kinds of meetings, either organized or not. These spaces, however, could not have worked in the way that they did without the time needed for their production.

From the Saturday half-holiday (1843) to "the weekend" later in the twentieth century, this spacetime created has, until recently, been understood as a time for collective "rest" (even if that rest was gendered and therefore unequally experienced). Gradually, during the twentieth century, the remuneration of those who worked "unsocial hours" during the nighttime, at weekends, and on "national" holidays, was subject to a premium, acknowledging the sacrifice of relinquishing the social time of association with others. This particular slice of time was, perhaps in class terms, a social leveler, in that "time off" was not confined to one class group. In fact, the weekend came to be synonymous with the urban working class, as its ubiquity in the content of popular cultural forms confirms.

Larsen, Urry, and Axhausen (2006: 4) identify five interdependent mobilities that they suggest characterize "the contemporary world": physical travel (people), physical movement (objects), imaginative travel, virtual travel, and communicative travel. Although this chapter does not discuss "the contemporary world," their taxonomy is still useful as an analytical tool for examining physical travel (walking, cycling, and travelling by train), "imaginative travel" (film and photographs), and communicative travel in the form of postcards, letters, and cards. The authors propose that "time-space compression" outlined by Harvey (1989), which "characterizes modern societies," seems to produce "time space distanciation"—a "spreading of people's networks." The movement of social actors beyond their immediate locale was facilitated both by technological developments and the temporal reorganization that produced the weekend. This combination allowed friendship and "political" networks to emerge outside of immediate locales, which will be discussed in the context of industrializing Manchester and the northwest of England in the second half of the nineteenth and the first half of the twentieth centuries. An examination will be made of how new times and spaces are produced and opportunities created for "meetings" of all kinds, whether for work, to see family, or to socialize with friends.

Although not everyone was able to afford travel by the new forms of transport, either train, omnibus, or bicycle, new imaginative technologies such as photography and film and, more important, communicative technologies such as postcards, meant that travel could be made imaginatively, either across the city, the region, across Britain, or even globally as postcards or letters were sent or films viewed at the cinema. The Saturday half-holiday produced new geographies of mobility, which were quickly codified, narrativized, and developed into commodities for the newly "leisured" publics to peruse. One such example was the 1844 *Half-Holiday Excursions or Topographical, Historical and Biographical Notices of the more picturesque and*

Remarkable Places Within an Afternoon's Walk from Manchester (Anon. 1844). Such texts allowed readers to imagine itineraries, as well as physically walk them, thereby facilitating a number of differently experienced mobilities.

The *Half-Holiday* handbook of "excursions" is introduced with a warning, reflecting both the anxiety felt by the bourgeoisie at the newly emancipated Saturday afternoons and setting out their prescription for and "warning" about this time "off." The author begins thus:

> The use or abuse of the Weekly Half holiday by the warehousemen of Manchester, during the approaching Summer, will probably determine, not merely the question of the continuance or otherwise of the relaxation here, but of its extension to other classes throughout the kingdom. If it is found that the leisure afforded on the Saturday afternoon is wasted in suburban taverns, cigar divans, music saloons or other objectionable places of resort, it will prove a bane instead of a blessing, and its withdrawal will be the inevitable result.
>
> (Anon. 1844: 1)

Particular means of mobilizing Saturday afternoons were therein suggested and might be seen as part of the discourse of "rational recreation," one of "moral improvement," which the middle classes advocated for the new leisure time of the working classes, aimed at preventing hedonism or political involvement on a Saturday night! The author of the *Half-Holiday* handbook, as well as a *Principal Places of Interest*, also provides a commentary on the mythical "working men" who he "meets" while walking through the places described. However, in addition to walking, he mentions the omnibus as a means of travel along with the "Swift Passage Boat" on the Bridgewater Canal. The title suggests an emergent tourist "gaze," but only for the rural "picturesque" and "remarkable sights," beyond the Manchester suburbs into leafy Cheshire.

That the "new times" of modernity and industrialization produced new mobilities and "spaces" during the nineteenth and early twentieth centuries is most evident in the postcards of the early twentieth century, a significant number of which are archived at the Manchester Records Office. As Gillen and Hall write in Buscher et al. (2011: 20), "the early twentieth century postcard can be seen as an astonishing instanciation of an era of revolutionary change in mobilities. . . ." The date on the postcards seen in the Manchester archive almost always refers to physical mobility taking place on a Saturday. Although the postcard is, in itself, a form of "mobility," the time afforded by the weekend was to make the scale of those mobilities "revolutionary." Gillen and Hall (2011: *Ibid.*) detail how the General Post Office and its "massive apparatus" made possible a new scale of communication and mobility. They suggest that the "huge network" of post offices and post boxes, the ability to post letters on the train, and deliveries

40   *Jill Ebrey*

"potentially many times a day" (*Ibid.*: 32), generated microcommunication between actors. The ubiquity of the postcard in the early years of the twentieth century in now familiar format, image on one side and text on the other, together with the expansion in postal services, led, Gillen and Hall suggest, "to an explosion in the use of the postcard" for interpersonal communication.

THE "POLITICAL" AND SOCIAL MOBILITY OF CLUBS AND SOCIETIES: THE CLARION CYCLING CLUB AND THE RAMBLERS ASSOCIATION

The ability to arrange "meetings" through the communicative facility of the letter and postcard was an outgrowth of technological advances, particularly in institutions, such as the post office, and new spaces and times for meeting, such as the city and the weekend. The processes of modernity made possible the development of admittedly gendered "chains of friendship" based on common interests. These were often rooted in the collectivities of clubs and associations. Solnit (2001: 156) writes that "the late nineteenth and early twentieth century was 'the golden age of organisations.' " She goes on:

> Some provided social cohesion for the displaced of a rapidly changing world; others offered resistance to industrialisation's inhuman appetite for the time, health energy and rights of workers. Many were organized around utopian or pragmatic change, and all of them created communities of Zionists, feminists, labor activists, athletes, charities and intellectuals. Walking clubs were part of this larger movement, and each of the major political walking clubs was founded in some kind of opposition to the mainstream of its society.

Solnit refers mostly to North America, but discusses, relatively briefly, organized rambling in Britain. Many of the clubs were those that centered on mobilities, and much of that mobility was practiced on Saturdays and Sundays. Weekend leisure mobilities enfranchised some groups of women. The Manchester Oxford Ladies Cycling Club (Manchester Record Office, Ref M522/5/1–4), founded in 1897, took rides out to various places around Manchester on Wednesday afternoons, Monday evenings, and Saturday afternoons to prearranged destinations detailed in mini-cloth-bound annual membership cards. A combination, then, of time, technology, and democracy created a space for some women to be mobile. Rubenstein (1977, quoted in Langhamer, 2000: 4) suggests that "Cycling brought the sexes together on equal terms more completely than any other sport or pastime. It also gave women a striking sense of independence and self-reliance."

The nineteenth century saw a rapid expansion in the mobilities of the working and middle classes. For instance, *Odds and Ends*, a nineteenth-century

Manchester manuscript journal, was a handwritten, illustrated precursor of pictorial magazines such as *Life* and *Picture Post*. Amongst its content about life and literature, it gave accounts of the new weekend mobilities of various organizations in the city. The Little Go Brotherhood (Manchester Record Office: M38/4: *Odds & Ends* Vol. XLIV 1898), for instance, went out into the country on weekends from Manchester via the train. Their philosophy is summed up in a quote from Shakespeare's *Henry V*:

> Our plot is a good plot as ever was laid: our friends true and constant, a good plot, good friends and full of expectation, an excellent plot, very good friends.

Their trips were recorded through writing and some very early photographs and sketches of the Lake District. Albert Jordan, one of their members, describes "the hospitable landlady" at their guesthouse, "The Tourists Rest," and their weekend rambles in Little Langdale. The journey to Keswick of its counterpart, The Ancoats Brotherhood,[2] in 1898 is remembered thus:

> To the city clerk, warehouseman, or man from the workshop or factory, a weekend at Keswick is an agreeable tonic. One hundred and twenty one miles is rather a long journey for so short a holiday time, but the railway ride is interesting. Of course from Manchester to Preston the traveller will see little that can be described as picturesque on the break. However, as we once heard a cotton salesman say "what is the good to a Manchester man of a landscape without factory chimneys. . . ."

He later went on to complain about the five-hour journey, particularly as each person was sitting in a carriage with seven others!

Women were mobilized into this emergent weekend tourism. Ruth Mary Shephard, for instance, wrote an account in *Odds and Ends* (293: *Ibid.*) of her "Cycle Ride to the Land of Burns," which, in common with many such accounts of weekend rural forays away from the city, discussed the aesthetics of the landscape in great detail, drawing on the discourse of romanticism to contrast the experience of the rural and urban. The mobilities represented by weekend railway journeys from Manchester to the Lake District were, at the same time, being practiced by the cyclists of the emergent Clarion Cycling Club.

THE CLARION "MOVEMENT" AND THE SATURDAY HALF-HOLIDAY

The arrival of the Saturday half-holiday in Manchester, as suggested earlier, was a moment of contingency, an unexpected arrival into the maelstrom of modernity. Research indicates that Manchester, as the first industrial city,

42 *Jill Ebrey*

may have been amongst the first to designate Saturday afternoon thus. The half-holiday was incrementally and unevenly adopted both across the U.K. and within towns and cities, depending on place and sector of employment. In addition, for those, mostly women, undertaking paid work in retail or domestic service, Saturday afternoons would not necessarily have been a holiday. By the 1890s, many regions and industries conformed to a Saturday afternoon off.

Hobsbawm (1975: 10) refers to the years between 1848 and 1875 as the "age of capital," a time of capitalist consolidation and the embedding of bourgeois culture, succeeding the "age of revolution." He details the 1848 revolution in France and its "rapid and wide" spread through the southwest German states, Bavaria, Berlin, Vienna, Hungary, Milan, the Italian states, and Sicily. Despite defeat, Hobsbawm argues, "the revolutions of 1848 made it clear that the middle classes, liberalism, political democracy, nationalism, even the working classes were henceforth permanent features of the landscape. The defeat of the revolutions might temporarily remove them from sight, but when they reappeared they would determine the actions of even those statesmen who had the least sympathy for them" (1995: 26).

Although Britain experienced no revolution at this time, the radical politics of the Chartists and others, combined with the insurrections in mainland Europe, produced anxiety among the British ruling classes. The Saturday half-holiday was perhaps a response to their concerns. As Hobsbawm points out, the shadow of the revolution created political spaces for new actors to find their way on to the public stage, in both politics and cultural life. Heterogeneous associations were formed in the rapidly developing cities, drawing on newly developing technologies, spaces of consumption, and pieces of time, through which identities based around leisure, as well as politics, could be constructed. The Clarion "movement" was such an association, based entirely around the time of the weekend and national holidays such as Easter, when the annual meeting of members and their cycles was held. Individual Clarion Cycling Club membership booklets (Working Class Movement Library, Salford: various years) detail times of bicycle rides, all planned on Saturday and Sunday afternoons.

The Clarion newspaper first appeared in Manchester on December 12, 1891, and was published in the city until December 1894. Although espousing a rather nationalist viewpoint, supporting the second Boer War and speaking against some of the organizations associated with women's suffrage, it was the precursor of an extraordinary left-leaning network of cultural, social, and political activities. By the early years of the twentieth century, the Clarion Club owned or leased a series of clubhouses across the country, two of them being the London Clubhouse at Nazeing, Essex, and the Nelson Clubhouse in Lancashire, with the Manchester area being accommodated by a clubhouse at Handforth in Cheshire. This web of citizen-organized, weekend refuges from everyday life and work in the industrial cities, owned or rented by a socialist/left-leaning organization, seems an unlikely phenomenon in contemporary Britain, given the inflated prices of property and land and high rents. There is little chance, then, for a contemporary "Clarion" with the same spatial presence—a powerful illustration of the consolidation of capital and power into fewer hands since the late nineteenth century.

The Clarion Cycle Club was an important and enduring section of the whole Clarion enterprise. Their members' access to clubhouses in which to stay, or adjoining land on which to camp, made the affordability and utility of cycling or walking much more possible, potentially extending access to greater numbers of people. The first club was set up in Birmingham, others spread quickly across the country, organized eventually at both the national and the local level. Members' cycling activities were based around weekend time: Saturdays and Sundays were the only times when extended rides were possible. Its annual Easter meet, first held in 1895, still takes place over the Easter weekend in towns relatively close to northern industrial conurbations such as Buxton and Chester.

The Clarion movement, and similar organizations based around leisure mobilities (see Solnit earlier), emanated from a moment of modernity when "all that was solid was melting into air" (Marx and Engels 1997). They produced spaces and communal movements across space in which the lower-middle and working classes could have a visible social, political, and cultural presence in public life. Footpaths were forged across the hills and moors (members sometimes faced prosecution for accessing private land, e.g. Kinder Trespass, April 1932) and cycling routes were plotted along lanes and roads. The Clarion played a key role in allowing women to create spaces of mobility and thus have a public presence. In 1895, Manchester Clarion Cycle club put out a call for Clarionettes to join them:

> I desire to call to the attention of Manchester and District Cycling "Clarionettes" to the advertisement on page 4 calling for all who are interested in joining a strong Clarion Cycling Club in Manchester. The meeting will be held at the Labour Church Institute, 3 St John's Parade, Deansgate, Manchester on Wednesday evening next, the 16th January 1895, at 8 pm. Ladies are especially invited; and political differences will be no bar to membership, providing they are only readers and believers in the Clarion and its good work.
>
> En avant! Mes Camarades, come join the Clarion crew.

(2)

The first Clarion guesthouse based near Manchester was inaugurated at Bucklow Hill, Cheshire, just south of Manchester. Emmeline Pankhurst was part of its organizing committee, and Julia Dawson, active in the Independent Labour Party and a prominent advocate of women's rights, particularly amongst the Lancashire cotton workers, too, was a Clarion member.

44   *Jill Ebrey*

The Clarion "movement" was indeed an organization that produced a nexus of mobilities that linked their members through a variety of activities. It mobilized members through appeals to both their sporting and political desires, although the latter was surpassed by the former as the mid-twentieth century approached. Clarion Clubs were keen on various forms of association that promoted "fellowship" and solidarity, both nationally and internationally. The political side of their enterprise was, at one point, bolstered by the purchase of Clarion vans that promoted socialist ideas through the use of posters and loud hailers. The Clarion vans forged a new kind of political mobility using new mechanical technologies to tour locales and challenge the hegemony of the ruling classes.

The precedent for the chain of Clarion Club guest houses stretching across the U.K. was Bucklow House and Camp at Tabley Brook in Cheshire, founded in 1895. Formed with the idea of "developing comradeship" and giving opportunities "to get out into the fresh air at reasonable cost," two thousand people visited it during its first eighteen days in operation. Dr. Pankhurst (possibly Emmeline Pankhurst's husband, Richard) opened the first Clarion Club guesthouse in rented property in 1897. Groom, a prominent member of Clarion, makes the connection between weekends and mobilities:

> It was as if a new era had dawned. To be able to wheel out on Saturday or Sunday—after the week's toil and moil in the dingy warehouse, the stuffy warehouse, the reeking slum, the enervating mill, workshop or mine, to one's own house, situated within walking distance of quaint old Rostherne . . .
>
> (Groom: The First Socialist Guest
> House 016/3 Manchester Record Office)

Socialist ambitions and mobilities informed much of the imagery produced by the Clarion. Its logo and rather blunt motto, "Fellowship is Life—Lack of Fellowship is Death," was used on most pieces of communication as an early form of corporate (shared) identity. Images were either proclamatory (a bugle interwoven with the word "Clarion"; a Walter Crane design of an angel with wings outspread blowing a bugle underneath a scroll, with National Clarion Cycling Club at the top and the "fellowship" message on either side) or represented some kind of mobility (e.g., a ship for the Manchester Clarion Café). However, even though it was not overtly signified, the bugle acted as a signifier for political mobility across continents, as well as for the more physical mobility of cycling, walking, swimming, football, or other sports.

Archival material demonstrates the strength of the organization (still active today, although not necessarily "politically" active) and its national and international presence. Its visibility was increased through a considerable quantity of ephemera distributed through the postal service and the more informal routes of weekly and monthly local and regional meetings, as well as the Annual General Meeting (AGM) taking place (and still happening) at the annual Easter meet, alternating between places such as Buxton and Chester. These were marketed carefully through printed programs detailing the timetable and places to stay and meet.

Postal communications associated with the Clarion demonstrate this mobility on several levels: the spread of political ideas, the mobilities of ephemera, the mobilities of actors as they met and rode their bicycles to various places, and the joining of groups at the annual meet, as well as overseas meetings. In 1913, for instance, Robert Robertson, a member of the Scottish Miners Federation Friendly Society, wrote to ask for a "Clarion Fellowship Badge" and promised, if he could find sufficient interested fellow cyclists, to consider setting up a Clarion Cycling Club section. In the same year, an official of the Federation Sportive Athletique Socialiste—Monsieur Laine of Paris—wrote to Tom Groom, the chair of the club, in 1913–1914 regarding a visit to Paris, ending the epistle with "*J'espere pouvoir manger ensemble plusieurs fois*" ("I hope to do more eating together"), thereby emphasizing the social interaction that the chains of mobility produced. During the Clarion Cycling Club AGM of 1913, a communication from the Workers Cycling Federation of Germany was discussed, as well as another letter from France. Some twenty or so years later, once again at the AGM, the antifascist political focus of the club was demonstrated in resolutions that deplored "capitalist wars," criticized the location of the 1936 Olympic Games in Berlin, and supported the International Brigades in Spain.

Larsen, Urry, and Axhausen (2006: 261) discuss contemporary "geographies of social networks" by emphasizing how "ordinary people in prosperous societies are increasingly on the move and communicating more to connect with absent others." Although not disagreeing with this, the example of the Clarion cultural "network" demonstrates how mobilities of various kinds operated in the late nineteenth and the first half of the twentieth centuries. They were less "dense," perhaps, but nonetheless performed the same function of "spreading social networks," of stretching sociability beyond the local into the regional, national, and even international levels. Although criticized in its earlier years for its support of imperialist wars in its newspaper, the *Clarion*, the organization eventually became international, or at least European, in its outlook and displayed signs of a nascent cosmopolitanism. Harvey (2009: 770) cites Kant's "cosmopolitan quest" as trying to work out "by what set of institutional arrangements might all the inhabitants of planet earth hope to negotiate, in a peaceful manner, their common occupancy of a finite globe?" In a very small way, perhaps, the Clarion "movement" tried to imagine how the new spaces and times of modernity might be mobilized to produce everyday lives that were fairer, more pleasurable, and more democratic through "fellowship." The weekend, with its

46 *Jill Ebrey*

new times and consequent spaces, produced the possibility of movement in space towards meetings and friendships, a greater visibility and presence in the world, and greater understanding at the regional, national, and international levels, as well as at the local level.

CONCLUSION

This chapter has discussed, firstly, the new spaces and times of modernity. It has suggested, with particular reference to Harvey (1989, 2009), that space and time are contingent upon each other. It has proposed that the weekend (or at least in the first instance, the Saturday half-holiday) was an unintended consequence of industrialization that set in motion both a space for consumption (capital) and a utopian imaginary (social actors). The latter was rehearsed in the nineteenth and early twentieth centuries through the various spaces of association and friendship promoted through a number of different instances of mobility. We have seen how the time of the weekend worked in symbiosis with various spatialities, such as that of the railways or the webs of Clarion activities. At the end of the nineteenth and the beginning of the twentieth centuries, newly created leisure spaces and forms of mobility, like railways, had to be accompanied by concomitant times during which they could be used. The Saturday half-holiday, later to evolve into the weekend, was crucial: this "time" was as important as the railways in the reorientation of time and space.

From this spatial and temporal reorganization, new spaces of pleasure and friendship were created, which were stretched out from the local to the regional, national, and even international levels. New mobilities were created that produced the new spaces and "stretchings." The Clarion movement, remarkable for its ability to make a visible presence through a panoply of ephemera, buildings, and bikes, provides evidence of the mobilization of human subjects towards a different kind of world. Strangely, the new times and spaces of the weekend were also those that produced political resistance. Indeed we could argue that the rush of the crowd or the group travelling together, nowhere in particular, on a Sunday afternoon, might offer some food for thought for the twenty-first century.

NOTES

1. Anon (1844). *Half-Holiday Excursions, or Topographical, Historical and Biographical Notices of the most Picturesque and remarkable Places within an afternoon's walk from Manchester: Rostherne, Bowdon, Dunham Park and Altrincham*, Manchester: The Advertiser and Chronicle Office, Market Street and Oldham St., Manchester. This was printed in response to the Saturday half-holiday and gives some account of a supposed walk-out with some male beneficiaries of the half-holiday.

2. *The Ancoats Brotherhood* was founded by Charles Rowley in 1878 and based in Ancoats, the industrial center of Manchester. Its purpose was to "bring art and literature to the working classes." Among their invited speakers was William Morris and, interestingly, in this edition of *Odds and Ends*, was a "tipped in" William Morris design on paper.

WORKS CITED

Anon. *Half-Holiday Excursions, or Topographical, Historical and Biographical Notices of the most Picturesque and Remarkable Places within an Afternoon's Walk from Manchester: Rostherne, Bowdon, Dunham Park and Altrincham.* Manchester, Anon., 1844.

Buscher. M., J. Urry, and K. Witchger (eds.). *Mobile Methods.* London, Routledge, 2011.

Clarion archive (accessed Feb/March 2012). Ref 0161/1–11 Greater Manchester County Record Office.

Clarke, J., and C. Critcher. *The Devil Makes Work: Leisure in Capitalist Britain.* Basingstoke, Macmillan, 1985.

Clarke, S. H. *The Development of Leisure in Britain after 1850.* Web. 1996. http://www.victorianweb.org/history/leisure2.html.

De Sapio, Joseph. "Transient Communities: Travel, Knowledge, and the Victorian Railway Carriage, 1840–90." *Mobilities* 8 (2013), no. 2, p. 201–219.

The First Socialist Guest House: An Historical Sketch. Greater Manchester Record Office (Ref 0161/1–11).

Flanders, J. *Consuming Passions: Leisure and Pleasure in Victorian Britain.* London, Harper Collins, 2006.

Goldstone, Jack A. "Initial Conditions, General Laws, Path Dependence, and Explanation in Historical Sociology." *American Journal of Sociology* 104 (1998), no. 3, p. 829–845.

Gillen, J., and N. Hall. "Any Mermaids? Early Postcard Mobilities." In: M. Buscher, J. Urry, and K. Witchger K (eds.), *Mobile Methods.* London, Routledge, 2011.

Harvey, D. *The Condition of Postmodernity.* Oxford, Blackwell, 1989.

———. *Cosmopolitanism and the Geographies of Freedom.* New York, Columbia University Press, 2009.

Kidd, Alan J. *Manchester* (3rd ed). Edinburgh, Edinburgh University Press, 2002.

Langhamer, C. *Women's Leisure in England.* Manchester, Manchester University Press, 2000.

Larsen, J., J. Urry, and K. Axhausen. *Mobilities, Networks, Geographies.* Aldershot, Ashgate, 2006.

Malcolmson, R. "Popular Recreations Under Attack in Popular Culture Past and Present." In: T. Bennett, G. Martin, and B. Waites, Popular Culture Past and Present. London, Routledge, 1981.

Marx, K., and F. Engels. *The Communist Manifesto: A Modern Edition.* 1848. London, Verso, 1998.

Odds and Ends. Vol. XXXIX. Greater Manchester Records Office Ref M/38/4/239.

Reid, D. "The Decline of Saint Monday, 1766–1876." *Past and Present* 71 (1976), p. 76–101.

Rose, Michael E. "Culture, Philanthropy and the Manchester Middle Classes." In: A. J. Kidd and K. W. Roberts (eds.), *City, Class, and Culture.* Manchester, Manchester University Press, 1985, p. 103–147.

Rubenstein, David. "Cycling in the 1890's." *Victorian Studies* 21 (1977), no. 1.

Silverstone. R. *Television and Everyday Life.* London, Routledge, 1997.

48 *Jill Ebrey*

Slater, D. "Looking Backwards." In: M. Lee (ed.), *The Consumer Society Reader*. Oxford, Blackwell, 1997, p. 177–185.

Solnit, R. *Wanderlust*. London, Verso, 2001.

Slugg, J. *Reminiscences of Manchester Fifty Years Ago*. 1881. Shannon, Irish University Press, 1971.

Urry, J. *Sociology Beyond Societies*. London, Routledge, 2000.

4 Towards a Better Understanding of Bicycles as Transport

Peter Cox

INTRODUCTION

Historically, the bicycle provided the first mass-produced, affordable means of independent, individualized mobility. In 1912, Edwin A. Pratt, in his *History of Inland Transport and Communication*, was able to characterize its role thus:

> Cycles have materially developed the taste for travel; they have led to indulgence in outings or pleasure trips at home and abroad to an extent previously unknown; they have vastly increased the means of communication; they have exercised a powerful influence on our general social conditions, and they have become, in a variety of ways, and with different modifications of the bicycle or the tricycle principle, an important auxiliary to the despatch of business.
>
> (473)

By the middle of the twentieth century, this auxiliary and leisured role had been transformed into the most numerous means of personalized mobility on European roads. Bicycles accounted for the majority of urban traffic in most industrialized cities, excepting those in the United States. Yet, by the late 1960s, its use as everyday transport in Europe had dwindled to the exception, only for the bicycle to reemerge as a leisure consumer item, followed by a slow rise again as transport in the twenty-first century.

Today, policy guidance and strategic planning for sustainable urban mobility, from World Bank/Global Environment Facility development strategies, through national governmental arenas, down to local city and community plans, has refocused attention on the bicycle as an important component in sustainable urban transport networks. Despite the enthusiasm of advocacy, the actual use of bicycles as everyday transport remains sporadic and geographically distinct. Moreover, significant questions remain concerning bicycle mobility. Why did it never attain the status as a means for mass transport in the United States? Why did it disappear so rapidly in Europe? Why did it not decline in other regions? As a contribution to

50   *Peter Cox*

the debate over these questions, this chapter examines some of the factors responsible for the growth (or lack thereof) of cycling as transport in the first half of the twentieth century.

Until relatively recently, the bicycle remained all but invisible in narratives of transport history (see, for example, Bagwell and Lyth 2002). When it did appear, its role was frequently simplified to that of a proto-motorcar, whose demise after a brief period of mass use was all but inevitable. Where bicycle mobility is considered as part of future mobility scenarios, its treatment is frequently limited and without basis in analysis of existing or historical models of use (see both Vuchic 1999 and Banister 2005 for examples). The appearance and coordination of academic studies on cycling since around 2006 has changed the picture somewhat, and this chapter contributes to an expanding literature, particularly in journals such as *Transfers* and the *Journal of Transport History*.

A further problem is that even the best scholarly bicycle histories have been dominated by accounts focusing on the technology of the machine itself, and consequently are weighted toward the nineteenth century (typified even in McGurn's [1999] social history and Herlihey's *Bicycle* [2009]). Characteristically, a composite picture of the (European) development of bicycle mobility emerges in this literature. A European invention, the bicycle was taken up by bourgeois social elites in a number of nations, keen to embrace symbols of a new modernity. Its design, subject to initial contestation, reached stabilization in the safety bicycle. By the start of the twentieth century, the technology of the solo bicycle reached a relatively mature stage or, using a social construction of technology (SCOT) perspective, closure. A boom in use during the last decade of the nineteenth century was followed by general diffusion across other social classes, resulting in mass use as an affordable and ubiquitous mode of transport, a period that lasted until rapid decline during the 1950s. A slow reemergence is visible from the mid-1970s onwards, primarily as leisure, but latter as transport. This latter period, although less spectacular, has been dubbed a "renaissance" and, although uneven, is at its most visible in the Netherlands, Denmark, and Germany (Pucher, Komanoff, and Schimek 2001; Stoffers and Cox 2010).

This account is problematic on a number of levels. First, it fails to recognize the diversity of historical trajectories in different locations. Second, this linear narrative introduces a potentially "naturalized" periodization, implicitly suggesting that the bicycle, as a stable technology, must pursue a predetermined "life-course" in which it is inevitably surpassed by the advent of motor vehicles. Neither of these readings facilitates comprehension of the historical events and social and political forces that change the practices and meanings of cycle use in any given time and place. Third, being primarily derived from a Northern European perspective, it not only fails to adequately provide a comparative study, but introduces a developmentalist, colonialist perspective: Eurocentric normativity creates a center to which all other experiences are peripheral and against which the experiences of "other" users are measured (Nandy 2008). Significant independent innovations and counternarratives—especially the rickshaw and bicycling in Asia—are hidden or only mentioned in passing. Efforts to turn towards a more global account of the history of cycling have drawn attention to the diversity of historical patterns of cycle usage (Boal 2001; Steele 2010). Although the diversity of contemporary cycle usage across nations is obvious, the significance and extent of differences in the historical trajectories through which they have arrived at these patterns is less well explored. It is notable that this volume opens with the explicit discussion of walking and cycling as transport modes. In mitigation, the omission of these modes in previous studies owes a lot to the very real difficulties in obtaining consistent data. It is to these varied problems that this chapter addresses its considerations. Even so, for practical purposes, its scope is largely limited to Western Europe, North America, and East Asia from 1890 to 1945.

Before comparing the emergence of mass cycling across a number of locations, we can sketch two contrasting narratives of cycling outside Europe. In the United States, the initial boom of the 1890s was followed by significant collapse of the industry as the bicycle fell out of fashion. Although cycles were still constructed, purchased, and ridden, this deployment did not translate into use as mass transport. Rather, cycling continued principally as a leisure activity and transport for children. Adult urban transport needs were met initially by the rapid expansion of mass-transit systems, and later by the use of the automobile. These developments are further linked with different patterns of land use, demographic distribution, urban growth, and population densities, which by the mid-1950s had made car use the only really viable transit option (Wells 2012). By contrast, in Japan, where the first bicycles also appeared on the streets very early, there is minimal evidence of a 1890s boom–bust cycle. Rather, comparatively steady growth in use through the twentieth century was perturbed by a periods of rapid growth and decline arising from external events, in particular warfare (and its cessation). Neither was there a rapid decline in the 1950s. Consequently, Japan continues to have one of the highest levels of global cycle use in the first decade of the twenty-first century (Steele 2012). In order to understand why the same technology was used so very differently, a comparative approach allows distinctions to be made between regions and within them, as well as between varying user (and nonuser) groups. This also allows us to isolate mechanisms that may account for changes in use and users, and explain how similar changes occur within different timescales in different regions. Not only do use patterns differ, but the relationship of the bicycle to other forms and practices of mobility may be markedly different, too. It is further worth noting that the changes in bicycle use and users may also reflect other broader changes in mobility, not just those arising from technological innovation.

52 *Peter Cox*

BOOM–BUST CYCLES, MODERNITY, AND INDUSTRIAL CAPITALISM

The development of the pneumatic-tire safety bicycle created a versatile machine suitable for riding in most conditions on a wide variety of surfaces and easily adapted for carrying luggage. In other words, the bicycle became, in potential at least, a practical conveyance. Its use as such, however, depended on both the travelling public's need for such a vehicle and its affordability to those with such a need.

The fortunes of the bicycle during the 1890s are frequently characterized by descriptions of the rapid expansion of production and soaring rates of use, during which the solo bicycle was heralded as a signifier of modernity (Norcliffe 2001). It was an object of conspicuous consumption, displayed and used in public by a newly confident upper middle class. Ownership reflected the possession of considerable social (as well as financial) capital by its users. As Veblen (1889) wrote in describing the general boom of consumer goods in the United States, "goods which contain an appreciable element of cost in excess to what gives them serviceability for their ostensible mechanical purpose are honorific" (94). The mobility provided by the bicycle was by no means necessary, indeed, the bicycle fit into the realm of a luxury good, fitting with the new desire for touristic travel. Given this emphasis, Pratt's (1912) statement (quoted above) is more reasonably understood as pointing towards the increase of luxury travel afforded and the adjunct to business alluded to as opening new possibilities for trade, not for individual worker mobility.

The bicycle's viability as a symbol of modernity was, however, a fragile commodity, wholly dependent on its novelty as a mobility mode (Ameye, Gils, and Delheye 2011, 205). Motorized vehicles—two, three, or four wheeled—powered by electricity, steam, or internal combustion, very soon offered an even more visible means of mobility display with the advantage of even greater exclusivity, maintaining, even reinforcing, the social order for the proud car owner who could employ a chauffeur. Although writers of the 1890s understood the utility of the bicycle as a means of transporting goods and persons together with basic luggage, solo machines were generally not retailed on that basis at that time (Albermarle and Hillier 1896). Carrier tricycles, although developed extensively during the mid-1890s, were sold as objects for trade, not consumer, purchase ("Built for Business" 1895, 94; "An Original Carrier" 1896, 52).

The boom–bust pattern was most extreme in the United States, fuelled by the innovation of mass production and the Pope Manufacturing Company's attempts at monopolizing the cycle trade. Although Norcliffe (1997, 269) describes Pope as being "well poised to benefit from the bicycle craze of 1895–[18]97," the introduction of new manufacturing processes during the preceding years (replacing batch production) were themselves a significant factor in enabling the boom to occur. Equally dramatic was the collapse of the industry after 1897. Gross overproduction and a saturated market led to a collapse, only partially mitigated by exporting surplus cycles at a significant markdown to Europe. The scale of this shift is indicated by the rapid changes in U.S. cycle exports to Europe, which, in 1895–1896, amounted to $1,898,012. The following year this rose to $7,005,323, and in 1897–1898, $6,846,529. One-third of these went to England (Harrison 1969, 290). Surpluses created in the United States as a result of a particular form of capitalism were exported to Europe, where they assisted in fuelling expansion in European cycle use among a less elite population, for whom locally produced cycles remained expensive.

Even with surplus production capacity after the turn of the century, the bicycle never attained a role as a mass transport technology in the United States. Rubenson identifies the use of cheap but impractical single-tube tires as one factor. Epperson (2000, 300) argues for the salience of the structure and ideology of U.S. cycle manufacturing, especially the legacy of Albert Pope's attempts to monopolize the U.S. cycle industry during the 1880s. The American Bicycle Corporation, also chaired by Pope, made a similar attempt in 1899–1903. The dismantling of the ABC and the transfer of its assets into the Pope Manufacturing Company, and the attendant financial problems of that company, were not conducive to creating a new market for bicycles as transport. Bicycles promised only low margins and little of the captive lucrative accessory trade visible in the car market, to which the company was committed through its production of the Columbia Electric Car (Pope 1995; Kirsch 2000). Throughout his enterprises, Pope identified firmly the affluent urbanite of the emerging clerical and administrative classes as the target consumer (Petty 1995, 100). Pope's consistent strategy through his diverse enterprises was to establish complete control in one area and maintain profit margins either through patent control and price fixing or by slashing production costs when patents were no longer valid (Epperson 2010). As Norcliffe (1997, 273) notes, Pope himself explained to the *New York Record* on July 17, 1894, that "bicycle prices will drop when the patents run out, as did the price of sewing machines."

Beyond these technological and industrial factors, however, American urban transport needs were already well served by the proliferation of a dense network of tramways, despite their reputation for poor quality and service (Filarski 2011). By the turn of the century, the cycling trade press in the United States was itself attributing the disuse of the bicycle to the increase in trolley (tram) use ("No Horseless Age" 1900; "The Measure of Cycle Use" 1900). Despite some attempts to revive the U.S. cycle industry from 1906 onward, 1909 marked a low point of production. Simultaneously, Japanese indigenous manufacture was beginning to take off, and continental Europe was moving towards mass use, requiring more affordable machines. In the United States, the bicycle was still perceived as a luxury good, which highlights the United States' isolation from trends elsewhere (Herlihey 2004). Another relevant factor in understanding the formation

54   *Peter Cox*

of the bicycle market and the social practices of cycling in the post-1900 era is the organization of labor. Although the United States could boast relatively high wages in skilled industries, compared to Europe, the broad masses of the American working classes were weakly organized and poorly paid, and attempts to organize were actively discouraged (Thompson and Bekken 2006, passim). Thus, the bicycle never acquired the symbolic value for labor that it did in Germany or Denmark.

In the U.K., the bicycle boom did not fundamentally transform the cycle industry, which continued to rely on high-price and high-margin sales. But in France and Germany, it "stimulated the expansion of the indigenous cycle trades and put them on a more satisfactory commercial and technological footing" (Harrison 1969, 288). Canada, Australia, and New Zealand were directly linked by their positions within the British Empire and, as in the mother country, the bicycle provided not only an important means for demonstrating fashionable status, but also began to provide more utilitarian transport (Toohey 2010, 214; Lehr and Selwood 1999, 3). Yet the end of the boom did not see automatic translation of the bicycle from toy to transport. Indeed, the aftermath of the bicycle boom in the U.K. also occurred at the same time as a significant expansion of municipally owned electric tramways, due to the maturing of the municipal purchase rights established in the Tramway Act of 1870, and, after the turn of the century, new motor-buses augmented, then succeeded, existing horse-bus services (Hibbs 1989; Filarski 2011). After the bicycle boom, much of the growth of mundane urban mobility for large numbers of people in Europe and the United States was fulfilled largely by the expansion of other services, not by individual bicycle use. What is clearly visible in the U.K. is that the first decade of the twentieth century saw a marked transition in the social class of cycle users.

After 1898, the bicycle ceased to be a rapidly changing novelty. Design features quickly stabilized with one year's model virtually indistinguishable from the last (Oddy 2007, 26). Standardization marked a decline in new-purchase prestige and made the secondhand market more viable (because older machines were less visibly obsolete). Roadster types, not racy or sporting models, dominated sales. Together these factors point towards the bicycle's changed status and prevalence among the middle and lower-middle classes. Membership of the Cyclists' Touring Club (CTC) fell away rapidly after 1905, in large part due to an intransigent clinging to bourgeois identity. Overall bicycle sales did not taper off so rapidly, suggesting a slow but steady increase in U.K. ridership in the first decade of the twentieth century (unlike in the United States). The bicycle boom, as with rapid expansions in other consumer products, is less a factor of the technology than of the socioeconomic situation itself: Large-scale production capacity coincided with the availability of surplus income in a sufficiently large section of the population. As with other twentieth-century consumer goods, initial exclusivity and high desirability followed by rapidly increased production created an initial boom prior to later diffusion. With mass adoption, however, came a lowering of the social cachet attached to the good itself, as ownership moved across social classes. Where the bicycle differs is that the meanings and practices attached to it are also subject to change. To understand the working classes' adoption (and nonadoption) of the bicycle in industrial capitalist societies, and to comprehend the cycle's transformation from a leisure item to a mundane, quotidian form of transport, we need to look at its use in greater depth.

THE BICYCLE AS AN ADJUNCT OF BUSINESS

A corollary of the expansion of solo bicycle production and use in the 1890s was intense lobbying by manufacturers to further increase the potential applications of their novel product. The utilitarian possibilities of cycles had been recognized almost since their inception. During the era of the ordinary (i.e., high-wheel bicycle), experimentation with the bicycle's form continued. Tricycle designs by Starley and numerous imitators intended to be more suitable for the locomotion of society ladies—who could not be seen mounting a high bicycle in polite company—were far more easily adapted to transport goods as well as persons.

Subsequently, with the safety bicycle produced in both diamond- and open-frame designs (the latter marketed specifically for the "Lady" rider), manufacturers in Europe and America demonstrated new uses for pedal vehicles amongst different user groups. In the United States, Pope "advocated the use of bicycles to conduct several public activities including policing, fire protection, post and telegraph delivery" (Norcliffe 1997, 278). Similar applications were envisaged by European manufactures, ranging from a human-powered fire crew transport to a complex, multirider ambulance cycle (Kielwein and Lessing 2005, 140, 150). If the 1890s are to be regarded as the period of stabilization of the safety bicycle as a design, they should also be understood as simultaneously a period of diversification where the technologies of the safety bicycle were deployed in a variety of different ways for goods carriage.

However, human-powered options for such transport uses are restricted by weight limitations. Complex vehicles requiring multiperson power sources were rapidly rendered obsolete by the development of motor traction for the same functions. But for urban deliveries and functions served formerly by handcart traffic, utility tricycles and carrier bicycles of numerous designs proved to be practicable. Much of their advantage over either motorized forms or animal traction arose from their capacity for immobilization. The constant stop-start of postal or other doorstep deliveries of relatively lightweight goods, as well as mobile sales to households, ensured roles for human-powered vehicles that have lasted, largely unchanged, to the present day. And unlike animal traction, feeding and watering the motive power need not necessarily be the responsibility of the employer.

56   Peter Cox

Design of work bikes, unlike the solo bicycle, remained localized and diverse, reflecting small-scale manufacturing applied to specific purposes. For example, the newspaper industry in Paris used bicycles as a means of distribution from the 1890s, even organizing annual races as a further means of publicity. The *Criterium des Porteurs de Journaux* was first run (in both men's and women's editions) in 1895 (Metz n.d.). By the turn of the century, two- and three-wheeled delivery tricycles (*bi-* and *tri-porteurs*) were also being used (and were still being raced until the 1960s). Delivery tricycles have been developed wherever bicycles are in use, and their design simply depends on the particular needs for which they are constructed. Overall, however, the most undoubtedly important form of nonsolo cycle is the cycle rickshaw. Mating the mechanical efficiency of the bicycle with the passenger- or goods-carrying trade of the hand-pulled rickshaw, the cycle-rickshaw rapidly became emblematic of transport across South Asia in the 1930s and continues in a variety of local variants to the present (Gallagher 1992; Wheeler and l'Anson 1998).

Why the rickshaw has been so consistently overlooked not only in transport studies but also in bicycle studies may have something to do with its status as an autonomous product of the semi-periphery, derived from modern knowledge produced outside of the core of western modernity (Santos 2005; Samanta and Roy 2013, 62). One of modernity's distinguishing features is that technological innovation is presumed to be an exclusive quality of the metropolitan center, because that is the very reason for the imperial center's advantage over its "other" territories. This technological marginalization is not only visible in colonial terms but also in those of gender (Leonard 2003). That the periphery, or even semi-periphery, may be the origin of a "better," "more useful," or "appropriate" technology is almost unthinkable for the core. The post-1948 concept of "development" is conceptually predicated on the technological obsolescence of the "underdeveloped" vis-à-vis the "developed" world (Rist 2008, 72). Dubey's (2007) study of rickshaws in India uses this analysis to explain attempts at suppression by governmental authorities and the way in which, although ignored and sometimes banned, rickshaws persist. Ambiguously trapped between modernity and obsolescence, the same problem that has isolated knowledge of the rickshaw is also characteristic of the bicycle in contemporary transport analyses. Cycle transport is complicated not only by being shaped through colonialist discourse, but also through the more conventionally recognizable categories of class and gender differences.

SOCIALISM AND CLASS STRUGGLE: THE BICYCLE AS A TOOL OF APPROPRIATION OR CONCILIATION

For European socialists, what made the bicycle such a desirable commodity during the growth years was its clear potential for more universal distribution of social goods through the access granted by increased mobility. Across Europe, wherever there were societies of organized labor, the advent of socialist bicycle clubs was not far behind. Similarly, for women, the bicycle was also recognized as a vehicle of liberation, offering independence and unchaperoned autonomy in public spaces (Carstensen and Ebert 2012, 27). Indeed, Crystal Eastman (1978), reflecting on a lifetime of feminist action, stated boldly, "I believe bicycles were the beginning of women's emancipation" (216). Where the two impulses diverge is over the issue of class. The success of working-class societies, their ability to ensure supply of machines at affordable prices to desiring nonusers, correlates with the relative strength of organized labor and varies between locations. The clearest and strongest example may be seen in Germany.

The corollary of the antisocialist legislation passed in Germany from 1878, which originated from fears of enfranchised laborers, was the legitimization of the state's role in promulgating policies designed to "heal the wounds of modern society" (Barmayer 2002, 98). If the role of welfare legislation was thus to forestall insurrectionary activity, state provision of transport networks and systems as further means by which to promote social inclusion and cohesion is part of the same process. Hence the expansion of electric tramways in Prussia from the 1880s served workers (especially more independently minded, white-collar workers), expanding into the mobility sphere state interventions first seen in relation to more conventional forms of social security.

Organized labor grew stronger after the repeal of the *Sozialistengesetze* in 1890 (Geary 1989). Unionization also created cultural and sporting organizations, of which the cycling club *Solidarität*, the Worker's Cycling Organization (1896), was an important part (Rabenstein, 162). The use of the bicycle by its 130,000 members in the early days, at least, was not primarily as quotidian transport but as a claim on privileges previously exclusive to the bourgeoisie: a form of emancipation. As Ebert (2004) argues, even this "appropriation by a large group of society, i.e. the working class, did not automatically result in its recognition as an important mode of transport and the incorporation in to a national framework" (349). It did, however, provide the mechanism for cycling's transition from an elite activity to a more generalized one.

In Britain, organized union activity had far less structured engagement with the political process and relatively little power. There were socialist cycling clubs, and the National Clarion Cycling Club, which united the various local Clarion Clubs (named after the title of Blatchford's weekly socialist newspaper, which had proposed their formation), provided a signal demonstration of the potential of social organization. Nevertheless, they remained relatively small in number compared with their German counterparts, and even in Britain itself their numbers were overshadowed by the membership of the Cyclists' Touring Club, which maintained a more firmly bourgeois stance and firmly opposed the Clarion. Additionally, the cycle

58   *Peter Cox*

trade maintained an effective cartel on sales, enforcing price ceilings and vigorously pursuing those seeking to lower prices to a level affordable to the majority of laborers (Millward 1995, 101). Consequently, cycling in the U.K. did not truly become a mass activity until after the First World War.

The success of Danish workers' political organization at the turn of the twentieth century was also paralleled in the rise of socialist cycling organizations (Hoffman 2008). Early Danish socialist cycling clubs (e.g., the ABC—Arbejdernes Bicykle Club—formed 1895 and still in existence) were rooted in the urban milieu, which was dominated by Copenhagen, but bicycling did not long remain limited to urban regions given the geography of the country. By 1930, a third of the population of Copenhagen was reckoned to move by bicycle (Herlihey 2004, 328). So essential was the bicycle to general mobility throughout the country that during the Nazi occupation a decade later German sources were at pains to deny rumors that bicycles would be confiscated by the occupiers. Cycles remained in widespread use by civilians, as well as by the Nazi authorities, through the war years, even to the extent that a "Pedal Exhibition" was organized in September 1941. Authorities insisted that cycles should remain available to the public, because a lack of mobility would have jeopardized agricultural production levels because laborers would have been unable to reach their work. The only limitation was the shortage of rubber for tires, a situation similarly problematic in all occupied territories.

The importance of organized worker movements in the spread of cycling is twofold. First, they encouraged desire for the democratization and diffusion of mobility and access, which previously had been afforded to only a privileged few, to all classes. Second, in practical economic terms, workers' successes in ensuring wage increases and the breakup of sales cartels was necessary in order to make the bicycle an affordable commodity. However, although socialist organization facilitated bicycle use in Germany and Denmark, an antithetical movement provoked the growth of cycling in the Netherlands.

Examining the rapid and early adoption of the bicycle as a primary mode of transport in the Netherlands reveals the extent to which Dutch exceptionalism is the product of a number of unique political forces. At the end of the nineteenth century, the Netherlands Touring Club (ANWB) made concerted efforts to portray the bicycle as a vehicle "acceptable" to the bourgeoisie. Their success enabled disparate, "pillarized" elite interests to agree that the bicycle could simultaneously calm the threat of socialist unrest and promote civic virtue and liberal values: "Cycling was being presented as a way to promote 'traditional' Dutch virtues, i.e. independence, self-confidence, self-control, balance and consistency, which needed to be preserved and reasserted in a changing world" (Ebert 2004, 356). Using a national cycling policy, the Netherlands incorporated a nascent, self-conscious, working class into the bourgeois state by ensuring access to public goods. McGurn (1999), drawing on a 1923 Jubilee publication of the ANWB, observes that cycle roads in the Netherlands were seen as a means by which the rural hinterlands could be better incorporated into the modern nation state: They were a means by which to spread education and increase social intercourse (82).

The construction of the Dutch network of cycle paths—more properly, cycle roads—newly constructed in rolled macadam, was a unique corollary of a political response from social elites to perceived threats of socialism. Existing road and path networks could not be practically promoted for this purpose because of the predominance of brick and gravel surfacing, neither of which were particularly suitable for bicycle traffic, unlike the macadamized surfaces, asphalted or not, that predominated in Britain (Cox 2011, 19; Mom 2004, 76; Mom 2007, 33). That transport could even be considered an arena for legitimate state intervention also depended on other political preconditions. Canals and roads were already state-sponsored construction ventures in the Netherlands, another profound contrast with the *laissez-faire* conditions in Britain. Dutch neutrality in 1914–1918, while disrupting trade and isolating the country, did allow for greater social continuity, and it is not surprising that we see the Netherlands characterized as a cycling nation by 1921, with levels of bicycle use rivalled only by similarly neutral Denmark.

The transition of cycling from an exclusive bourgeois pastime to a means of everyday mundane mobility, and the bicycle's mass adoption, was by no means "natural." Ebert (2004) describes the transition as a "general diffusion" arising from a "trickle-down process" (347). Yet even her study shows that very specific mechanisms can account for very different meanings of the bicycle in Germany and the Netherlands. Based on further international examples, we can see in greater detail that interlinked social, political, and economic forces played important roles. The common characteristic, however, in all but the United States, is that by the 1930s the bicycle was the most numerous vehicle on the road. A few examples hint at the varied routes by which this position was reached.

BECOMING A MASS ACTIVITY

Growth of bicycle use in Japan, as elsewhere, is closely related to the growth of early industrial manufacturing capacity. Although the first Michaux-type (front-driver) velocipedes were imported in the late 1860s, the simultaneous development of the *jinrikisha*—the human-pulled rickshaw—provided the urban transport revolution while bicycle design was going through its developmental stages (Steele 2010). When John Foster Fraser (1889) wrote his account of travelling through Japan in 1899, he commented on the popularity of obviously homemade machines in Nagoya. These were scooted rather than pedal driven, reflecting the limited capacity of local production at the time. Fraser saw conventional bicycles as the imported preserve of Americans

60 *Peter Cox*

and Europeans, as did Frank Lenz in 1892 (Herlihey 2010). Some local production was initiated alongside assembly of imported machines, and, in 1894, *The Wheel and Cycle Trade Review* (May 18, 1894, 44) reported that the first Japanese bicycle export was a shipment of six machines to Russia in 1894. Horror stories circulated in the U.S. cycling press about the imminent threat of Japanese production during the boom of 1896, but these proved groundless (*The Wheel and Cycle Trade Review* January 31, 1896, 94).

After the turn of the century, cycling clubs under the patronage of prominent local citizens provided incentives for more sophisticated local manufacturing, but indigenous manufacturing only began to take off in any volume after the end of the Russo-Japanese War (1905). The similarity between the industrial production processes necessary for handguns and bicycles should be noted: both BSA (Birmingham Small Arms) in England and Miyata in Japan moved from gunsmithing to cycle manufacturing (T. Takeuchi 1991). Although relatively slow by international terms, local production, supplemented by assembly from imported parts and production using imported machines, was soon able to provide sufficient numbers for the bicycle to become a serious modal component of the domestic transport fleet (T. Takeuchi 1991). Bicycle export in the form of CKD (complete knock down) for assembly in the importing nation remained an important feature of the international cycle trade in the early twentieth century and enabled bulk export, as well as providing a means to avoid import taxes in some cases. Japanese cycle ownership increased by as many as 200,000–500,000 units per annum after 1910, and a Tokyo traffic survey of 1925 listed bicycles as accounting for 2.4 million out of a total of 4.4 million registered vehicles (Saito 2001, 76). By 1925, domestic production amounted to 90% of total cycle sales. By 1930, total numbers were over five million, with over eight million in 1940, as compared to a prewar motor vehicle fleet peaking at 50,994 vehicles in 1937 (Steele 2010). Bicycle production in the 1930s was not only for domestic consumption. By the middle of the decade, Japan was exporting machines through India, China, and Southeast Asia, including Australia. Only through restrictive regulation were Japanese cycles kept from the British market.

Closely linked with the fortunes of the Japanese bicycle industry and its products were the fortunes of cycles in China. As in Japan, the bicycle at first was encountered through the aegis of missionaries and other European colonists. Although bicycles represented an almost insignificant element of the traffic profile until the early 1920s, by the end of the decade they were almost twice as numerous as the combined motor-vehicle fleet and two-thirds of the number of (hand-pulled) rickshaws. Bicycle imports from Japan increased rapidly from 1934–1935 to well over 50,000 per annum by the end of the decade. It was Japanese imperial expansionism and occupation that stifled Chinese production, but it also left a legacy of manufacturing plants in the occupied zone that formed the basis of China's postwar, mass cycle industry, augmented by numerous smaller independent firms (Tao 2011, 460).

Towards a Better Understanding 61

In Switzerland, licenses allow us to calculate the number of bicycles in use relatively accurately. Bicycle use remained relatively limited before 1914, but expanded steadily through the 1920s. The early 1930s saw an almost complete stagnation, corresponding to the prevailing economic climate, but growth rates had more than recovered by 1934–1935. The number of bicycles continued to increase through the latter years of the decade, with automobile use remaining almost stagnant. In 1941, over 150,000 new cycle registrations were recorded, while car numbers fell by 50,000, but both modes remained relatively static until 1945 (Meyer 2008). Unspectacularly, the bicycle was simply adopted and used for its obvious practicality. In neither case did the bicycle become a symbolic identifier of social class.

In postwar Britain, the Crane family established Hercules explicitly to supply affordable bicycles for the masses. Previous attempts at cheap sales by the firm had been curtailed through legal action by the trade cartel. Hercules rapidly became the largest manufacturer and brought about an irrevocable change in the industry. However, with mass use, the bicycle also became identified even more powerfully as a symbol of class difference, especially in the aftermath of the General Strike of 1926 (Cox 2012a, 15). Although Britain had the highest use of cars in Europe, automobiles nevertheless remained the province of the wealthy British middle classes and social elites. Indeed manufacturers' lower-cost cars did not sell well (O'Connor 1998, 22). The class divide between cyclists and motorized road transport users played out in rising levels of conflict, as road accident rates rose dramatically through the latter part of the 1920s. The rise in casualties became a subject of national public and media concern because the ownership of the mass-circulation newspapers was the province of the political right and social elites, who were ideologically committed to the expansion of private motoring. Road death was presented as a problem caused by the presence of bicycles—logically solvable by their removal.

In 1926 Britain, 1,715,000 motor vehicles were registered and 4,886 road fatalities were recorded. Bicycle numbers were rarely counted. In parliament, estimates of approximately ten million riders were accepted as a fair assessment—the total population being some forty-six million. Numerical superiority made little impact on the experience of riders. Many felt embattled and outmaneuvered by hostile motoring forces. Despite rapid rises in casualties, stabilizing between 6,500 and 7,300 in the decade from 1929, concerted opposition campaigns were mounted by a variety of cyclists' groups against the introduction of compulsory rear lights, centering on the argument that it should not be the victim's task to guard against an "oppressor." Parallel campaigns were mounted against the introduction of segregated cycle paths, because these were seen to remove the cyclists' long-established and hard-earned right to be on the road. Fears were also voiced that separate infrastructure would be inferior in quality, relegating the cyclist to the condition of a second-class traveler—fears that were later vindicated by the cycling infrastructure that was constructed.

62   Peter Cox

In Germany during the 1930s a number of high-profile restrictions on cycling were enacted that accompanied the construction of motor traffic–only highways. The construction of cycle paths was advocated for the explicit function of removing cycles from the highways so that they would be less of an impediment to motor traffic (Ebert 2004, 361). Car ownership in Germany, however, remained at a significantly lower level than ownership in France or Great Britain. In 1938, Germans possessed 27.9 cars per thousand inhabitants, as opposed to 42.1 per thousand inhabitants for France and Great Britain—only Italy and Russia had lower levels of motorization (Filarski 2011, 91; Zeller 2013, 52). The *Autobahnen* served to propagandize the motorcar in its relative absence, not serve it. Simultaneously, this attention occluded the reality of continued reliance on other forms of mobility. With relatively high bus travel prices, this meant a continued reliance on bicycle traffic. Indeed, bicycle manufacturers such as Torpedo responded to neocorporatist Fascist social policy by deliberately marketing the bicycle as a classless machine—equally suitable for blue- and white-collar workers—and produced special models for party members. Production levels of about two million bicycles a year were on a par with U.K. levels, reflecting the continued salience of the bicycle in the modal split of transport practices (Herlihey 2004, 328).

In Italy, another early adopter and an important cycle producer, restrictions on bicycle mobility were introduced in the 1929 Highway Code, but these were frequently relaxed as the necessity of maintaining bicycle mobility was understood. Bicycles continued to outnumber motor vehicles by a ratio of at least 10:1 throughout the interwar period (Caracciolo 2009, 20). Part of the reason for the hostility by the regime can be attributed to the manner in which the bicycle had been heralded by the political left as a weapon in waging class warfare. At the first national congress of "Red Cyclists" in Imola, the bicycle itself had even been presented as the vanguard for revolutionary communication and propaganda: as if the bicycle itself was an agent of change. Conversely, the imagery of fascism revolved around speed and motorization, despite the reality not matching the rhetoric. As Caracciolo (2009) perceptively observes, as the numbers of bicycles increased, their social value decreased (25). In Italy, levels of ownership and use varied dramatically across regions, reflecting broader inequalities in wealth. For example, in 1934 in Emilia there was one cycle for every 4.4 persons, whereas in Basilicata, the poorest region of Southern Italy, only one for every 289 persons was recorded (Foot 2011, 67).

With cycle use proliferating across Europe, innovation prospered despite the impact of economic recessions and instability. Users and artisan manufacturers cooperated to produce numerous types and models of trailers and sidecars to adapt solo or tandem bicycles to carry luggage or passengers. Most radical of the engineering innovations was Mochet's four-wheel Velocar and two-wheel, recumbent Velocar designs. Other manufacturers followed suit with a range of similar models (Cox 2012b, 22).

In Denmark, the first Sofacyckel was built in 1934 and heralded as a "future bicycle." The design relocated the cranks slightly further forward of the saddle than on most bicycles, enabling the rider to stand stationary in the saddle while keeping his or her feet on the ground. Other technical developments in the application of light alloys, derailleur gearing, and further advances in hub gearing all reflected a relatively healthy market even in the midst of consumer economic limitations (see both Berto 2005 and Hadland 1987 for examples).

WAR AND ITS AFTERMATH

The Second World War had a dramatic impact not only on levels of cycling but also on the productive capacities that dictated cycling levels. It also created a visual and symbolic legacy that shaped attitudes towards bicycles and bicycle use in the postwar years. Among the major combatant nations, Germany had by far the greatest use of cycles by the military, having correspondingly lower levels of motorization. The bicycle was a pragmatic choice of vehicle that was employed and annexed wherever possible. Importantly, the bicycle's independence from other support structures (petrol or fodder) lent itself to the more mobile patterns of warfare from 1939 to 1945. The bicycle's potential had been trumpeted as an important innovation in the First World War, but the reality of static trench warfare and mass bombardment rendered it largely irrelevant. Little was said in praise of the bicycle in 1939, demonstrating just how mundane it had become. Yet it was a significant means of mobility not only on the battlefront, but also on the home front, as petrol rationing and the reallocation of transport provisions toward the support of militarization affected peoples' options for mobility alongside the transformation of working practices. Restrictions on the availability of steel tubing restricted some forms of production, but the main problem was the loss of rubber sources for European and American manufacturers.

Japanese soldiers commandeered bicycles wherever they went during the Japanese Army's advance through South Asia in order to produce the army's legendary mobility (Fitzpatrick 2011). We should observe the implicit assumption about the ubiquity of bicycles throughout Malaya and other South Asian regions: The military knew that they would not need to take bicycles with them, only the power and authority to seize local machines. The commandeering of local bicycles by occupying forces in Europe lent them an iconic quality for forces of resistance, as witnessed by accounts in Denmark, the Netherlands, Italy, and France.

In Italy, war brought a general resurgence in bicycle use. Before the Allied invasion, it was even the subject of state promotion as a means of leisure and practical mobility. In contrast, Romagnoli (2009, 135) records that during the turmoil of 1943–1944, with Rome under German occupation, a decree forbade bicycle use anywhere in the city because of their widespread

64   *Peter Cox*

employment by partisans, "it took care of practically 80% of the Roman means of Transportation." He recalls that, in response, people welded a third wheel or trailer onto their (former) bicycles to get round the ordinance. Ironically, this wartime use led to even greater rejection of cycling in the postwar era, because the bicycle was so firmly grounded as a wartime symbol that the population wanted to leave behind.

Postwar reconstructions are beyond the scope of this chapter, but the economic growth and drop in relative energy prices of the 1950s led to a dramatic decline in bicycle use in western nations and the relocation of the locus of global cycling, both in usage and subsequently in manufacturing, from Europe to East Asia.

The position of the bicycle in transport is a complex one. Its mass adoption was neither inevitable nor universal. From a brief and necessarily limited comparison of select cases, it is possible to distinguish a range of relevant social, political, and economic factors external to the machine itself. Much work remains to better understand the changing fortunes of bicycle transport, but comparative study reveals similarities and contrasts that can be correlated with other factors and forms of agency in social change.

WORKS CITED

This chapter has benefitted from the use of a number of background archive sources, including the author's own collection of trade and club journals, the photographic collection of the Resistance Museum, Copenhagen, and the archives of the Deutsches Museum, Munich.

Albermarle, The Right Hon. The Earl of, and G. Lacy Hillier. *Cycling* [New edition Thoroughly Revised 1895, reprinted with amendments 1896]. London and Bombay, Longmans, Green & Co., 1896.
Ameye, Thomas, Gils Bieke, and Pascal Delheye. "Daredevils and Early Birds: Belgian Pioneers in Automobile Racing and Aerial Sports during the Belle Époque." *The International Journal of the History of Sport* 28 (2011), p. 205–239.
Banister, David. *Unsustainable Transport: City Transport in the 21st Century*. London, Routledge, 2005.
Bagwell, Philip, and Peter Lyth. *Transport in Britain 1750–2000: From Canal Lock to Gridlock*. Hambledon, Continuum, 2002.
Barmayer, Heidi. "Bismark and the Origins of the Modern Welfare State in 19th Century Germany." In: Henrik Jensen (ed.), *The Welfare State: Past, Present, Future*. Pisa, Editizioni Plus—Università di Pisa, 2002, p. 87–110.
Berto, Frank J. *The Dancing Chain: History and Development of the Derailleur Bicycle* (2nd ed.). San Francisco, Van Der Plas Publications/Cycle Publishing, 2005.
Boal, Ian. "Towards a World History of Cycling." In: Andrew Richie and Rob Van der Plas (eds.), *Proceedings of the 11th International Cycle History Conference*. San Francisco, Van Der Plas Publications, 2001, p. 16–22.
"Built for Business." *Wheelman and Cycle Trade Review* November 8, 1895, p. 52.
Caracciolo, Carlos Héctor. "Bicicleta, circulación vial y espacio público en la Italia Fascista." *Historia Critica* 39 (2009), p. 20–42.

Carstensen, Trine Agervig, and Anne-Katrin Ebert. "Cycling Cultures in Northern Europe: From Golden Age to 'Renaissance.' " In: John Parkin (ed.), *Cycling and Sustainability*. Bingley, Emerald, 2012. p. 23–58.

Cox, Peter. "The Co-construction of Cycle Use." Paper delivered to Re/Cycling Histories: Users and the Paths to Sustainability in Everyday Life, Rachel Carson Center, Munich, May 27–29, 2011.

———. " 'A Denial of Our Boasted Civilisation': Cyclists' Views on Conflicts over Road Use in Britain 1926–1935." *Transfers* 2 (2012a), p. 4–30.

———. "Human Powered Vehicles in Britain 1930–1980." In: Andrew Ritchie (ed.), *Cycle History 21*. London, Cycle History Publishing, 2012b, p. 19–26.

Dubey, Abhay Kumar. "The Rickshaw Refuses to Go Away: The Struggle of the Co-Traveller of Asian Modernity." In: Ravi Rajendra (ed.), *The Saga of Rickshaw: Identity, Struggle, and Claims*. New Delhi, VAK, 2007, p. 29–65.

Eastman, Crystal. "What Is Real Protection?" [excerpted from *Equal Rights*, February 19, 1927]. In: Blanche Cook (ed.), *Crystal Eastman on Women and Revolution*. Oxford, Oxford University Press, 1978, p. 215–219.

Ebert, Anne-Katrin. "Cycling Towards the Nation: The Use of the Bicycle in Germany and the Netherlands, 1880–1940." *European Review of History* 11 (2004), p. 347–364.

Epperson, Bruce D. "Failed Colossus: Strategic Error at the Pope Manufacturing Company, 1878–1900." *Technology and Culture* 41 (2000), p. 300–320.

———. *Peddling Bicycles to America: The Rise of an Industry*. Jefferson NC, McFarland & Co., 2010.

Filarski, Ruud. *Shaping Transport Policy*. Den Haag, SDU, 2011.

Fitzpatrick, Jim. *The Bicycle in Wartime: An illustrated History*. Revised ed. Kilcoy, Australia, Star Hill Studio, 2011.

Foot, John. *Pedalare, Pedalare: A History of Italian Cycling*. London, Bloomsbury, 2011.

Fraser, John Foster. *Round the World on a Wheel*. 1899. London, Chatto and Windus, 1982.

Gallagher, Rob. *The Rickshaws of Bangladesh*. Dhaka, University Press, 1992.

Geary, Dick. "Socialism and the German Labour Movement before 1914." In: Dick Geary (ed.), *Labour and Socialist Movements in Europe before 1914*. Oxford, Berg, 1989, p. 101–136.

Hadland, Tony. *The Sturmey Archer Story*. Birmingham, John Pinkerton, 1987.

Harrison, A. E. "The Competitiveness of the British Cycle Industry, 1890–1914." *The Economic History Review* [New Series] 22 (1969), p. 287–303.

Herlihey, David. *Bicycle: The History*. New Haven, CT, Yale University Press, 2004.

———. *The Lost Cyclist*. Edinburgh, Mainstream, 2010.

Hibbs, John. *The History of British Bus Services* (2nd ed.). Newton Abbot, David & Charles, 1989.

Hoffman, Aage. "Arbejderidrættens Forhold Til Socialdemokratiet ca 1880-ca 1925." *Arbejderhistorie* (2008), p. 96–115.

Keilwein, Matthias, and Hans-Erhard Lessing (eds.). *Kaleideskop früher Fahrrad-und Motorradtechnik—Vollständige Artikelsammlung aus Dinglers Polytechnischem Journal 1895–1908, Band 1*. Leipzig, Maxime, 2005.

Kirsch, David A. *The Electric Vehicle and the Burden of History*. New Brunswick, Rutgers University Press, 2000.

Lehr, John C., and H. John Selwood, "The Two-Wheeled Workhorse: The Bicycle as Personal and Commercial Transport in Winnipeg." *Urban History Review* 28 (1999), p. 3–13.

Leonard, Eileen B. *Women, Technology and the Myth of Progress*. Upper Saddle River NJ, Prentice Hall, 2003.

66   *Peter Cox*

McGurn, Jim. *On Your Bicycle.* York, Company of Cyclists, 1999.

"The Measure of Cycle Use." *The Wheel & Cycling Trade Review* (New York & Chicago) XXV.10, August 2, 1900, p. 649.

Metz, Joel. *Criterium des Porteurs de Journaux.* Web. http://www.blackbirdsf.org/courierracing/journaux.html.

Meyer, Benedikt. "Vorwärts, Ruckwärts. Baisse und Renaissance des Fahrradfahrens in der Schweiz 1960–1980" (PhD thesis, Historisches Institut Uni Bern, 2008).

Millward, Andrew. "The Founding of the Hercules Cycle and Motor Co. Ltd." In: Rob van der Plas (ed.), *Proceedings of the 5th International Cycle History Conference, Cambridge, England, September 1994.* San Francisco, Bicycle Books, 1995, p. 99–106.

Mom, Gijs. "Inter-artifactual Technology Transfer: Road Building Technology in the Netherlands and the Competition between Bricks, Macadam, Asphalt and Concrete." *History and Technology* 20 (2004), p. 75–96.

———. "Constructing Multifunctional Networks: Road Building in the Netherlands, 1810–1980." In: Gijs Mom and Laurent Tissot (eds.), *Road History: Planning Building and Use.* Neuchatel, Alphil, 2007, p. 33–62.

Nandy, Ashis. *Time Treks: The Uncertain Future of New and Old Despotisms.* Oxford, Seagull Books, 2008.

"No Horseless Age." *Wheel & Cycling Trade Review* XXV, July 24–26, 1900, p. 10.

Norcliffe, Glen. "Popeism and Fordism: Examining the Roots of Mass Production." *Regional Studies* 31 (1997), p. 267–280.

———. *The Ride to Modernity: The Bicycle in Canada 1869–1900.* Toronto, University of Toronto Press, 2001.

O'Connor, Sean. *The Car in British Society: Class Gender and Motoring 1896–1939.* Manchester, Manchester University Press, 1998.

Oddy, Nicholas. "The Flaneur on Wheels?" In: Dave Horton, Paul Rosen, and Peter Cox (eds.), *Cycling and Society.* Aldershot, Ashgate, 2007, p. 25–46.

"An Original Carrier." *Wheelman and Cycle Trade Review*, February 14, 1896, p. 94.

Petty, Ross D. "Peddling the Bicycle and the Development of Mass Marketing." In: Rob Van der Plas (ed.), *Cycle History 5: Proceedings of the 5th International Cycle History Conference, Cambridge, England, September 1994.* San Francisco, Bicycle Books, 1995, p. 99–106.

Pope, Albert. (1995) "Colonel Pope and the Founding of the U.S. Bicycle Industry." In: Rob Van der Plas (ed.), *Cycle History 5: Proceedings of the 5th International Cycle History Conference, Cambridge, England, September 1994.* San Francisco, Bicycle Books, 1995, p. 95–98.

Pratt, Edwin A. *A History of Inland Transport and Communication.* 1912. Newton Abbot, David & Charles, 1970.

Pucher, John, Charles Komanoff, and Paul Schimek. "Bicycling Renaissance in North America? Recent Trends and Alternative Policies to Promote Bicycling." *Transportation Research Part A* 33 (2001), p. 625–654.

Rabenstein, Rüdiger. "The History of German Workers' Cycling Association, Solidarity." In: Rob Van der Plas, *Cycle History 11: Proceedings of the 11th International Cycle History Conference.* San Francisco, Van der Plas Publications, 2001, p. 160–168.

Rist, Gilbert. *The History of Development: from Western Origins to Global Faith* (3rd ed.). London, Zed, 2008.

Romagnoli, G. Franco. *The Bicycle Runner: A Memoir of Love, Loyalty and the Italian Resistance.* New York, St. Martin's Press, 2009.

Rubenson, Paul. "Patents, Profits, and Perceptions: The Single Tube Tire and the Failure of the American Bicycle 1897–1933." In: Rob Van der Plas (ed.), *Cycle*

History 15: Proceedings of the 15th International Cycling History Conference, Vienna, 1–4 September 2004. San Francisco, Van der Plas Books, 2005.

Saito, Toshihiko. "The Bicycle and Transportation Policy in Japan." In: Rob Van der Plas (ed.), *Cycle History 11: Proceedings of the 11th International Cycle History Conference.* San Francisco, Van der Plas Publications, 2001, p. 72–80.

Samanta, Gopa, and Roy Sumita. "Towards a Subaltern Paradigm of Mobility: Hand-pulled Rickshaws in Kolkata." *Transfers* 3 (2013), p. 62–68.

Santos, Boaventura de Sousa. "Reinventing Social Emancipation: Towards New Manifestos." In: Boaventura de Sousa Santos (ed.), *Democratizing Democracy.* London: Verso, 2005, p. xvii–xxxiii.

Steele, M. William. "The Speedy Feet of the Nation: Bicycles and Everyday Mobility in Modern Japan." *Journal of Transport History* 31 (2010), p. 182–209.

———. "The Making of a Bicycle Nation: Japan." *Transfers* 2 (2012), p. 70–94.

Stoffers, Manuel, and Peter Cox. "Beyond Technology: The Bicycle Renaissance as a Case in the History of Mobility." Paper presented to Mobility and the Environment workshop held at Rachel Carson Center for Environment and Society, Munich, June 3–5, 2010.

Takeuchi, Johzen. *The Role of Labour Intensive Sectors in Japanese Industrialization.* Tokyo, United Nations University Press, 1991.

Takeuchi, Tsuneyoshi. *The Formation of the Japanese Bicycle Industry: A Preliminary Analysis of the Infrastructure of the Japanese Machine Industry.* Working paper HSDRJE39/UNUP-241. Tokyo, United Nations University, 1991.

Tao, Xu. "Bicycle Trade Organizations in Modern Shanghai Mobility." *Urban History* 38 (2011), p. 457–474.

Thompson, Fred W., and Jon Bekken. *The Industrial Workers of the World: Its First Hundred Years: 1905–2005.* Cincinnati, IWW, 2006.

Toohey, Michael S. *Amateurs, Cash Amateurs, and Professionals: A Social And Cultural History of Bicycle Racing in New Zealand, 1869–1910* (PhD thesis, Lincoln University, NZ, 2010).

Veblen, Thorsten. *The Theory of the Leisure Class.* 1899. Mineoloa, USA, Dover, 1994.

Vuchic, Vukan R. *Transportation for Liveable Cities.* Brunswick NJ, CUPR Press, 1999.

Wells, Christopher. *Car Country: An Environmental History.* Seattle, University of Washington Press, 2012.

The Wheel and Cycle Trade Review, January 31, 1896, p. 94.

Wheeler, Tony, and Richard I'Anson. *Chasing Rickshaws.* Hawthorn, Victoria, Australia, Lonely Planet, 1998.

Zeller, Thomas. *Driving Germany: The Landscape of the German Autobahn 1930–1970.* Oxford, Berghahn, 2013.

5 Mobile Worths
Disputes over Streets

Jim Conley

INTRODUCTION

Roads and streets have long been objects of controversy. From the invasion of automobiles that challenged pedestrian control of streets in early twentieth-century cities and movements against urban freeways in the 1960s to cyclists' opposition to automotive domination of city streets at the beginning of the twenty-first century, disputes about the meanings and uses of urban streets and sidewalks reappear continually in different contexts. Contention over street space has consequently been the subject of much recent historical work on transport and mobility. Recent studies of historical and contemporary conflicts between drivers, pedestrians, and cyclists over streets and roads have shown that participants have viewed the issues normatively, as matters of justice (Norton 2008), traditional rights and responsibilities (Cox 2012), moral choice (Green, Steinbach, and Datta 2012), social acceptance of aggression (Möser 2003), moral strategies (D. Weber 2012), moral panics (Ladd 2008), and worthiness of different identities (Skinner and Rosen 2007). This chapter seeks to contribute to this literature by outlining a pragmatist approach to the moral or ethical dimension of conflicts on, around, and about roads.

In contrast to older approaches in which the triumph of car transportation appeared as the smooth, evolutionary development of technology responsive to consumer choices (e.g., Volti 1996, 2006; Foster 2003), more recent scholarship has emphasized a variety of groups and the tensions between them in debates over roads (e.g., McShane 1994). Three ways of understanding these group tensions and conflicts appear in this literature. One approach assumes historical agents to be rational individual or collective actors (such as occupational groups, industries, and classes) that mobilize power resources to advance enduring interests defined by their position in social structures. In contrast, for social construction of technology theorists (e.g., Bijker 1995; Norton 2008), "relevant social groups" coalesce around unstable technological frames in periods of interpretive flexibility concerning new technologies. Although criticized for ignoring broader cultural changes and social forces affecting the fate of technological artifacts and sociotechnical ensembles (Rosen 2002), constructionist approaches reveal the fluidity and contingency of technological change. Finally, the governmentality approach focuses on the constitution of disciplined mobile subjects through dominant discourses (e.g., Packer 2008; Paterson 2007; Seiler 2008; Green, Steinbach, and Datta 2012; D. Weber 2012).

None of these approaches address fully the moral dimensions of disputes over streets, which inherently concern distributive justice, or what roads are for and who belongs on them. In both everyday disputes and public debates over streets, questions of the common good and the worth of different ways of being mobile are at issue. The pragmatist model of justification and critique formulated by Luc Boltanski and Laurent Thévenot in *On Justification* (2006) provides a framework for considering disputes at both mundane and political levels, integrating existing approaches, and highlighting dimensions they neglect. In this model, six worlds, or "orders of worth," provide a repertoire of evaluation used in western societies to justify and criticize social arrangements. In each world, a "higher common principle" is invoked to establish the relevance and worth of humans, objects, and their relations. The model consists of inspired, domestic, fame, civic, market, and industrial orders of worth, each supported by a different, incommensurable conception of the common good. Building on Thévenot's (2002) analysis of disputes over a highway project in the Pyrenees, the chapter extends this model to disputes over streets and sidewalks, illustrating its heuristic value by analyzing commentaries on a violent incident between a bicycle courier and a driver that occurred in Toronto's Kensington Market in 2006. The chapter concludes with some reflections on characteristics of mobile social worlds that shape mobile worths and the implications of this approach for research on mobility disputes.

AN INCIDENT

On January 26, 2006, in Toronto's Kensington Market, a several-block area of small shops and restaurants, there was a brief confrontation between a car driver and a cyclist/pedestrian. Seeing the driver drop a hamburger and its wrapping onto the street, a passing bike courier (who was walking her bike) picked it up, opened the car door, and "returned" it to him. Getting out of his car, the driver threw coffee at her, and then grabbed her by the helmet. In the ensuing scuffle, the key the courier carried on a bracelet scratched his car (the driver reported it as a deliberate act; the courier said it was an accident). Encouraged to leave by people on the street, the driver instead parked and ran back as the cyclist was getting on her bike to ride home. A passing photographer (Adam Krawesky) chanced to document what happened next (*citynoise* 2010). The driver grabbed and upset the courier's bike, knocking her down. He then stamped on her rear wheel, and the two scuffled until passersby subdued him. When the photographer went to take a picture of

70 Jim Conley

his license plate, the driver took a baseball bat from the trunk, threatened him with it, and then drove away. The police later picked him up, but said that if they charged him they would also have to charge her with mischief for scratching his car, so she let the matter drop.[1] After the photographer posted his photos on a local blog (*citynoise* 2010), a vigorous debate erupted, and other Toronto media picked up the story, including the *Toronto Star* newspaper and the Canadian Broadcasting Corporation (CBC).[2]

Although trivial in and of itself, the Kensington market incident links everyday experiences of car drivers, cyclists, and pedestrians to broader political issues concerning legitimate and illegitimate uses of urban streets. As public spaces that are used for both private purposes and public political claims (e.g., Blomley 2011; Thelle 2013), streets and sidewalks are settings where different principles of assessment come into conflict and require public justification. Luc Boltanski and Laurent Thévenot's pragmatic sociology of justification and critique provides a framework for understanding these conflicts.

THE PRAGMATIC SOCIOLOGY OF CRITIQUE AND JUSTIFICATION

How do people reach legitimate agreements in public disputes without resorting to violence or force? In *On Justification* (2006), Boltanski and Thévenot answer that they "rise in generality" from the contingent particularities of the contentious situation to principles of the common good, applying "tests" specific to each to establish the relative worth of actions, actors, and objects. In their model, six worlds, or "orders of worth," based on "polities" (*cités*) constructed in western political philosophy constitute a repertoire of conventional principles by which persons make cognitive and evaluative judgments and engage in critique and justification. Disputes over streets involve issues of distributive justice—the distribution of road space and priority in its use—raising questions of relative worth that require reference to higher common principles if these distributions are to be judged legitimate, thus constraining the naked exercise of power (Boltanski and Thévenot 2006; Boltanski and Chiapello 2005).

Streets and roads are examples of "an equipped humanity" (Thévenot 2002) in which humans, objects, and the relations among them are "qualified," or categorized differently in different worlds and have different relevance and "worths," or values. As Latour (1992) has argued, objects or nonhumans are actants in situations; they objectify conventions and compromises in ways that are difficult to reverse, and they "order and orchestrate" conduct (Boltanski 2012; Boltanski and Thévenot 2006). The actions of car–driver assemblages, bike–rider assemblages, and pedestrians are shaped by all the other objects that make up streets, from the materials of the road surface to the various other "actants" in and around them: signs and signals, lane markings, curbs, guard rails, parked vehicles, lights, trees, buildings, children playing, and so on, which serve to define the situation and the conduct appropriate to it.

In disputes, the question arises of what sort of "beings" (persons and things) "belong" in the situation (Thévenot 2002). "Qualification" is an operation that provides a cognitive and evaluative answer by invoking a "higher common principle" as a convention of equivalency for comparing and ranking the worth (*grandeur*) of relevant beings. In *On Justification* (2006), Boltanski and Thévenot construct a model of inspired, domestic, fame, civic, market, and industrial orders of worth that may be used to qualify roads and their users.[3] Although compromises between worlds are possible and frequent, the six worlds provide incompatible modes of justification, each supported by different conceptions of the common good. The worlds thus involve different "orders of worth," or rankings, and what is worthy in one world may be irrelevant, or unworthy and out of place, in another.

In the contemporary, secular incarnation of the inspired world, non-conformity, creativity, emotion, and authenticity are valued (Boltanski and Thévenot 1999). Taking risks, acting spontaneously, and following one's own path qualify a person as worthy. A road or street would be inspired to the extent it affords spontaneous expression in defiance of convention, such as the "alley-cat" races of bike messengers (Kidder 2011). Such a street would facilitate artistic and lifestyle experimentation.

In the domestic world, worth derives from tradition, ties to persons and places, trustworthiness based on personal reputation, and loyalty, "the domestic value *par excellence*" (Boltanski and Chiapello 2005, 67). Exemplary conduct, emphasizing good manners and propriety, is conveyed through anecdotal testimony, and "locality and ties to place are revered" (Thévenot, Moody, and Lafaye 2000, 250). A domestic road or street would be used by residents and richly layered with locally shared meanings, the opposite of Augé's (1995) "non-places."

In the polity of fame or renown, the mediated opinion of anonymous others (not specific, copresent others, as in the domestic world) confers recognition and esteem based on arbitrary signs and images. The famous streets that every tourist must visit (such as Champs-Élysées in Paris or Unter den Linden in Berlin) or, more fleetingly, streets or areas that are "trendy" would be examples in spaces of mobility.

The civic polity legitimates a world of solidarity and equality, in which persons are qualified as citizens serving the common good, not as private individuals pursuing private interests. This is a world of public spaces, collective objectives, and laws and regulations. Civic legitimacy can take the more "republican" form of solidarity found in France or a more liberal "equal rights" form found in North America (Thévenot, Moody, and Lafaye 2000). A civic street is a public space open to all, where diverse members of the collectivity encounter each other as equals and develop common purposes or exercise subjective rights.

72 Jim Conley

In the market polity the common good is served by free competition for commodities, and worth derives from purchasing power. It is a world of buying and selling, of private property and monetary value where "social relations are governed by private interests" (Moody and Thévenot 2000, 285). More than just a commercial street, a market street is a public space that is justified by generating wealth.

Finally, functional efficiency, long-range planning, expertise, and scientific measurement confer worth in the industrial world. Efficient traffic flow, predictability, reliability, and avoidance of breakdowns, accidents, and disruptions qualify a road or sidewalk as worthy in both an engineering and legal sense (Blomley 2011).

For Boltanski and Thévenot (1999), legitimation of orders of worth requires that equivalences be sought in higher common principles. Justifications are generalizable, not dependent on the specifics of the situation. In a car crash, it is not relevant that one of the drivers was upset because of an argument at work; it is relevant that one of them broke the law by driving through a stop sign. The higher common principle furnishes criteria by which the persons and objects in dispute can be evaluated in a test, trial, or proof.[4] The question thus concerns the principle that allows us to compare these beings (people or things) such that a legitimate, in other words justifiable, ranking of worth can be determined, and legitimate relations between these beings established—what Max Weber (1968, 31) would call a "legitimate order."

JUSTIFICATION IN WORLDS OF MOBILITY

Boltanski and Thévenot's model of six worlds enables us to see how people perform pragmatic operations of justification and critique in mundane situations of daily life. How is it relevant to the Kensington Market altercation? Justification and critique require a reflexive break in action that in this case was precluded by the rapidity of an act of violence. The required delay in the course of interaction can be recovered after the fact, however, in moments of reflection when parties to, or observers of, the interaction can consider what happened, draw on higher common principles to find equivalences between the persons and objects involved, and judge their worth. Such cognitive and evaluative judgments appear in twenty-six signed letters commenting on the episode that were solicited and published by the Canadian Broadcasting Corporation (CBC News). Thanks to the photographer's posting of his photos on the *citynoise* blog, and its subsequent dissemination by news media, a confrontation that would have been visible only to a few bystanders became public and subject to the imperative of justification "at a distance" (Boltanski 1999).

For the letter writers, three acts serve as tests of the capacities of the driver and the cyclist: the driver's initial act of littering on the road; the cyclist's act of opening the car door and "returning" the litter; and the driver's subsequent assault on the cyclist. Like most moments of everyday life, the Kensington Market incident was not a specially formulated test limited to one world (Joseph 1998). Nonetheless, "ordinary disputes raise the same kind of issues [of the common good and orders of worth] when the level of generality in the cognitive treatment of people rises. At such moments, public qualifications are used to criticize and justify, and those qualifications fit into constructions of the common good" (Thévenot 2007, 415). The letter writers rise from the uncertain, contingent particularities of the situation to issues of the common good. In their commentaries, the observers treat the incident as a test to the extent that they judge the actions of the driver and the bike messenger as revealing the capacities and worth of the actors (Boltanski 2012, 287 n2).

Because it is an ambiguous, "composite situation" (Boltanski and Thévenot 2006) in which beings relevant in different worlds are present, the observers are uncertain about what kind of situation it is and are faced with an initial task of qualification, deciding what world is involved and what test to apply. They comment on different actions, using each as an informal test of a different world rather than of the situation as a whole, and the same letter writer may combine critiques and justifications from different worlds. The majority invoked two orders of worth, six stayed within one, and another six referred to more than two worlds.[5]

Most writers justify the cyclist: "I totally support the cyclist," "I fully support the courier," "Good for her!" "The courier was totally right," "I admire the courier," "Fantastic! Congrats to the biker!" "I take my hat off to the cyclist," "I . . . applaud her." Although there are also critiques of the cyclist, the driver is almost always denounced.[6] Evaluations come primarily from the civic and domestic worlds, to a lesser extent from the industrial world, and even less from the world of fame. Inspired and market logics are virtually absent.

CIVIC JUSTIFICATIONS

Civic justifications refer to a higher common principle of the solidarity of an anonymous and general public good represented by legitimate authorities. Civic justifications for the courier are often combined with critiques. On the one hand, she is qualified as a worthy being in the civic world. She is commended for "being a good citizen," "doing his [sic] civic duty," and having "a civic conscience." "Good for her for being a good citizen"; "We should all stand against" people like the driver.

On the other hand, the courier is also denounced from the civic world for opening the car door and throwing the litter at the driver. She should have "report[ed] the matter to the authorities. She is a citizen and should have responded more appropriately"; "It would have been much better to

74   Jim Conley

have taken the plate number of the van and organized a couple of witnesses"; "Far better to keep a cool head and report the matter to police"; "Let the authorities deal with people like this." One critic recognizes that the authorities are unlikely to act: "Obviously law enforcement officers could not make a case against a litterer with just here [*sic*] say so an incident report to the police would be also be futile." Another writer uses the lack of enforcement (which could also be said of many traffic laws) to justify the courier's actions from a civic world: "If our laws which cost millions of tax dollars to write up are not respected then let the citizens who actually give a darn about this city take matters into their own hands." Adds another, "There is little enforcement of litter laws" and therefore "What is left is for each of us to take steps we feel are necessary to bring attention to the problems on the road and to do what we can to correct them—individually. This is what this cyclist did. Even if she did go too far, at least arguably, at least she did not simply do nothing like happens all too often." Apathy is the enemy of the general will, and the courier is worthy in the civic world because she made herself its embodiment: "I support the courier for taking a stand. Too many people just stand by and refuse to get involved. Not getting involved doesn't solve anything." Another speaks of "complacency and apathy" as a challenge to dealing with problems of "waste and pollution."

An explicit appeal to a higher common principle that also denounces systemic violence is worth quoting in full:

> As a cyclist first and a driver second I fully empathize with the courier. Drivers throw things out the window a lot and often deliberately target cyclists including yells and insults in the barrage. I haven't yet had the opportunity to catch up with these offensive cagers [slang for automobile riders and drivers] but I can certainly see me returning the litter if I did! I was even once chased down a sidewalk by a large diesel pickup truck late one night purely for the amusement of the cagers inside. Drivers need to learn that they don't have any special rights to the road. I pay taxes too.

There is a compromise here (see Boltanski and Thévenot 2006, on compromises), as in the last sentence the author qualifies her civic justification with a market one, in which roads are commodities to which those who pay deserve access, implicitly excluding those who do not pay (Norton 2008).

DOMESTIC JUSTIFICATIONS

In the domestic world, protection and support, trustworthiness, personal character, loyalty, good manners and propriety, and attachment to place are valued attributes. For the letter writers, the domestic world appears mainly in the form of denunciations of the driver generalized to people like him: "Too many people have no respect for others"; they are "inconsiderate jerks"; "lazy, thoughtless, witless, stupid slobs." In addition to being classed as an unworthy human in the domestic order, the driver is sometimes disqualified as a nondomestic animal—"a litter bug" or "pig." The object, in other words, the litter, is also qualified as "matter out of place" (Douglas 1985) in a proper household, and the same person who called the driver a "a litter bug" also referred to "pollution, and waste." He added that he sometimes picks up garbage that people have deliberately dropped, asking them "Do you do this in your own house?" Another identifies all streets (not just his own) as domestic spaces: "I look at the street as an extension of my living space and for someone to throw garbage on it is like throwing it through my living room window." In the words of yet another: "How would that man like it if we dumped garbage on his front yard?!" One writer makes a link between a high-speed automotive world and ritual pollution (in the anthropological sense) of domestic spaces: "It *sickens* me to walk down the street and see the litter that lies everywhere, whether thrown by driver, cyclist, or pedestrian. There are areas within Toronto that I have visited that are disgusting. Certain on ramps to the major highways are the worst, probably because few if any people would bother to pick it up, as there are no pedestrians in the area."

Finally, the driver is criticized for violating a domestic hierarchy of protection and support in this rhetorical question: "OK here we have a guy, throws out trash on the street, throws coffee on a woman, attacks a woman and we are asking who is in the right?" This denunciation is combined with the only violent proposal in this sample: "The people who separated the scuffle should have beaten this clown into a coma and left him on the street." Another writes, "So not only is this fine gentleman, a litterer, but he is also one to abuse women."

The courier is also criticized for conduct unbecoming of the domestic world: "She should have acted with manner and courtesy. For example: Talking to the man in a kind voice." Another writer advises exemplary conduct: "Be a positive example and pick up trash you see on your travels," and goes on to refer to the number of people who "respect our streets, sidewalks, parkways, and yards." A third writer reflects, "However, did she go too far in opening the door and throwing the bag at the driver [?] Hmmmm. By opening the door and depositing the bag back where it came, one would have to say no, not at all. By throwing it at the driver, if that is what happened, perhaps." He goes on to emphasize propriety and consideration for others, using a gardening metaphor for dealing with those who are disqualified in the domestic order of worth: "When I lived in the city, I saw many bike couriers being inconsiderate on our roads as well. But two wrongs don't make a right. The drivers out there who have little consideration for the other users of the road, cyclists and pedestrians primarily, have to be weeded out, and quickly." Finally, another, less concerned about two wrongs not making a right, wants to violate the driver's domestic space in

76   Jim Conley

retaliation: "I've always wanted to nab their license plate and leave all the garbage they've tossed out their window in their car (or if locked, on their front porch)." That the driver's house can substitute for the interior of his car draws on the meaning of car interiors as "domestic" spaces, "a living room on wheels" (as a 1949 Ford brochure put it).[7]

INDUSTRIAL JUSTIFICATIONS

The common good is served in the industrial world by efficiency, predictability, reliability, and the contribution of persons and objects to the satisfaction of social or organizational needs. Breakdowns, accidents, and disruptions indicate lack of worth in this world. Justification and critique from the industrial world appear in two ways in these letters. First, as critiques of the driver's action from the point of view of cyclists' safety: "As a commuting cyclist, similar incidents have happened to me . . . trash, cigarettes, and paper also constitute hazards to other vehicles including bikes. I have been hit with a cigarette, paper and in one very memorable incident with an empty can of pop." She goes on to connect this to the particular assemblage that is the car and driver: "A motorized vehicle seems to give the occupants a sense of being removed from what happens around them." Another writer states, "I drive a car and I ride my bike, regularly. Does the average citizen know just how difficult it is to dodge impediments on the road and vehicles who have little regard for cyclists when they are approaching them? A cyclist is vulnerable on our roads." Another refers to drivers' littering as "reckless and dangerous behavior." The road here is not a domestic or a civic space, it is a functional space for safe and smooth travel.

Second, the industrial world also appears in critiques of the cyclist's actions. On the one hand, they created unsafe conditions for others, "a potentially dangerous situation. . . . Her actions might have caused a traffic accident." Another writes, "The act of opening a car door and throwing material at the driver could cause a traffic accident and or injury to the occupant(s) of the vehicle." On the other hand, she was criticized for putting herself in danger: "She did take a personal risk throwing the garbage back in the vehicle." Another: "By opening his van door, she overstepped and put herself into a dangerous situation. Thank goodness it was just coffee—it could have been a gun he pulled." A third: "Opening the car door of the driver was crossing the line and opening herself up to possible charges, not to mention a heightened possibility of a road-rage incident." Finally, a cyclist and defensive driving instructor points out the difference between automotive and bicycle assemblages: "Whenever I'm on my bike, I try to keep in mind that whatever satisfaction I might get from immediate retaliation could quickly turn to disaster at the hands of a driver controlling a weapon more deadly than any firearm." What would be valued in an inspired world—taking a risk, or authentically expressing one's emotions—is disqualified in an industrial world as dangerous and disruptive.

FAME JUSTIFICATIONS

Fame justifications appear infrequently. One writer advocates public shaming to overcome the anonymity conferred by the automobile: "A motorized vehicle seems to give the occupants a sense of being removed from what happens around them, so a little 'trash back' or yelling to shame them publicly is a good idea." Another echoes this, "Yelling at him and embarrassing him would have been as far as she should have gone." In other words, infamy is proposed as a sanction for the driver.[8]

Others commend the bike courier for drawing public attention to the problem of littering. (They should really be commending the photographer who took and posted the photos.) "This publicity may make others think twice about throwing their garbage on the street"; "What i [*sic*] like MOST of the story however, is that in doing so, she brought much needed publicity to the issue." As in scandals and affairs (Adut 2007; Boltanski and Claverie 2008) publicity is key, because it raised the incident from a private matter between two persons to a public dispute requiring justification going beyond the particular situation.

MOBILE SOCIAL WORLDS

The comments made by writers to the CBC website show that urban streets can be considered spaces of civic, public interactions; inhabited domestic spaces to which people are attached; and industrial spaces for the safe, unimpeded flow of foot, bicycle, or automotive traffic. The diversity of assessments is attributable in part to the place where the incident occurred, which like most streets is the material and institutional realization of a compromise between a variety of worlds of evaluation or mobile social worlds.

Bounded by Spadina Avenue on the east, Bellevue Avenue on the west, College Street on the north, and Dundas Street on the south, Kensington Market consists mainly of converted Victorian houses and two- or three-story buildings. It hosts an eclectic mix of small independent shops selling food (bakers, fishmongers, greengrocers, butchers, vendors of cheese, spices, products from Latin America, and so forth), discount and vintage clothing, shoes, army surplus, crafts, and music, as well as restaurants and coffee shops. These establishments are often open to the street or display goods on the sidewalk. It is surrounded by older houses on small narrow lots, often divided into flats. To the east, a broad commercial street (Spadina) has a profusion of Asian restaurants and shops.

78 *Jim Conley*

Kensington Market's streets contain slow-moving automobile and delivery truck traffic, and pedestrians walk on both the street and the narrow sidewalks that border it. Although many people from outside the area come there to shop, eat, or experience the ambience, it has a neighborhood feel to it. With rare exceptions, the small shops are owner operated, some of them family businesses of long standing. Because of the succession of Jewish, Portuguese, Italian, Caribbean, South Asian, Chinese, and Latin American communities that have lived and worked in the area, it is a National Historic Site (Parks Canada 2011), but gentrification has been advancing.

This description of Kensington market brings out the location of action and operations of cognitive and evaluative qualification that are both afforded and constrained by the material and social arrangements of situations.[9] With the characteristics described, Kensington market can appear, depending on the circumstances, as a domestic space (home and neighborhood), a market space (of buying and selling), and a space of fame (a trendy, gentrifying, National Historic Site). As a composite space, the order of worth or world of evaluation that actors mobilize in judgments depends in part on its material and institutional arrangement and in part on the actors' relationship to the space. Actors have the critical capacity to use several modes of justification, passing from one order of worth to another in different situations. The letters to the CBC show that the same person can mobilize different types of justification and critique about the same situation because, first, the situation is ambiguous, or complex and composite, and, second, they are not parties to the action, but are only observing it from a distance. It also depends on the form of mobility with which they encounter it: driving, walking, or cycling.

Automobile traffic is a distinctive form of social life combining physical copresence with limited opportunities for social interaction between drivers. Face-to-face interaction is difficult and in some circumstances almost impossible in automobile traffic (Conley 2012). First, as one of the letter writers noted, the automotive assemblage of metal, glass, and plastic forms a barrier—often serving as an "invisibility cloak"—shielding its occupants from the occupants of other vehicles and other road users, limiting contact between persons inside and outside the vehicle.[10] Second, above a certain speed (thirty to forty kilometers per hour or so), eye contact between drivers becomes difficult, if not impossible (Vanderbilt 2008). Road designs often exacerbate this, with high-speed roads reducing them to the point that there is hardly social interaction at all. The most extreme examples are divided highways—which can be qualified as "industrial" because of their emphasis on efficient, continuous, high-speed flow with long sight lines, and few distractions—where interaction is face-to-tail rather than face-to-face and possibilities for communication between drivers are seriously impaired (Katz 1999). In contrast to face-to-face interaction, traffic lacks what Goffman (1963) terms "richness of information flow and facilitation of feedback" (17).

The distinctiveness of automobile traffic is highlighted by its contrast with walking (Goffman 1971; Wolff 1973) and cycling. Pedestrians are bodily copresent, providing so many opportunities for social interaction that all of Goffman's devices of civil inattention are required to avoid unwanted interaction. Cyclists are somewhat in the middle. Like automobiles, they move more quickly than pedestrians, creating an obstacle to interaction, but, except in congested traffic, they are generally not as fast as the former. Like automobiles, they are machine–human assemblages, but they lack the protective shell of the former. Having nearly the maneuverability of pedestrians, they can stop for interaction or, in many circumstances, ride side by side, as what Ole Jensen (2010) has called "mobile withs." Marc Augé (2008) suggests that a distinctive kind of sociability is possible on bicycles:

> The intoxications of solitude thus do not exclude forms of sociability, which I believe is one of the enduring virtues of cycling. . . . Cyclists at the most humble level are conscious of a certain solidarity, of trials and shared moments, of a little something that distinguishes them from others.
>
> (34–35, author translation)

Despite these differences, it would be a mistake to draw the contrast between automobility and other forms of mobility too sharply. Rather than one "autoworld," there may be several. The "invisibility cloak" furnished by the automotive shell remains more or less a constant, but even so, at slower speeds (and even at high speeds in some circumstances), there are possibilities for interaction, mutual recognition, and the ritual courtesies described by Jonasson (1999) and by Jørgensen (2008).[11] Differences between autoworlds are not just a matter of speed, they are also a matter of the humans and the nonhuman objects that are appropriate on and around roads, and the proper relations between them. Drivers and cyclists may make local accommodations to each other—such as the deference of the stronger toward the weaker when a driver yields the right of way to a cyclist (Goffman 1967). Such accommodations do nothing to reduce the dominant position of automobiles on roads, however, and it is only when there are disputes that broader political issues arise.

The distinctiveness of automotive interactions may be conducive to such disputes. Boltanski and Thévenot argue that complex societies such as ours require that people be able to recognize different situations and switch rapidly between them, and make judgments about the "suitability" of objects, things, and actions (Boltanski 2012; Boltanski and Thévenot 2006; Thévenot 2006). Although there is evidence that drivers are able to do so (Renouard 2000), it also seems that at least some of the time they have difficulty switching from the high-speed "industrial" situation of freeways and thoroughfares to more "domestic" residential roads or the "civic" spaces of urban streets that combine pedestrians, cyclists, and automobiles. Such

80   Jim Conley

failures to adjust are subject to informal social sanctions, often (as in the case examined here) in the form of so-called "road rage" in the absence of legal enforcement (Katz 1999).

The street has different meanings for drivers, cyclists, and pedestrians: As one of the letter writers cited above stated, in their metal, plastic, and glass cages, drivers are insulated from their environment and are less likely than cyclists or pedestrians to notice or consider relevant features such as litter. A cyclist or pedestrian is "closer to the ground" and more aware of her surroundings, noticing and valuing its idiosyncrasies and particularities that have no place for a driver on her way somewhere else. As Augé (2008) puts it, the bike is in itself a small object, an object that is embodied and not a space that is inhabited, like a car (67–68). In addition, the size, weight, suspensions, and stability of cars make features of streets irrelevant for the car–driver assemblage that for the cyclist–bike assemblage are a discomfort, if not a danger: litter, broken glass, wet leaves, patches of ice, potholes, grates, and street-car tracks. Consequently, drivers, cyclists, and pedestrians are, in many ways, in different situations on the road.

Second, the speed of automobile travel (and the opportunities it provides for escape) means that there is little time to justify actions, and little opportunity to communicate justifications, excuses, and other remedial actions (Goffman 1971), or to reflect and try to find agreement on the higher common principle that would legitimate the distribution of road space. Consequently, disputes are often resolved outside a regime of justification. On the one hand, they are resolved through force: the intimidation of the larger vehicle against the smaller, more vulnerable one or of the risk-taking driver against the risk-averse driver. As the Kensington Market incident shows, in car–bike or car–pedestrian interactions the rider–bicycle assemblage or the pedestrian is more vulnerable than the driver–car assemblage. In contrast, "reference to justice presupposes that force is shackled in such a way that relations of force can be redefined as relations of worth" (Boltanski and Chiapello 2005, 107, translation modified). On the other hand, disputes can be ended (or avoided) outside the regime of justice through forgiveness (Boltanski 2012), pardoning, or tolerance (Boltanski and Thévenot 2006; Lemieux 2007).

Alternatively, disputes can be resolved within a regime of justice by agreeing on and applying a test from one world or by compromising between two worlds (keeping an orientation to the common good while avoiding clarification of the incommensurable principles on which agreement is grounded). The ambiguity of road spaces, as revealed by the mixture of arguments in the letters analyzed here, means that except on roads where other users are excluded (such as limited-access freeways) compromise is a necessary feature of road spaces in which people on foot, in the saddle, or behind the wheel must interact. Thus in the politics of urban transportation, arguments over the allocation of road space to bikes and cars tend to be clashes involving different worlds, but the disputes themselves are likely to be resolved through compromises that are stabilized in the material arrangement of the streets, sidewalks, and other objects and in the institutionalized and conventional social arrangements that serve as resources and constraints on the coordination of mobile action and interaction.

CONCLUSION

Disputes over roads display multiple modes of moral judgment. On the one hand, this is because people in modern societies have a plurality of incommensurable orders of worth available to them; on the other hand, it is due to the frequently composite character of spaces of mobility, and the characteristics of walking, cycling, and driving as forms of mobility in them.

By emphasizing the everyday pragmatics of disputes involving "ordinary" people, the approach adopted here addresses theoretical and methodological issues in mobilities research. In contrast to the more organized groups emphasized by the social construction of technology and the dominant discourses of the governmentality approach, it allows subordinated orders of worth to be brought to light. In contrast to rational actor approaches, it recognizes that actors are not simply or only rational; they make judgments or are called to account using the conventional standards that Boltanski and Thévenot have proposed.

Judgments in the orders of worth discussed here are reported in different forms (Thévenot 1989), with consequences for the research methods and sources used by mobilities researchers. Inspired worth is revealed in images, symbols, or displays of emotion showing that an observer is moved, overwhelmed, or awed (Thévenot, Moody, and Lafaye 2000). Domestic worth is typically conveyed in anecdotes concerning exemplary actions, such as might be found in conversations, letters, or memoirs. Fame will be discovered through visibility, especially in the form of images in the mass media (Heinich 2012). Civic worth appears in judgments based on laws, rules, and norms of political conduct emphasizing solidarity and equality. Market worth can be reported as current monetary value or its equivalent in signs of wealth (expensive vehicles, construction materials, and so on). Industrial worth is conveyed in reports concerning efficiency, cost-effectiveness, functional relations, and the like, according to scientific and engineering standards. The usual archival and public documentary sources available to historians and social scientists may privilege civic and industrial orders of worth over other, less readily accessible ones.

Disputes over streets are disputes about what legitimately belongs there, about the worthiness of different modes of transport, and different ways of using those modes. Disputes over worth occur at multiple levels, from political and policy disputes (about the construction of roads versus other forms of transport infrastructure, the routing of such infrastructure, and its amenities, design speeds, and so forth) to mundane clashes between road users,

82　*Jim Conley*

such as the incident in Kensington Market described here. There is unlikely to be any shortage of material for historians of transport and mobility, and this chapter suggests that approaching such disputes, at whatever level is involved, using the pragmatic sociology of critique and justification will help to elucidate those conflicts.

NOTES

1. Source: Accounts by the photographer (Adam Krawesky), and the courier, in *citynoise* (2010). The driver did not present his side of the story.
2. As of March 20, 2012, the blog on which the photos were posted reported, "This article has been viewed 532796 times in the last 6 years." The last substantive comment appeared on September 30, 2011.
3. Other emerging polities have been proposed subsequently: the project (*cité par projet*) (Boltanski and Chiapello 2005) and the green or environmental (Latour 1998; Thévenot, Moody, and Lafaye 2000, 256–263), but the focus here is on the original six.
4. The French term *épreuve* has all of these connotations, which are only partly conveyed by the English term "test." "Reality test" is perhaps the best translation (see Boltanski and Thévenot 1999, 367).
5. Some authors get the story wrong: They mistake a van that is visible in the photos for the driver's car; one refers to the courier as a male; most assume that the courier deliberately keyed the driver's vehicle. Our concern here is not with the factual accuracy of the writers' statements, but with the orders of worth they use to evaluate the actions and actors in the situation.
6. One exception: "We do not know why the man threw the garbage out the window. . . . The man may not have known why a complete stranger was throwing garbage in his car. We do not know what he was thinking." This writer is suggesting that the driver may have had good reasons for his actions, in other words, that they were justifiable. He thus emphasizes uncertainty, and uses that uncertainty to criticize the cyclist.
7. See, for example, Marsh and Collett (1987, 10–11) and Miller (2001). For an analysis of feminized domesticity opposed to masculinized freedom in automobile advertising, see Conley (2009).
8. This is ambiguous, however, because notoriety is a form of fame, and the least worthy state in a world of fame is nonrecognition; public shaming should perhaps be considered part of the domestic world.
9. See Lemieux (2007, 69).
10. I owe this use of the term to a Harry Potter–influenced student in my sociology of the automobile course.
11. "More or less" because open windows, and convertibles with their roofs down, increase the visibility of occupants and the possibility of visual and oral communication.

WORKS CITED

Adut, Ari. *On Scandal: Moral Disturbances in Society, Politics, and Art.* Cambridge UK, Cambridge University Press, 2008.
Augé, Marc. *Non-places: Introduction to an Anthropology of Supermodernity.* London; New York, Verso, 1995.

———. *Éloge de la Bicyclette*. Paris, Éd. Payot & Rivages, 2008.

Bijker, Wiebe E. *Of Bicycles, Bakelites, and Bulbs: Toward a Theory of Sociotechnical Change*. Cambridge MA, MIT Press, 1995.

Blomley, Nicholas K. *Rights of Passage: Sidewalks and the Regulation of Public Flow*. London, Routledge, 2011.

Boltanski, Luc. *Distant Suffering: Morality, Media, and Politics*. Cambridge UK, Cambridge University Press, 1999.

———. *Love and Justice as Competences: Three Essays in the Sociology of Action*. Cambridge, Polity, 2012.

Boltanski, Luc, and Eve Chiapello. *The New Spirit of Capitalism*. London, Verso, 2005.

Boltanski, Luc, and Élisabeth Claverie. "Du Monde Social en tant que Scène d'un Procès." In: Luc Boltanski, Élisabeth Claverie, Nicolas Offenstadt, and Stéphane Van Damme (eds.), *Affaires, Scandales et Grandes Causes: De Socrate à Pinochet*. Paris, Stock, 2007, p. 395–452.

Boltanski, Luc, and Laurent Thévenot. "The Sociology of Critical Capacity." *European Journal of Social Theory* 2 (1999), p. 359–377.

———. *On Justification: Economies of Worth*. Princeton, Princeton University Press, 2006.

CBC News. "Cyclist–Driver Clash Photos Spark Online Debate." Web. January 31, 2006. http://www.cbc.ca/canada/story/2006/01/31/toronto-fightphotos060131.html.

CBC News Viewpoint. "Cyclist–Driver Clash Photos Spark Online Debate." Web. February 1, 2006. http://www.cbc.ca/news/viewpoint/yourspace/cyclist_driver.html.

citynoise. "Motorist vs Courier." Web. October 18, 2010. http://citynoise.org/article/2770.

Conley, Jim. "Automobile Advertisements: The Magical and the Mundane." In: Jim Conley and Arlene Tigar (eds.), *Car Troubles: Critical Studies of Automobility and Auto-mobility*. Farnham, England, Ashgate, 2009, p. 37–57.

———. "A Sociology of Traffic: Driving, Cycling, Walking." In: Phillip Vannini (ed.), *Technologies of Mobility in the Americas*. Oxford, Bern & New York, Peter Lang, 2012, p. 19–36.

Cox, Peter. " 'A Denial of Our Boasted Civilisation': Cyclists' Views on Conflicts over Road Use in Britain, 1926–1935." *Transfers* 2 (2012), p. 4–30.

Douglas, Mary. *Purity and Danger: An Analysis of the Concept of Pollution and Taboo*. London, Routledge, 1985.

Foster, Mark S. *A Nation on Wheels*. Belmont, Thomson, Wadsworth, 2003.

Goffman, Erving. *Behavior in Public Places; Notes on the Social Organization of Gatherings*. New York, Free Press, 1963.

———. *Interaction Ritual: Essays on Face-to-face Behavior*. Garden City NY, Anchor, 1967.

———. *Relations in Public; Microstudies of the Public Order*. New York, Harper and Row, 1971.

Green, Judith, Rebecca Steinbach, and Jessica Datta. "The Travelling Citizen: Emergent Discourses of Moral Mobility in a Study of Cycling in London." *Sociology* 46 (2012), p. 272–289.

Heinich, Nathalie. *De la Visibilité: Excellence et Singularité en Régime Médiatique*. Paris, Gallimard, 2012.

Jensen, Ole B. "Erving Goffman and Everyday Life Mobility." In: Michael Hviid Jacobsen (ed.), *The Contemporary Goffman*. New York, Routledge, 2010, p. 333–351.

———. "Negotiation in Motion: Unpacking a Geography of Mobility." *Space and Culture* 13 (2010), p. 389–402.

Jonasson, Mikael. "The Ritual of Courtesy—Creating Complex or Unequivocal Places?" *Transport Policy*, 6 (1999), p. 47–55.

84   Jim Conley

Joseph, Isaac. *Erving Goffman et la Microsociologie*. Paris, Presses Universitaires de France, 1998.

Jøvrgensen, Anette J. "The Culture of Automobility: How Interacting Drivers Relate to Legal Standards and to Each Other in Traffic." In: Tanu Priya Uteng and Tim Cresswell (eds.), *Gendered Mobilities*. Aldershot, Ashgate, 2008, p. 99–111.

Katz, Jack. *How Emotions Work*. Chicago, University of Chicago, 1999.

Kidder, Jeffrey L. *Urban Flow: Bike Messengers and the City*. Ithaca, Cornell University Press, 2011.

Ladd, Brian. *Autophobia: Love and Hate in the Automotive Age*. Chicago, University of Chicago, 2008.

Latour, Bruno. "Where Are the Missing Masses? The Sociology of a Few Mundane Artefacts." In: Wiebe E. Bijker, Thomas P. Hughes, and Trevor J. Pinch (eds.), *The Social Construction of Technological Systems: New Directions in the Sociology and History of Technology*. Cambridge MA, MIT Press, 1992, p. 225–259.

———. "To Modernise or to Ecologise? That Is the Question." In: Bruce Braun and Noel Castree (eds.), *Remaking Reality: Nature at the Millennium*. London, Routledge, 1998, p. 221–242.

Lemieux, Cyril. "L'accusation Tolérante. Remarques sur les Rapports entre Commérage, Scandale et Affaire." In: Luc Boltanski, Élisabeth Claverie, Nicolas Offenstadt, and Stéphane Van Damme (eds.), *Affaires, Scandales et Grandes Causes: De Socrate à Pinochet*. Paris, Stock, 2007, p. 367–394.

———. "Du Pluralisme des Régimes d'Action à la Question de l'Inconscient: Déplacements." In: Marc Breviglieri, Claudette Lafaye, and Danny Trom (eds.), *Compétences Critiques et Sens de la Justice: Colloque de Cerisy*. Paris, Economica, 2009, p. 69–80.

Marsh, Peter E., and Peter Collett. *Driving Passion: The Psychology of the Car*. Boston, Faber and Faber, 1987.

McShane, Clay. *Down the Asphalt Path: The Automobile and the American City*. New York, Columbia University Press, 1994.

Miller, Daniel. "Driven Societies." In: Daniel Miller (ed.), *Car Cultures*. Oxford, Berg, 2001, p. 1–33.

Moody, Michael, and Laurent Thévenot. "Comparing Models of Strategy, Interests, and the Public Good in French and American Environmental Disputes." In: Michèle Lamont and Laurent Thévenot (eds.), *Rethinking Comparative Cultural Sociology: Repertoires of Evaluation in France and the United States*. Cambridge UK, Cambridge UP, 2000, p. 273–306.

Möser, Kurt. "The Dark Side of 'automobilism,' 1900–30: Violence, War, and the Motor Car." *Journal of Transport History* 24 (2003), p. 238–258.

Norton, Peter D. *Fighting Traffic: The Dawn of the Motor Age in the American City*. Cambridge MA, MIT Press, 2008.

Packer, Jeremy. *Mobility without Mayhem: Safety, Cars, and Citizenship*. Durham, NC, Duke University Press, 2008.

Parks Canada. "Kensington Market National Historic Site of Canada." Web. July 20, 2011. http://www.pc.gc.ca/apps/cp-nr/release_e.asp?bgid=890&andor1=bg.

Paterson, Matthew. *Automobile Politics: Ecology and Cultural Political Economy*. Cambridge, Cambridge University Press, 2007.

Renouard, Jean-Marie. *As du Volant et Chauffards: Sociologie de la Circulation Routière*. Paris, L'Harmattan, 2000.

Rosen, Paul. *Framing Production: Technology, Culture, and Change in the British Bicycle Industry*. Cambridge MA, MIT Press, 2002.

Seiler, Cotten. *Republic of Drivers: A Cultural History of Automobility in America*. Chicago, University of Chicago Press, 2008.

Skinner, David, and Paul Rosen. "Hell Is Other Cyclists: Rethinking Transport and Identity." In: Paul Rosen, Peter Cox, and David Horton (eds.), *Cycling and Society*. Aldershot, Ashgate, 2007, p. 83–96.

Thelle, Mikkel. "Subversive Mobilities: The Copenhagen Riots, 1900–1919." *Transfers* 3 (2013), p. 7–25.

Thévenot, Laurent. "Économie et Politique de l'Entreprise; Économies de l'Efficacité et de la Confiance." In: Luc Boltanski, Laurent Thevenot, and Alain Desrosières (eds.), *Justesse et Justice dans le Travail. Cahiers du Centre d'Études de l'Emploi, 33.* Paris, Presses Universitaires de France, 1989, p. 135–207.

———. *L'action au Pluriel: Sociologie des Régimes d'Engagement.* Paris, La Découverte, 2006.

———. "Which Road to Follow? The Moral Complexity of an 'Equipped' Humanity." In: John Law and Annemarie Mol (eds.), *Complexities: Social Studies of Knowledge Practices.* Durham, NC, Duke University Press, 2002, p. 53–87.

———. "The Plurality of Cognitive Formats and Engagements: Moving between the Familiar and the Public." *European Journal of Social Theory* 10 (2007), p. 409–423.

Thévenot, Laurent, Michael Moody, and Claudette Lafaye. "Forms of Valuing Nature: Arguments and Modes of Justification in French and American Environmental Disputes." In: Michèle Lamont and Laurent Thévenot (eds.), *Rethinking Comparative Cultural Sociology: Repertoires of Evaluation in France and the United States.* Cambridge UK, Cambridge University Press, 2000, p. 229–272.

Vanderbilt, Tom. *Traffic: Why We Drive the Way We Do (and What It Says about Us).* New York, Alfred A. Knopf, 2008.

Volti, Rudi. "A Century of Automobility." *Technology and Culture* 37 (1996): 663–685.

———. *Cars and Culture: The Life Story of a Technology.* Baltimore, Johns Hopkins University Press, 2006.

Weber, Donald. "The Morality of Motoring: The Emergence of the Automobile in Belgium, 1895–1940." *Transfers* 2 (2012), p. 31–55.

Weber, Max. *Economy and Society: An Outline of Interpretive Sociology.* Berkeley, University of California Press, 1968.

Wolff, M. "Notes on the Behavior of Pedestrians." In: Arnold Birenbaum and Edward Sagarin (eds.), *People in Places; the Sociology of the Familiar.* New York, Praeger, 1973, p. 35–48.

6 Urbanization and Transport Restructuring before World War II

A Comparison between London and Osaka

Takeshi Yuzawa

INTRODUCTION

The object of this chapter is to examine the chaotic transit modes in big cities that resulted from rapid urbanization at the beginning of the twentieth century, especially after World War I. Railways, underground lines, trams, omnibuses, taxis, and private automobiles coexisted and competed amongst each other, which led to serious traffic congestion. The question this chapter addresses is how big cities integrated and governed these transit modes, and how urban policies "locked-in" the direction of the coordination regime.

The chapter will compare the history of transport in London with that of Osaka, Japan, because both cities had similar mobility problems at the beginning of the twentieth century and struggled to solve them, although the scale and graveness was different between the two cities. London had an advantage over Osaka due to the development of a single authority, the London Passenger Transport Board (LPTB), in 1933. However, it took more than twenty years to finalize the LPTB through seemingly endless discussions among politicians, municipalities, and various business interests. They clashed with each other at various stages in the creation of the authority, but eventually compromised and agreed to form the LPTB.

Osaka offers an important point of comparison with London. It was the second largest city in Japan at that time, known as the "Manchester of the East," and the cotton industry prospered there. This city developed a progressive transport policy and launched the first municipal tram and underground lines in Japan. Osaka was more advanced in its transport policy than Tokyo at the time. Both London's and Osaka's approaches to solving their transport problems shared common elements, although their methods differed, and officials in both cities were strongly influenced by German transport policy ideas.

The first part of the chapter discusses the changing pattern of urban transport modes in London, which resulted in serious traffic competition and congestion. Political antagonism among members of the Tories and the Labour Party, as well as municipalities and various transport enterprises, made the solution difficult and complicated. Strong leadership was required

Urbanization and Transport Restructuring 87

to coordinate stakeholders and realize a new transport system. Herbert Morrison and Lord Ashfield were major players in this drama.

The second part of the chapter describes the historical background of Osaka's transport system, and makes comparisons with Tokyo and its municipal transport policy. It seeks to understand why Osaka was so progressive in its transport policy. In order to address this question, it is important to investigate the role of Hajime Seki, the mayor of Osaka, who promoted the modernization of Osaka's transport system after resigning from a professorship at Tokyo Higher Commercial School (now Hitotsubashi University). His ideas regarding transport and urban policy were largely formed while he was studying in Europe, especially in Germany.

Lastly, the chapter will compare how London and Osaka, which faced similar traffic problems, arrived at solutions to their transport concerns. In both cities, strong leaders with very different ideological backgrounds tackled the transport difficulties and eventually reached similar solutions for coordinating various transport modes.

SOLVING LONDON'S TRAFFIC PROBLEMS

The Situation at the Beginning of the Twentieth Century

At the end of Victorian era, both London's population and area had expanded rapidly. By 1921, the population in the county of London was 4.5 million, and in Greater London it had reached 7.5 million. As the size and population density of the London metropolis increased, residents began to commute from the suburbs to the city via various transport modes. The trunk railways for long-distance journeys terminated in London, but the terminal stations were located separately: for instance, at Euston (London and North Western Railway), Paddington (Great Western Railway), King's Cross (Great Northern Railway), St. Pancras (Midland Railway), Liverpool Street (Great Eastern Railway), Waterloo (London and South Western Railway), London Bridge (London, Brighton and South Coast Railway), Charing Cross (South Eastern and Chatham Railway), and Victoria (L.B. &S.C. and S.E.&C Railways).

At first, the trunk railway officials, except those with the Great Eastern Railway, were reluctant to ease urban traffic congestion in London, because they were competing against each other and were primarily concerned with long-distance, rather than cross-city, services. Many passengers had to transfer from one terminal to another by tram, omnibus, or underground line. Local railways, including underground services, were more important players in urban transport than the trunk railways (Yuzawa 1985, 5–8). However, the role of local railways in the London transport milieu was declining compared with tramways, and especially omnibuses, which were increasing their presence in London significantly as they replaced horse-drawn transport (Table 6.1).

88 Takeshi Yuzawa

Table 6.1 Passenger journeys in Greater London (millions of passengers carried)

| | \multicolumn{3}{c}{Railways and} | Tramways | Omnibuses | Total |
	Local	Trunk	Total			
1902	277 (25%)	188 (17%)	465 (42%)	361 (33%)	280 (25%)	1,106 (100%)
1925	556 (16%)	319 (9%)	875 (25%)	979 (28%)	1,671 (47%)	3,523 (100%)

Source: London Labour Party 1927, 3

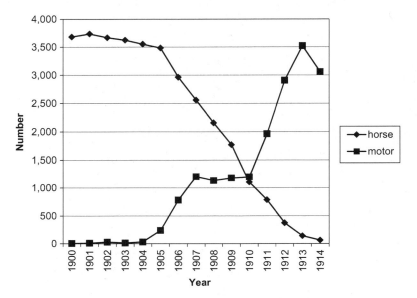

Figure 6.1 Numbers of buses driven by horses and motors in London
Source: Munby 1978, 562–565

The number of horses working in London at the end of nineteenth century was estimated at more than 150,000 (Turvey 2005, 49), and, needless to say, the manure from the horses created serious hygiene problems. The replacement of horse trams and horse-drawn coaches with electric trams and automobiles, respectively, was an urgent public health concern, and Figure 6.1 illustrates the drastic decline of the number of horses in London from the beginning of the twentieth century. According to Fouquet (2012), the conversion from horse-drawn vehicles to railway, tram, and omnibus services reduced energy consumption tremendously—in the case of motor cars by more than one-third. The modern mechanical traction systems were also superior in speed and capacity to horse-drawn conveyances.

However, mechanization of transport required tremendous capital. As a result, individual and small-scale firms were driven out of business or forced to merge into larger companies. The London General Omnibus Co. (LGOC), which originated as the Compagnie Generale des Omnibus de

Londres in 1855, dominated horse-drawn transport in London. It began to introduce motorized omnibuses in 1903 and finished the conversion from horse-drawn to motorized vehicles in 1911.

As for the underground systems, two types of underground railways existed in London: Railway carriages pulled by steam locomotives in shallow tunnels and rail cars moved by electric traction deep underground and known as "The Tube." The Metropolitan Railway, the first underground line in the world, was run by steam locomotives beginning in 1863. Its gauge and carriages were the same as those found on trunk railways. The Metropolitan established the Metropolitan District Railway (District) as a sister firm in 1868 to construct the Circle Line. The Metropolitan would take charge of the northern part of the Circle Line and the District would operate the southern part. Eventually, both railways were supposed to merge to create the Circle Line as part of the system. However, Metropolitan and District officials came into conflict with each other regarding divisions of financial interest and operating policies. Above all, both firms were more interested in extending their lines towards outer London individually than in completing the Circle Line together. Although the Circle Line was eventually completed in 1884, sixteen years after work began, the two companies pursued their own policies and never merged their lines as they had intended initially.

In 1898 the Board of Trade implemented a policy of electrifying the underground railways to prevent sulfurous smoke. The Metropolitan had the financial wherewithal to begin electrifying its line party through its own capital reserves. However, the District was too weak financially to launch the electrification project and asked Charles Yerkes, the American financier and traction magnate, to fund it. He established the Metropolitan District Electric Traction Co. in 1901 to tackle the project.

Yerkes came to London after the failure of his elevated electric railway (the "L" line) in Chicago, where he was known as the king of the street railroad. His first acquisition in London was the Charing Cross, Euston, and Hampstead Railway (CCE&HR, currently part of the Northern Line) in 1900 with the assistance of Speyer Brothers, the American financiers. The CCE&HR had parliamentary permission to build a deep-level tube, but had been unable to raise the money for its completion.

Yerkes organized the Underground Electric Railway Co. of London (UERL), which he used as a holding company for controlling the deep-level electric railways (tubes), the District Railway, and the London General Omnibus Company (LGOC). The UERL was called the "Combine"; it also ran tramway groups, such as London United Tramways and Metropolitan Electric Tramways.

Yerkes died in 1905, and although the significance of his role in London transport development is debatable, he had a great impact on the electrification of London's transportation infrastructure. Edgar Speyer, a financier, succeeded Yerkes, but had no knowledge or experience running railways and buses. Albert Stanley (1874–1948), who had emigrated from Britain to

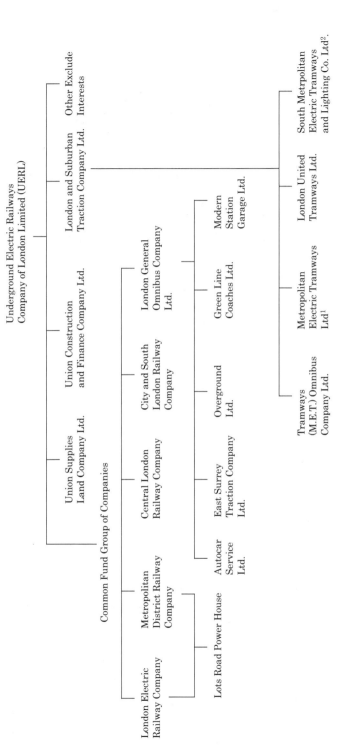

Note (1) Including shares in North Metropolitan Electric Power Supply Company Ltd
(2) Including Electricity Undertaking

Figure 6.2 Organization of UERL group
Source: Morrison, 1933, 11

the United States and had experience operating a tramway in Detroit was therefore, invited to run the firm. He became general manager of UERL in 1907 and joined the board of directors. He played a pivotal role in building the modern transit system in London. The UERL developed into the largest transport combine in London, with the LGOC's rapid transition from horse-drawn vehicles to motorized buses. Stanley coped with wartime transport problems during the First World War and was appointed president of the Board of Trade in 1916. After the war, he returned to the Underground group of companies, becoming chairman, as well as managing director, of the parent company and its subsidiaries. He was ennobled a baron and adopted the title of Baron Ashfield in 1920. Figure 6.2 shows the structure of the UERL.

Although the Metropolitan Railway was the largest underground company in London, the UERL group of firms surpassed it in terms of total passengers and receipts. Table 6.2 compares the UERL group with the Metropolitan Railway, which merged with the Great Northern & City Railway in 1913. The UERL group controlled 66.2% of the total number of passengers and 66.0% of the receipts of London underground services.

As for tramway traffic in the London area (Table 6.3), the London County Council (LCC) promoted the municipal tramway network vigorously by amalgamating a number of different firms. The LCC controlled

Table 6.2 Comparison of UERL group and Metropolitan Railway in 1910

	Passengers Carried (millions)		Total Receipts(£)	
UERL tubes	161.9	45.7%	1,224,558	42.2%
(District)	72.7	20.5%	691,128	23.8%
Metropolitan	108.2	30.5%	905,866	31.3%
(G. North. & City)	11.8	3.3%	78,729	2.7%
Total	354.6	100%	2,900,281	100%

Source: Barker and Robbins 1963, 49

Table 6.3 Tramways in the Greater London area controlled by LCC and UERL

	Length of Lines (miles)		Number of Cars		Passengers Carried (millions)	
LCC	177	39%	1,778	61%	533	65%
UERL	136	30%	703	24%	160	20%
Others*	146	31%	417	15%	127	15%
Total	459	100%	2,898	100%	820	100%

*Others include ten municipalities.

Source: Barker and Robbins, 1963, 190

92 Takeshi Yuzawa

65% of the total passengers carried in 1912, although it controlled only 39% of the lines in Greater London. The LCC occupied a profitable position, particularly compared with the UERL, whose tramways carried only 20% of the total passengers in spite of controlling 30% of the total mileage.

As shown in Table 6.1, omnibuses were the largest conveyor of passengers in London in 1925, carrying 47% of the total volume, compared to 28% carried by tramways, the second largest mode of transport. Omnibus firms engaged in cutthroat competition amongst themselves, while at the same time they faced a threat due to the entry of motor cars into the transport scene. The LGOC, under the control of UERL since 1912, dominated the omnibus business and transported 88.7% of omnibus passenger traffic in London in 1925. Its share increased to 95.7% in 1930. However, omnibus profits were inferior to those generated by tramways (see Table 6.4). Omnibus lines produced greater revenues than tramways, but their net receipts were about half those of tramways.

Overall, the UERL established the largest transport network in London in 1920s. It carried more than half of all underground passengers—although the Metropolitan remained the largest independent underground company—had the largest network of tramways next to that possessed by the LCC, and dominated omnibus services.

Table 6.5 indicates the dominant position of the UERL in terms of receipts. The UERL group pooled its receipts as a result of special statutory authority granted by parliament in 1915. The UERL, including London &

Table 6.4 Revenue and expenditure of tramways and omnibuses in 1923 (£000)

	Revenue	Working Expenditure	Net Receipts
Tramways	6,490	5,684	806
Omnibuses	8,704	8,303	400

Source: London Labour Party, 1927, 5–6

Table 6.5 Traffic receipts and net revenues of principal undertakings, 1931 (£000)

	Traffic Receipts	%	Net Revenues	%
UERL	15,487	65.9	2,976	65.2
London & Suburban				
Traction Group	2,340	9.9	100	2.2
Metropolitan Railway	1,549	6.6	802	17.6
LCC Tram	4,135	17.6	687	15
Total	23,511	100	4,565	100

Source: National Archives, MT46/23

Suburban Traction Group, shared 75% of traffic receipts and 67.4% of the net revenue in the total London transport system.

Attempts to Address the Traffic Problems in London

The Royal Commission on London Traffic was established in 1903 to investigate the city's traffic problems and the possibility of creating a new organization to control transportation in London. One of the difficulties of controlling traffic in the metropolitan region was that administrative districts and the transport network did not completely overlap. These administrative districts were also different from the area controlled by the Metropolitan Police. The Commission analyzed the traffic congestion, the various existing traffic regulations, and the means of coordinating different transport modes—including railways (trunk lines, local railways, and undergrounds), tramways (horse-drawn or electric), and omnibuses. It published a seven-volume report in 1906 that recommended creating a traffic board to control transportation in London. A London Traffic Board was established under the Board of Trade in 1907. It was responsible for collecting information and statistics bearing on traffic and transport problems and preparing an annual report for parliament. However, the London Traffic Board was disbanded in 1916.

After the First World War, the Select Committee on Transport (Metropolitan Area) was established in 1919 to deal with the urgent problem of London traffic. The Select Committee expressed a strong conviction that a supreme traffic authority was essential for implementing and enforcing a solution that would address all transport modes. In November 1919, the Advisory Committee on London Traffic was set up under the chairmanship of Kennedy Jones, a journalist and Member of Parliament (MP), who recommended the creation of a small statutory body that would operate under the Ministry of Transport. However, the Advisory Committee opposed the idea of a municipal traffic authority, because the "123 local bodies concerned were so numerous, and their personnel so changing, and their interests on occasions so divergent." Moreover, it insisted that "there was no possibility of a selection from these sources of a small body such as is required for effective action which would in any way be considered as representative of the whole. Indeed, any authority constituted on these lines would be unwieldy, and the difficulties of obtaining a wide range of vision and of carrying out a continuous policy would be insuperable" (London Municipal Society and National Union of Ratepayers' Association 1923, 4).

The London County Council and the representatives of omnibus firms met with the Ministry of Transport in 1920 and admitted that a unified structure for operating local passenger transport services in Greater London was necessary. They also agreed that it was desirable to set up a traffic control authority. The LCC passed a resolution confirming these principles and suggested that the municipal traffic control authority should be appointed by the local authorities affected. The council recommended that railways and tramways carrying urban and suburban traffic should be operated in large systems, under regulations suitable "to protect the interests of the public," and that a traffic board, appointed by the central government and "possessed of special knowledge and experience and giving continuous attention to all questions affecting locomotion and transport in London" should be established. The council also stated that "opinions may differ on minor points, but the fact remains that traffic problems of Greater London MUST be tackled without further delay" (London Municipal Society and National Union of Ratepayers' Association 1923, 10).

The views of the Royal Commission on the Greater London Government, which was established in 1923, with regard to the problems of London traffic were important because the commission received evidence from witnesses representing a large majority of the local authorities in Greater London. The evidence represented the most authoritative and up-to-date expression of the opinions of the local governing bodies in Greater London on the question of traffic regulation. The London and Home Counties Traffic Advisory Committee, as part of the Royal Commission on Greater London Government, was formed under Wilfred Ashley, who was minister for transport from 1924 to 1929, and although he was a strong antisocialist, he seriously considered addressing the London transport problems via some means of public control.

Since the middle of 1926, discussions had also been proceeding between the representatives of the Combine and the members of the LCC as to the possibility of joining each other's passenger networks in London. They eventually agreed to coordinate the traffic under a common fund and common management. The general idea of a common fund was that the balance of the gross revenues earned by the members, after deducting their respective revenue liabilities, would be pooled and thereafter distributed or applied in accordance with the rules proposed. A common management was defined as "one or more persons forming an executive actually engaged in the task of maintaining, working, renewing and developing the combined undertakings, and responsible to the proprietors of several undertakings for the results of his or their entire management." It was thought that considerable economies would result from common management.

The Traffic Advisory Committee recommended a common fund and common management for London's transport system in a 1927 report. The report also explained the principles by which such a system would be managed. For the protection of both the public and the private firms involved, several points were suggested: "The combined undertakings shall at all times be operated as a single system of transport so that adequate travelling facilities are provided for the public . . . the combined undertakings shall be managed and worked so that the earnings shall be sufficient to meet all proper charges against them and provide a reasonable return upon the capital invested" (London and Home Counties Traffic Advisory Committee 1927, 7–9; Barker and Robbins 1963, 210–214).

The Traffic Advisory Committee introduced the Coordination of Passenger Traffic Bill, but it was severely criticized by the Labour Party, and particularly by Herbert Morrison, a transport expert in London. He argued that the bill establishing a common fund and common management was intended to copy the successful business model of UERL, although management of the transport entities would be led by the municipalities and supervised by the Ministry of Transport. The following section will examine how and why the Passenger Traffic Bill was modified to better treat the various interests affected by it and to gather support from the major parties who had opposed it.

Herbert Morrison and Lord Ashfield

Herbert Morrison (1888–1965) joined the Independent Labour Party at the age of eighteen, and then became secretary to the London Labour Party. When the First World War began, he declared himself to be a conscientious objector, and stated that "I belong to the Independent Labour Party and Socialism is my religion." He became mayor of Hackney from 1920–1921, and was also elected to the LCC in 1922 and became an MP in the general election of 1923. When Ramsay Macdonald organized the second Labour cabinet, he appointed Morrison as the minister of transport from 1929 to 1931. After he lost his seat in the general election in 1931, Morrison continued to sit on the LCC and in 1934 became its leader. In this post he oversaw the development of London's housing, health, education, and transport services. Morrison's main achievements in London included the unification of the transport system and the creation of a "green belt" around the suburbs.

In early 1922, Morrison wrote a memorandum on London transport. In his view, the new authority for Greater London "should not only be empowered to control traffic, but also itself operate the various passenger traffic services proper to its area." The London Labour Party scheme for Greater London emphatically declared that the ownership and operation of the various traffic services should be in the hands of a directly elected body governing a new regional council distinct from the LCC. In 1922, the Labour Party opposed a joint committee, board, or indirectly elected board running London Traffic, and preferred a directly elected body (London Municipal Pamphlet 1929, 2–3).

On December 13, 1926, seventeen members, including London Labour Party executive representatives, London Labour Party MPs, LCC Labour Party members, and the Parliamentary Labour Party Executive gathered and discussed London's traffic problems. Participants asserted that "the old idea that competition was beneficial to the consumer is, with certain reservations, untrue as far as London Traffic is concerned. All the wasteful expenditure must be met, in the main, either by passengers in unnecessarily high charges or by the workers in unnecessarily low wages, whilst the financial insecurity of the undertakings leads to limitations on enterprise and development and prevents the scrapping of useable but really

96   *Takeshi Yuzawa*

out-of-date rolling stock, with the result that the passenger suffers in comfort and convenience." It was proposed that the undertakings should be owned and operated by a public authority and that there should be complete coordination by merging London passenger services into one public service. Morrison was secretary for that committee and no doubt played an important role in writing the pamphlet that came out of the meeting (London Labour Party 1929, 3–7).

As minister of transport, Morrison had stressed three objectives for his transport policy in London: first, the restriction of excessive competition between transport modes; second, the unification of management into a single organization; and third, public control, while retaining the principle of efficiency and profitability. He attacked the Coordination Passenger Transport Bill, asserting that "the scheme of the Tory L.C.C. [was] a fraud, a delusion and a snare" and that "the scheme secures the permanent subordination of municipal interests to private interests." He mocked the bill, promoted by the Tory LCC and the Combine, as "the London Private Traffic Monopoly (enabling) Bill," and claimed that its purpose was to permit the profit-seeking concern known as the London Traffic Combine to run the London County Council tramways, which were the property of ratepayers. He insisted that "monopoly must be a public monopoly, the management of which is accountable to the people" (Morrison 1929, 3, 9). He wrote that the "[Labour] Party is of the opinion that complete public ownership and control is highly desirable in view of the vital character of the service and the public interests affected." However, he added that "we would not be unwilling to consider a joint municipal and private company, provided that a majority of the directors were municipal representatives. This form of combining private and public capital to ensure a predominance of public control, assisted by private commercial experience, is not uncommon on the Continent, and it has attractions not to be ignored" (21).

The Labour Party looked to Germany, where socialists were in favor of combining municipal and private enterprises, for a transport model. Such a combination actually existed in Berlin, where Ernst Reuter, a member of Social Democratic Party (SPD), had played a key role in establishing the *Berliner Verkehrs-AG* (BVG) in 1928. His ideas and policies may have had an influence on the London Labour Party, but it is not clear if members of the London Labour Party and Reuter were in contact at either an organizational or a personal level. The London Labour Party viewed the German system as a success due to the fact that "it avoids the grave danger of political influence in the management of the concern, the granting of unprofitable concessions to the public, 'padded pay rolls,' as they say in the United States, undue size of staff, lavish and uneconomic management" (London Municipal Pamphlet 1929, 8). It is important that the Labour Party viewed the German system, where municipal representation on the board of management, as a general rule, was less than private representation in order to shield public transport from political strife, as a solution to the transport dilemma. Morrison, who preferred municipal leadership, accepted the German system as a model for reorganizing the London Transport Board.

Another important player in the transport debate was Lord Ashfield, formerly Albert Henry Stanley. As previously noted, he was recruited by the UERL in 1907 and contributed not only to the development of the UERL and the Combine, but also to the British government as a minister of transport during the First World War. He worked as chairman and managing director of the UERL (1910–1916 and 1910–1933) and the Metropolitan District Railway (1910–1916 and 1919–1933).

At first, Lord Ashfield promoted the Coordination Passenger Transport Bill that introduced a common fund and common management to the LCC. The proposed framework was similar to the organization of the Combine, which was part of his enterprise group. He agreed to the conditions stipulated by parliament and the LCC, although the common management model proposed by these groups was different from that used by the Combine. He endeavored to secure good terms with the shareholders of the Combine regarding the rate at which their shares would be exchanged for shares of the new corporation. Eventually, he promoted the resulting London Passenger Transport Bill, compromising with Morrison and the Labour Party.

At the beginning of the negotiation, Morrison and Ashfield disagreed about the direction of London traffic policy, but gradually they reached an understanding that a single agency with the majority of the board of directors consisting of representatives from the private sector was the only solution. Both men were sufficiently flexible to adopt elements of each other's proposals, which made a common view possible. Barker and Robbins (1963) suggest that "perhaps Morrison moved farther than Ashfield did" (273). Morrison insisted initially on a policy of public ownership based on socialist values, but eventually conceded that operations should be left in the hands of professional managers with business expertise.

The London Passenger Transport Act was enacted in 1933. Ashfield became the first chairman of the London Passenger Transport Board (LPTB) in 1933 and remained in the position until 1947. Barker and Robbins (1963) write that "without Ashfield the thing could never have been done" (273). His experience managing the Combine, in addition to his political skill acquired as president of the Board of Trade during the war, were essential for the new organization (Yuzawa 2008, 64–70).

EASING TRAFFIC CONGESTION IN OSAKA

Comparing Osaka with Tokyo and London at the Beginning of the Twentieth Century

In 1921, London was the largest city in the world with a population of about 7.5 million people and an advanced transport system. Tokyo was

98 Takeshi Yuzawa

about half the size of London, and Osaka was half again the size of Tokyo. Thus, the size of Osaka was roughly one-fourth the size of London. But as far as urban transports were concerned, Tokyo was backwards and Osaka resembled cities in the developed nations of Europe.

Although Kyoto served as the capital of Japan prior to the Meiji Restoration, the country's economic center lay approximately fifty kilometers southwest in Osaka for more than a thousand years. Even after the Meiji Restoration in 1868, Osaka remained the largest commercial center in the country, and many major companies had their head offices there. In terms of population in 1921, the top five cities in Japan were Tokyo (2.17 million.), Osaka (1.25 million), Kobe (0.61 million), Kyoto (0.59 million), and Nagoya (0.43 million). From 1911 to 1924, including the economic boom during the First World War and the depression after the war, the population in Greater Osaka increased by 33%. This increase was caused mainly by rapid growth in the city's suburbs, where the population grew by 159%, compared to 7% in the urban core. This meant that the central part of Greater Osaka had become crowded and that people had moved to the suburbs. When the city of Osaka expanded by merging with neighboring counties, towns, and villages in 1925, it overtook Tokyo in terms of population, but Tokyo surpassed it when it merged with adjacent counties and towns in 1932. Both Tokyo and Osaka were typical cities in Japan, the former a center of the East and the latter a center of the West. However, Osaka began to decline from the 1970s onwards as many large companies moved their head offices to Tokyo and business activities and the population base increasingly concentrated in the Tokyo metropolitan area. Today, Osaka is the third largest city after Tokyo and Yokohama.

According to *The Handbook* published in 1928 by Osaka City, we can point out several key differences between Osaka and Tokyo. Osaka had the larger population in 1925 because it expanded its boundaries earlier than Tokyo and covered an area twice as large. The size of Tokyo's budget (236 million yen) was similar to Osaka's budget (207 million yen), including the amount of unredeemed bonds. Osaka had about 3,906 companies compared to 3,510 in Tokyo, but in terms of the paid capital for the companies Tokyo (3,997 million yen) was twice as large as Osaka (1,946 million yen), and Tokyo (68) surpassed Osaka (44) in the number of banks, as well as the size of their deposits. This was due to the fact that the economy of Osaka consisted of small and medium-sized enterprises. Osaka (4,228 factories and 151,340 employees) exceeded Tokyo (3,025 factories and 67,740 employees) in the number of factories and employees. Osaka flourished mainly due to its textile factories with a large number of female workers who accounted for 37% of all employees, compared to 15% in Tokyo. Based on various statistics, total factory output in Osaka was 854 million yen, by far exceeding Tokyo's 330 million yen. Osaka was the largest industrial city in Japan, and popularly called the "Manchester in the East."

Table 6.6 Transport in Tokyo and Osaka in 1925

	Railway		Cars	Trucks	Motorcycles	Bicycles	Rickshaws
	Rail stations	Passengers (million)					
Tokyo	22	103.8	3,437	1,742	962	162,433	8,112
Osaka	18	18.9	1,625	533	1,335	166,661	3,492

	Municipal trams		
	Miles	Passengers (million)	Revenue (million yen)
Tokyo	164	471.2	31.2
Osaka	109	304.6	17.2

Source: Osaka City 1928

Compared with Tokyo, Osaka's transportation infrastructure was lacking. The number of passengers on railways in Tokyo was far larger than that of Osaka, and the number of passenger cars and trucks in Tokyo also exceeded those found in Osaka (Table 6.6). However, Osaka had more motorcycles than Tokyo and a similar number of bicycles. Osaka developed its tramway network proportionally to that of Tokyo, although its revenue was slightly poorer than the revenue from Tokyo tramways.

Overall, Osaka was a flourishing industrial city, but public transport did not respond to the increasing traffic, and that is the reason why Osaka had to implement a unique transport policy. The person who played a crucial role in this process was Hajime Seki.

Hajime Seki

Hajime Seki (1873–1935) graduated from Tokyo Higher Commercial School (THCS, now Hitotsubashi University) in 1893. He became a professor at Tokyo Higher Commercial School and lectured on transport, social policy, and city planning. He studied in Belgium and Germany between 1898 and 1901, and was strongly influenced by German scholars like Gustav von Schmoller, Adolph Heinrich Wagner, and Lujo Brentano. He attended Georg Simmel's lectures (Hanes, 4J, 48J). He was impressed especially with Schmoller's ideas regarding transport policy (Shibamura 1987).

On the way back to Japan from Europe in 1901, Seki travelled through southern Germany, Switzerland, the Netherlands, and Belgium and boarded a ship for New York from Antwerp on August 21, 1901. He was strongly impressed by New York's progressive, urban transport system and visited Chicago where he watched the "L" train. He took a ship bound for Yokohama from Seattle. He resumed teaching at Tokyo Higher Commercial School, but

100   Takeshi Yuzawa

was invited to be deputy mayor of Osaka City in 1914, and then became mayor of Osaka in 1923, a position he retained until his death in 1935.

Seki published many books and articles, including a work titled *Koruson shi no kotsu seisaku* (*Clement Colson's Transport Policy*) in 1903, based upon Colson's *Transports & Tariffs* of 1898. Clement Colson (1853–1939) was a French civil engineer and scholar on transport, who taught at the Ecole Polytechnique and the Center of High Military Studies. Colson was close to Alfred Marshall, and assumed to be a liberal, but he stressed the state's legitimacy to deal with education and public services: "The real character . . . is unable to be organized without the use of coercive power." He explained precisely the fare system in transport and stressed the "user-pays" principle (Fujii 2000, 106–112).

Seki published *Tetsudo Kogi Yoryo* (*Epitome of Lecture on Railway*) in 1905. He concentrated on the fare system in a railway economy. Colson's influence was evident. Seki pointed out four characteristics of a railway: the concentration of capital, monopolistic aspects, service to the public, and interconnections with other railways. A railway needed tremendous capital for land, locomotives, carriages, rail, and so on, and that was the reason why railways were established as joint-stock companies or subsidized by the government, or even constructed and owned by the government itself. The railway had two kinds of monopoly: a natural and an economic monopoly. The railway would be built on the best routes for the populated area in addition to the technological reasons for the construction of the lines; once the railway is constructed in the best location, it enjoys a monopolistic profit because passengers cannot easily use an alternative railway. Seki also explained the two public aspects of the railway. The railway was essential for a nation in terms of political, military, social, and economic purposes. At the same time, the railway had a public obligation as a common carrier to serve customers fairly, and public authorities had to watch and control the railway. The transport industry required the standardization of technologies and managerial practices in order to link with other companies.

Seki stressed that even though the railways were owned by the public authorities, they should seek profit with efficient management. He agreed with the 1906 nationalization of the seventeen major railway companies in Japan, which took place a year after the publication of his book.

He wrote several articles on municipal enterprises, which had introduced the modern urban transport system in Europe. From the end of the nineteenth century, municipal authorities in Europe started tramway businesses by issuing bonds. As for criticism against the municipal enterprises, Seki emphasized that the public utilities funded by issuing bonds eventually belonged to the citizens after the redemption of the bonds (Seki 1911). He argued in an article published in 1928 that the municipal enterprises and the joint-stock companies were similar in terms of their management, even though their enterprise forms looked quite dissimilar, and that the professional managers of both enterprises assumed pivotal roles in running the businesses (Seki 1928). Thus, he discussed the separation of ownership from management before the publication of *The Modern Corporation and Private Property* by Adolf Berle and Gardiner Means in 1932.

Seki, who has been called a liberal reformer, had a strong interest in social and urban problems as well as labor relations. He was one of the founders of the Society for the Social Policy in Japan in 1907. There were three ideological groups in the society; left, middle, and right. The left wing had sympathy with socialism and labor movements, the middle was liberal and sought social reform and a philanthropic approach to labor problems, and the right stressed the role of the state and its protection for society and labor. According to Shibamura, Seki's position was close to the middle. Seki debated with Hajime Kawakami, a famous Marxist at the University of Kyoto, on social policy, and disagreed with the Marxism's doctrine of determinism, although he had a keen interest in the labor problem, not from a class standpoint, but from the perspective of social and urban policies.

According to Jeffrey E. Hanes (2002), "rather than rejecting Marxism outright, contemptuous of its rigid determinism and fantastical internationalism, [Seki] painstakingly historicized Marxist class analysis and integrated it into his prescription for labor reform in Japan's late-developing capitalist society" (104). "In the end, Seki was able to conflate the competing visions of modernity proffered by Marx and List through his domestication of class analysis" (105).

It is difficult to sketch briefly Seki's entire corpus of ideas on public and transport policies, because he wrote numerous papers even after he became mayor. The following section will examine how Seki conducted the modernization of transport in Osaka as deputy mayor and later mayor through his extensive academic background in transportation policy and contemporary knowledge of transport in the western world.

Seki and Osaka Transport

Before Seki came to Osaka, there was already an established tradition of municipal enterprise. While Sadakichi Tsuruhara (1857–1914) was mayor of Osaka from 1900 to 1905, he realized that mitigating traffic congestion in the central area was one of the most urgent problems in the city. At that time, Osaka did not have the financial resources to tackle its growing urban problems and needed a new source of revenue to fund the city budget. He persuaded Osaka's municipal assembly that if Osaka had a municipal tram, it would be able to control its fare system and protect the interest of its citizens, which would be profitable and supply money for the general budget of Osaka.

Tsuruhara asserted that public transport in the city should be in the hands of city officials and carried out the policy of constructing the tram.

102 *Takeshi Yuzawa*

It is not clear how Tsuruhara acquired the knowledge to implement such a strategy. He had been a diplomat in London between 1885 and 1887, where he saw trams driven by horses, but not by electricity, because the first electric tram operated by the London County Council did not begin operations until 1903. Tsuruhara missed the chance to see the electric tram in London firsthand, but he could have received information about public transport in modern cities before becoming mayor of Osaka. Tsuruhara saw the successful electric trams in Kyoto (opened in 1895) and in Nagoya (opened in 1898), and may have gained confidence to proceed with his plan based on these precedents, all of which were operated by joint-stock companies.

He had the idea of municipal trams in 1899, and succeeded in getting the permission for the construction from the government at the end of 1902. Osaka City started its municipal tram in 1903, which was only three miles long. It was the first tram run by a municipality in Japan. The tram was constructed not based on some ideal, but for the practical reason that the city wanted to connect the newly built harbor with the city center by tram (Osaka Shi Denkikyoku 1943, 4). Moreover, the tram was aimed at supporting the fifth National Fair in Osaka, organized to promote industries in Japan. If the municipalities had granted the right for the construction and management of the trams to the private sector, and then levied taxes and various charges, they could have avoided the risk of financial failure. Osaka was flourishing at the time, and there were many proposals from entrepreneurs to construct trams. Tsuruhara stood firmly against their proposals, and insisted on the municipality building trams. It was significant that Osaka attempted to establish a tradition of public transport in Japan.

Following Tsuruhara, Shiro Ikegami (1857–1929) was nominated the sixth mayor of Osaka in 1913. He had been a police officer since 1877 and the head of the police department in Osaka. As soon as he became mayor, he sought a right-hand man to help him with administrative tasks, and invited Hajime Seki to become deputy mayor in 1914. With Seki's support, Ikegami promoted the municipalization of the electricity and water services, and planned the widening of Midosuji as the main street in central Osaka, which was 4,027 meters long and 43.6 meters wide with six car lanes. While he was deputy mayor, Hajime Seki had idealistic plans for the modernization of Osaka, which he tried to implement. He improved the living conditions of people in Osaka by building council houses and parks.

After he became mayor in 1923, Seki promoted the construction of the first municipal underground line in Japan (now part of the Midosuji Line), which opened in 1933. Seki knew about urban transport systems in London, Paris, and Berlin, where underground lines were assuming important roles in public transport. He missed a chance to take the underground in Berlin because it was completed in 1902, after he had already left Germany, but he could have ridden the Metro in Paris at the World Fair in 1900 (Shibamura 1987, 979). No evidence has been located that Seki made direct contact with Ernest Reuter, but Reuter is supposed to have been influenced by Lujo Brentano in Munich while he was studying there, and, as previously mentioned, Seki learned much from Brentano.

When Seki had the idea to construct an underground in Osaka, he already had information about the Tokyo Underground, the first underground railway in Japan, which had been constructed not by the public, but by the private sector. Noritsugu Hayakawa (1881–1942), a pioneer of underground line development in Japan, visited London in 1914, where he received a positive impression of the underground system, and, after his return to Japan, he asked the government to construct a similar transport mode in Tokyo. But the government was reluctant to discuss his proposal because of a budget shortage. Therefore Hayakawa organized the Tokyo Underground Company in 1920. The first part of the line between Asakusa and Ueno (2.2 kilometers), in spite of interruption by the Great Kanto Earthquake in 1923, opened in 1927 and today is a part of the Ginza Line.

When Seki planned the underground in Osaka, he asked *Teikoku Tetsudo Kyokai* (the Imperial Railway Association) and *Doboku Gakkai* (the Institute of Civil Engineers) to investigate the feasibility of his plan. He felt that it was a good idea to have his plan certified by the authorities. They submitted a report to the Osaka administration in October 1924, *Osakashinaigai Kosoku Tetsudochosakai Hokokusho* (*Report of the Investigation on the Rapid Train in Osaka City and Its Suburbs*). It showed that Osaka's population was increasing, which was creating serious transport problems, and that there was no space for construction of new tramways, because the existing tramways already filled the main streets. Therefore, Osaka needed a new transport mode, called a rapid underground train (Teikoku Tetsudo Kyokai 1924, 3). The report compared Osaka with Tokyo, Paris, and Berlin, but London was only briefly referred to in the report, because London rapid trains (undergrounds) and omnibus services were already fully developed (Teikoku Tetsudo Kyokai 1924, 49, 55). The construction cost for the underground was estimated at 165.66 million yen, and the report recommended that the system be owned and run by Osaka City. The idea of municipal tram systems could be easily applied to the new transport mode. Indeed, there were many railways run by the central government and joint-stock companies that served Osaka and its suburbs, but it was not realistic to transfer control of all of them to the Osaka government, because their lines extended beyond Osaka's municipal area (Teikoku Tetsudo Kyokai 1924, 65).

CONCLUSION: COMPARING LONDON AND OSAKA

London and Osaka, although the latter's population was one-fourth of London's population and its transportation infrastructure was much less developed compared with the former, had similar traffic problems at the beginning of the twentieth century. London possessed advanced urban transport methods, but suffered from serious traffic congestion. Although

104 *Takeshi Yuzawa*

the Combine controlled a large part of London's passenger transport, most observers felt that London transport should be controlled by a single organization. The Combine and the LCC tried to establish a new organization for coordinating passenger transport facilities through a common fund and common management. Morrison and the Labour Party were opposed to leaving management to a joint committee of municipal and private-sector representatives. Morrison insisted on public ownership with officials elected, ideally, by the public. But Morrison and the Labour Party recognized the success of the German model, and acknowledged the risks of political intervention in management.

Osaka was a developing city at that time, and Mayor Tsuruhara, who foresaw the future of public transport and benefitted from access to a wide range of information on western cities, started the first municipal tram in Japan. Seki benefitted from his study in Europe, especially in Germany. He understood Marxism, but he did not agree with its deterministic ideologies and tried to solve the social problems and traffic congestion in Osaka by practical and realistic policies. He championed the construction of the underground, the first municipally owned and managed underground in Japan.

Both cases highlight the underlying characteristics of the transport industry, where competition within and among different modes of transport in the same market eventually led to a natural monopoly essential for a networked industry, which, in turn, was conducive to public ownership or at least strong public control or regulation. An open question was who should exercise this ownership or control: the central or the municipal governments? In London, the socialist Herbert Morrison insisted on public ownership largely for ideological reasons, whereas Hajime Seki considered the transport system indispensable for the modernization of Osaka. Seki asserted that the structure of joint-stock companies and municipal enterprises were similar due to the role of professional managers in large businesses. At first Morrison adhered to public ownership, but he acknowledged the role of professionals with knowledge and experience. Kevin Hey (2010) asserted that "Whereas co-ordination appealed to those with socialistic tendencies who saw a political opportunity to nationalize the transport sector, non-socialists were able to support the case for public or common ownership on the grounds of superior operational efficiency and effectiveness" (39). Likewise, both London and Osaka sought an ideal business form for urban transport, though their ideologies were different, but both cities were influenced strongly by the German system which was already in place in its public transport sector.

WORKS CITED

Material for this chapter was drawn from the National Archives (London), the London Metropolitan Archives (London), the London School of Economics Archives (London), and the Osaka City Central Library Archives (Osaka).

Urbanization and Transport Restructuring 105

Barker, T. C., and M. Robbins. *A History of London Transport: Passenger Travel and the Development of the Metropolis*, Vol. 2. London, Allen and Unwin, 1963.

Fouquet, Roger. *Trends in Income and Price Elasticities of Transport Demand* (1850–2010). Basque Center for Climate Change, 2012.

Fujii, Hideto. *Kotsuron no Sokei-Seki Hajime Kenkyu* [The Origin of Transport Theory. A Study of Hajime Seki]. Tokyo, Hassaku sha, 2000.

Hanes, Jeffrey E. *The City as Subject: Seki Hajime and the Reinvention of Modern Osaka*. Berkeley, University of California Press, 2002.

Hey, Kevin, "Transport Co-ordination and Professionalism in Britain: Forging a New Orthodoxy in the Early Inter-War Years." *Journal of Transport History* 31 (2010).

London and Home Counties Traffic Advisory Committee. *Report of the London and Home Counties Traffic Advisory Committee to the Minister of Transport Giving Particulars of a Scheme for the Co-ordination of Passenger Transport Facilities in the London Traffic Area*. 1927. London, 1972.

London Labour Party. *London's Traffic Problem: How to Secure Low Fares, Better Services and Greater Comfort: Being the Report of the Special Joint Committee Representing the London Labour Party*. London, 1927.

London Municipal Pamphlet. *Memorandum on the London Traffic Scheme of the Labour-Socialist Government*, no. 36. London, 1929.

London Municipal Society and the National Union of Ratepayers' Association. *The Greater London Traffic Problem: A Scheme for its Solution*. London, 1923.

Morrison, Herbert. *The London Traffic Fraud: Being the True Story of the London Traffic Monopoly Bills*. London, Labour Party Publication, 1929.

———. *Socialisation and Transport: The Organisation of Socialised Industries with Particular Reference to the London Passenger Transport Bill*, London, Constable, 1933.

Munby, D. L. *Railways, Public Road Passenger Transport, London's Transport*. Oxford, Clarendon Press, 1978.

Osaka Shi [City]. *Rokudai Toshi Hikaku Tokei Yoran* [A Handbook of Comparative Statistics for Six Largest Cities]. Osaka, 1928.

Osaka Shi Denkikyoku [Department of Electricity of Osaka City]. *Osaka Denkikyoku 40nenshi* [Department of Electricity in Osaka, Forty Years]. Osaka, 1943.

Seki, Hajime. "Shiei jigyo ron" [Theory of municipal enterprises]. *Kokumin Keizaizasshi* 10 (1911), no. 5.

———. "Shiei Jigyo no Keiei" [Management of Municipal Enterprises]. *Kokumin Keizaizasshi* 45 (1928), no. 2.

Shibamura, Atsuki. "Seki Hajime no ryugaku nikki" [Hajime Seki's Diary at the time of studying abroad]. *Bunkashi Ronso* ge [History of Culture, vol. 2], 1987.

———. *Seki Hajime-Toshi Shiso no Paionia* [Hajime Seki-Pioneer of Urban Idealists]. Shoreisha, 1989.

Teikoku Tetsudo Kyokai [Imperial Railway Association] and Doboku Gakkai [Institute of Civil Engineers]. *Osakashinaigai Kosoku Tetsudochosakai Hokokusho* [Report of the Investigation on the Rapid Train in Osaka City and Its Suburbs], 1924.

Turvey, Ralph. "Horse Traction in Victorian London." *Journal of Transport History* 26 (2005).

Yuzawa, Takeshi. "The Introduction of Electric Railways in Britain and Japan." *Journal of Transport History* 6 (1985).

———. "Rondon Joukyaku Yusou Iinkai no Keisei" [The Formation of London Passenger Transport Board]. GEM Bulletin, Gakushuin University, 2008.

7 Why the "Los Angelization" of German Cities Did Not Happen

The German Perception of U.S. Traffic Planning and the Preservation of the German City

Christopher Kopper

German and American historians have frequently asked whether West German society underwent a process of self-Americanization after 1945. At first glance, lower- and middle-class Germans seemed fascinated with American civilization's high attainment. This fascination prevailed even among the educated strata of German society. The silhouettes of skyscrapers and the amazing numbers of sophisticated cars on urban streets and highways represented a level of individual and collective wealth that Germans considered unachievable in the 1950s, but they also offered a tantalizing glimpse of a brighter future. However, these general impressions do not properly represent the modernity of German town planning before and after the war and how elite German urban planners perceived American modernity and adapted the concept of a mass-motorized city to meet the demands and desires of German urban planning.

Already by the 1930s German town planners who worked on National Socialist urban projects for cities such as Berlin and Munich began to anticipate the requirements of a mass-motorized society. At a time when the *Volkswagen* was still nothing more than a political vision of the Nazi regime in general, and the *Deutsche Arbeitsfront* in particular, planners of new towns such as Salzgitter and Wolfsburg took the mass adoption of the *Volkswagen*, which would serve as an engine of mass motorization, for granted. The plans for the city of Wolfsburg—originally named "*Stadt des KdF-Wagens*"—by the renowned town planner Peter Koller displayed all the specifics of National Socialist architectonic monumentalism and triumphalism, including a huge *Stadtkrone* (city crown) with dominant administrative buildings on a natural elevation and huge squares for hosting mass manifestations of uniformed German *Volksgenossen* on the secular holidays of Nazism. The wide streets from the residential areas to the center of the city and the *Volkswagen* factory were designed as *via triumphalis* (triumph streets) for the marching columns of uniformed storm troopers on National Socialist secular holidays. But apart from these symbolic meanings as stages of Nazi manifestations, the wide thoroughfares were meant to fulfill a functional purpose as traffic arteries.

Architecture and town planning historians such as Werner Durth and Niels Gutschow (1993) have noted that the functionalist core of Koller's plan was hardly distinguishable from the blueprints of contemporary British and French town planning. The monumental squares in the center of Wolfsburg provided ample parking space for Germany's anticipated, mass-motorized population. The width of the main thoroughfares and the plentiful space between the residential streets and the apartment blocks demonstrated more than simply the generosity of modern town planning. The wide spaces along the residential streets provided sufficient parking space for the cars of future Volkswagen workers who were supposed to be able to afford the vehicles they manufactured.

The plans for the future city of Salzgitter—the company town of the Reichswerke AG "Hermann Göring"—developed by Göring's favorite city planner, Herbert Rimpl, displayed similar patterns of urban planning. Wide thoroughfares and off-curbside parking spaces in residential areas anticipated necessary infrastructural requirements after the expected breakthrough of mass motorization, but still at a time when the commercial success of the *Volkswagen* lay in the balance. The detailed and diligent study of Hans Mommsen and Manfred Grieger (1996) about the Volkswagen works under the Nazi regime has demonstrated that the National Socialist vision of a motorized *Volksgemeinschaft* was built on flawed calculations by the *Deutsche Arbeitsfront* and the non-self-fulfilling euphoric prophesies of its leader, Robert Ley. The calculations by the National Socialist management that the *Volkswagen* could be sold at a price of only 990 Reichsmark were flawed and idealistic from the very beginning. The purchasing power of the ordinary, middle-class German in the 1930s would not have allowed him (or her) to purchase and maintain a car even at this unrealistically low price.

Due to a lack of material resources and labor, the ambitious city construction of Wolfsburg and Salzgitter was postponed during the war. After 1945, Koller de-Nazified his design for Wolfsburg by deleting the monumentalist National Socialist symbolism from his blueprints. The neoclassical monumentalism and the architectonical self-representation of a totalitarian state were replaced by the symbolic language of democratic town planning. The new architectonical language of modesty, soberness, and decency discarded the National Socialist inheritance of broad, triumphant, axis-like main streets and dominant, even overwhelming, monumental public buildings. But some patterns of the town plan from the Nazi age survived: The big thoroughfares to the city center were stripped of their propagandistic purpose for National Socialist body politics and refilled with a purely nonpolitical designation—as functional traffic arteries for the anticipated future of mass motorization. In 1948, the original traffic flow charts for Wolfsburg reappeared in an influential textbook on urban planning. They served as an example of the functional disadvantages of an axial and centralist urban design—but all hints about their National Socialist origins had been deleted.

After the end of the war, German town planners engaged in a vivid and emotional debate about the principles of reconstruction. A group of traditionally minded reconstructionists argued for the rebuilding of traditional block structures and street grids, whereas the modernist school argued in favor of a functionalist rebuilding along the guidelines of Le Corbusier's Charter of Athens. In some cities, such as Münster and Munich, traditionalist planners implemented the reconstruction in a traditional style, whereas the advocates of a functionalist modernity paved the way for modern architecture in cities like Hannover and Frankfurt.

Planners oriented toward tradition saw no reasons to rebuild their cities on a completely redesigned street grid. But even the avid admirers of Le Corbusier had no opportunity to rearrange the street grid from scratch in a functional pattern. Sewers, water and gas pipes, and power and phone lines had often survived air raids or were, at least, not destroyed beyond repair. The material value of urban streets with their supply grids was too great to abandon all prior infrastructural investments. City planners in big cities such as Hamburg, Düsseldorf, and Frankfurt had to restrict themselves to the widening of important thoroughfares and the construction of some wide, tangential streets, such as the Ost-West-Straße (in Hamburg), the Berliner Straße in Frankfurt, and the Berliner Allee in Düsseldorf (Deutsche Akademie für Städtebau und Landesplanung 1961). In the case of Hamburg's Ost-West-Strasse, the destructions of the war provided the city planners with the opportunity to implement a prewar concept from 1939 (Düwel and Gutschow 2013).

During the 1950s, Hannover evolved as the textbook example of modern urban planning in postwar West Germany. The heavy destruction of Hannover's city center during the war and the municipal administration's patient and skillful communication strategy provided Hannover's chief city planner, Rudolf Hillebrecht, with unique opportunities to redesign the street grid inside and at the edge of the Central Business District (CBD). In an early and seemingly overly optimistic anticipation of the growth potential of motorization, Hillebrecht's master plan from 1948 paved the way for a four-lane, inner-city ring; widened main streets; and generously dimensioned, tangential thoroughfares as traffic arteries (Dorn 2012). The concept of widening the thoroughfares and rerouting the main traffic around the CBD was highly acclaimed by fellow town planners and public opinion leaders (such as the news magazine *Der Spiegel*) in the German mass media.

In the 1950s, the idea of a functionalist and car-friendly town planning was adopted by some of the most influential members of the town planning community. Urban planners Johannes Göderitz and Hubert Hoffmann's highly influential textbook (Göderitz, Rainer, and Hoffmann 1957) about modern town planning was published in 1957, but based on an unpublished draft from 1944. The elite of German urban planners had studied continuously the development of British, French, and Scandinavian urban planning

"Los Angelization" Did not Happen   109

and had never isolated themselves from their peers in the international epistemic community of planners, even during the war.

The German concepts for the construction of new residential areas did not differ significantly from comparable plans in other Western European countries. Town planners such as the renowned Hans Bernhard Reichow developed the concept of the *gegliederte und aufgelockerte Stadt* (organized and decompressed town) with an elaborate network of main thoroughfares, residential streets, and separate footpaths and bikeways. The idea behind this concept was the full functional separation of traffic to maximize traffic safety, noise protection, and residents' convenience. Reichow's concept of the organized and decompressed town dated back to 1941 and demonstrated amazing similarities to British town planning of the same decade. At this time, the mass motorization of Germany was already anticipated, but was postponed until after the final victory (*Endsieg*).

In the 1950s and 1960s, the concept of the organized and decompressed town became a model for planning new residential areas. During the 1950s, Reichow rebranded his cultural concept from the "organic art of town planning" (*Organische Stadtbaukunst*) (Reichow 1948) to the functionalist "car-friendly town" (*Autogerechte Stadt*) (Reichow 1959). The practical reason for the rebranding of his original concept was certainly the fact that car-friendly urban designs had become a major concern during the course of the 1950s. The cultural reason behind this rebranding may have been to make the concept more compatible with those of their European peers. The term "organic" carried a conservative connotation and rather concealed the positive notion of modernity through functionalism.

The German model of the organized and decompressed town displayed many functional similarities with American planning concepts, but also contained one symbolic difference. Reichow's neighborhood and town models were based on organic patterns, whereas residential areas in American towns were built on rectangular grids. Reichow's town design took the mass-motorized future into account, but his concept of neighborhoods was still based on a society of pedestrians and bikers that attended small, decentralized schools and shopped in small grocery stores within walking distance from home. Unlike the inhabitants of postwar American suburbs, their inhabitants were not compelled to buy a car and adopt a car-centered lifestyle. The German concept of the organic pattern carried both a functional purpose and a cultural meaning. The main functional benefit was the replacement of rectangular intersections with intersecting traffic from four different directions by T-shape intersections with only three different directions of traffic. German planners like Reichow considered the avoidance of rectangular intersections and the spatial separation of cars, bikes, and pedestrians to be an important safety benefit. The organic pattern was perceived as an antithesis to the nonorganic, and allegedly soulless and inhumane, concept of modern planning that was culturally incompatible with

110   Christopher Kopper

the German tradition of urbanity. The organic pattern, however, did not reflect the conservative idea of an organically developed society. Reichow's ideas of esthetics, housing, and lifestyle were definitely modern and detached from conservative role models.

As both German and American urban planners followed the path of car-friendly urban designs, one might assume that similar principles and objectives ruled on both sides of the Atlantic. German urban planners such as Otto Sill, head of the municipal traffic-planning department in Hamburg, had already anticipated major parking problems in 1951. His idea of a coming parking crisis was based on the prognosis that Germany would reach a car density of 100 vehicles per one thousand inhabitants—still rather later than sooner, but within the long-term timeline of urban planning. At the time of his publication in 1951, Germany's car density was only about fourteen cars per one thousand inhabitants and ranked considerably below other Western European nations. But the swift progress of reconstruction and the optimism about West Germany's economic prospects gave planners good reasons to believe in a future mass-motorized society. In relation to his professional peers, Sill was not overly optimistic. Already in 1949, his fellow planner, Rudolf Hillebrecht, anticipated one hundred cars per one thousand inhabitants as the final saturation rate of individual motorization in West Germany (Röhrbein 1993). In order to predict the coming demand for parking space and to anticipate possible solutions like off-street parking and parking ramps, Sill diligently studied contemporary U.S. research literature on urban and traffic planning. Sill learnt that a deficit of parking space had already contributed to the decline of retail shops in CBD's and concluded that the traffic problems of city centers could not be solved without improvements in the quality and quantity of public transport (Sill 1951). Los Angeles, the most prominent and most obvious example of urban sprawl, had already witnessed the decline of public transport and the beginning of car-related traffic planning in the 1920s (Bratzel 1997).

Already in 1948, the renowned city planner Konstanty Gutschow projected a flyover for a major intersection in the CBD of Düsseldorf (Kreuter 2009). Before 1945, Gutschow had been the chief planner for the gigantic project to transform Hamburg's Elbe shoreline into a monumental gateway to Germany's biggest port. The former member of Albert Speer's staff for the reconstruction of destroyed German cities (*Wiederaufbaustab*) switched seamlessly from Nazi monumentalism to American functionalism and found inspiration in images of modern American cities in international research journals. From the early 1950s, urban planners in Germany got the chance to see the future of traffic on field trips through the United States. Because the United States was approximately three decades ahead of Germany in terms of mass motorization (measured by the ratio of cars per one thousand inhabitants), German planners had the unique chance to avoid the pitfalls of urban planning in a mass-motorized future. But during the 1950s, planners like Rudolf Hillebrecht started to dissociate themselves from the results of American urban planning. In 1959, a key story in the German news magazine, *Der Spiegel*, reported that Hillebrecht was aware of the dangers of uncontrolled urban sprawl and the decline of retail and shopping in America's CBDs. At a meeting with real estate owners on a major street in the CBD of Hannover, Hillebrecht argued for wider streets in order not to deter motorized shoppers. Hillebrecht painted a dark picture of decaying CBDs where the shops and department stores had disappeared. The American experience of sprawling suburban malls and decaying CBDs was shocking enough to convince the real estate owners to transfer a portion of their lots to the city of Hannover. Under the anticipated pressure of a motorized society, shop owners relinquished financial compensation for their property as a *quid pro quo* for wider streets with more parking space and parking ramps—in order to provide more convenience and higher accessibility for motorized shoppers.

Hillebrecht and many of his fellow planners traveled through the United States in the 1950s to see Germany's potential future in the age of mass motorization. Trips to the United States provided them with firsthand experience about how cities in the age of mass motorization would look if planners paved the way for cars without taking care of the historical urban environment. Hillebrecht realized that CBDs would lose their attractiveness to shoppers and service industries. Because inner city streets' capacity to accommodate curbside parking and parking ramps was limited, he and his fellows planned to enhance both car and public transportation.

In the early 1960s, the problems of suburban sprawl and decaying inner cities in the United States attracted growing attention beyond the epistemic community of professional urban planners. Jane Jacob's famous 1961 book *Death and Life of Great American Cities* (Jacobs 1961; Sparberg 2006) was published in German in 1963 and received considerable attention in widely read weekly magazines such as *Die Zeit* and *Der Spiegel*. Well-known sociologist and prominent critic of contemporary urban planning Lewis Mumford's equally influential 1961 book *History of the City* (Mumford 1961), was translated into German in the same year. Already in 1958, Hamburg's first-mayor, Max Brauer, rejected the Hamburg city planning department's proposal to build a freeway through the city. Brauer, a former émigré to the United States with a good knowledge of contemporary American affairs, based his contempt for this idea on Mumford's recently published book, *The Highway and the City*, and stated explicitly that wider streets and highways would increase traffic rather than alleviate congestion. Apart from critical sociologists, cultural critics like the conservative journalist and publisher Wolf Jobst Siedler (1964) bemoaned the continuing loss of historically and esthetically valuable buildings and the progress of a soulless functionalism. Siedler deplored the sacrifice of architectonical heritage for the convenience of motorized traffic. Despite the hegemony of modernists among the city planners, the culturally conservative Siedler was neither a nostalgic outsider nor someone isolated from the cultural mainstream of

112   *Christopher Kopper*

his time. The enormous loss of architectonical heritage through the course of the war contributed to the idea that the surviving old buildings, squares, and streets were precious and should not be sacrificed to the concept of the car-friendly city.

German urban planners coined the term *Los Angelisierung* ("Los Angelization") as a metaphor for uncontrolled urban sprawl, the decline of urbanity, and the decay of the inner cities. "Los Angelization" served as a descriptor for purely car-oriented urban development that would inevitably result in the destruction of German, or more generally European, cities. German planners considered the American way of urban development and the ensuing mobility patterns to be both impracticable and unacceptable. The concerns about the consequences of motorization and urban sprawl emerged at a time when the number of cars in Germany was still below the level of mass motorization. In 1961, fewer than one in five households owned a car. The German car ownership ratio (cars per one thousand inhabitants) was still below one hundred and only half of what the U.S. car ownership ratio had been at the end of the 1920s.

In 1962, the number of cars per one thousand inhabitants finally exceeded 100. During the early to mid-1950s, traffic planners and motorization experts expected this level to be the saturation point of private motorization in Germany (Sill 1951; Schühe 1986). But in the early 1960s, West Germany had already reached the second stage of postwar suburbanization, but on a far smaller scale than in the United States. The first stage of suburbanization had taken place during and shortly after the war when air raid victims and expellees (*Vertriebene*) were relocated to the undestroyed suburbs of the bigger cities. The second stage of suburbanization took off during the 1950s and gained momentum in the following decade when a growing number of big city dwellers voluntarily opted for a suburban lifestyle. Between 1939 and 1961, the population in the twenty-kilometer perimeter around the five biggest West German cities (Hamburg, München, Köln, Frankfurt, and Stuttgart) doubled from 689,000 to 1,364,000 (Kopper 2007). But unlike in the United States, the suburbanization of the 1940s and 1950s was not based primarily on the availability and affordability of cars.

The majority of suburban commuters did not own a motorized vehicle and used public transportation for their journeys into the city, but a growing minority made use of personal vehicles for commuting. By 1961, about one-third of German commuters used a motorized vehicle for their daily commute. The share of scooter and motorcycle users was still significant within this group, but was declining steadily. Taking the swift growth of individual car ownership into account, urban planners did not need a strong imagination or prophetic skills to expect growing problems with motorized traffic. The affordability and availability of cars reduced the time necessary for a daily commute considerably and was perceived as an important pull factor for suburbanization. Conversely, the decision to relocate to a suburban residence worked as a push factor for the decision to buy a car.

"Los Angelization" Did not Happen   113

In the early 1960s, urban planners, city administrators, and transport politicians of the *Länder* governments agreed on a consensus that the future problems of urban growth and mobility could only be solved by a balanced concept of wider thoroughfares and investments in new mass transportation systems. Transportation economists forecasted continuous growth rates of motorization until a saturation level of about three hundred cars per one thousand inhabitants would be reached in 1975 (Schühle 1986). This revision of the saturation level exceeded the traffic planners' forecasts of the 1950s by a factor of three. Urban planners had to cope with a rising number of cars at a time when motorization had already started to cause congestion problems in the inner cities.

In 1961, the German Bundestag followed the example of a British Royal Commission and commissioned a team of respected planners to issue an expert report on the future of urban traffic infrastructures and mobility. The extensive report was published in 1964 (Bericht der Sachverständigenkommission 1964) and provided ample material for long-term programs of urban traffic improvement. The report was a compilation of municipal investment programs for urban transportation infrastructures. It served as a blueprint for the following decade of enthusiastic long-term and large-scale urban planning and demonstrated the start of a new age of social engineering. The report demonstrated that the urban planning departments were prepared for large-scale programs, which, until 1966, had to be shelved for a lack of funds. Even fiscally conservative politicians such as the minister of economic affairs and transport in the *Land Nordrhein-Westfalen* (the state of North Rhine-Westphalia) agreed that large-scale urban street building programs alone would be insufficient to keep up with the growth of individual mobility. Instead, public transport construction programs should enhance the attractiveness and competitiveness of public transport networks in order to keep the growth of car traffic within manageable limits (Kienbaum 1966).

Historians have coined the term "decade of planning enthusiasm" for the ten years between 1966 and 1975 (Metzler 2005; Ruck 2009). This delimitation is true for the stage of implementation, but does not adequately represent the stage of conception. Many comprehensive plans (*Stadtentwicklungspläne* and *Generalverkehrspläne*) for the modernization of urban traffic infrastructures had already been designed between the late 1950s and 1966, but the cities lacked the financial means for their implementation.

By 1954, Hannover's chief city planner, Hillebrecht, began to consider a future underground tramway network through the CBD of Hannover. The majority of urban planners perceived tramways as obstacles to continuous traffic flow and slow and inflexible competitors for the limited space on the streets. But unlike in the United States, the consequence was not the abolition of streetcars and their substitution by buses, but rather their upgrade to a light rail (*Stadtbahn*) network with separate, and preferably underground, tracks. Already during the 1920s, downtown shop owners

114 *Christopher Kopper*

in American cities and particularly in Los Angeles blamed streetcars for clogging the streets and inhibiting the flow of cars. The alternative solution of banning curbside parking was unacceptable for the shop owners for the following reason. In Los Angeles, shop owners in the CBD criticized a decline in returns of 25–35% after the city council had implemented a short-lived ban on curbside parking. According to their unscientific findings, car owners spent more on shopping than streetcar passengers. Apart from this, American shop owners believed, with good reason, that the number of motorized shoppers would inevitably rise to the disadvantage of streetcars (Norton 2008; Bratzel 1995). As a consequence of the swift rise of individual motorization in Los Angeles during the 1920s, the average, middle-class Los Angeleno shared this negative perception of streetcars as onerous obstacles to the free flow of car traffic. The transition to fully motorized society with the car as the dominant transport model became irreversible in the course of the post-Depression recovery. In 1937, the modal split of cars in Los Angeles reached 80%. The transition to a car-dependent society had already taken place at a time when the construction of freeways had not yet begun.

In the postwar United States, the streetcar was doomed to perish. This happened partly as a consequence of rigid and obsolete fare regulations for streetcars that caused a steady growth in operating deficits. Because U.S. streetcar companies were forced to invest their diminishing revenues to cover the cost of maintaining their transport infrastructure, the transition from streetcars to buses seemed to be the cheaper and inevitable alternative for the transit companies. The disappearance of streetcars from American cities between the end of World War II and the late 1950s helped German transportation planners to understand the negative long-term effects of a thorough modernization policy. As in the United States, but to a significantly lesser degree, the municipal public transportation companies in Germany had to fight the popular perception that streetcars were an outdated technology that had reached the stage of obsolescence in the car age (Norton 2008).

West Berlin and Hamburg, the two biggest West German cities, made the decision in the 1960s to phase out streetcars and replace trams with buses. Unlike American cities in the 1940s and 1950s, however, the municipal transit administrators avoided negative side effects of the decision. West Berlin and Hamburg had already decided to upgrade their subway networks by extending old lines and building new ones. Except for a few locations such as Kiel, Münster, and Wiesbaden, most of the German cities with a population between 200,000 and a million inhabitants decided to keep their streetcar networks. The concept of a shared space for private cars and public trams was altered by reserving street space for the cars and moving tramways below the surface. But this solution required high investments in public transport infrastructures and significant cofunding by the federal government and the *Länder*, neither of which were available in the early 1960s.

German planners, like their American peers, had to cope with similar challenges to urbanity—but opted for different solutions. Similar discourses among planners yield different results if the normative priorities of planners, the institutional settings, and the economic conditions allow for different results. In the early 1960s, the destruction of traditional urbanity by the car had already become an irreversible fact for American cities—but was still reversible in Germany. German city planners obtained firsthand impressions of the destruction of urban areas through elevated freeways and decided to build them only in exceptional cases. The construction of light rail subway systems was a rather expensive but highly functional and esthetically painless alternative to elevated streets and freeways.

The main institutional bottleneck for new urban thoroughfares and light railway systems was the federalist partition of taxes. Germany's federal government was the sole recipient of the gas tax (*Mineralölsteuer*), whereas the *Länder* governments received all the revenues from the vehicle registration tax (*Kraftfahrzeugsteuer*). The level of the local property tax (*Grundsteuer*) was too low to permit sufficient funding of urban freeway and public transport projects. Unlike in the United States, property tax revenues did not increase with the value of real estate. Urban and suburban real estate owners profited from improved streets and roads, but were not taxed for these external benefits. The modernization of the urban street grid was not a self-financing *perpetuum mobile* and needed a financial boost from the federal and state levels.

The *Länder* passed some of their vehicle registration taxes to the municipalities, but consumed the larger part of their car-related revenues for maintaining and upgrading state roads (*Landesstrassen*). Apart from this, the growth of the vehicle registration tax lagged behind the growth of the gas tax. After the enactment of the federal road financing law (*Strassenverkehrs-Finanzierungsgesetz*) in 1960, the federal government generated sufficient gas tax revenues to finance an extensive program for extending interstate highways (*Autobahnen*) and upgrading federal roads (*Bundesstrassen*). The federal road financing law was obviously inspired by the legislation of the Eisenhower administration that earmarked the federal gas tax for the gigantic and highly popular interstate highway program (Kopper 2007; Klenke 1995).

On the other hand, the Urban League (*Deutscher Städtetag*) and prominent mayors complained about the growing discrepancy between the public task of providing adequate streets and public transportation infrastructure and the big municipalities' financial means to do so. The discrepancy between the public demand for infrastructure investments and the financial means of public administrations was rather low on the federal level, relatively higher on the state level, and reached a breaking point at the municipal level by the 1960s. Many big municipalities, such as Essen, Cologne, and Frankfurt, had already completed extensive plans for light rail subway

116 Christopher Kopper

networks in the early 1960s (Kienbaum 1966; Müller-Raemisch 1996), but were compelled to shelve them due to a lack of funds.

The conditions needed for improving municipal traffic infrastructure changed dramatically when the Christian Democratic Party and the Social Democrats constituted the "Great Coalition" and formed a federal government in December 1966. The increase of the federal gas tax by four *Pfennige* (cents of *Mark*) per liter was one of the first laws of the new coalition. These additional revenues were earmarked for the funding of municipal investments in streets, freeways, and light railway systems. This legislation would not have passed the *Bundestag* and the second chamber (the *Bundesrat*) unanimously if the law had not promised a silver bullet for the growing problems of traffic and mobility in cities (Kopper 2007). Both the new secretary of economic affairs (*Bundeswirtschaftsminister*), Karl Schiller, and the new secretary of finance (*Bundesfinanzminister*), Franz Josef Strauss, considered the implementation of "shovel ready" municipal investments to be a rapid means for resolving the German economy's recession at the time. The desire for urban renewal coincided with the new age of a demand-side Keynesian economic policy. Thus, the backlog of investments in modern, urban, mass transit systems gave way to a planning and construction euphoria that would change city maps during the following decade.

WORKS CITED

Bericht der Sachverständigenkommission über eine Untersuchung von Maßnahmen zur Verbesserung der Verkehrsverhältnisse der Gemeinden. In: Deutscher Bundestag, Drucksache 4/2661.

Bratzel, Stefan. *Extreme der Mobilität. Entwicklung und Folgen der Verkehrspolitik in Los Angeles.* Basel, Birkhäuser, 1995.

———. "Der verkehrspolitische Misserfolgsfall Los Angeles. Eine Pathogenese städtischer Mobilität." In: Hans-Liudger Dienel and Barbara Schmucki (eds.), *Mobilität für alle.* Stuttgart, Steiner, 1997, p. 183–210.

Deutsche Akademie für Städtebau und Landesplanung, Deutscher Städtebau nach 1945, Essen, 1961.

Dorn, Ralf. "Auf dem Weg zur autogerechten Stadt? Zur Verkehrsplanung Hannovers unter Stadtbaurat Rudolf Hillebrecht." In: Rolf Spilker (ed.), *Richtig in Fahrt kommen. Automobilisierung nach 1945 in der Bundesrepublik Deutschland.* Bramsche, Rasch, 2012, p. 204–219.

Durth, Werner, and Niels Gutschow. *Träume in Trümmern. Stadtplanung 1949–1950.* München, dtv, 1993.

Düwel, Jörn, and Niels Gutschow. *"A Blessing in Disguise": War and Town Planning in Europe 1940–1945.* Hamburg, DOM Publishers, 2013.

Göderitz, Johannes, Roland Rainer, and Hubert Hoffmann. *Die gegliederte und aufgelockerte Stadt.* Tübingen, Wasmuth, 1957.

Jacobs, Jane. *Death and Life of Great American Cities.* New York, Vintage Books, 1961.

Kienbaum, Gerhard. *Ökonomische Probleme des modernen Stadtverkehrs.* Göttingen, Vandenhoeck & Ruprecht, 1966.

Klenke, Dietmar. *Freier Stau für freie Bürger.* Paderborn, Schöningh, 1995.

"Los Angelization" Did not Happen 117

Kopper, Christopher. *Die Bahn im Wirtschaftswunder*. Frankfurt, Campus, 2007.

Kreuter, Bernd. "Auf dem Weg in die autogerechte Stadt. Verkehrsplanung und Verkehrsbau der Zwanziger-bis Vierzigerjahre am Beispiel von Düsseldorf." In: Susanne Anna (ed.), *Architektenstreit. Wiederaufbau zwischen Kontinuität und Neubeginn*. Düsseldorf, Droste, 2009, p. 139–164.

Metzler, Gabriele. *Konzeptionen von Adenauer bis Brandt. Politische Planung in der pluralistischen Gesellschaft*. Paderborn, Schöningh, 2005.

Mommsen, Hans (with Manfried Grieger). *Das Volkswagenwerk und seine Arbeiter im "Dritten Reich."* Düsseldorf, Econ, 1996.

Müller-Raemisch, Hans-Reiner. *Frankfurt am Main. Stadtentwicklung und Planungsgeschichte seit 1945*. Frankfurt, Campus, 1996, p. 98–115.

Mumford, Lewis. *History of the City*. New York, Harcourt Brace, 1961.

Norton, Peter: *Fighting Traffic: The Dawn of the Motor Age in the American City*. Cambridge MA, MIT Press, 2008.

Reichow, Hans Bernhard. *Organische Stadtbaukunst*. Braunschweig, Westermann, 1948.

———. *Die autogerechte Stadt—ein Weg aus dem Verkehrs-Chaos*. Ravensburg, O. Maier, 1959.

Röhrbein, Waldemar (Bearb.). *Anpacken und Vollenden. Hannovers Wiederaufbau in den 50er Jahren—ein Quellenlesebuch*. Hannover, Historisches Museum, 1993.

Ruck, Michael. "Gesellschaft gestalten. Politische Planung in den 1960er und 1970er Jahren." In: Sabine Mecking (ed.), *Zwischen Effizienz und Legitimität*. Paderborn, Schöningh, 2009, p. 35–47.

Schühle, Ulrich: *Verkehrsprognosen im prospektiven Test*. Berlin, TU Berlin, 1986.

Siedler, Wolf Jobst. *Die gemordete Stadt*, Herbig, Berlin 1964.

Sill, Otto. *Die Parkraumnot*. Berlin, Schmidt, 1951.

Sparberg, Alexiou. *Jane Jacobs. Urban Visionary*. New Brunswick, Rutgers University Press, 2006.

8 Automobility, Utopia, and the Contradictions of Modern Urbanism, Concerning Karel Teige

Steven Logan

> *All optimism, whatever kind of hope, is only an addictive narcotic, which leads to new disappointments and a worse hangover. On the contrary: radical pessimism and the most apathetic detachment in the face of the swarm of the outer world.*
>
> —Karel Teige, 1947

Karel Teige expressed these words in a letter to fellow surrealist Marie Popíšilova. They were a marked change from the hope and optimism of his many manifestos of the interwar period. In "Images and Prefigurations," Teige inaugurated the 1920s with fighting words: "Everything has to be done . . . This is life and we are here so that we can build it anew, right? *We will once again build a new life a new society, we will build again our days and our nights* . . ." (Teige 1947:25).

Karel Teige was born in 1900 in Prague. He was a prolific writer, editor, urban and architectural theorist, typographer, and book designer. Following the end of the First World War in the newly formed Czechoslovak Republic, he became one of the key figures of Europe's most diverse and active avant-garde movements, Devětsil, an interdisciplinary group of leftist artists, architects, and intellectuals. In 1922, Teige traveled to Paris, where he met Le Corbusier for the first time. In addition to meeting Teige during his visit to Paris, Le Corbusier lectured in the Klub architektů in Prague in January 1925, a series of lectures that also featured Adolf Loos, Walter Gropius, and J. J. P. Oud. In 1925, Teige traveled to Moscow and Leningrad to see firsthand the fruits of the Bolshevik revolution, meeting with Russian Constructivists such as Vladimir Tatlin and Kazmir Malevich (Honzík 1963:72). Although well situated between Paris and Moscow, Prague is largely absent from standard accounts of modernity's "complex historical geography," which bypasses Prague in favor of Paris, Berlin, Vienna, and Moscow (Harvey 1989:24).[1]

Teige was especially influenced by Le Corbusier's idea that both the dwelling and the city are tools to be discarded when they no longer function. On a fall day in 1924, not long before his lecture in Prague, Le Corbusier had an epiphany standing on the Champs-Élysées, which he recounted in the opening pages of *Urbanisme* (1924). Prizing circulation above all else, Le Corbusier made a defiant break with the past: If the automobile was to be accommodated, then the old cities would have to be destroyed and rebuilt, their clogged arteries freed up by the doctors of urbanism, and new cities and garden cities constructed from scratch.

In addition, 1924 marked an important year for Teige in the formation of his ideas. On a spring evening, Teige and fellow poet Vitěslav Nezval, sitting in one of their favorite bars, enacted their own form of symbolic destruction, liquidating old ideas of art in favor of a new kind of art, which they called "poetism," the art of living well. Poetism would break down the barriers between art and everyday life, between art and its singular creator. Then, in June, Teige and the modernist architect Jaromír Krejcar formed The Club for New Prague as a response to the Club for Old Prague, which was founded in 1900 as a response to the planned "modernization" of Prague's Old Town (Švácha 1985:102). Jean-Louis Cohen (2000:38) writes that Teige and Krejcar were prepared to impose their own version of Le Corbusier's *Plan Voisin* in Prague by knocking down most of the city's medieval core, save for a few choice historical monuments, and erecting an administrative center in its place whose roads, unlike the narrow, winding streets of the medieval core, would be able to accommodate modern forms of traffic. The Club for New Prague was "for" the acceleration and extension of an affordable and cheap means of transport and "against" the "superstition of the *genia* loci." In their view, the form of the modern city should reflect "modern organization of work." Above all, the building of cities, they claimed, was a "scientific, not an artistic problem" (Club for New Prague, 1925:13).

These two moments illustrate the contradictory tension in Teige's approach to architecture and the city that will be explored in this chapter. This tension manifests itself between a rational, scientific approach to the city as a product to be produced like an object manufactured in a laboratory or on an assembly line: repeatable, efficient, and perfectible, and; a poetic approach where the city is produced as a collective work of art. The chapter will illustrate this dialectical tension by looking at three aspects of Teige's writings on architecture and the city. First, it will address his revolutionary poetics and aesthetics through what he called, in English, the "magic-city." Then, it will turn to his socialist critiques of dwelling and transportation. The last part of the chapter will consider Teige's vision for an "architecture without architecture," a deurbanized landscape that will be referred to here as "a city without a city," drawing on the work of German architect and planner Thomas Sieverts.[2] This last section will consider most explicitly Teige's relevance for the present.

By the mid-1930s, Teige had become disillusioned with Stalin's Soviet Union following reports from Krejcar, who had been working in Moscow in 1934–1935. Teige became openly critical of Stalinist authority and

120 *Steven Logan*

especially its monumental architecture. In 1947, he revisited his ideas on architecture and urbanism in an introductory essay to architect Ladislav Žák's book *The Inhabited Landscape*. In that essay, Teige wrote that the machine for living, upon which he believed would be the starting point of architecture and urbanism, had turned into a "dwelling for a machine, a mechanized human" (Teige 1947:289).

After World War II, Teige was increasingly marginalized by the new regime. In 1950, the ruling Communist Party began a press campaign discrediting Teige (Dačeva 1999:381). In October 1951, a short while after this campaign, Teige died of a heart attack while waiting for a tram (Dluhosch 2002: xi). His apartment was sealed by the police, and most of his personal papers and his library were taken, never to be seen again. His death was followed by the suicides of his two long-time female companions Jožka Nevařilová (on the same day) and, ten days later, Eva Ebertová (Aulický 1999:386).

PRODUCING URBAN SPACE: THE *OEUVRE* AND THE PRODUCT

Although one of Teige's primary focuses is on architecture and individual buildings, this chapter will primarily focus on his critiques of urbanism and urban planning.[3] It will first situate Teige's approach through the work of Henri Lefebvre (1974:124), who traces the modern production of space to the urban and industrial social practices of the 1920s. The link between these processes manifested itself in the influence of industrial spaces and products on both the form of dwellings and urban space as a whole. Dwellings and the city would take inspiration from the efficiency and productivism of the workplace, particularly the factory. Lefebvre writes that the historical importance of the Bauhaus can be attributed to the emergent idea that space could be produced. Lefebvre argues that this form of producing space was "expressly industrial in nature." It was a space in which "reproducibility, repetition, and the reproduction of social relationships are deliberately given precedence over works [*oeuvres*]" (Ibid. 120).

The *oeuvre*, or work, was Lefebvre's foil for critiquing modern urbanism's near fascistic attention to the functionality of the plan. Lefebvre identified works with unique and singular cities like Venice or Florence, cities that emerged over time and that were slowly secreted by the everyday practices and representations of the inhabitants. Here, chance, unpredictable encounters, and sensuous experiences were characteristic of the city as oeuvre, as opposed to the city produced as if it were a product from a factory that had been laid like a transparency over the existing landscape. In *Right to the City*, Lefebvre (1967:174) argued that the city dweller had the right to affordable housing and good public transportation, but also the "right to the oeuvre," to participating in and appropriating the city for her- or himself.

Michel de Certeau (1988:93) offers a similar interpretation of urban space in his work "Walking in the City." For de Certeau, the city as oeuvre is less a physical plan than a spatial practice that "slips into the clear text of the planned and readable city". He calls it a "mobile city" or "metaphorical city." The rational city "makes room for a void . . . it opens up clearings . . . it 'allows' a certain play within a system of defined places" (Ibid. 106). De Certeau calls this area of free play a *Spielraum*, the creation of a new mobile space in the face of the strict productivism of the functional city. The notion of *Spielraum* was also important to Walter Benjamin's understanding of art in the age of mechanical reproducibility. Benjamin (2002:124) writes that because "technology aims at liberating human beings from drudgery, the individual suddenly sees his scope for play, his field of action [*Spielraum*] immeasurably expanded. He does not yet know his way around this space. But already he registers his demands on it". De Certeau and Benjamin's formulations of *Spielraum* draw out the potential for a productive relationship between the work and the product, in the sense that the latter opens up space for the former.

In his book on Lefebvre's architectural and urban research, Lukasz Stanek (2011:40) delineates the two meanings of production in Lefebvre's work. Production in its wide sense refers to "social practice defined as the material and 'spiritual production' simultaneously". Production in the "narrow sense" refers to its strict economic association with industrialization, repeatability, and reproducibility in contrast to the uniqueness of the work (*Ibid.*). In *The Production of Space* (1974:72), Lefebvre writes that the concept of production in its more general sense has been annexed by the narrow view of an "ideology of productivism" and a "crude and brutal economism". The "rationalism of the 'principle of economy' " and its "minimum expenditure" contrasts with the "non-productive" spaces of play, art, and festival; that is, those spaces that do not contribute to economic and industrial growth. Production in its narrow sense should only be the means for the realization of urban society, not the end (Ibid. 177).

The production of space is not simply about a binary between the work and the product, but rather overcoming their separation through a broader understanding of production. This means the production of space on the model of art, but not art as a singular work "isolated by and for the individual" (Lefebvre 1974:422). Lefebvre (1967:173) imagined that art would become "*praxis* and *poiesis* on a social scale. The art of living in the city as a work of art".

AESTHETICS AND A REVOLUTIONARY POETICS OF THE CITY

This chapter will consider Teige's approach to art and the city, particularly through the Devĕtsil collective. Teige was also critical of an idea of art as the unique product of a creative genius (like Le Corbusier). Teige believed that art and technology had a necessarily political and social role to play whether it was film and photography or cars, trains, and ships. In 1923, Teige became

122   Steven Logan

the editor of *Stavba* (*Construction*), a monthly journal devoted to modern architecture, purism, and constructivism, and which took up many of the themes that Le Corbusier and Amédée Ozenfant addressed in their journal *L'esprit Nouveau*. Teige translated many of the articles from that journal for *Stavba* and also wrote on many of Le Corbusier's ideas, in particular the idea that a dwelling should be a machine for living "mass produced and just as available and cheap as a Fiat model 509, a Ford, or a Citroen" (Teige 1923:139). In this article, entitled "Machines for Living," Teige wrote that industrialization made possible the utopian promises of the past (Ibid. 136).

Very much like Le Corbusier, Teige (1932:135) made the leap from the car and the dwelling, objects perfected through mass production, to the city as a machine for living. The "wholesale reconstruction of cities" that were designed for "pedestrians and horse and buggy" must "serve modern means of transport". In order to organize traffic rationally, the old city had to be discarded. And in many ways, Teige's writings of the 1920s and early 1930s reiterate many of the problems that the modernists associated with the industrial city. In *Modern Architecture and Czechoslovakia* (1930:264), images of Czech functionalist and constructivist architecture are accompanied by text claiming that contemporary cities are "useless for modern life".

Although it would appear Teige's views did not differ from Le Corbusier's, Teige did offer a scathing critique of one of Le Corbusier's designs. Teige (1929:89) wrote: "Le Corbusier sins against harmony, having formulated such a clear and comprehensible notion as the 'machine for living,' he depreciates it by adding vague attributions of dignity, harmony and architectonic potential, through which he can then embrace all aestheticism and academicism".

The flashpoint of Teige's criticism was that architecture should create instruments and not monuments to timeless ideas of aesthetics, which are mere expressions of "ideological and metaphysical imagination" (Teige 1928–1929:90). To call itself modern, architecture should be dictated by actual social need, not by "formal appearance and pompous monumentality" (Teige 1932:183). Unlike Le Corbusier, Teige's definition of modernist architecture was inseparable from his radical socialist critique of the capitalist city, which will be addressed in the next section of the chapter.

Le Corbusier (1929:93) responded, claiming that "this is the first time I have replied to criticism". Fittingly enough, Le Corbusier began his response, entitled "In Defense of Architecture," while riding on the train from Paris to Moscow. Aside from his comments on the specific project and issues at hand, Le Corbusier's response was quite personal. He addressed Teige directly: "You speak in a way that contradicts your thought and suggests the opposite of what you really are: a poet". Although Teige claims to be a "passionate devotee of *objectivity*," he and his friends had come to Paris to "breathe in the streets (the women, the shops, the cars)" and not to visit the "cruel places . . . of ruthless Taylorism" in the suburbs (Ibid. 106). Emphasizing Teige's poetic side, Le Corbusier also remarks that the "Czechs have shone so brightly in the emerging sky of the new times" because of the poems, journals, manifestos and the people—"Teige, Nezval, Krejcar, etc."—"who know so well how to make a stay in Prague captivating" (Ibid. 94). It is significant that Le Corbusier singles out the city here because it was central to the formation of the ideas of Devětsil.

Taking inspiration from the new technologies of film and other technologies of reproducibility, Teige collapsed the distinction between art and everyday urban life in his theory of poetism as an art of life, an "art of living and enjoying life" (Teige 1924:122). In the first manifesto of poetism written in 1924, Teige declared that this new art is not to be found in cathedrals or galleries, but "outside on the streets, in the architecture of the cities . . . in the heat of industry that satisfies our primary needs" (Ibid. 121). Freed of its connections to literature, poetry becomes "gleaming cafes, intoxicating alcohol, and lively boulevards," and "silence, night, calm and peace" (Ibid. 128). Poetism in this description is about bringing together art and the city so that the city itself becomes a place where art is encountered not as the works of individual artists, but as the collective products of industrial and socialist society.

Devětsil's rejection of the singular work of art reflected its collective nature. Teige (1933:7) wrote that the collective emphasis of Devětsil was more important than the actual individual creative achievements. Although there was a voluminous output of works, as Derek Sayer notes in *Prague, Capital of the 20th Century* (2013:202), the artists of Devětsil did not see themselves as producing artworks in the way that making art is currently understood; rather, their efforts were directed ultimately to creating a new society.

That collective experience was an irreducible urban experience. Devětsil was made in and through the experiences of the city, in the cafes, dance halls, bars, and streets of old Prague. In the National Cafe and in Cafe Slavia—the main cafes of Devětsil between 1923 and 1928—"the fighting words of purism and poetism" were first formed (Honzík 1963:55).

Karel Honzík (1963:59), founding member of Devětsil's architectural wing, recalls that it was the nighttime walks through Prague that "were the most rich for recognizing the goals of our work". Nezval also wrote that poetism was created by the "believers in modernity" on long nighttime walks through the city (Teige 1928:199). Honzík (1963:68) describes the mood on these walks: "We spoke about the future of the world, about the future of creativity. Global revolution was knocking at the door. How would one work, live? How would cities be built? How would one eat? Sit? Travel? Fly?". They would walk "from the moment the street lamps were lit until the moment they were extinguished" traversing the old city out to the surrounding inner suburbs of Vinohrady and Smichov (*Ibid.*).

This idea of recreating the world culminated in what Teige called the "magic-city" (English in the original). In the concluding pages to *A World which Laughs* (1928:89), Teige challenges poetism to organize in the constructivist city of work and production, an "Epicurean garden of poetry, a magnificent and entertaining . . . magic-city". The "magic-city" would be

124   *Steven Logan*

a city of noise, sounds, color and light, and above all movement, "the fundamental element" of the magic-city. In the magic-city, there should be no "immobile emptiness." The idea of the magic-city as a city of encounters is the ultimate realization of poetism as a poetry "for all the senses." Teige called his second manifesto of "Poetry for the Five Senses," and it allowed him to bring together his Marxism with his poetism, by drawing upon Marx's *Economic and Philosophical Manuscripts 1844*, in which Marx writes that "the *forming* of the five senses is a labor of the entire history of the world" (qtd. in Teige, 1928:233).

Although Teige's writing suggests this magic-city is a place—perhaps somewhere in the suburbs, like Epicurus' own Garden—poetism might be better thought of as precisely no-place, a city on the move in contrast to the rational, functional city that Teige himself advocated. The magic-city appropriates its own kind of mobility or circulation, but one very different from the dominated spaces of the functional city. The magic-city and the nighttime strolls of Devětsil's members where poetism was invented literally on the move, might be better conceived as the "mobile city" or "metaphorical city," one that makes a space for play, a *Spielraum*, within the confines of the functional city.

In *Right to the City* (1967:171), Lefebvre takes a broad notion of play freed from its "subordination to the industrial and commercial production of culture" as a heuristic principle for the right to the city. For Lefebvre, what attracts people to the urban is "movement, the unpredictable, the possible and encounters" (Ibid. 172). Thus, the magic-city becomes a kind of playful (yet utterly serious), mobile intervention into the rational, planned city, not just its necessary complement, but as an immanent critique of the productive spaces of circulation and exchange. Without the notion of play, of a magic-city, the city is reduced to the stereotypical environments associated with the legacy of the modernist functional city. Teige believed that mass production and automation would lead to the free time necessary to build the magic-city, liberating human beings—the working classes in particular—from drudgery, long commutes, and substandard apartments.

ON THE LEFT FRONT: TRANSPORTATION AND DWELLING

Poetism may have embraced the beauty of modern technologies like the automobile, yet at the same time, it was the automobile, along with the single-family house in the suburbs, that was occupying people's free time (and occupying space) and preventing the appropriation of space as a poetist and specifically socialist and collective space. If the poetist spaces of the magic-city are a kind of oeuvre, then its corresponding product, in the narrow sense discussed above, would be extensive networks of public transport linking the so-called minimum dwellings for the working classes:

single-celled apartments for one individual with enough space for a bed to sleep on and a desk at which to read and work.

Devětsil disbanded in 1931, and Teige's focus shifted to *Leva Fronta* (The Left Front), formed in 1929. He founded its architectural section, ASLEF, in 1930, and led it until 1934, when it became the *Svaz socialistických architektů* (Association of Socialist Architects). The focus of ASLEF and the Association was the "socialist reorganization of dwelling and the city" (Effenberger 1994:689). Teige was at his most politically active in this period, and although he supported the Communist Party, he did not (nor did he ever) become a member.

The Minimum Dwelling (1932) along with "Toward a Sociology of Architecture" (1930) were two of his most significant critiques directed at urban planning, both in Prague and abroad (Cohen 2000:38). *The Minimum Dwelling* addresses themes that were taken up in the second meeting of the International Congress of Modern Architecture (CIAM) in Frankfurt in 1929 entitled, "Habitation minimum," or "*Wohnung fur das Existenzminimum*," where different plans for small, standardized, affordable apartments were presented. Teige did not take part in the 1929 meeting, but he did attend the 1930 meeting in Brussels, and his book was a direct response to the Frankfurt meeting. At the request of director Hans Meyer, Teige gave a series of lectures at the Bauhaus in January 1930 on typography and contemporary literature and was scheduled to give a lecture on "Sociology of the City and Housing" in March of the same year (Spechtenhauser and Weiss 1999:235, 251).[4]

The Minimum Dwelling was not intended to be a "handbook of designs for new apartments," but rather a thorough critique of the capitalist city. Teige sums up the crisis of the contemporary city thus: "overcrowding, congested streets, energy wasted, time lost . . . transport paralysis, and tubercular housing" (Teige 1932:135). Only urbanism, defined as the "scientific and rational approach to managing cities," (Ibid. 124) can overcome the crises that cities face. This marked Teige's idea of modern architecture as a science that insisted upon a "complete negation of aesthetics" (Švacha 1985:326).

In Teige's view, modern architecture was not about innovative design elements—"a flat roof or steel furniture"—which Teige (1932:12) called "fashionable design fetishes". He singled out the single-family house, and in particular the nineteenth-century bourgeois house, which the "ruling class" had elevated to the "status of a work of art" (Ibid. 164). And even though modern architects had removed the ornaments, the dwelling remained a "special, isolated object, posing as a work of art" (Ibid. 165). It was in this context that he critiqued the star architects who called themselves modern, but who designed villas for the elite. By 1929, and with a pressing housing shortage and economic crisis in Czechoslovakia and throughout the world, Teige criticized Le Corbusier, "who spoke about machines for living and the simplicity of Diogenes' barrel," but "wastes his time building villas fit for a

126 *Steven Logan*

Midas" (Teige 1928–1929:182). He called Mies van der Rohe's Tugendhat Villa in Brno the "pinnacle of modernist snobbism" (Ibid. 7).

If the dominant figure of the magic-city is the Prague poetist-walker inspired by new technologies, here it is the architect as a social scientist who approaches architecture and city planning through careful analysis of statistics on dwelling, pollution, transportation, and so forth. Architectural theorist Rostislav Švacha notes that architects and planners could only become true experts provided that they take a "strictly rational and desubjectivized approach" and ignore the wishes of private capital in favor of the common, public good. Teige, in essence, argues for a kind of dictatorship of technocrats, agreeing with Le Corbusier on the need to create a "ministry of public works independent of the 'whims of parliament'" (Le Corbusier, qtd. in Švacha 1985:125).

Teige's thesis in *The Minimum Dwelling* is unequivocal: The single-family house is "utterly inconceivable" as a solution for housing shortages. The existing "cramped garden colonies" are "further proof of the irrationality of petit bourgeois ideology and the sentimental illusion of their highly touted cottage dreams" (Teige 1932:317). Teige's writings were part of larger shift in Depression-era Prague urban policy away from building garden cities with single-family houses towards apartment complexes with small apartments affordable to the working classes (Švacha 1985:304). Teige lambasted the garden city approach for solving the problems of the city, arguing that it merely exacerbated transportation problems. Free time is wasted commuting between work and home on crowded public transport.

The *existenzminimum* as a solution to the housing shortage might now seem antiquated, an idea flogged to death long ago. Its rather unfortunate name is more likely to conjure up images of a dystopian world out of the mind of filmmaker David Cronenberg than utopian images of a magic-city. The minimum dwelling has been understood by critics as "the absolute minimum amount of space for human existence" (Gartman 2009:105) or with its "minimum facilities" and "programmed environment" the "lowest possible threshold of tolerability" (Lefebvre 1974:316). Lefebvre argued that it marked the end of dwelling or residing as a poetic act, which Teige opted to virtually ignore, and the beginning of the "functional abstraction" of housing.

Teige's writing of this period, in marked contrast to the poetics of the magic-city, does just this as he embraces a scientific, rational approach to dwelling and the city. Parts of *The Minimum Dwelling* are dedicated solely to apartment designs that maximize the efficiency of space and minimize movement within the apartment; he suggests the elimination of long hallways to improve energy efficiency and shorten "domestic communication distances" (Teige 1932:248). His commitment to rational and efficient circulation in the city was structured similarly as he criticized the inefficient transport system where cars and streetcars are stopped by traffic lights and gridlock, whereas "in a modern factory a conveyer would never be allowed to get stuck so many times" (117). Teige wrote that a city is also a "huge factory . . . whose operations must be rationally ordered" 183).

And it was in this context that Teige (1922:77) was sharply critical of the automobile, which was a break from his earlier work where he praised the automobile as "the beauty of reality and pure form, which does not need to be covered in ornaments or talked about in poems". In *The Minimum Dwelling* he decries it as a "wasteful personal luxury," and in any city where public and private interests do not collide private automobiles should disappear altogether (Teige 1932:316).

In 1931, a year before the publication of *The Minimum Dwelling*, Jaromir Krejcar, Teige's friend and collaborator (the same Krejcar with whom Teige envisioned the destruction of the center of Prague) published *Krise pražské dopravy (Prague's transportation crisis)*. A key aspect of the book was Krejcar's proposal to a Prague regional transportation competition in 1928. In Teige's review of Krejcar's proposal—called "Public Transport for All"—he writes that the street is "dominated by a disorderly herd of private automobiles and should be returned to public transport" (Teige 1933:143). Krejcar proposed removing cars completely from the city center and replacing them with a network of trolleybuses for the narrow streets, trams on the wider roads, the space for which would be freed up by the elimination of cars, and a surface railway for longer trips to and from the city. The proposal was not successful, which Teige attributed to the official thinking of the time, rooted in the idea that trams did not belong on the streets of the inner cities and that it was better to put people underground on metro lines so that the automobile could have its "privileged position" on the streets and roads. Teige (1947:226) called Krejcar's plan the urban equivalent of Friedrich Engels' *The Housing Question*, and even though unrealized, he would later recall it as one of the major works of functional urbanism in Czechoslovakia.

In Teige's (1932:316) vision for the "quiet city," all "high-intensity traffic" would be placed underground, so that the city would be free of "intolerable, nerve-racking street noise" and the "chaos of uncontrolled traffic". Even pedestrians would be inserted into this circulatory network on moving sidewalks that would bring people from their houses to the metro stations. Teige's quiet city stands in direct contrast to the magic-city of light, noise, and movement. The irony here is that in texts like *The Minimum Dwelling* there is no sign of the Devětsil walkers, no sign of people walking on the street at all. And this is one of the main critiques of modernism that Lefebvre levels. He writes in *Production of Space* that the "homogeneity" of the "architectural ensemble conceived as a 'machine for living'" actually presupposes a fracturing of space as the dwelling no longer bears any relation to the street or city spaces (Lefrebvre 1974:303). With so much attention given to rational and functional circulation, the street itself is lost, the street that was the setting for the emergence of poetism in the first place. There was no basis to Teige's claims that given the strict rational ordering of the city,

128   *Steven Logan*

people would then spend their free time living the convivial poetic life like the members of Devĕtsil.

ARCHITECTURE WITHOUT ARCHITECTURE IN THE DEURBANIZED LANDSCAPE

Teige's attention to quiet, green cities was likely influenced by the 1930 competition in the Soviet Union for a decentralized, socialist, green city outside of Moscow and one that brought designs from many of the Soviet constructivist architects (Mumford 2000:44). What is clear from *The Minimum Dwelling* is that Teige's model for this quiet city was the Soviet *sotsgorod*, or socialist city, a linear city with no definable center, and which was comprised of an industrial and agricultural area, collective dwellings, and a greenbelt. Teige was largely influenced by the writings of Lenin, Marx, and Engels—particularly from the latter's 1882–1883 pamphlet, *The Housing Question*—on overcoming the antithesis between city and country by producing qualitatively different settlements, neither city nor village. This process was called deurbanization (*desurbanisace*), which is sometimes rather erroneously translated as antiurbanism. Deurbanization did not mean the rejection of the city, but rather reducing its importance economically and administratively (but not culturally, in Teige's opinion). As Buck-Morss writes in *Dreamworld and Catastrophe* (2000:123), the Russian Constructivists approach to dwelling was "implicitly critical of the social hierarchy fostered by urban centralization". Following Engels, Teige (1932:377) defined deurbanization as the "planned route toward dispersed and uniform new types of socialist settlements" of which collective living would be the primary form of dwelling.

One of the bases of deurbanization, particularly in the influence from the Russian Constructivist architects, was that it implied a high degree of mobility—or at least a readiness for mobility—on the part of the inhabitants. The Russian Constructivists preoccupied themselves with mobility and mobilization (Buck-Morss 2000:121). Buck-Morss cites the post-Soviet theorist, Vladimir Paperny (2002:32), who writes that people were ready to relocate at any time to such a degree that "no permanent residence is necessary". Paperny contrasts the movement and mobility of people, objects, and ideas that were central to Soviet avant-garde constructivism with the monumentality, stasis, and immobility of the Stalin area, which Teige explicitly rejected. Inspired by the Italian futurist architect Antonio Sant'Elia's claim that for every generation a new dwelling, Teige (1932:351) himself asks: "why should a dwelling, which is much like a suitcase accompanying our life's journey, be dragged along like a heavy burden"?

In the conclusion to *The Minimum Dwelling*, Teige wrote that by the end of the twentieth century there would be "complete deurbanization"

(Teige 1932:376).That Teige misread the processes of urbanization is an understatement. However, the focus on mobility and new types of sustainable settlements offers an interesting historical perspective to what Thomas Sieverts (2003) calls today's *Zwischenstadt*, or the city without a city. Encompassing whole city regions, the *Zwischenstadt* is an urban landscape that defies description, combining elements of cities, villages, suburbs, and so on. The majority of people do not live in traditional cities, nor suburbs, but in the new urban–rural landscapes that characterize the anonymous peripheries of cities, and which can include the post-World War II suburbs, modernist housing developments (Keil and Young 2011:4), or the sprawling Asian and South American cities of twenty and thirty million inhabitants (Sieverts 2003:3). Inasmuch as Teige's description of the deurbanized socialist city may now appear unrealistic, his visions of distributed settlements that are neither traditional city nor garden suburb—both of which he explicitly rejected as models for the future—are the distant cousin to the urbanized landscape that Sieverts describes.

Sieverts (2011:23) argues that one of the biggest challenges in understanding the fragmented urban landscapes is to develop an aesthetic relationship with them. To handle the *Zwischenstadt* on its own terms means cultivating a capacity for aesthetic perception of the nonaesthetic "reverse side of our rational-technological world" (Sieverts 2003:94–95). Sieverts understands aesthetics as an "awareness beyond the functional and instrumental realm" and not simply the inclusion of a marquee, attractive building (Sieverts 2007:209). If the poetist magic-city is not a place, but rather a kind of urban methodology, then it can offer a model for addressing the nonaesthetic side of the *Zwischenstadt*, heeding Sieverts' call for city and landscape planning to "enter into a discussion with art and general cultural theory" and "again become an 'art' " (2003:115). It is in this context that Teige theorist Peter Zusi (2004:113) argues that poetism, at least in theory, was to lead to the periphery of the city, "redeeming these zones from the stigma of being extra-aesthetic".

The idea that the nonaesthetic has come to dominate the peripheries of cities was a major focus for Teige in his last work on architecture and urbanism, an extended introduction to *The Inhabited Landscape*, written by the architect Ladislav Žák (1947). In this essay he writes that the very same technologies he once praised have become part of the problem, particularly in the postwar landscape ravaged by both war and the expansion of capitalist economies. Teige criticized the technocratic, nonaesthetic approach to architecture, which turns "woods, meadows and rivers into . . . the asphalted, paved world with street lamps, ribbons of highways, billboards, gas stations, reservoir dams, noisy power stations, factories and train stations" turning dwellings and cities into "the 'world we live in,' but where it is impossible to live" (Teige 1947:283). But he did not turn to beautiful works of architecture as a response. In keeping with both his rejections of monumentality and the capitalist city, he did exactly the opposite. Teige

130   *Steven Logan*

(1933:286) rejected all pretenses to architecture in his vision of "the earth and nature as the people's dwelling without palaces, without temples, without architecture". In his early work, Teige applied the term "architecture without architecture" to the austere design for a train station, which was a reaction to the desire to add decorative elements to a functional building (18). In this sense, the phrase had a very programmatic meaning that related to his claim in the debate with Le Corbusier that architecture should create instruments that are dictated by social needs and not monuments to aesthetic ideas that do not ostensibly serve any immediate purpose.

But the phrase also has a meaning beyond this strictly functional perspective of the antidecorative and implies an understanding of the relationship between the dwelling and the environment or landscape in which it would be situated. Teige's architecture without architecture morphs further into a vision of cities without cities in his arguments for deurbanization. In keeping with the title of Ladislav Žák's book—*The Inhabited Landscape*—Teige shifts his emphasis from the metropolis to the region or the landscape. It is in the deurbanized landscape, rather than in the city, that Teige brings together ideas of surrealism and poetism with the plans of modern urbanism.

Teige attempts to creatively handle this landscape through what he calls "surrealist space" and the "surrealist landscape," an important prevision to Sieverts' own call for the aesthetic rehabilitation of the urbanized landscape. Most fantastically, the urban landscape would become a vast, regional park inspired by landscape painting: "In a time when landscape painting as an artistic field has died away, having climaxed in impressionism, landscaping develops as a branch of architecture, and the landscape, before composed in two-dimensional painting, steps out of the frame into the three-dimensional space of reality" (Teige 1947:284). Teige believed that it was in the power of modern urbanism to turn the regional (unloved) landscape into a park, where art and nature, dwelling and culture would intertwine. In these urban landscape parks, asks Teige, why should one not find the "artfully balanced compositions of Calder's mobiles, which move in the wind like aspen leaves" (Ibid. 286).

And with Teige's surrealist deurbanized landscapes we are—in perhaps a surreal fashion—back to the work of Henri Lefebvre. At first glance, deurbanization would appear to be completely the opposite to Lefebvre's own writings on the global urban society, but as we have seen, they shared the same appreciation for restructuring the urban along the lines of the work of art, and in *Right to the City*, Lefebvre (1967:173) expressed the same appreciation for the gardens and landscapes that surrounded and were an integral part of the city. In his own take on the magic-city, Lefebvre wrote that "the ideal city would involve the obsolescence of space: an accelerated change of abode." Lefebvre called this ideal city "the *ephemeral city*, the perpetual oeuvre of the inhabitants, themselves mobile and mobilized for and by this oeuvre." The ephemeral city, like the magical-city and the surrealist landscape, are the "apogee of play and supreme oeuvre and luxury" (Ibid. 173).

CONCLUSION

The same year that Teige rejected the capitalist city and suburb in his essay on the surrealist landscape, Theodore Adorno and Max Horkheimer first published the *Dialectic of Enlightenment*. The opening of the essay on "The Culture Industry" begins with a critique of architecture, both capitalist and socialist, very similar to the one Teige makes. The urban planning projects that were to give individuals their own spaces in "hygienic small apartments" have turned into "dismal . . . residential blocks" that "subjugate them . . . more completely to their adversary, the total power of capital" (Adorno and Horkheimer 2002:94). It was in this context that Teige claimed in the epigraph to this chapter that optimism was an "addictive narcotic" and the only position left was "radical pessimism" and "the most apathetic detachment."

Why did utopia turn into dystopia for Teige? To a certain degree, this was part of some of the more glaring contradictions in Teige's writing that he believed would be resolved under socialist conditions. One is reminded, then, of the dangers of putting too much faith in both technology and historical progress, as if given the socialist relations of production, industrial technologies would "generate the socialist imagination capable of producing a brand new culture" (Buck-Morss 1989:123). The dialectical relationship of art and technology, "fantasy and function," "meaningful symbol and useful tool" was the "very essence of socialist culture" (Ibid. 126), but it most often appears in Teige's writing as two separate things.

This chapter argued that the contrast between function and fantasy is best perceived from the standpoint of what Lefebvre called the product and the *oeuvre*, or what de Certeau called the functional city and the mobile or metaphorical city. The oeuvre was something impermanent, an urban methodology constantly being worked upon within the spaces of the functional city. The work of Teige and his Devětsil comrades provides an unwitting example of this; however, with the dissolution of Devětsil in 1931 came the dissolution of this necessary corollary to the scientific, functional city. Teige did turn to surrealism in the 1930s, but aside from his idea of the surrealist landscape, it was much more separate from urbanism than was poetism. And as Lefebvre (1974:124) notes in *The Production of Space*, although the work of the 1920s avant-garde architects and urbanists may have seemed "rational and revolutionary," without its poetic aspects it was actually "tailor-made for the state—whether of the state-capitalist or the state-socialist variety".

The tragic ending to Teige's life is perhaps a warning against putting too much hope in concrete visions for the future. Whether one agrees with collective dwellings as the solution is beside the point, and as history has shown they did not find a ready audience. There are only two examples of such collective dwellings in evidence in today's Czech Republic: one has been converted into a hotel; in the other, the common dining room was

132 Steven Logan

rarely used and is now an art gallery. And there is no shortage of inadequate apartment blocks the world over completely lacking in basic infrastructure and public spaces.

Does this mean abandoning utopian thinking? What this chapter has tried to gesture toward is thinking about the dialectical relation between works and products. Although it was not always clear from Teige's writings, the rational city needed the magic-city, the scientist needed the poet, and vice versa. They are not mutually exclusive, but inhere in one another, gaining meaning through each other.

As this chapter has shown, many of the problems Teige and others faced in their time resonate with the problems of today's urban society—albeit on a much larger, global scale. It has been the aim of the chapter to offer a historical perspective on the twentieth-century struggle with dwelling and transportation, and to suggest that in looking forward, urban planners, philosophers, and architects might do well to first look backward.

NOTES

1. Derek Sayer's *Prague, Capital of the Twentieth Century: A Surrealist History* (2013) is the most recent attempt to fill that gap.
2. *Cities without Cities* is the title of the English translation of German planner and architect Thomas Sieverts' book *Zwischenstadt*. The chapter will draw on Sieverts' work primarily, but not exclusively, in the final section.
3. A number of English-language publications have addressed the dual nature of Teige's approach, focusing on the question of style (Zusi 2004), art and architecture (Dluhosch and Švacha 1999), architecture and urbanism (Cohen 2000), and dwelling (Dluhosch 2002).
4. Spechtenhauser and Weiss (1999) note that there is no documentary evidence to confirm if the lecture actually took place. The Bauhaus director at the time, Hans Meyer, with whom Teige had close ties, was dismissed on August 1, 1930 (237). An article based on the lecture was published in *ReD (revue Devětsil)* under the title "Towards a Sociology of Architecture" (1930).

WORKS CITED

Adorno, Theodor, and Max Horkheimer. *Dialectic of Enlightenment: Philosophical Fragments*. Stanford, Stanford University Press, 2002.

Aulický, Miloš. "Postscript: My Uncle, Karel Teige." Translated by Eric Dluhosch, in: Dluhosch and Švacha, p. 384–387.

Benjamin, Walter. "The Work of Art in the Age of Its Technological Reproducibility: Second Version." 1936. Translated by Edmund Jephcott and Harry Zohn, in: Howard Eiland and Michael W. Jennings (eds.), *Walter Benjamin: Selected Writings*, Vol. 3. Cambridge MA, Belknap Press of Harvard University, 2002, p. 101–133.

Brabec, Jiri, et al. (eds.). *Osvobozování života a poezie: Studie ze čtyřicátých let* [The Liberation of Life and Poetry: Studies from the 1940s]. Prague, Aurora, 1994 (Vol. 3 of *Karel Teige: vybor z díla*. 3 vols., 1966–1994).

Automobility, Utopia, and Contradictions   133

———. *Svět stavby a báseň: Studie z dvacátých let* [World, Building and Poem: Studies from the 20s]. Prague, československý spisovatel, 1966. (Vol. 1 of *Karel Teige: Výbor z díla*. 3 vols., 1966–1994).

Buck-Morss, Susan. *The Dialectics of Seeing: Walter Benjamin and the Arcades Project*. Cambridge MA, MIT Press, 1989.

———. *Dreamworld and Catastrophe: The Passing of Mass Utopia in East and West*. Cambridge MA, MIT Press, 2000.

Cohen, Jean-Louis. "Introduction." In: Karel Teige, *Modern Architecture in Czechoslovakia and Other Writings*. Translated by Irena Žantovská Murray and David Britt. Los Angeles, Getty Research Institute, 2000, p. 1–55.

Club for New Prague. *Sedum přednášek o architektuře* [Seven Lectures on Architecture]. Prague, Klub architektů, 1925.

Dačeva, Romjana. "Appendix: Chronological Overview." Translated by Eric Dluhosch, in: Dluhosch and Švacha, p. 348–383.

De Certeau, Michel de. *The Practice of Everyday Life*. Translated by Steven Rendall. Berkeley, University of California Press, 1988.

Dluhosch, Eric. "Introduction." In: Teige, *The Minimum Dwelling*, p. xi–xxvi.

Dluhosch, Eric, and Rostislav Švácha (eds.). *Karel Teige: L'enfant Terrible of the Czech Avant-Garde*. Cambridge MA, MIT Press, 1999.

Effenberger, Vratislav. "O podsatnost tvorby" [The Substance of Creative Work]. In: *Osvobozování*, p. 679–727.

Gartman, David. *From Autos to Architecture: Fordism and Architectural Aesthetics in the 20th Century*. New York, Princeton University Press, 2009.

Harvey, David. *The Condition of Postmodernity*. Cambridge MA, Blackwell, 1989.

Honzík, Karel. *Ze života avantgardy* [From a Life of the Avant-Garde]. Prague, československý spisovatel, 1963.

Keil, Roger, and Douglas Young. "In-Between Canada: The Emergence of the New Urban Middle." In: Young, Wood, and Keil (eds.), p. 1–18.

Le Corbusier. *Urbanisme*. Paris: G. Cres & cie, 1924.

———. "In Defense of Architecture." 1929. Translated by Nancy Bray, et al. Introd. George Baird. *Oppositions*, 4 (1974), p. 93–108.

Lefebvre, Henri. *The Production of Space*. 1974. Translated by Donald Nicholson-Smith. Cambridge MA, Basil Blackwell, 1991.

———. *Right to the City*. 1967. In: Eleonore Kofman and Elizabeth Lebas (eds.), *Writing on Cities*. Cambridge MA, Blackwell Publishers, 1996.

Mumford, Eric. *The CIAM Discourse on Urbanism, 1928–1960*. Cambridge MA, MIT Press, 2000.

Paperny, Vladimir. *Architecture in the Age of Stalin: Culture Two*. Translated by John Hill and Roann Barris. New York, Cambridge University Press, 2002.

Sayer, Derek. *Prague, Capital of the Twentieth Century: A Surrealist History*. Princeton, NJ, Princeton University Press, 2013.

Sieverts, Thomas. *Cities without Cities: An Interpretation of the Zwischenstadt*. Translated by Daniel de Lough. New York, Spon Press, 2003.

———. "The In-Between City as an Image of Society: From the Impossible Order Towards a Possible Disorder in the Urban Landscape." In: Young, Wood, & Keil, p. 19–28.

——. "Some Notes on Aesthetics in a 'Städtebau' on a Regional Scale." In: Richard Heil et al. (eds.), *Tensions and Convergences*. New Brunswick, USA, Transaction Publishers, 2007, p. 199–212.

Spechtenhauser, Klaus, and Daniel Weiss. "Karel Teige and the CIAM: The History of a Troubled Relationship." Translated by Eric Dluhosch, in: Dluhosch and Švácha, p. 216–255.

Stanek, Lukasz. *Henri Lefebvre on Space: Architecture, Urban Research, and the Production of Theory*. Minneapolis, University of Minnesota Press, 2011.

134   *Steven Logan*

Švacha, Rostislav. *The Architecture of New Prague 1895–1945*. Translated by Alexandra Buchler. Cambridge, MIT Press, 1995. Translation of *Od moderny funkcionalismu*. Prague, Odeon, 1985.

Teige, Karel. "Foto kino film." 1922. In: Brabec et al., p. 64–90.

———. "Mundaneum." 1928–1929. Introduction by George Baird, in: *Oppositions* 4 (1974), p. 83–91.

———. "K sociologii architektury" [Towards a sociology of architecture]. 1930. *RED, měsíčník pro moderní kukturu*. Vol. 3. Wurzburg, Germany, jal-reprint, 1970, p. 163–223.

———. "Modern Architecture in Czechoslovakia." 1930. In: Jean-Louis Cohen (ed.), *Modern Architecture in Czechoslovakia and Other Writings*. Translated by Irena Zantovská Murray and David Britt. Los Angeles, Getty Research Institute, 2000.

———. *The Minimum Dwelling*. 1932. Translated by Eric Dluhosch. Cambridge, MIT Press, 2002.

———. "Moderní architektura v československu." 1947. In: Brabec et al. (eds.), *Osvobozování*, p. 186–234.

———. "Obrazy a předobrazy" [Images and Prefigurations]. 1920. In: Brabec et al. (eds.), p. 25–32.

———. "Obývací stroje" [Machines for Living]. *Stavba* 4 (1925–26), p. 135–146.

———. "Poetismus." 1924. In: Brabec et al. (eds.), *Svět*, p. 121–128.

———. *Práce Jaromíre Krejcara: monografie staveb a projektů* [The Works of Jaromír Krejcar: Buildings and Projects]. Praha, Nakl. Václav Petr, 1933.

———. "Předmluva o architektuře a přírodě" [Prolegomena to Architecture and Nature]. 1947. In: Brabec et al. (eds.), *Osvobozování*, p. 257–290.

———. *Svět, který se směje* [A World which Laughs]. 1928. Jiří Thomáš (ed.). Prague, Akropolis, 2004.

Young, Douglas, Patricia Burke Wood, and Roger Keil (eds.) *In-Between Infrastructure: Urban Connectivity in an Age of Vulnerability*. Praxis (e) Press, 2011. www.praxis-epress.org.

Zusi, Peter. "The Style of the Present: Karel Teige on Constructivism and Poetism." *Representations* 88 (2004), p. 102–124.

9 The Conquest of Urban Mobility
The Spanish Case, 1843–2012

Alberte Martínez and Jesús Mirás

INTRODUCTION

Reflecting on changing patterns of mobility over time may help to better focus current analyses of mobility problems. This chapter will contribute to the debate about the sustainability of the current model of urban mobility by analyzing how the constraints imposed by different technological models affected the evolution of urban mobility over the long term. In order to address this question, the chapter is structured according to the successive technologies of public transport.[1] However, this does not mean that the analysis will adhere to a linear, deterministic vision of the evolution of mobility. Instead, it will demonstrate that different types of transport have coexisted and have been more or less complementary over time. It will also show that the choice of the dominant transport model is explained not only by technological factors but also by economic, social, political, and cultural factors (Divall and Bond 2003). In any case, the chapter will focus on technological and economic factors responsible for changes in transport mobility with brief references to other constraints.

THE START OF MODERN URBAN MOBILITY: ANIMAL TRACTION, 1843–1895

The first stages in the emergence of networked transport regimes can be traced to the development of vehicles employing animal traction inside cities (e.g. omnibuses and the rippert) that were used by the middle and upper classes (McKay 1976). The first trams emerged in the United States in the 1830s and spread rapidly due to the strong process of urbanization, the expanded urban model, and the rapid growth of per capita income. The United States remained the technological leader in the sector for decades, although Germany started to challenge American technological hegemony at the end of the nineteenth century as transport systems began to be electrified (McKay 1988).

136 *Alberte Martínez and Jesús Mirás*

The scale of tram service was dependent on market size, population volume, urban surface area, topography and climate, population density, level of income, available capital, and investors' profit expectations. These factors help to explain the diffusion of tramway technology across the globe and particularly in Spain (Lewis 2008), where twenty-four cities implemented such a service. During the first wave of tramway construction from 1871 to 1887, tramways were built primarily in large cities, but between 1890 and 1906 most tramway networks were constructed in medium-sized towns.

Due to the intrinsic inefficiency of the tramway business model, fares were high, especially in relative terms. This explains the elitist character of this means of transport, which was mainly used by the bourgeoisie. This characteristic was further reinforced by tramway routes, which primarily served new bourgeois residential areas (the *Ensanches*) that were built during the second half of the nineteenth century (Monclús and Oyón 1996). Their use primarily for accessing leisure activities or in times of festivals led to the development of timetables with peak service on Sundays and during the summer months, which hindered the efficiency and profitability of the lines (Oyón 1992). Growing awareness of these limitations led to demands for electrifying the lines, but process was far from easy in small and medium-sized towns due to investors' lack of confidence, because electrification required high capital requirements and profit expectations were uncertain. This led occasionally to local concessions being transferred to Belgian investors, because they had greater financial resources and experience in the sector (Alvargonzález 1990; Martínez, Piñeiro, and Velasco 2006).

THE PROCESS OF TRAM ELECTRIFICATION, 1895–1929

The use of electric traction for urban transport required a series of trials during the 1880s to determine the most effective technology for tram use. The design employing overhead contact wires eventually triumphed (McKay 1988, 10). At the time, compared to other Western European nations, Spanish delays in implementing new technologies were notorious (Tables 9.1 and 9.2). In the case of animal traction, Spain lagged nearly four decades behind other European nations, though to some extent this was due to the need for a larger and more sophisticated technological system and a greater and better-refined business model. This helps to explain why the Spanish technological matrix was Anglo-Saxon, utilizing an American patent and English and Belgian implementation. Although British companies dominated business and financing of Spanish lines and developed the first tramway systems at the beginning of the 1870s in large cities such as Madrid and Barcelona, tramway electrification technologies were imported from the United States and especially from Germany. The most sophisticated traction engines came from the latter nation, whereas Belgian associates dealt with the chassis and rails. Companies that carried out the electrification of

Table 9.1 Length of tramlines (km) in Europe in 1895, according to the type of traction employed

Country	Animal traction (km)	Steam (km)	Electric (km)	Total (km)	Animal traction (km)	Steam (%)	Electric (%)
Italy	248	2,478	40	2,766	9.0	89.6	1.5
Germany	927	233	491	1,651	56.1	14.1	29.7
France	566	798	130	1,495	37.9	53.4	8.7
Great Britain	935	200	68	1,202	77.8	16.6	5.6
Belgium	119	1,056	26	1,200	9.9	87.9	2.1
Spain	200	47	14	261	76.5	17.9	5.6
Switzerland	26	224	32	282	9.1	79.4	11.4

Source: Ernest Gerard, "Statistics and growth of European tramways," *Bulletin of the International Railway Congress* XI (1897): 297–299.

Table 9.2 Length of electric tramlines in Europe (in km), January 1, 1934

Country	Length (km)
Italy	2,884
Germany	1,990
France	1,370
Great Britain	1,354
Spain	1,122
Switzerland	583
Belgium	349

Source: Anuario de ferrocarriles y tranvías XXXIX (1935).

existing networks were usually Belgian, but electrotechnical German capital (AEG and Siemens) also had a strong presence (Martínez 2012).

During the early years of electrification at the turn of the twentieth century, the process advanced slowly due to the technological requirements necessary for electrical power production (thermal generation), which made investments more expensive (see Figure 9.1). The process accelerated during the decade before the First World War. Hydroelectric power generation and technological advances in long-distance power transport allowed a substantial cost reduction and permitted the spread and diversification of power grids. The difficulties of the Great War and the subsequent economic crises put a halt to the growth of electrified networks and to the substitution of animal traction and steam. Nevertheless, electrification of the tram system resumed during the mid-1920s, coinciding with economic

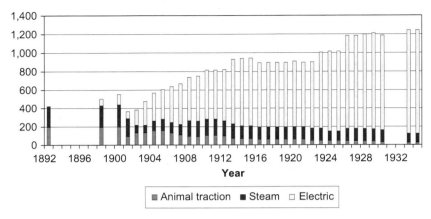

Figure 9.1 Total length (km) of tramlines in operation, according to their type of traction, 1892–1934

Sources: For 1892: *Memorias de Obras Públicas*, 1892. For 1898–1900: Ministerio de Fomento. Dirección General de Obras Públicas, *Estadística de las obras públicas de España* (Madrid: Minuesa, 1898–1900). For 1901–1930: José G. Ceballos, *Historia económica, financiera y política de España en el siglo XX* (Madrid: El Financiero, 1932), 381. For 1931–1934: *Anuario Estadístico de España*, 1931–1934.

expansion, urbanization, and concentration of businesses. Consequently, on the eve of the Spanish Civil War, the dual process of expanding and electrifying tram networks had practically concluded.

THE IMPACT OF ELECTRIFICATION ON MOBILITY

Traditional public transport using animal traction had serious limits for satisfying urban populations' demands for mobility (e.g., low capacity, reduced speed, rigidity), which resulted in higher fares. These restrictions limited tram services to middle- and upper-class users. Compared to steam power, electrified traction had a lower environmental impact, lower operating costs, and offered the possibility of mastering steeper gradients. By overcoming these obstacles, electrification helped to bring about a real revolution in urban transport, facilitating what may be considered "the conquest of mobility." This transformation formed part of a larger process of modernization of Spanish society and, especially, its cities (urbanism, public services) during the first third of the twentieth century.

Electrical traction allowed the speed and frequency of tram service to increase, although trams' dependence on electricity made them more vulnerable to technical failures. Carriages could be made larger, which enabled them to hold larger numbers of people in more comfortable conditions. The high cost of the fixed infrastructure and the rolling stock encouraged more intensive use of the system to recoup costs more quickly. This led to an

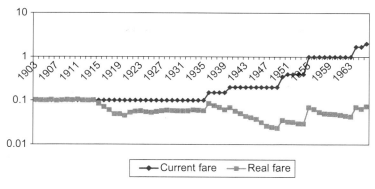

Figure 9.2 Current fare and fare in 1913 pesetas for A Coruña, 1903–1966
Source: A Coruña Tramways Company, Board of Directors' Reports.

increase in kilometers travelled by railcars. Lines could extend to the suburbs and across hilly terrain. The advantages of electricity were particularly evident for lines that carried intense traffic or traversed long distances, particularly over hills, provided that concessions were granted for a sufficient time to allow a return on the high capital investments necessary to build the lines (*Congreso* 1901, 273–279). Large companies that were involved in unifying and electrifying tram networks aimed to secure greater line concessions. On the whole, they secured concessions that lasted until the end of the Spanish Civil War.

The increase in the scale of tram operations permitted cost reductions. Fares also declined, but the drop was due to the inflationary effects of the First World War and the postwar years, because the nominal fares remained the same (Figure 9.2). From a long-term perspective, it is evident that later changes in traction, such as trolleybuses in the 1950s and 1960s, were accompanied by an increase of nominal tariffs that were justified by improvements in service and inflation (although they did not manage to compensate for the effects of this).

The reduction of fares led to a gradual increase both in the number of users and the annual average number of journeys (Figure 9.3). Tramways progressively became a more popular means of transport,[2] and were used increasingly for daily commutes, not simply for weekly or yearly social activities. Nevertheless, increased mobility depended on the size of populations in urban centers and on the substitution of an industrial model of production, whereby working and living took place in separate spaces, for the earlier artisan model of working and living in the same residential space (Capuzzo 2000, 631–632).

Another very important aspect of the electrification of transport, through the development of urban transport networks, was its impact on urban structures and the location of economic activities, above all commercial, for

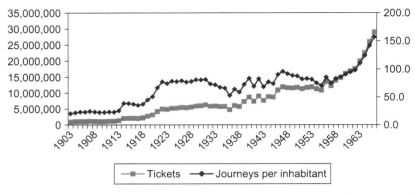

Figure 9.3 Tickets and journeys per inhabitant of A Coruña, 1903–1966
Source: A Coruña Tramways Company, Board of Directors' Reports.

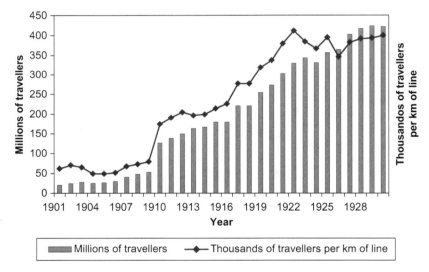

Figure 9.4 Travelers transported by tram, 1901–1930
Source: Ceballos, *Historia económica*, 381.

which visibility and accessibility were key (Mirás 2005). The tram acted as a vector of urban growth, reinforcing a radial structure that linked the center to the periphery, initially to upper-class districts but later to lower-class neighborhoods. Compared to the modest networks employing animal traction that had linked the city center with the railway station and upper-class neighborhoods, electrified networks were denser and more complex. They favored slow homogenization of urban spaces and growth towards peripheral and suburban areas, which established the basis for future underground transit system (Monclús and Oyón 1996; Divall and Bond 2003). Spain followed this trend, despite a small time lag compared to more developed countries. An increase in the number of travelers took place during the second decade of the twentieth century, coinciding with the extension of networks and their electrification. This increase was also visible in the number of travelers per line. However, although the number of users continued to grow during the 1920s, albeit at a slower pace, the number of travelers per line tended to decline. During this stage, the growth of public transport was extensive and based on the expansion of networks, but the new peripheral lines were less attractive with respect to the number of travelers, because they faced growing competition from other means of transport such as underground lines in large cities and buses in suburban areas (Figure 9.4).

CRISIS, TECHNOLOGICAL OBSOLESCENCE AND THE FIRST TRANSITION: THE TROLLEYBUS, 1930–1951

Unlike other European countries where a significant municipalization of public services (including urban transport) took place beginning in the early twentieth century (Dogliani 1988), this phenomenon arrived very late in Spain, proved to be of little importance for transit, and was mainly focused on waterworks. This meant that the ownership of tram companies remained in private hands during the interwar period. The services were municipalized after the Spanish Civil War but only in the larger cities. The most significant change was the replacement of the Belgian firms by Spanish companies that were financially supported by banks (Martínez 2002). During the interwar years the tramway sector reached maturity. The only threat for tram companies (although it was still incipient) came from small, local entrepreneurs who put peripheral bus lines into operation, which represented a serious source of competition, but only in the suburbs at the time (Martínez, Piñeiro, and Velasco 2006).

The design of the public transport system did not change substantially during the 1930s despite the slow and hesitant introduction of bus services. Public transport remained practically stable until the end of the 1940s in most Spanish cities. The evolution of business in Spain during the 1930s is marked by three events: (1) the general economic crisis, which had repercussions for urban transport; (2) the Civil War, which aborted attempts to develop a transport system with buses in the suburbs; and (3) the economic policy of Franco's dictatorship, which exerted intense pressure on operational margins by freezing fares despite inflation and cost increases.

Demand for public transport did not stop increasing during the 1940s,[3] due, above all, to demographic growth, reduction in the number of motor vehicles, and frozen fares, which reduced the real cost of journeys, even when lower income levels during the postwar period are taken into account. The biggest problems for tram companies was a shortage in energy supplies, which was primarily due to national economic policies. Energy shortages

142   *Alberte Martínez and Jesús Mirás*

were very significant for businesses, such as urban transport systems, that depended on constant energy supplies. Energy was produced domestically, but there was a significant disparity between supply and demand. The supply deficit grew due to the scarcity of petrol (a political weapon employed by the United States, but also due to shortages of foreign currency) and, to a lesser extent, coal. Likewise, the regime's price-control policy decapitalized businesses and prevented necessary technological investments to increase production (Catalán 1995, 257–264). There were, moreover, difficulties importing necessary implements and tools for electrical production due to insufficient currency reserves and the frequent and corrupt diversions of assigned currency quotas (Sudrià 1987, 332–335).

Transit companies' activities in the period after the war were clearly constrained by a lack of materials, not only to implement expansion projects and rebuild networks, but also to carry out ordinary repairs. Many firms found themselves obliged to reduce the number of cars in service. The impossibility of importing parts and equipment meant that tramway projects and autobuses evolved towards a system of trolleybuses with electrical traction.

In the tramway business, the evolution of operations was delayed by three circumstances: (1) fluctuation in electrical supply (especially intense during the summer due to droughts affecting hydroelectric production); (2) a decline in the value of personal incomes (as a consequence of inflation); and (3) difficulties in obtaining the necessary supplies for vehicle and network maintenance. These limitations, particularly the failure of energy supplies, led to frequent and repeated service suspensions. These anomalies were especially numerous and relevant in the early 1940s when the service often had to be reduced, above all due to summer droughts.

Due to the precarious economic situation, many tramways came dangerously close to bankruptcy (with the exception of municipal companies). This meant that the national government ordered the creation of commissions to study alternatives for the economic viability of these businesses.[4] There were essentially four alternatives at that time: updating fares, subsidies, municipalization, or the abandonment of existing services and the substitution of more "efficient" technologies. Tariff increases were authorized but were not sufficient to cover costs. The delicate situation of the public treasury meant that increasing expenditures, via subsidies, for trams, which were depicted as inefficient technologies, was seen as a bad investment. Municipalization was carried out in some cities, primarily in the largest ones where economic and social factors increased the gravity of the situation (Alemany and Mestre 1986; Martínez 2002). On the whole, though, there was a preference for accelerating the substitution of trams by buses. This process was favored by the government through the approval of a legal-economic framework that was favorable for the transformation of these systems.[5]

A constellation of reasons, thus, encouraged the substitution of buses for trams. Major reasons included the deterioration of the tram network, the fact that many concessions would soon expire, and social awareness of the "technological obsolescence" of tramways. The process began in 1940 and culminated in 1951 in the case of trolleybuses. Trolleybuses were claimed to be economically more efficient per kilometer travelled compared to trams, mainly because the cost of track construction and maintenance disappeared and the cost of road building and maintenance was borne by other agencies.

Unlike the electrification of tramways, the substitution by trolleybuses for trams was not a national phenomenon—it took place in ten cities (mainly the largest)—nor was it complete, because the new buses coexisted with a variety of preexisting traction systems. Besides social and political inertia, the great size of the existing tramway networks required huge (and not available) sums of capital to implement a complete technology shift.

THE SUBSTITUTION OF TRAMS AND TROLLEYBUSES BY BUSES, 1952–1989

Due to its scale, the Spanish tram system resisted the first wave of change, but in the long run the system continued to deteriorate as economic difficulties plagued its operation. Additionally, trolleybuses made advances over trams in certain aspects (e.g., a lower cost of infrastructure and vehicles, higher flexibility), although, over time, similar faults were found with trolleybuses. In fact, compared to autobuses, trolleybuses were considered more expensive to install and maintain, not only due to the necessary electrical infrastructure but also due to the higher cost of vehicles. Their vulnerability was also criticized, because an electrical fault could paralyze the entire system. Finally, they were considered to be slower, less flexible, and less adaptable to rapid route changes than buses.

The prevailing urban configuration in Spain played an important role in the disappearance of tramways and trolleybuses during the 1960s and 1970s (Figure 9.5). The strong increase of per capita income led to an accelerated growth of the private vehicle fleet (Figure 9.6). All Spanish cities began to be redesigned for cars, and urban streets were considered exclusive areas for nonpedestrian traffic, preferably for private vehicles. Any element that interfered with the circulation of cars was seen as an obstacle to progress that had to be removed (Oyón 1999). In this sense, tramways and trolleybuses, with their rails and overhead electrical lines, were seen as competitors with cars for urban space. This competition worsened with the significant urbanization that accompanied the economic development policy of the 1960s and 1970s and led to significant changes in the traditional structure of the transport network, with the construction of rapid-access roads and highways, the opening or closing of streets, new construction of industrial and commercial parks, and so on (Jürgens 1992). This changed the traditional street network and led (along with significant migration from

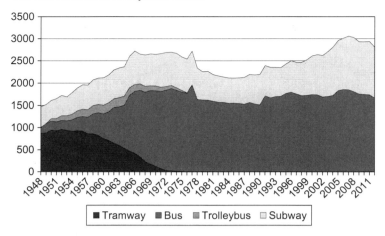

Figure 9.5 Urban transport in Spain, 1948–2012, in millions of passengers

Source: Albert Carreras and Xavier Tafunell, eds., *Estadísticas Históricas de España. Siglos XIX y XX* (Bilbao: Fundación BBVA, 2005), 557–558, and INE.

the countryside to the city during these years) to the spatial redistribution of urban populations.

These problems were compounded by the transport companies' lack of dynamism, because they were used to having a monopoly over urban transport and lack of competition had routinized management.

In this respect, the introduction of the bus was not merely technological, but it also greatly affected models of business organization and methods of management. Buses did not require high investments in dedicated infrastructure like tramways and trolleybuses did. Their greater flexibility allowed them to adapt more easily to changes in demand. Entry (and exit) barriers for the urban transport market were much lower than those of the tram and favored an inrush of new companies in the sector, or at least significant changes in shareholders and management. The business model of the tram era was based on a company with strong financial backing due to high capital demands for infrastructure. Corporate stock ownership had been concentrated progressively since the 1920s, and financial control was largely in the hands of a few families, originating from the local bourgeoisie, who oversaw management and shared the more representative tasks. Organization of these firms was relatively complex and had become rigid and bureaucratic over time. Stability and routine, in short, characterized tramway firms, which was in line with a mature sector. All in all, the tram and bus industries represented the Schumpeterian contrast of mature and youthful entrepreneurial companies. The growing business difficulties due to a changing social and technological environment led to control of these older businesses being transferred to a new type of businessman occasionally originating from outside the city in which the firm was located and with an initial accumulation of capital that was sometimes viewed as controversial.[6] The business transition was not easy and sometimes resulted in confrontations and even conflicts (Martínez, Piñeiro, and Velasco 2006). This transition process happened in a number of Spanish cities, such as Vigo, Ferrol, and Granada.

As studies of technological innovation have emphasized, diffusion is largely conditioned by users' proficiency in applying new technologies (Rosenberg 1982). In the case of the electric tram, setting up new systems required hiring drivers and mechanics from other companies, at least temporarily, until personnel were familiar with the new technology. In the case of buses, the process of learning was formalized through educational institutions for professional training. In both cases, the change of technology implied a readjustment of personnel functions. Nevertheless, it is worth pointing out that in the case of buses, companies used the change of traction to save manpower, thus intensifying personnel workloads and benefiting the firm's bottom line. This kept the growing burden of salaries in check, and productivity increased. From a business standpoint, the process of reshuffling was finalized in the 1980s with a major restructuring of bus lines both to ensure that they satisfied social demands and that they were profitable. Finally, innovative criteria for rate structuring replaced the old, haphazard system of fare increases and guaranteed stable and balanced operational methods (Martínez, Piñeiro, and Velasco 2006).

The traction transition reduced costs and improved the economic viability of transit companies during the 1970s. Nevertheless, their economic situation deteriorated during the decade. On the one hand, this was due to the inflation during the economic recession of the era and to union claims in the context of political transition. On the other hand, insufficient and irregular fare increases did not provide a stable source of operating capital for management. These problems tool place during the peak of private motoring in Spain (Figure 9.6). Transit firms would eventually address the situation, although not without tension, by restructuring service and staff in the 1980s (Martínez, Piñeiro, and Velasco 2006).

Transforming tramway and trolleybus concessions into bus concessions meant not only implementing technological and business innovations, but also changing the legal structure under which concessions operated. Whereas tramway and trolleybus operators generally depended on the central government for concessions, town halls granted concessions to bus companies. The different competences also meant that the levy paid by the concessionaire for the transport concession and any fees for installations and materials (at the time of reversion) were directed to different administrations. To support the transition, the state granted similar bonuses to concessionaires approved to operate trolleybuses. The fact that the substitution of routes and services allowed concessionaires to depend on town halls rather than the central government for support favored the change in traction and was facilitated by the legislation of 1973, which was approved before the oil crisis.

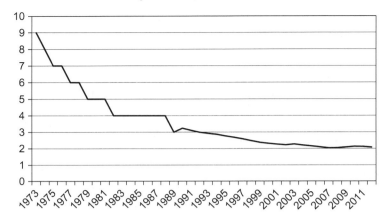

Figure 9.6 Inhabitants per car in Spain, 1972–2012

Source: http://www.dgt.es/portal/es/seguridad_vial/estadistica/parque_vehiculos/series_historicas_parque.do. Accessed September 17 2013.

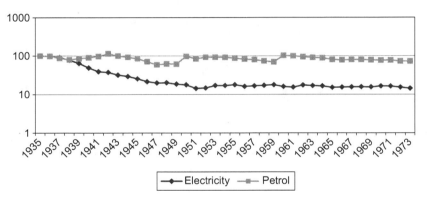

Figure 9.7 Wholesale real prices of electricity and petrol in Spain, in index numbers, 1935–1973

Source: Carreras and Tafunell, *Estadísticas Históricas*, 433–436.

One cannot overlook the cultural factors, such as convenience, independence, flexibility, and modernity, associated with buses and particularly private motorcars (Yago 1984; Thrift 1996; Urry 1999). One must also not lose sight of multinational oil firms' interest in promoting a new transport system that held the potential to generate a huge demand for petroleum products and might be stimulated by a suitable price policy (Rutledge 2006). It is also important to recognize that the differential between the energy costs of the two systems of transport (electricity and petrol) had dropped since the 1950s (Figure 9.7), after a sharp fall in the actual price of electricity due to a governmental decision to block tariffs during the 1940s.

A similar process had occurred with the interest shown at the start of the century by foreign financial groups (Belgian–German mainly) in promoting electrical traction as a means for introducing their metallurgic and electromechanical products to the Spanish market (Martínez 2003; Hausman, Hertner, and Wilkins 2011).

This reorientation of the transport regime can be linked, although not in a mimetic way, to the sharp increase in the number of businesses tied to the motor industry (e.g., petrol refineries; fabricators of cars, lorries, and buses; and tire manufacturers) compared with the electrical sector, a sector that was already mature at the time, in rankings of the largest Spanish companies.

THE PROGRESSIVE CONVERGENCE TO EUROPEAN PATTERNS OF MOBILITY AND SUSTAINABILITY, 1989–2012

The transformation of the economic and territorial structures, which occurred during and after the 1980s, altered mobility patterns (Miralles 2002) in Spain, and the widespread use of private motor vehicles gradually replaced public transport (Barker 1996). Spanish cities today are characterized by privatized mass mobility, to the point that such a model negatively affects the urban transport system as a whole (Santos and de las Rivas 2008, 15).

In the 1980s, the larger Spanish metropolitan areas faced serious bottlenecks in their transport systems, because the dominance of private cars generated serious traffic congestion problems.[7] After many years of focusing on private transport, a change took place at the end of that decade that facilitated a transition to a new urban model similar to that embraced by other European countries. The municipalities gradually overcame administrative barriers, which helped to consolidate several metropolitan areas. The growth of the larger urban areas, with the traffic problems that this entailed, boosted support for public transport (Ordóñez 1992). The most striking outcomes were the extensions of the subway networks in Madrid and Barcelona and the construction of an underground system in Bilbao; moreover, in this city, a significant investment in commuter rail was made. Other cities, such as Valencia, rediscovered the utility of trams, and elsewhere railways once again played a significant (albeit forgotten for a long time) role in urban development (Fernández de Alarcón 1998, 37).

From an organizational standpoint, urban public transport services in Spain are basically comparable to those found elsewhere in Western Europe (except the U.K.). The level of public intervention is high. Despite this, however, competences are widely dispersed among national, regional, and local administrative levels, which hinders the development of an integrated urban transport system (Fernández de Alarcón 1998, 41).

The provision of urban public transport services in a standard Spanish city would be characterized by a company operating as a monopoly that is

148   *Alberte Martínez and Jesús Mirás*

protected by legal entry barriers (de Rus 1991, 232). For private companies, the long concession periods and the tradition that these concessions are rarely forfeited, eliminate, *de facto*, the threat of new competitors. This affects cost structures, tariffs, and service as a whole. Once the network is implemented, the public authority has no effective control on the firm's expenses, which can lead to productive inefficiencies. Hence, public subsidies are the most common mechanism of financing the firms (de Rus and Nombela 1997).

However, the evolution of the economic system has caused a rapid change in the organization of the geographical territory, which is inducing new patterns of economic and residential settlement. Mobility has increased, as has the tendency for metropolitan sprawl to become more accentuated (Cervero 1996). Thus, mobility patterns have changed because urban structures are increasingly polycentric (Van der Laan 1998) as a result of a deep suburbanization processes (Clark and Kuijpers-Linde 1994).

In the 1990s, citizens and institutional agents involved in urban transport began to react to this new reality. It was often claimed that public transport in developed countries was undergoing a crisis. The situation in America seemed to be more serious (Fielding 1995), but in Europe urban centers also suffered serious problems of congestion and mobility (Simpson 1992). Therefore, there was an increasing perception that the existing transportation system was not sustainable (Black 1996).

Consequently, new challenges to mobility were posed that demanded different solutions. Large European cities increasingly linked their urban development to public transport with some success. These formulas were copied in the United States and Canada, where the idea of creating public authorities that could implement new transport systems gradually spread. In North America, the concept of *growth management* emerged. Responsible management of urban growth through the use of tools to control territorial transformation and achieve the difficult balance between economic growth, social equity, and environmental sustainability was the intended outcome (Geurs, Boon, and Van Wee 2009). This is why the idea of *transit-/transport-oriented development* appeared in the United States (Santos and de las Rivas 2008, 28).

Although many of these initiatives did not crystallize, they did help to put new solutions into practice (Thompson 2005, 160)—systems such as the tram-train (opened in 1992 in Karlsruhe, Germany), light rail trains, or other intermediate solutions (bus rapid transit, bus mass transport, and so on). These systems require less investment than rebuilding tram networks (a rather popular alternative in Europe), even though they seem to have reasonably high demand thresholds (Lillo, Wensell, and Willumsen 2003).

In Spain, the twenty-first century has marked the consolidation of supramunicipal models in transportation management (Valenzuela, Soria, and Talavera 2011). In 1994, the government approved an Infrastructure Master Plan 1993–2007, which contemplated intermodal transportation planning for large metropolitan areas such as Madrid, Barcelona, Valencia, Seville, Bilbao, Málaga, Saragossa, and Cadiz. These intermodal plans were conceived as an instrument at the service of the territorial development policies (Aparicio 1994). The two most prominent examples of integrated management of public transport have been implemented in the nation's two largest metropolitan areas: Madrid and Barcelona.

In Madrid, a transport company owned by the regional government was founded in 1985 (*Consorcio Regional de Transportes de Madrid*). The firm instituted a major reform of the metropolitan transport system aimed at improving intermodality (Anguita, Flores, and Muñoz 2010). This was achieved in 1986 by transferring and consolidating management and regulation of public transport in the region from all administrations involved to a consortium (Vasallo and Pérez 2008, 43).

The transport system that was implemented has maintained an efficient level of operation, thanks to successful integration at administrative and tariff levels. According to the latest survey of metropolitan mobility (2004), in Madrid, the distribution of mobility modes was relatively balanced: public transport (34%), private vehicles (34.9%), and pedestrians (31.1%). Four transport modes have been successfully combined, two of them typically urban (the underground system, which includes a light rail line in the urban periphery, and urban buses) and two of them that are metropolitan (commuter rail and interurban buses). Likewise, the management system is mixed. *Metro de Madrid* (the firm that absorbs a higher demand) is publicly owned, because it belongs to the city council. The *Empresa Municipal de Transportes* manages and operates urban buses. The public body *Renfe-Operadora* runs the commuter rail, whereas interurban buses are operated by private companies through concessions (Vasallo and Pérez 2008, 43, 55).

However, despite the wide range of public transport options, Madrid residents still make excessive use of private vehicles. Decentralization of businesses and facilities, urban development policies, and the location of new mobility generators (shopping and leisure centers, specialized cities, and so forth), which are not easily accessible from nodes of public transport, are exhausting the capacity of the whole system (Monzón and de la Hoz 2009, 61, 70).

Meanwhile, in Barcelona, transport suffered severe congestion due to increasing car ownership (Junyent and Jiménez 1989). To address these problems, in 1997, the *Autoritat del Transport Metropolità* was established.[8] Due to increased demands for transport in the metropolitan area, this organization approved the *Plan Director de Infraestructuras* in 2002, which consolidated several initiatives in public transport infrastructure (especially the introduction of a tram system in one of the metropolitan corridors). The regional and national government carried them out from 2001 to 2010 (García and Vizcaíno 2005, 69).

More recently, European Union (EU) policies have exerted a strong influence on planning decisions by urban public transport authorities in Spain. In

150 *Alberte Martínez and Jesús Mirás*

July 2005, the national government approved a strategic infrastructure and transport plan that stressed the need for rationalizing urban public transport. After the publication of a green paper by the Commission of the European Communities entitled, *Towards a New Culture for Urban Mobility*, and the implementation of the EU's Sustainable Development Strategy, the Spanish government approved the Spanish Strategy of Sustainable Development. Finally, in 2009, the Spanish Strategy of Sustainable Mobility was passed.

CONCLUSIONS

In the long term, the evolution of urban transport companies and the service itself was led by societal and economic shifts, which were marked by the introduction of innovative technologies. Its modes of realization (following the theory of path dependency) were conditioned by its previous situation. Technological innovation in the sector presents two key moments with exogenous inventions (electricity and the internal combustion engine) that were applied to transport in a schematic cluster layout. These innovations meant significant discontinuities, because they led to noticeable changes in business models and organizations.

Electrification of tramways was the innovation with the biggest breakthrough. It popularized mobility in a context of increasing demand for public transport. Strong financial backing often came from abroad (Belgian–German). The service became more complex and vulnerable, with a network that made its organization more arduous.

The second change of traction (the internal combustion engine) had less relevant, though not negligible, effects in public transport, but it changed private mobility radically. It was carried out in a less drastic and less rapid manner than electrification with the trolleybus as a technology of transition, probably due to the significance of the investment already made in tramways (the repayment of which still needed to be made). On the other hand, the introduction of autobuses occurred in a period of stalled public transport demand due to the dramatic expansion of private motoring. In any case, this innovation was also accompanied by a significant change of business models, with an inrush of new companies that were smaller and more dynamic, which introduced important service and organizational reshufflings.

All the changes in traction occurred when services underwent strangulation and when companies experienced difficulties due to the limits of current technologies. In this sense, the innovation helped to overcome these situations and led to clear improvements in business outcomes. On the whole, this is a sector where technological transfers had significant discontinuity effects, which followed a scaling model.

The 1970s witnessed significant changes in mobility patterns in urban areas, leading to transport bottlenecks during the following years. The lack of coordination between urban and transport policies between the 1950s and the 1960s hampered an effective response to the changes that were taking place. The dominance of private transport during the previous decades was answered in the 1980s by a greater effort to improve public transport, particularly in larger cities.

However, the growth of metropolitan areas in Spain has hindered transport management since the late twentieth century. The increasing mobility demands (which were generated as a result of the consolidation of polynuclear cities) have resulted in intermodal transport systems at a supramunicipal level. But despite this, citizens have a positive outlook regarding the use of urban public transport.

NOTES

1. The study does not include private means of mobility, such as walking, bikes, or motorbikes, which are very important but are still scarcely researched in Spain (Hass-Klau 1990). In British cities, some 59% of all journeys to work were undertaken on foot in the 1890s (Pooley, Turnbull, and Adams 2006). For bikes, see Anaya and Gorostiza (2014).
2. In European cities in 1910, transport consumed 2.5–4.5% of the salary of a qualified worker (Capuzzo 2000, 630–631).
3. This decade also witnessed a surge in cycling, which began to decline in the 1950s with the spread of the motorbike and, especially, from the 1960s onwards, due to the increased use of motor vehicles (Anaya and Gorostiza 2014, 38–39). Travel by bicycle also peaked in Britain in the 1940s when it accounted for almost 20% of journeys to work (Pooley, Turnbull, and Adams 2006).
4. Decree of February 10, 1952.
5. The decrees of October 5, 1940, and June 16, 1954, established bonuses and discounts to facilitate the substitution of trams by trolleybuses and buses, respectively (Armengol 2012).
6. Selling on the black market (illegal commerce was very widespread in Spain in the 1940s), for example, or having good connections with the political power (Núñez 1999).
7. Despite some delays, strategic town planning was developed in European cities during the 1960s and 1970s, followed in the 1980s by so-called *urban management* (Aparicio 1993, 8).
8. This is an interadministrative consortium. Any administration managing public transport services in the metropolitan region of Barcelona may join this organization. These administrations are: the regional government (51%) and local governments (49%), which are formed by Barcelona City Council, Barcelona Metropolitan Area, and the *Agrupación de Municipios titulares de servicios de Transporte Urbano de la región metropolitana de Barcelona*. http://www.atm.cat/web/es/autoritat/presentacio.php.

WORKS CITED

Alemany, Juan, and Jesús Mestre. *Los transportes en el área de Barcelona. Diligencias, tranvías, autobuses y metro*. Barcelona, TMB, 1986.

152 Alberte Martínez and Jesús Mirás

Alvargonzález, Ramón. *Los tranvías de Gijón.* Gijón, Compañía de Tranvías de Gijón, 1990.

Anaya, Ester, and Santiago Gorostiza. "The Historiography of Cycling Mobility in Spain in the Twentieth Century." *Mobility in History* 5 (2014), p. 37–42.

Anguita, Francisca, Sandra Flores, and Juan P. Muñoz. "Los intercambiadores de transporte público como factor determinante de la intermodalidad: el caso de la ciudad de Madrid." *Análisis local* 92 (2010), p. 47–60.

Aparicio, Ángel C. "Autopistas y ciudad: ¿una reconciliación posible?" *Revista de Obras Públicas* 140 (1993), no. 3324, p. 7–18.

———. "El P.D.I. y el transporte en las grandes ciudades." *Revista de Obras Públicas* 141 (1994), no. 3331, p. 25–38.

Armengol, Ferrán. "La regulación de los transportes urbanos en España: intervencionismo estatal contra autonomía local 1859–1987." *VI Congreso de Historia Ferroviaria* September 5–7, 2012, Vitoria, Fundación de los Ferrocarriles Españoles.

Barker, Theo C. "The World Transport Revolution." *History Today* 46 (1996), no. 11, p. 20–26.

Black, William R. "Sustainable Transportation: A US Perspective." *Journal of Transport Geography* 4 (1996), no. 3, p. 151–159.

Capuzzo, Paolo. "La conquista della mobilità. Contributo ad una storia sociale dei transporti urbani in Europa (1870–1940)." *Richerche Storiche* XXX (2000), no. 3, p. 621–639.

Catalán, Jordi. *La economía española y la segunda guerra mundial.* Barcelona, Ariel, 1995.

Cervero, Robert. "Mixed Land-Uses and Commuting: Evidence from the American Housing Survey." *Transportation Research Part A: Policy and Practice* 30 (1996), no. 5, p. 361–377.

Clark, William A., and Marianne Kuijpers-Linde. "Commuting in Restructuring Urban Regions." *Urban Studies* 31 (1994), no. 3, p. 465–483.

Congreso internacional de ferrocarriles, tranvías y electricidad celebrado en París en 1900. Memorias de los ingenieros de caminos, canales y puertos. Madrid, 1901.

De Rus, Giner. "Análisis del mercado de servicios de transporte público en España: costes, demanda, precios y nivel de calidad." *Investigaciones Económicas* 15 (1991), no. 2, p. 229–247.

De Rus, Giner, and Gustavo Nombela. "Privatization of Urban Bus Services in Spain." *Journal of Transport Economics and Policy* 21 (1997), no. 1, p. 115–129.

Divall, Colin, and Winstan Bond (eds.). *Suburbanizing the Masses: Public Transport and Urban Development in Historical Perspective.* Aldershot, Ashgate, 2003.

Dogliani, Patrizia. "Il dibattito sulla municipalizzazione in Europa dall'inizio del Novecento alla Prima Guerra Mondiale." In: Aldo Berselli, Franco della Peruta, and Angelo Varni (eds.), *La municipalizzazione nell'area padana: storia ed esperienze a confronto.* Milano, Angeli, 1988, p. 222–256.

Fernández de Alarcón, Rafael. "El sistema de transporte en las ciudades y la intermodalidad (una visión dinámica)." *OP. Obra Pública* 45 (1998), p. 36–43.

Fielding, Gordon J. "Congestion Pricing and the Future of Transit." *Journal of Transport Geography* 3 (1995), no. 4, p. 239–246.

García, Marc A., and Javier Vizcaíno. "El tramvia de Barcelona, endavant." *Mobilitat Obligada* 13 (2005), p. 69–74.

Geurs, Karst T., Wouter Boon, and Bert Van Wee. "Social Impacts of Transport: Literature Review and the State of the Practice of Transport Appraisal in the Netherlands and the United Kingdom." *Transport Reviews* 29 (2009), no. 1, p. 69–90.

Hass-Klau, Carmen. *The Pedestrian and City Traffic.* London, Belhaven Press, 1990.

Hausman, William J., Peter Hertner, and Mira Wilkins. *Global Electrification: Multinational Enterprise and International Finance in the History of Light and Power, 1878–2007.* Cambridge, Cambridge University Press, 2011.

Junyent, Rosa, and Rafael Giménez, "Societat i transport a les aglomeracions de Barcelona, París i Milà." *Revista Catalana de Geografia* 9 (1989), p. 43–51.

Jürgens, Oskar. *Ciudades españolas: su desarrollo y configuración urbanística.* Madrid, MAP, 1992.

Lewis, Colin. "Capital, tecnología y nacionalismo: economía política de los tranvías urbanos en América Latina, 1850–1960." *TST. Transportes Servicios y Telecomunicaciones* 14 (2008), p. 42–89.

Lillo, Enrique, Ulises Wensell, and Luis Willumsen. "Innovación en el transporte urbano: Bus Transit Systems." *Economía Industrial* 353 (2003), p. 65–72.

Martínez, Alberte. "Las empresas de tranvías en Madrid, del control extranjero a la municipalización, 1871–1948." In: Manuel Benegas, María J. Matilla, and Francisco Polo (eds.), *Ferrocarril y Madrid: historia de un progreso.* Madrid, Ministerio de Fomento, Ministerio de Educación, Fundación de los Ferrocarriles Españoles, 2002, p. 149–179.

———. "Belgian Investment in Trams and Secondary Railways. An International Approach, 1892–1935." *Journal of Transport History* 24 (2003), no. 1, p. 59–77.

———. "Energy, Innovation, and Transport: The Electrification of Trams in Spain, 1896–1935." *Journal of Urban Technology* 19 (2012), no. 3, 2–24.

Martínez, Alberte, dir., Carlos Piñeiro, and Carlos Velasco. *Compañía de Tranvías de La Coruña (1876–2005). Redes de transporte local.* Madrid, Lid, 2006.

McKay, John P. *Tramways and Trolleybus. The Rise of Urban Transport in Europe.* Princeton, Princeton University Press, 1976.

———. "Comparative Perspectives on Transit in Europe and the United States, 1850–1914." In: Joel Tarr and Gabriel Dupuy (eds.), *Technology and the Rise of the Networked City in Europe and America.* Philadelphia, Temple University Press, 1988, p. 3–21.

Miralles, Carme. *Transporte y ciudad. El binomio imperfecto.* Barcelona, Ariel, 2002.

Mirás, Jesús. "The Spanish Tramway as a Vehicle of Urban Shaping. La Coruña, 1903–1962." *Journal of Transport History* 26 (2005), no. 2, p. 20–37.

Monclús, Francisco J., and José L. Oyón. "Transporte y crecimiento urbano en España, mediados s. XIX–finales s. XX." *Ciudad y Territorio* 107–108 (1996), p. 217–240.

Monzón, Andrés, and Daniel de la Hoz. "Efectos sobre la movilidad de la dinámica territorial de Madrid." *URBAN. Revista del Departamento de Urbanística y Ordenación del Territorio* 14 (2009), p. 58–71.

Núñez, Gregorio. *Raíles en la ciudad. Ciudad y empresa en torno a los tranvías en Granada.* Granada, Ayuntamiento de Granada, 1999.

Ordóñez, José L. "Transportes urbanos colectivos. El regreso del tranvía." *Revista del Ministerio de Obras Públicas y Transportes. MOPT* 403 (1992), p. 19–23.

Oyón, José L. "Transporte caro y crecimiento urbano: el tráfico tranviario en Barcelona 1872–1914." *Ciudad y Territorio* 94 (1992), p. 107–123.

———. "Transporte público y estructura urbana (de mediados del s. XIX a mediados del s. XX): Gran Bretaña, España, Francia y países germánicos." *Ecología Política* 17 (1999), p. 17–35.

Pooley, Colin, Jean Turnbull, and Mags Adams. "The Impact of New Transport Technologies on Intra-urban Mobility: A View from the Past." *Environment and Planning A* 38 (2006), no. 1, p. 253–267.

Rosenberg, Nathan. *Inside the Black Box: Technology and Economics.* Cambridge, Cambridge University Press, 1982.

Rutledge, Ian. *Addicted to Oil: America's Relentless Drive for Energy Security.* New York, I.B. Tauris, 2006.

Santos, Luis, and Juan L. de las Rivas. "Ciudades con atributos: conectividad, accesibilidad y movilidad." *Ciudades* 11 (2008), p. 13–32.

Simpson, Barry J. "Transporte público: problemas a los que se enfrentan hoy los centros urbanos." *Ciudad y Territorio* 91–92 (1992), p. 183–190.

Sudrià, Carles. "Un factor determinante: la energía." In: Carles Sudrià, Jordi Nadal, and Albert Carreras (eds.), *La economía española en el siglo XX. Una perspectiva histórica*, Barcelona, Ariel, 1987, p. 313–364.

Thompson, Gregory L. "The Birth of the Light Rail Movement in North America and its Results." *TST. Transportes, Servicios y Telecomunicaciones* 8 (2005), p. 142–164.

Thrift, Nigel. *Spatial Formations*. London, Sage, 1996.

Urry, John. *Sociology beyond Societies: Mobilities for the Twenty-first Century*. London, Routledge, 1999.

Valenzuela, Luis M., Julio A. Soria, and Rubén Talavera. "Hacia la integración de los planes y proyectos andaluces de movilidad metropolitana." *Scripta Nova. Revista Electrónica de Geografía y Ciencias Sociales* XV (2011), no. 349. http://www.ub.edu/geocrit/sn/sn-349.htm.

Van der Laan, Lambert. "Changing Urban Systems: An Empirical Analysis at Two Spatial Levels." *Regional Studies* 32 (1998), no. 3, p. 235–247.

Vasallo, José Manuel, and Pablo Pérez de Villar. "Equidad y eficiencia del transporte público en Madrid." In: *Revista de Obras Públicas* 155 (2008), no. 3494, p. 41–58.

Yago, Glenn. *The Decline of Transit: Urban Transportation in German and US Cities 1900–1970*. Cambridge, Cambridge University Press, 1984.

10 Shifting Transport Regimes
The Strange Case of Light Rail Revival

Massimo Moraglio

Streetcars, transit systems, and the social and cultural values behind those transport devices can appear, unexpectedly enough, in a children's movie.[1] Such is the case in the 1988 Walt Disney live action and animated production, *Who Framed Roger Rabbit*. Set in 1947, Toontown is in danger of being destroyed by Judge Doom, the villain—ridiculously clad in black clothing—who wants to remove the streetcar fleet and build a network of freeways in Los Angeles.

The characters, including Roger Rabbit's femme fatale wife, Jessica, and Detective Valiant, elucidate the broader plot premise:

> *DOOM:* "Who's got time to wonder what happened to some ridiculous talking mice when you're driving past at 75 mph?"
>
> *JESSICA:* "What are you talking about? There's no road past Toontown."
>
> *DOOM:* "Not yet! Several months ago I had the good providence to stumble upon a plan of the city councils. A construction plan of epic proportions. They're calling it, a freeway."
>
> *VALIANT:* "A freeway? What the hell's a freeway?"
>
> *DOOM:* "Eight lanes of shimmering cement running from here to Pasadena. Smooth, straight, fast. Traffic jams will be a thing of the past."
>
> *VALIANT:* "So that's why you killed Acme and Maroon? For this freeway? You're kidding."
>
> *DOOM:* "Of course not. You lack vision. I see a place where people get off and on the freeway. On and off. Off and on. All day, all night. Soon where Toontown once stood will be a string of gas stations. Inexpensive motels. Restaurants that serve rapidly prepared food. Tire salons. Automobile dealerships. And wonderful, wonderful bill boards reaching as far as the eye can see . . . My god, it'll be beautiful."
>
> *VALIANT:* "Come on. Nobody's gonna drive this lousy freeway when they can take the red car for a nickel."
>
> *DOOM:* "Oh, they'll drive. They'll have to. You see, I bought the red car so I could dismantle it."

156 *Massimo Moraglio*

We have here, in condensed dialogue, a long train of concepts, cultural values, and countercultural beliefs. Remarkably, for an American movie, we can detect the inversion of ideals, the notion that American inner values are better represented by a transit system than by car ownership. The villain, Doom—with his freeways—does not represent notions of progress, efficiency, and speed, but rather those of loneliness and deprivation. As a corollary, there is also the claim of an open contradiction between community-based behaviors and practices and mass motorization: once the freeways are open, there will be room for only billboards, precooked food, and occasional meetings in petrol stations. We can deduce, thus, that the dominant transport system is one of the key factors in shaping the social fabric, forging the latter according to physical displays and the symbolic value of transport regimes.

The second central point is the conspiracy theory, in which the car lobby acted in bad faith to destroy the streetcar network, thereby pushing end-users to buy cars (or be constrained in immobility). The best way to implement such a plot was to buy the network and then, according to Doom, destroy it. This premise implies that without underhanded actions, transit could still be used and enjoyed by end-users. Although this conspiracy theory has been discredited by scholarly investigations (Post 2010; Ladd 2008; Bianco 1998), such a representation of the past remains popular in the publics' imagination.

The third point is the construction of a recognizable narrative of success and failure. Although, naturally, Toontown survives and probably prospers (is not *Who Framed Roger Rabbit* a comedy with a happy ending, after all?), through litotes the scriptwriters give us the message of another world, one in which the car finally became dominant and swept away the tramways. Of course, Walt Disney did not always herald transit for Toontown's future. Actually, quite the opposite: in the 1968 movie *The Love Bug*, the car (here a Volkswagen Beetle) was not only the main character of the film, but it acted autonomously and in an anthropomorphic way. Exactly because it was anthropomorphized, the car explored and openly conquered the most remote niches of its environment, including a meeting room, a pathway, and the eaves of a modern building. What happened between those two movies that changed, so dramatically, the perception of cars and tramways?

Under pressure by several factors over a forty-year period, including environmental issues and the failure of private mobility, officials in European cities found renewed interest in light rail systems, an upgraded form of tramways. This chapter aims to investigate the history behind the tram renaissance and will focus primarily on Europe. It will examine the revival from a long-term perspective, and argue in favor of considering a new narrative of the transport models and regimes that western countries experienced during the past two centuries. It will focus on the reasons behind the revival of light rail, discuss the factors that played a role in its resurgence, and address how such a constellation of elements changed, mutated, and found new legitimating elements during the 1980s and 1990s.

A STEP BEHIND

During the past centuries, cities experienced dramatic improvements in mobility, which consumed large quantities of both space and energy. Speed and accessibility increased significantly as a result of new, massive transport infrastructure performance improvements, which were often depicted as indispensable means for obtaining improved urban standards, shrinking time and space, and achieving modernity. In this respect, after the era of horse-powered streetcars, the electric tram at the end of the nineteenth century has been one of the most powerful means for improving mobility, enhancing capacity, increasing speed, and lowering transit costs. The final price of a tram ticket was, thus, clearly cheaper than that of a horse streetcar, to the point of opening the tramway market to lower-income strata (McKay 1976). Although successful from the start, electric tramways in North America and Western Europe reached their peak in terms of line numbers, passengers transported, and fleet size in the early 1920s in the United States (Post 2010) and in the late 1930s in Europe (Capuzzo 2003). Impressive as a large sociotechnical system, tramway infrastructure networks included not only the tram tracks and rolling stock, but also the electricity production and distribution apparatus necessary to move the vehicles. It is possible to estimate that on both side of the Atlantic the development of surface tramway networks was achieved in most cities with populations of 50,000 to 100,000 inhabitants, and very often even in smaller towns (McKay 1976; Schatzberg 2001).

However, at each stage of their development, tram systems faced several challenges, including the aesthetic impact of catenary wires (especially in older European city centers), and the speed of trams on city streets. Noise, bumpy journeys, sparks, and lack of appeal made trams subject to broader critiques in the 1920s, as the parallel development of the car industry and car technology—with its relevant impact in the public's imagination—led to a push for radical alternatives (Post 2003). During that decade, trams reached their peak in terms of passengers and lines, at least in Europe, but they also began to lose their appeal as electrified trolleybuses and buses with internal-combustion engines began to appear. Two main reasons were responsible for the shift. First, buses offered better commercial performance, not only because they required fewer staff, but mainly because infrastructure costs were lower due to public agencies paying for road construction and maintenance, whereas transit firms had to cover the cost of maintenance for tramway tracks. Such a change was particularly appealing to tramway firms that had lower passenger volumes. Second, buses were more appealing in crowded area, such as urban centers. The increase in motor-vehicle ownership made urban public space an even more valuable asset and led to clashes among users of different motorized transit modes. Trams, which had marveled users with their speed in the late nineteenth century, were accused of slowing down automobile traffic due to having to stop in order to drop

158   Massimo Moraglio

off and collect passengers (thus forcing vehicle traffic to stop, too), being cumbersome, and being rigid in the layout of their lines. For these reasons, urban policy makers in the United States made an effort to remove tram tracks from some cities in the 1930s, replacing them with buses, which were perceived as being more flexible in terms of route selection and how they dealt with obstructions created by other vehicles (Whalen 1920; for a critical assessment, see Passalacqua 2011). It was, however, not before the mid to late 1950s that tramway lines were removed from many European cities and replaced by buses (Jago 1994; Post 2010).

This is the dominant narrative regarding tram history, although we face at this point two sets of problems. The first one is more general and encompasses the question of a historical narrative that depicts mass motorization as an irresistible phenomenon that swept away other transport systems. Descriptions and representations of automobiles' success have not only condemned public transport to a *damnatio memorie* in the collective public imagination, but, subtly and powerfully, have bent historical analysis to focus mainly, if not obsessively, on motor-vehicle culture. Such a narrative makes the car's success appear to be inevitable, preordained, and indisputable (Seiler 2008; Norton 2008).

The second problem has to do with how twentieth-century transport history has been depicted as following a common path on both sides of the Atlantic and even further afield. The "basic chronology—the horse bus (1830–1860) and tram (1860–1890), electrification (1890–1918); the motor-bus (1919–1945); motorization (1945–)—did not however represent much of an advance on the popular accounts of lay historian and enthusiasts who otherwise dominate the literature" (Divall and Schmucky 2003: 2). Naturally, by looking closely at national and regional decision making, we can identify divergences from the dominant narrative. For instance, maintaining our focus on tramway networks, in the United States mass transit systems were largely in the hands of private companies, which often had very poor reputations and attracted bad press. In Europe, however, public transport networks were very often, if not exclusively, run by municipal entities. These municipal entities also frequently ran companies devoted to electricity production and distribution (McKay 1976). Additionally, the United States was an oil exporter, whereas Europe was an oil importer, thus making autobus service less desirable for transit suppliers due to the difficulties of acquiring petrochemical fuel sources.

The issue appears even more complex when we consider technological choices, cultural perceptions, and decisions by urban elites. Improvements in diesel engine technology during the 1930s meant that these engines were used increasingly in trucks and buses, paving the way for further development due to the cheaper cost of diesel fuel (Post 2010). Additionally, in the 1920s, the traffic congestion in European capitals, especially London and Paris, was a major factor in municipal decisions to dismantle urban tramways. However, the authorities' decision to remove urban tracks in these two European capitals was *not* mirrored by the actions of municipal authorities in other great and small European cities for a couple of decades. Even in the late 1950s, when removing tramways appeared fashionable across Europe, networks not only survived and prospered in many countries (including West Germany, Switzerland, Belgium, and Austria), but even automotive company towns, such as Turin (FIAT's headquarter) and Gothenburg (Volvo), kept their tramways running throughout the twentieth century. These examples do not even consider the transport regimes on the other side of the Iron Curtain, where transit systems, and trams in particular, were pillars of urban mobility. These disparities among European urban center are underrepresented in the literature (see Jago 1994; Haefeli 2008; Schmucki 2010), but they offer both unexpected ways of examining transport history and a broader means for understand the social compromises and the urban management strategies that lay behind these systems. Based on the aforementioned analysis, this chapter will examine how in the 1960s and 1970s tramways (and underground lines) were not obsolete technological dinosaurs of an earlier age, but rather a solid and successful means for moving millions of inhabitants on a daily basis in many European urban areas.

IN THE BOTTLENECK

There are many reasons to reconsider the role and relevance of mass motorization in Western Europe. It is certainly true that motor-vehicle ownership was a major goal of post–World War II generations. The car's success as an object of fulfillment for generations of Europeans had a cascading effect on the environment of many European cities, which needed to accommodate hundreds of thousands of vehicles on already chaotic city streets. Such astonishing and rapid development of private-car ownership was regarded by many westerners as evidence of the success of the western model. While Europeans, en mass, began enjoying travel by car (and women especially found privacy and freedom in motor vehicles), clouds began to appear on the horizon. Although evident from the early days of the car's existence, in the 1960s and beyond, a major public debate emerged about the negative effects of mass motorization (Ladd 2008). Motor vehicles were blamed for the many inconveniences they created. Following Mackett and Edwards' (1998) works, as well as Ladd's analysis and the large body literature now coalescing on the theme (Norton 2008), the chapter will attempt to systematize these critiques into the following categories: i) the urban and social perspective; ii) the efficiency perspective; iii) the energy perspective; and iv) the pollution perspective.

In the early 1960s, once Europe experienced mass motorization for the first time, the city emerged, in the opinion of several writers and intellectuals, as a space empty of people and full of cars, deprived of social life and, in

160 *Massimo Moraglio*

their view, organized by policy makers to accommodate only private motor vehicles. Transport regimes were held to have a major impact on urban life, and motor-vehicle users' overuse of streets was believed to be destroying the very concept of public space, namely as a venue for hosting lively and traditional face-to-face encounters. The transformation of urban space into mere traffic lanes was—in the early 1960s—the target of well-developed critical works by authors such as Jane Jacobs (1961) and Lewis Mumford (1963) in North America and Alexander Mitscherlich (1965) and Alfred Sauvy (1968) in Europe.

The core concepts of these critiques may be said to belong to an urban and social perspective. The city is accused of having lost its appeal as a dense, intriguing, and surprising environment; the remaining space is insufficient for true relations among the individuals who populate the urban cosmos. These critiques did not simply depict the city's failure, but—as noted above—also identified a culprit—car dominance—and a possible solution. The latter could be found in a transition back to a less frantic pace of movement and more physical space for meeting peers, all targets easily achievable once the number of cars in the city had been reduced. But, naturally, such a move could have a detrimental effect on the ability of city inhabitants to move freely at their pleasure. In order to keep the high standard of mobility usually found in cities, and because mobility was considered to be one of the pillars of post–Enlightenment western society, a reduction in the number of motor vehicles should be accompanied by in improvement in other transport systems that had less of an impact on social encounters. Public transport and bicycles fit that requirement quite well (Iliich 1973).

This line of thinking ran in parallel with, though it did not overlap, the ideas of another group of discontents, who framed the problems of mass motorization as a failure of economic efficiency. For this crowd, mainly transport and urban planners and transport practitioners, the "automobilization" of the transport regime had negative effect because it was a less efficient (or even irrational (UITP 1979)) means for moving people around space compared to public transport networks. Although motor vehicles' mobility offered better performance when operated singularly, guaranteeing speedy, door-to-door service, and no requirement to adhere to outside schedules, at the very moment private motorization became a mass institution the situation changed dramatically, at least in urban areas. City streets were simply not able to accommodate hundreds of thousands of cars, and once motor-vehicle drivers tried to exercise freedom of movement, the result was the shift from personal mobility to collective forced immobility. Not only that: once motorcars conquered the streets, they became stuck in congestion, which soon engulfed surface public transport entities, such as buses. As early as the mid-1950s, European public transport experts and managers discovered—with horror—how buses, whose flexibility had been presented as a key factor in navigating the busy streets of cities, were slowed or stopped by traffic jams caused by private motor vehicles (Schmucki 2003).

The use of public spaces, which streets are, therefore became a central point of contention, as the most prophetic (and iconoclastic) planners in the 1920s had already anticipated. In order to accommodate cars, the latters proposed to destroy *completely* the old city and build a new one that would be able to accommodate cars in large numbers (Ladd 2008: 69). More modestly, other planners and transit representatives constantly demonstrated how cars were space-dissipating, in absolute numbers as well as per capita, although no action was suggested, mainly because European transport stakeholders (and even automotive industrialists) believed that mass motorization would not reach the lowest economic rungs of society, and instead would be contained amongst the lower-middle-class and the blue-collar aristocracy. However, once car ownership became a real mass phenomenon, it meant perennial traffic bottlenecks, street congestion, and time lost in queueing (Metz 2008). The final outcome of mass motorization, once in evidence in the city, was, indeed, highly inefficient transport, both for the individual driving his or her motor vehicle and for the community as a whole. Additional inefficiency was found in car parking, which not only exploited—for a very mundane and trivial task—valuable urban street space, but also had a negative impact on the greater efficiency of the city's transport system as a whole, because a large portion of its space was "immobilized" and not available for movement (or other purposes) (Buchanan and Crowther 1963).

In other words, although largely ignored by advocates for social issues, efficiency advocates claimed, although not as openly, that mass motorization was a self-contradictory phenomenon: once the number of cars circulating reached a saturation point, car mobility was simply impossible. Such a situation was inevitable, an "iron law," regardless of any ameliorating policy applied to the urban spatial setting. If broader streets and new urban motorways were built, they would induce demand for more traffic. Any smooth traffic condition after the road expansion would quickly disappear as more drivers used the new roads and inevitably the roads would become jammed with traffic, just as they had been before the improvements. Mass motorization and traffic congestion were twin phenomena: urban congestion was mass motorization's self-fulfilling outcome (Buchanan and Crowther 1963).

FOR A BETTER LIFE: LIGHT RAIL AS A SOLUTION

Based on the aforementioned analysis, we can easily understand how, well before the 1973 oil crisis shocked western end-users, and well before any concerns about pollution and global warming became widespread, automobilism faced radical critiques, which demonstrated from various perspectives its incompatibility with the urban arena and, even more dramatically, with its own development.

In the late 1960s, urban policy makers and politicians faced the dilemma of favoring both car diffusion, as desired by voters and the automotive

162 *Massimo Moraglio*

lobby, and the need to take action to prevent further collapse of urban transport systems. The 1920s-era development plans that proposed completely rebuilding the urban fabric were simply not feasible; not only due to the huge financial resources necessary to accomplish such an imposing goal, but mainly because achieving such an outcome would mean altering the core identity of the city. Even the more modest, but high-impact, 1960s urban motorways projects faced widespread opposition, and were eventually withdrawn in many cases, making it impossible for planners to achieve the original development program (Mohl 2008; Ladd 2008: 97). This does not mean that any program was suddenly ended. On the contrary, many of these motorway plans were implemented, and car diffusion, at least in Europe, continued to develop at a steady pace. But, although the general public enjoyed car ownership (and complained of longer queues) and car culture reached its zenith, in some intellectual milieus and in many planners' discourses car culture was seen as troublesome.

In 1973, the year of the oil crisis, the core concept of western development, including its corollary of mass motorization, began to be questioned in the public imagination. In retrospect, the 1973 and 1979 oil crises simply slowed down, for short periods, the pace of motorization, which continued to prosper in Europe, the United States, and other parts of the world. Far from leading to the end of motor vehicles, however, the energy crisis forced many to rethink the values and the preconditions of car development on both sides of the Atlantic, values and preconditions taken for granted and never openly discussed previously. During the 1970s, national governments in Europe were intensely aware of their high dependence on oil imports, and made numerous efforts to reduce such dependency. Cars not only consumed significant amounts of energy, but, even worse, they used massive (costly) quantities of imported oil. In contrast, urban, electric, public transport systems, such as tramways, could use electricity, which could have differentiated sources of production (such as hydroelectric power stations or nuclear plants).

Thus, once the cultural debate on progress in western societies began to fade away, the question of energy usage entered the discussion and provided additional tools for those in favor of efficiency. Once scrutinized under the lens of energy efficiency, motor vehicles ranked very low, being only slightly better than airplanes. The single-occupant motor-vehicle regime was, indeed, very inefficient compared to a filled bus, and not just in terms of space utilization and street congestion, but also in the use of another (suddenly precious) resources: energy. We know that in the long run the price of gasoline influenced very marginally the use of motor vehicles, reflecting a very inelastic market demand (European Commission 2012: 45), but during the mid-1970s, western drivers experienced several shocks, including circulation bans, lack of petrol, hostile atmospheres, and, naturally, very high prices for fuel. The question of energy use became central in planners' and policy advocates' political and social agendas, and they demonstrated how the transport sector consumed large quantities of energy and performed extremely poorly. Transit advocates found a well-grounded and highly convincing basis for promoting public transport as a central policy, or at least for lobbying in favor of it (UITP 1979). But the twin oil crises were not isolated economic shocks. In the same decade, the world financial system moved away from the U.S. dollar standard, the western economies suffered stagflation, and the Keynesian social compromise entered a deep crisis. These elements affected all branches of the public sectors on both sides of the Atlantic, forcing governments to reduce budgets and review policies (Kelly 2005). Public transport was naturally a major part of this retrenchment process, which left less room for implementing big infrastructural plans, such as building underground transit lines, making these projects achievable politically and socially only in special circumstances (such as in Barcelona for the 1992 Olympic Games).

The deindustrialization of many European towns also offered a new perspective on pollution in the urban environment and provided more evidence for the impact of the transport sectors in this field. Although the debate about polluted cities may be as old as the city itself, the modern discourse addressed the question of zoning polluting activities, or escaping the city, such as through suburbanization in satellite cities. Now, suddenly, transport-related pollution became a social and political question, in which—once again—motor vehicles contributed the lion's share of negative consequences (Sachs 1992).

ON THE ROAD AGAIN

The oil crisis was thus a turning point in the general discussion of transport policy: after 1973 officials from many (if not all) European cities questioned the motor vehicle's dominance, and a discussion of possible alternatives to the car entered the debate about urban transport. A spell was broken and car ownership would never be the same. Based on social and political conditions, and particularly the energy imperative, advocates offered strategies to mitigate the negative effects of car use and eventually roll back mass motorization. The arguments discussed prior to 1973, as well as the counteractions to mass motorization envisioned from the different perspectives, were, suddenly, at center stage, largely backed by concerns about future energy constraints.

As early as 1975, the Italian government halted new motorway construction, while in the same year the French minister of transport, Marcel Cavaillé, launched a call for reintroducing the tram in France, also with the aim of standardizing national urban rolling stock technology. In 1976, the Union International de Transport Public (UITP) created a *Commission international des Métro légers* (International Committee of Light Rail). Already by this stage, the *bon veil* tram was rebaptized *Métro légers* in French, as

164 *Massimo Moraglio*

commercially branded by Alsthom, a French producer (Demongeot 2011: 181). The name was translated into *Metropolitana leggera* in Italian and *Tren ligero* in Spanish, although the origin of the English appellation "light rail," according to Thomson, had already been coined in the United States in 1972. It was a fortunate choice for it presented an old technical system (the tram) to an urban audience with an appealing new name, which—at least in the Latin languages—exploited the attractiveness of underground metropolitan systems, but in a "light" version. The name in French shows also the dilemma faced by public transport suppliers who were urged to take action in order to implement new networks, while also facing budget pressure and drastically reduced national infrastructure investment when compared to the previous decade.

Light rail, thus, presented a valid compromise by offering a transit-style system without the huge costs associated with building an underground network. After the bad publicity of the previous decade, the rehabilitation of the tram in the public eye was also possible due to the erosion of the idea of technological progress and the rediscovery of older and more traditional (slower) sociotechnical systems such as trams and bicycles (Illich 1973). The French case shows this cultural transformation clearly: while the 1960s were populated by many technological efforts to create new transit systems (Poma 2000; VAL, Aerotrain, and Aramis), the difficulties—or even the failures—of those attempts suggested that authorities should better utilize existing systems, such as tramways, highlighting the crisis of technological fetishism. As Thompson (2003: 26) claimed for North America, the light rail movement arose "amidst growing disillusionment with technological progress." The oil crisis thus spurred a more practical and less technologically intensive transport solution, in which "the idea of tramway is positioned at the core of the oil crisis debate, the energy autonomy as target and the civil atomic electricity production as instruments" (Demongeot 2011, 173, MM translation).[2]

However, reintroducing tramways in the city was not easy in any manner. The community of experts, the same group that had dismantled tram tracks fifteen years earlier, refused to simply return to tramways for the fear that the general public would refuse to use them, and instead preferred to rebrand the old tram with a new name.

Additionally, keeping our focus on France, in the mid-1970s many of the mayors and top urban civil servants were the same people who had led tram removal in the late 1950s, and this made them less than enthusiastic about contradicting themselves and inviting political mockery. Many of them discarded the tram option, preferring instead to lobby for underground systems, especially for the automated VAL system that was under development at the time, and which would offer more political glamour than a tram.

It was, thus, quite a surprise that in the late 1970s the city of Nantes, led by a young, outsider mayor, agreed to develop a tramway network, which finally opened in 1985, the first line completed in France since the

Shifting Transport Regimes 165

1930–1950s decline. The development of the network, however, faced significant resistance. The city mayor, Alain Chénard, who strongly backed the project, later considered his choice in favor of the tram to be a savvy decision, but at the time it was "political suicide." This was confirmed in 1983 when an election gave control to tram opponents in the middle of work on the project (Demongeot 2011). Similar successful tram development, accompanied by the political failure of its supporters can be seen in Turin's *Metropolitana leggera*, which was developed in the early 1980s, and probably other cases as well (De Magistris 1999).

BEYOND MOBILITY: LIGHT RAIL AS AN URBAN REGENERATOR

When Nantes' groundbreaking tram system was completed in 1985, the final product contained a mixture of different technical elements. The wagons were rather similar to designs from the 1950s; the right-of-ways were often fenced, like some German *S-Bahn* systems, but some innovations were introduced in the propulsion systems as well as in the use of public space, because the tram line used a slice of it (UITP 1987):

> At this stage, the promoters of the tramway envisioned it as a faster and superior service once compared to the bus, and not necessarily as a way to reduce motor-vehicles lanes. In this regard, once proposed, the reserved lanes for the tramway were thought for guarantying its speed and service, though keep at the minimum due to the negative reaction could develop. So, reserved lanes for tramway were [at the same time] indispensable for offering a credible service, but also the element which could make it "unacceptable."
>
> (Demongeot 2011: 179, author translation)[3]

Once the Nantes line opened, the factors that had legitimated the development of light rail in the mid-1970s were fading, but new innovative elements were introduced to the discussion. A new generation of stakeholders, technicians, and politicians entered the stage at a time when the memory of tram removal had also diminished. Pollution and traffic jams grew as car ownership in Western Europe continued to expand. Transport planners were rather convincing in showing how underground networks were commercially and technically a mistake in cities with populations below 500,000 inhabitants (for a critical view, see Mees 2010). The French government's commitment to develop tramways favored new requests for constructing tramway lines with new priorities:

> In the autumn 1982, Nantes is ahead in the tramway development, but other [French] cities show some interests, particularly Strasbourg and Toulouse, and even more Grenoble. Better, the local representatives began

166 *Massimo Moraglio*

to spell out specific questions. It is particularly the case of the Grenoble's experts, who openly ask vehicles accessible by impaired people.

(Demongeot 2011: 207, author translation)[4]

Grenoble's policy makers, for instance, stressed the relevance of accessibility for all the population layers and focused on public transport systems that could be used by people with reduced mobility or by "captives" (e.g., people without a car, thus held "captive" to the public transport system). They also stressed the potential role of social inclusion that a public transport network could foster. In Strasbourg, planners argued that trams would promote urban renewal and used the new tram network as a way to reshape the urban environment. The installation of light rail tracks was seen as a way to legitimate sweeping cars off downtown streets in order to reduce—or ban—motor-vehicle circulation and to relaunch the city's image and identity. Those two iconic cases in the late 1980s and 1990s unlocked the tram renaissance's potential to rethink and reshape the urban landscape with a major emphasis on the social and symbolic values of those projects (Siemiatycki 2006). In a broader context, during the 1990s, European cities were challenged by even higher levels of mass motorization, while the public debate rediscovered the architectonic and spatial value of historical centers, with the public realizing, suddenly, how these areas, often rich in historical significance, had been transformed into amphitheaters for motor vehicles carousels (UITP 1987).

Once the element of urban renewal entered the political agenda, the tram appeared on the horizon as a possible means for implementing this practice. Instead of being considered a pure transport device, able to fulfill mobility expectations for city inhabitants, in the 1990s, the light rail was presented more and more openly as a tool for developing a different kind of city. Because their infrastructure was space-demanding, trams effectively expelled other transport devices, such as cars, from urban streets. In other words, a tram line was a Trojan horse that permitted municipalities to engage in broader action, namely reshaping areas along the light rail line spatially and socially (Budoni 1997). This new stage of development of light rail, which reached its peak in the late 1990s, mixed old and new elements of public transport policies: first, the prolonged trend of smaller public budgets, in which trams were depicted as the second-best choice after underground systems (which were considered too expensive), and second, a more marked end of faith in technological progress, which made the rediscovery of old devices more agreeable, even to those stakeholders easily prone to technological fascination.

CONFLICTS AND INERTIA

This concept [of new surface transit] pushes to think that it will be compulsory to re-draw the traffic plans in any city once the modern tramways, or light rail, will be implemented. There is here a great issue, which will be questioned and refused especially by shops' runners and by who, with no limits nor restrictions, uses the private motor-vehicles. This new envisioned [urban transport] policy will thus find psychological obstacles, strong oppositions which will be systematically exploited politically on the local level.

(Vennin 1975: 9; author translation)[5]

In 1975, at the same moment that the idea of surface transport was presented to the French public, it was clear to the sector experts that the implementation of the projects would be difficult and politically challenging. Two categories were openly called into question: motor-vehicle drivers and resident communities, particularly the local shop owners. The first group was going to be harmed by a sensible reduction of space available for driving and parking, space that would need to be devoted exclusively for light rail tracks. Considering their vocal lobbies, car users' opposition was surely able to reach a wider audience and to influence the final decision. The local shop owners were also expected to offer up fierce opposition, because tram construction would disrupt their business due to the long process of construction, which would block roads for months or even years. Additionally, building light rail lines would mean less room for cars and less room for parking, thus reducing accessibility to the shops for drivers. The same local residents, though happy to benefit from a large infrastructure improvement, which was built to last and which would surely increase the economic value of their real estate assets, were rather unhappy to pay the price through interminable road works.

The lines above address the issue of end-users' involvement in urban projects and, in a broader sense, the role of users in shaping technology (Oudshoorn and Pinch 2003). This chapter is not intended to investigate such a topic, although the relevance gained by city inhabitants in the tram's revival is noticeable, and thus it deserves a closer look. We have here three relevant elements.

First, the larger an infrastructural transport project is, the more likely it is to assume a top-down posture. This does not mean that big projects do not influence the public imagination. On the contrary, although these plans have to meet audience expectations, they are designed and implemented with little or no involvement by citizens, and end-users have practically no opportunity to influence the final outcome. Second, in the transport field, public participation is weak (Schiefelbusch and Dienel 2009). Third, and more relevant for our theme, we have many historical elements and much anecdotal evidence that the tramway revival received tepid or apathetic responses from large sectors of the urban population, which often offered negative assessments of those projects (De Bruijn and Veeneman 2009; Siemiatycki 2006).

From many case studies, we can detect how such resistance had two main lines of expression. One was motor-vehicle users' fear of having less space

168   *Massimo Moraglio*

for their beloved cars once the tram was opened, despite the announced improvements expected by the light rail's implementation. In other words, car drivers would not switch to a new pattern of mobility, even though it was claimed to be more effective, less polluting, and more socially democratic. The second line of resistance was due to the annoyances caused by the long, disturbing, and highly impactful stage of implementation, which meant interminable construction disruptions, and once the work was done, the circulation of noisy trams.

The "losers" of the tram implementation conflict were usually noisy advocates against the project organized into various associations, whereas, on the other side, the "winners" were often neither organized nor vocal. Even so, it is impressive to note how practically any time city inhabitants were asked to give their vote for or against light rail projects, they rejected them. The result of the referendums held in Brest, Florence, and Barcelona show how the reintroduction of trams forced compromises with cities' previous use of urban spaces, due to consolidated mobility attitudes and infrastructural and urban path dependencies (Hommels 2005).

Policy makers and politicians were ambivalent towards these projects: often they simply refused to implement light rail projects, aware of the potential public backlash (Demongeot 2011). On some occasions, the urban elite were able to push through work on projects, but assumed a low profile when the time came to design the lines, well aware that the public might punish those who supported the project, and thus avoided any open challenge to the consolidated urban patterns. In other circumstances, supporters openly defied the urban fabric, though they incurred the risk of failure. In the last category, light rail advocates and their political supporters seemed to be overconfident in their projects due to their (self-evident) appeal. For project advocates, not only did trams offer a more efficient transport regime, but they also improved conditions for the lower income and lower mobility social strata, not to mention reducing pollution, noise, and congestion (Budoni 1997). As had happened with the electric tram in the late 1890s, light rail was presented as an essential tool for achieving better urban performance, shrinking space and time, and, finally, achieving a smart transport system. Too often those factors were so self-evident to the elite that they felt no extra explanation was needed for city inhabitants, and the constellation of factors (including a top-down approach by policy makers) obfuscated a clear legitimation action by residents (Regione Toscana 2003).

This means that any time a light rail project openly questioned current urban rhythms, end-users had very few means available for presenting their thoughts on the issue, and their reactions oscillated between tepid support and outright refusal. The lack of communication between planners and users not only impeded citizen involvement in planning and implementation of the projects, but fuelled tensions between different visions of mobility. The result was often a misunderstanding of reciprocal expectations, and actors displayed antagonistic approaches. This exasperated the clash and inevitably led to hostility from large sectors of the opinion-wielding public (De Bruijn and Veeneman 2009).

Soon, the most ambitious (top-down) projects were rejected, or planners were forced to compromise, which produced unsatisfactory outcomes for all involved. In particular, the Barcelona, Dublin, and Florence cases show how plans for reintroducing trams had to take into consideration cities' previous use of urban spaces. For instance, in Dublin, the tram was implemented successfully, but mainly by using abandoned train tracks or by using side roads and avoiding the historical center of the town. In Barcelona, the new light rail systems were accepted under the strict, but unwritten, condition that they not limit the number of lanes for motor traffic. A connection between the two networks was not implemented mainly because such a link would clash with the current use of the downtown and because it would change the "diagonal" city layout, city traffic patterns, and drivers' as well as residents' mental maps. In Florence, the first project for a tram line entering the city center and passing next to the *Duomo* failed, and in a contentious process, only one of three lines was implemented (Regione Toscana 2003).

CONCLUSION

As a transport device, light rail, as early as the mid-1980s, found its rationality and its motivation not necessarily in its transport performance, but more often beyond it. What emerges from the study of light rail construction is often that the implementation of new tram lines was not driven by the "best" choices available in the transport world. Instead, choices were determined (not necessarily explicitly by some policy makers) by several other factors.

According to the time frame in which they were experienced, or the local situations, different constellations of factors legitimated the construction of new light rail lines. Already in the 1960s, at the same very moment that mass motorization reached its zenith, a lively intellectual debate about the negative societal consequences of motor vehicles' diffusion emerged, as well as a technocratic discussion concerning the inefficiency of private car ownership and use once it reached a mass dimension. Mass transit was, thus, considered a true second-best option.

The 1973 oil crisis fueled the debate over transit from an energy-oriented perspective, and the tram was envisioned as a good alternative to gasoline-based transport systems, while environmental issues were raised for public consideration. During the late 1980s and the 1990s, social inclusion and city renewal (including city pollution) entered the scene, substituting for the issue of energy, while concerns over rolling back the presence of cars in city centers and addressing urban pollution stepped into the frame. The first decade of the 2000s witnessed the first crisis of the tram renaissance, as Bus Rapid Transit (BRT) was presented as a viable alternative solution that offered the same benefits as light rail with lower infrastructural costs

170 Massimo Moraglio

(Scheurer et al. 2000). However, despite the success of the new wave of light rail networks over the past thirty years, the results remain controversial. The new networks have had a very limited impact on the transport market and have produced few changes in mainstream urban mobility patterns (European Commission 2012). Additionally, their success was only due, partially, to a substitution effect, namely people swapping cars for transit; often light rail fulfilled a hidden need for mobility, mobilizing mobility that was not previously satisfied by other transit modes. The latter subject is emerging as a hot research topic, and it surely deserves additional, and more focused, study. On the other hand, new light rail lines unlocked urban potentials, offering a limited but sound alternative to the culture of car dominance.

NOTES

1. The research leading to these results has received funding from the People Programme (Marie Curie Actions) of the European Union's Seventh Framework Programme (FP7/2007–2013) under REA grant agreement no. 252489.
2. "l'idée du tramway se trouve placée au sein d'un argumentaire plus général sur le choc pétrolier comme problème, l'autonomie énergétique comme but et l'électricité nucléaire comme moyen" (Demongeot 2011, 173).
3. "À ce stade, les acteurs-promoteurs de la solution envisagent le tramway comme un service plus rapide et de qualité supérieure à l'autobus, pas comme un réducteur délibéré de l'espace automobile. Les sites réservés/protégés sont recherchés pour la qualité de service et de vitesse qu'ils assureront au nouveau système, mais redoutés pour les réactions qu'ils pourraient susciter. Les sites réservés/protégés sont ce qui doit rendre "crédible" la solution, mais aussi ce qui peut la rendre 'inacceptable' " (Demongeot 2011: 179).
4. "À l'automne 1982, lorsque le modèle commence à être au point, la DTT constitue un groupe de travail national, le 'Comité technique Tramway Français standard.' À ce moment en effet, Nantes s'apprête à prendre commande, mais d'autres villes manifestent un certain intérêt pour le futur véhicule, en pointillé dans le cas de Strasbourg et de Toulouse, très clairement en ce qui concerne Grenoble. Or, les élus locaux commencent à faire remonter des demandes spécifiques. C'est surtout le cas des élus grenoblois, qui exigent que le véhicule soit accessible aux personnes handicapées" (Demongeot 2011: 207).
5. "Ces considérations amènent à penser qu'il sera obligatoire de refaire les plans de circulation des villes dans lesquelles des tramways modernes ou métros légers seront installés. C'est là un grave problème qui soulèvera certainement des oppositions sérieuses venant notamment des commerçants et de la partie de la population habituée à se servir, sans restrictions et sans limite, de la voiture particulière. La nouvelle politique envisagée rencontrera donc des obstacles psychologiques sérieux, des oppositions difficiles qui seront systématiquement exploitées sur le plan politique local" (Vennin 1975: 9).

WORKS CITED

Bianco, M. J. *Kennedy, 60 Minutes, and Roger Rabbit: Understanding Conspiracy-Theory Explanations of the Decline of Urban Mass Transit.* Discussion Paper 98–11, Portland, Portland State University, 1998.

Shifting Transport Regimes 171

Buchanan, C., and G. Crowther. *Traffic in Towns*. London, Penguin, 1963.

Budoni, A., ed. *Tutti in tram. Trasporti collettivi e progetto della città*. Roma, CUEN, 1997.

Capuzzo, P. "Between Politics and Technology: Transport as a Factor of Mass Suburbanization in Europe, 1890–1939." In: C. Divall and W. Bond (eds.), *Suburbanizing the Masses. Public Transport and Urban Development in Historical Perspective*. Aldershot, Ashgate, 2003, p. 23–47.

De Bruijn, H., and W. Veeneman. "Decision-Making for Light Rail." *Transportation Research Part A* 43 (2009) no. 4, p. 349–359.

De Magistris, A. "L'urbanistica della grande trasformazione (1945–1980)." In: N. Tranfaglia (ed.), *Storia di Torino*, vol. 9. Torino, Einaudi, 1999, p. 189–238.

Demongeot, Benoît. *Discuter, politiser, imposer une solution d'action publique. L'exemple du tramway* (doctoral thesis, Université du Grenoble, 2011).

Divall, C., and B. Schmucky. "Introduction: Technology, (Sub)urban Development, and the Social Construction of Urban Transport." In: C. Divall and W. Bond (eds.), *Suburbanizing the Masses: Public Transport and Urban Development in Historical Perspective*. Aldershot, Ashgate, 2003, p. 1–19.

European Commission. *EU Transport in Figures 2013*. Luxembourg, Publications Office of the European Union, 2012.

Haefeli, U. *Verkehrspolitik und urbane Mobilität. Deutsche und Schweizer Städte im Vergleich 1950–1990*. Stuttgart, Steiner, 2008.

Hommels A. *Unbuilding Cities. Obduracy in Urban Sociotechnical Change*. Cambridge MA, MIT Press, 2005.

Illich, I. *Énergie et équité*. Paris, Le Seuil, 1973.

Jacobs, J. *The Death and Life of Great American Cities*. New York, Vintage, 1961.

Jago, G. *The Decline of Transport. Urban Transportation in Germany and US Cities 1900–1970*. Cambridge, Cambridge University Press, 1994.

Kelly, J. *Successful Transport Decision-Making. A Project Management and Stakeholder Engagement Handbook*. Aachen-London, European Commission, 2005.

Ladd, B. *Autophobia: Love and Hate in the Automotive Age*. Chicago, University of Chicago Press, 2008.

Mackett, R. L., and M. Edwards. "The Impact Of New Urban Public Transport Systems: Will The Expectations Be Met?" *Transportation Research A* 32 (1998), no. 4, p. 231–245.

McKay, J. P. *Tramways and Trolleys. The Rise of Urban Mass Transport in Europe*. Princeton, Princeton University Press, 1976.

Mees, P. *Transport for Suburbia: Beyond the Automobile Age*. London and Washington DC, Earthscan Press, 2010.

Metz, D. "The Myth of Travel Time Saving." *Transport Reviews: A. Transnational Transdisciplinary Journal* 28 (2008), no. 3, p. 321–336.

Mitscherlich, A. *Die Unwirklichkeit unserer Stadte. Anstiftung zum Unfrieden*, Frankfurt am Main, Suhrkamp, 1965.

Mohl, R. 'The Interstate and the Cities: The U.S. Department of Transportation and the Freeway Revolt, 1966–1973." *Journal of Policy History* 20 (2008), no. 2, p. 193–226.

Mumford, L. *The Highway and the City*. New York, Mentor, 1963.

Norton, P. *Fighting Traffic: The Dawn of the Motor Age in the American City*. Cambridge MA, MIT Press, 2008.

Oudshoorn, N., and T. Pinch, eds. *How Users Matters: The Co-construction of Users and Technologies*. Cambridge MA, MIT Press, 2003.

Passalacqua, A. *L'Autobus et Paris*. Paris, Economica, 2011.

Post, Robert. C. "Urban Railway Redivivus: Image and Ideology in Los Angeles, California." In: C. Divall and W. Bond (eds.), *Suburbanizing the Masses. Public Transport and Urban Development in Historical Perspective*. Aldershot, Ashgate, 2003, p. 187–209.

172 Massimo Moraglio

———. *Urban Mass Transit: The Life Story of a Technology*. Baltimore, Johns Hopkins University Press, 2010.Regione Toscana. *Piano Regionale della mobilità e della logistica*. Allegato 10, Firenze, Regione Toscana, 2003.

Sachs, W. *For Love of the Automobile. Looking Back into the History of Our Desires*. Berkeley, University of California Press, 1992.

Sauvy, A. *Les Quatre roues de la fortune. Essai sur l'automobile*. Paris, Flammarion, 1968.

Schatzberg, E. "Culture and Technology in the City: Opposition to Mechanized Street Transportation in Late Nineteenth Century America." In: *Technologies of Power: Essays in Honor of Thomas Parke Hughes and Agatha Chipley Hughes*. Cambridge MA, MIT Press, 2001, p. 57–94.

Scheurer, J., P. Newman, J. Kenworthy, and T. Gallengher. *Can Rail Pay? Light Rail Transit and Urban Development with Value Capture Funding and Joint Development Mechanisms*. Perth, ISTP, 2000.

Schiefelbusch, M., and H.-L. Dienel (eds.). *Public Transport and Its Users: The Passenger's Perspective in Planning and Customer Care*. Farnham, Ashgate, 2009.

Schmucki, B. "Cities as Traffic Machines: Urban Transport Planning in East and West Germany." In: C. Divall and W. Bond (eds.), *Suburbanizing the Masses. Public Transport and Urban Development in Historical Perspective*. Aldershot, Ashgate, 2003, p. 149–170.

———. "Fashion and Technological Change Tramways in Germany after 1945." *Journal of Transport History* 31 (2010), p. 1–24.

Seiler, C. *Republic of Drivers: A Cultural History of Automobility in America*. Chicago, University of Chicago Press, 2008.

Siemiatycki, M. "Return to the Rails. The Motivations for Building a Modern Tramway in Bilbao Spain." Research Paper 60, Glasgow, University of Glasgow, 2006.

Thompson, G. L. 'Defining an Alternative Future. Birth of the Light Rail Movement in North America." In: *Experience, Economics, and Evolution. From Starter Lines to Growing Systems, Proceedings of the Ninth National Light Rail Transit Conference*, November 16–18, 2003, Portland, Oregon, Transportation Research e-circular E-C058 (2003).

UITP. *The Long-Term Role of Public Transport*. Brussels, UTIP, 1979.

———. *Confort des Véhicules de métro léger et adaptation á l'environnement*. Brussels, UITP, 1987.

Vennin, J. "Éditorial." *Transports Urbains*, 30, janvier-mars 1975, quoted in Demongeot 2011, p. 186.

Whalen, G. *Replacing Street Cars with Motor Buses*. New York, National Automobile Chamber of Commerce, 1920.

11 The Creation and Perpetuation of an Automobile-Oriented Urban Form
Dispersed Suburbanism in North America

Pierre Filion

It is easy for North Americans to perceive the car-oriented, post–World War II suburb as the norm in terms of urban development—the way cities are built in an economically and technologically advanced society. After all, not only do a majority of North Americans reside in suburbs, but, for most of them, this is where they are born and spend most of their lives. The chapter attempts to counter this perception by arguing that there was nothing inevitable about this urban form, because it can be traced back to specific decisions that have led to its formulation and widespread adoption (see Marshall 2000). It concentrates on the impact of macroscale decisions, which reflect the political and economic conditions prevailing when they were made, and that set the context for microscale decisions, extending their impact over time.

An interpretive model that centers on the capacity of decisions to set in motion dynamics that perpetuate their effects summons up the path-dependence perspective. The chapter identifies the mechanisms that played the role of path dependencies by fostering the formulation of the car-oriented suburban model and assuring its proliferation and perpetuation.

The chapter concentrates on the relation between transportation and land use. It looks at the conditions that gave the automobile its unchallenged dominance and fostered the adaptation of land use to this supremacy, which further entrenched reliance on the automobile. The chapter investigates a unique case of mutual adaptation of transportation and land use. There is no comparable example of such a rapid and widespread synchronization of an urban form with a single mode of transportation. In other historical or contemporary urban patterns organized around mechanized forms of transportation, walking accounted for an important share of journeys. This is not the case in the type of suburban areas examined here, where functional walking has been marginalized.

By exposing factors contributing to the perpetuation of the North American, car-oriented suburb, the chapter casts light on the obstacles confronting efforts at departing from this development pattern. Any attempt at profoundly altering the North American suburban model will confront the cumulative effects of seventy years of decisions contributing to its

174   *Pierre Filion*

formulation and anchoring. By chronicling these decisions and investigating their origins and impacts, the chapter seeks to generate information relevant to strategies promoting alternatives to the suburbs that are less environmentally damaging, costly to build and service, and more conducive to physical activity and overall quality of life.

Throughout the chapter the term "dispersed" serves to connote the North American automobile-dependent suburb. In its present understanding, "dispersed suburbanism" refers to an urban morphology characterized by low density, specialized land use, and a scattering of workplaces, retailing, and institutions (hence the "dispersed" label) (Filion, Bunting, and Warriner 1999; Lang 2003). Dispersed suburbanism is intimately linked to automobile-defined accessibility patterns. In addition, the chapter occasionally uses the expression "form and dynamics" when referring to suburbs. "Form" alludes to how the built environment is structured, whereas "dynamics" pertain to behaviors taking place within the environment, including journeys. Finally, in this chapter North America refers only to the United States and Canada, two countries that have spawned similar post–World War II suburbs.[1]

The chapter unfolds in five sections. The first section introduces the societal context and the specific decisions that have defined dispersed suburbanism and encouraged its proliferation. The second section identifies the features of the dispersed suburban model, highlighting its evolution over time. In the next section, attention turns to critiques of dispersed suburbanism and recent attempts at departing from this form of development. This third section also examines motivations driving these transformative efforts, as well as their chances of success. The fourth section is given to an interpretation of the post–World War II history of the North American suburb from a path-dependence perspective. The last section proposes three scenarios depicting possible futures of the suburb, and assesses their respective likelihood in light of the path-dependence perspective advanced in the chapter.

THE SHIFT TO FULL AUTOMOBILE DEPENDENCE AND DISPERSED SUBURBANISM

Like any attempt at delimitating historical periods, the choice to make the origin of dispersed suburbanism coincide with the end of World War II can be contested. After all, by this time urban environments designed to fully accommodate the car had already been part of the imaginary of planners and the public, as evidenced by Frank Lloyd Wright's Broadacre City presented in 1932 and the popularity of automobile-oriented urban utopias in the U.S. world's fairs of the 1930s (Rydell and Burd Schiavo 2010). Arguably the main attraction of the 1939–1940 New York World's Fair was the General Motors pavilion's Futurama exhibit. Futurama, conceived by the architect Norman Bel Geddes, was an animated diorama that pictured the city of the future, as it would appear twenty years later, consisting of a mixture of high- and low-rise buildings traversed by numerous wide arterials and expressways. The futurist city presented here was fully automobile oriented. What is more, new low-density developments from the 1920s onwards increasingly relied on the automobile and began adopting development formulas that were adapted to the car. This was notably the case, for example, of Country Club Plaza, which opened in 1922 in a wealthy Kansas City neighborhood, and is deemed to be the first automobile-oriented shopping center.

Still, there are good reasons to set the origins of the dispersed suburbanism model in the postwar period. At the time, the continent was emerging from a fifteen-year urban development hiatus caused by the Great Depression and the war. Accordingly, even if planners and developers had been fantasizing about new urban forms that took advantage of the accessibility potential afforded by growing car use, they had little opportunity to realize their visions. Only with the end of wartime rationing did urban development take off. Another justification for the postwar juncture is that, although some aspects of the contemporary suburb were in place before, it is only after 1945 that the multiple dimensions of dispersed suburbanism take shape and that this type of development achieves sufficient scope to operate as a system (Halberstam 1993).

To make sense of the multiple decisions that have contributed to shape the suburban model and assure its quick spread, the chapter will first introduce the societal context in which they were adopted, and then divide them in three categories: First, political and planning decisions; second, corporate decisions; and third, decisions made by consumers. The section ends with a reflection on the respective influence of different types of decisions on the dispersed suburban form and dynamics.

Over the first part of the twentieth century, North Americans had been tantalized by the promises of a new modernist lifestyle defined by the mass consumption of cumulative waves of new technologies: the telephone, the radio, the television, home appliances, and, above all, the automobile. But for many, these aspirations had been deferred by the social polarization and the economic difficulties that marked the first half of the century. Under these circumstances, the pervasive adherence to modernist values in the postwar period, and the attendant rejection of the old and traditional, was not unexpected. Remarkably, however, in the post–World War II years, consumerism-driven modernism did not immediately extend to social values. The period was defined by a strong adherence to the nuclear family, a prevalence of stay-at-home mothers, and the high birthrates that produced the baby boom (Allan and Crow 1989; Hayden 2003).

Postwar macroeconomic policies played a key role in abetting mass consumption. Influenced by Keynesianism, and determined to avoid a return to the recessionary 1930s, governments adhered to demand-side economics. They adopted ambitious programs intended to stimulate consumption and,

176   *Pierre Filion*

thereby, facilitate the conversion of the war industry and promote an ongoing expansion of the production of consumer goods. The success of this strategy until the early 1970s yielded low unemployment; a rapidly expanding, consumerist middle class; and full public-sector coffers (Marglin and Schor 1990).

Suburban growth stimulated consumer demand, while itself benefiting from the postwar consumer-driven economic boom (Moulaert, Swyngedouw, and Wilson 1988). Of all instruments meant to fan consumption, federal mortgage loan and guarantee programs in the United States and Canada arguably had the strongest effect. Initially mostly targeted at veterans (the GI Bill), they were soon extended to wide segments of middle-class home purchasers. Not only does the construction of a new home generate employment, but so does the production of attendant household needs, such as furniture and appliances. As these mortgage programs were directed at new, single-family homes mostly erected in new subdivisions at the edge of the built perimeter, they also stimulated the purchase of cars (Hayden 2006; Miron 1988, 1993). From 1956, with the adoption of the National Interstate and Defense Highways Act the U.S. government funded, mostly from fuel taxes, 90% of the Interstate system (Brown, Morris, and Taylor 2009). In Canada, notwithstanding the availability of federal highway money in cities along the Trans-Canada highway, most of the financial support came from the provinces.

Beltways soon became magnets for suburban workplace, retail, and residential development. Central-city interests reacted by lobbying successfully for federally funded expressways within the built perimeter. They assumed that existing workplace and retail concentrations, most notably central business districts, would benefit from the automobile accessibility provided by radial expressways. Outcomes of this strategy were mixed. Downtowns that had achieved a sufficient critical mass to compete with suburban shopping and work locations, and that were rail transit hubs, kept on growing in absolute terms, if not as a share of metropolitan-wide retailing and employment. In other instances, the effect of the new urban expressways was to shift a proportion of traditional downtown markets to suburban activities by improving the accessibility of outlying locations from older urban areas (Bottles 1987; Jones 2008: 108–137; Muller 2004).

Taking advantage of the opportunities offered by the characteristics of the postwar suburban environment, economic interests contributed to further define dispersed suburbanism. Features of the suburb were engrained in large, private, master-planned developments, such as the four Levittowns in the United States, and Don Mills in Canada. The ubiquity of the automobile was mirrored in new retail formulas and building styles, such as the prominence of garages in single family–home layouts, and the popularity, in some cases long lasting and in others fleeting, of motels (i.e., motor hotels), curb service restaurants, drive-through services, and drive-in cinemas. More influential was the adoption of development formulas predicated on extended automobile accessibility sheds, such as increasingly large shopping malls and now power centers (unenclosed shopping centers with large-format retailing), as well as industrial and business parks (Hardwick 2004; Jones and Doucet 2000; Lorch 2005; Zukin 2005).

The adoption and spread of the suburban model was also a function of countless consumer decisions underpinning its form and dynamics. These decisions ranged from major choices that commit to a suburban lifestyle, such as those involving the type and setting of the home, the purchase of a car, and the location of a workplace, to those concerning day-to-day activities, such as shopping and visiting friends.

Dispersed suburbanism benefited from a period exceeding two decades when it was widely accepted as the norm for new urban development. There was a broad consensus around this model, although seeds of discontent were being sown by urban critics such as Lewis Mumford, for whom standardized suburban development contributed to the "orchestrated chaos" of the modern metropolis, and Jane Jacobs, who celebrated the diversity of traditional inner-city neighborhoods while dismissing modern planning formulas (Jacobs 1961; Mumford 1961). By the time shortcomings of dispersed suburbanism became common knowledge, the model was well established, which made it resistant to change. Interests vested in this pattern of development had mustered considerable economic and political power, and interrelations between its different aspects—most notably, transportation and land use—were solidly anchored.

THE DISPERSED SUBURBAN MODEL

All North American suburban areas developed since the end of the war share similar morphological features. They register generally low, although variable, densities. What is more, their land use is highly fragmented due to a rigid functional and housing-type segregation. As a result, they are composed of zones that are internally homogenous but sharply distinct from one another, which makes for contrasted suburban landscapes (Rowe 1991). Suburbs are also characterized by an absence of mixed-use clustering of activities, due a scattering of retailing, employment, and institutions in specialized, multiple functionally zones. Finally, suburbs are crisscrossed by expressways and arterials causing the formation of super blocks, each with its own lower-order street network (Southworth and Ben-Joseph 1995).

These common, land-use features can all be traced back to a near total reliance on the automobile. Lower densities are a natural outcome of enhanced accessibility profiles, which bring growing expanses of residential land within reach of activities urban residents must engage in on a regular basis. The larger the accessible area, the lower the cost of land, and the greater the space households can afford. Land-use specialization is equally related to heavy reliance on the car. For large, monofunctional zones to

178　*Pierre Filion*

exist, residents must be able to travel long distances in different directions to reach each of their regular activities. Only the automobile can respond efficiently to such needs. At the same time, the prevalence of driving makes it necessary to shield housing from the noise and hazards of traffic; hence the nestling of residential areas within super blocks.

The leveling of accessibility gradients brought on by generalized automobile use yields multiple sites with good expressway and arterial accessibility, in contrast with the single, public transit–induced downtown accessibility peak defining the previous centralized urban model. It is this flattened accessibility pattern that accounts for the dispersion of retailing, employment, and institutions. Such conditions are inimical to centralization. Were an important critical mass of activities to take shape in one of the points of good automobile accessibility, land prices would escalate therein. Activities would then be encouraged to seek another among the numerous locations offering comparable accessibility at a lower cost. There is a further car-related impediment to centralization in suburban areas. Considerable space is required for parking purposes. With so much of the surface of suburban locales given to the car, it is impossible for them to achieve the pedestrian-based interfunctional synergy that contributes to the appeal, and high land values, of successful downtown locations. Finally, as the dispersed suburb provides each activity with a range of equally accessible sites, there is necessarily some randomness in the assignment of land uses to different zones (Dear and Flusty 2002). This is especially the case because most suburban land uses can be placed side by side thanks to the segmenting effects of arterials and the abundant availability in dispersed suburbs of buffer space. Therefore, not only can the dispersed suburb, with its large monofunctional zones, be berated for its lack of fine-grained planning, but the arbitrariness of its zonal assignments makes it vulnerable to criticisms that it is the product of lazy planning.

Although fundamental characteristics, such as the enduring discipline imposed on suburban development by the combined effects of the super grid and near universal automobile reliance, have defined dispersed suburbanism since its postwar emanation, the stages of its evolution over the past seventy years have also left their mark on the model. In the early postwar years, suburbs took the form of a lower density extension of the grid pattern of the then-urbanized area. Yet, they already registered higher car reliance, and land uses, especially retail, were quickly adapted to the automobile, as exemplified by the 1950s car-dominated retail strips. For the reasons covered in the previous section, the North American suburb rapidly acquired its own morphology. If in their early years suburbs were predominantly the domain of the middle class, they diversified socially as they matured. They also became more complex urban forms as they came to accommodate all functions associated with urban living, leading to a widening range of densities (Kruse and Sugrue 2006; Lee, Gook Seo, and Webster 2006; Lucy and Phillips 2000, 2006; Phelps and Wood 2011). But suburban density peaks, such as those encountered in edge cities, remain far lower than those registered in traditional downtowns (Garreau 1991).

Differences in the manifestations of dispersed suburbanism also relate to variations in the extent to which suburbs are planned. One extremity of the spectrum is occupied by the *laissez-faire* suburb where, in the absence of strong regulations, it is automobile accessibility, the need to accommodate the car, and the attractive and repulsive effects of large traffic flows on different functions that determine suburban form. Although land-use specialization prevails within this type of development, it is more tolerant of exceptions than more regulated suburban patterns. Despite its generally orderly residential subdivisions, the laissez-faire suburb is mostly symbolized by the muddled strip, where virtually all types of activities stand cheek by jowl without apparent logic. Moreover, there is no attempt in these types of suburbs to organize retailing according to predetermined catchment areas—from the neighborhood to the regional scale. The different retail formats are free to locate where they choose, provided they do not infringe the loose zoning regulations of the *laissez-faire* suburb.

At the other end of the spectrum are master-planned communities, which are organized around a planning concept and whose development is tightly ordered by a single firm or a precise municipal plan (Checkoway 1980). Postwar, master-planned suburbs were inspired by Radburn, New Jersey, which was planned as a complete community but, due to the Great Depression, was only partially built. Radburn introduced the concept of pathway systems that separated pedestrian movements from motor traffic. Such pathways became a hallmark of the residential areas of subsequent master-planned communities (and often of non-master-planned suburbs as well). Radburn was followed by the Levittowns and many other such communities, including Reston, Virginia; Columbia, Maryland; and The Woodlands, Texas. In Canada, the Toronto metropolitan region features four such communities: Don Mills, Bramalea, Meadowvale, and Erin Mills (Sewell 2009). Note that master-planned communities represent an infinitesimally small proportion of North American suburban developments.[2] Most suburbs fall between the *laissez-faire* and master-planned extremes on the planning spectrum (Harris 2004).

Master-planned developments are distinguished from other suburban layouts by their strict zoning and rules guiding retail and service distribution. The size and location of retailing and services are defined in a hierarchical manner, whereby local retailing and services are placed in neighborhoods, and larger concentrations occupy more central locations. Especially in their more recent emanations, master-planned communities present an abundance of green space, much of it in the form of preserved vegetation. Despite obvious land-use distinctions, master-planned communities share with other variants of dispersed suburbs a heavy reliance on the car. Accordingly, their planning must conform to automobile-defined accessibility patterns and the need to accommodate cars. It follows that if the appearance of master

180　*Pierre Filion*

planned communities is distinctive, their structure and dynamics are not all that different from those of more run-of-the-mill dispersed suburbs.

Suburban development has been the object of two recent innovations. Since the early 1980s more than six hundred projects, most of them in suburban areas, have been planned according to New Urbanism principles. These principles call for higher density of use, a pleasant walking environment, the appropriation of design elements from pre–World War II towns or neighborhoods, a return to the grid, and efforts at deemphasizing the presence, if not the use, of the car (Duany, Plater-Zyberk, and Speck 2000; Talen 2000). In some instances, as with Celebration, Florida, entire communities have been planned according to these principles, whereas in others New Urbanism developments occupy one or more superblocks within otherwise conventional suburban layouts. The Toronto Cornell and Oak Park neighborhoods represent examples of New Urbanism enclaves within conventional suburbs (Grant and Bohdanow 2008).

The historical design themes of New Urbanism do not translate into distinct behavioral patterns on the part of their residents. They are just as dependent on the automobile as are other suburbanites. Attempts to create a retail main street configuration in New Urbanism neighborhoods have failed (with the exception of rare cases like Celebration, where these streets are heavily patronized by tourists) because residents typically use their cars to access large-format retailing (Grant and Perrott 2011). From this perspective, as master-planned communities, New Urbanism developments can be seen as a form of suburban area with a unique design, but undifferentiated dynamics.

Taking a different tangent than New Urbanism, there is presently a tendency in suburban areas to concentrate on the preservation of natural areas—creeks and their riparian zones, wetlands in general, woods, and other natural features. Such a tendency mirrors the influence of the environmental movement and of the principles advanced by the Landscape Urbanism school of thought. Landscape Urbanism perceives open spaces as the primary structuring elements of cities and, drawing from the work of Ian McHargh, promotes the organization of urban development around natural features (Hough 2004; McHarg 1969; Waldheim 2006). Unlike New Urbanism, which aspires to reduce dependence on the car, Landscape Urbanism takes advantage of automobile accessibility in its efforts to protect large expanses of green space. Doing so is indeed easier in dispersed suburban environments than within public transit–oriented compact areas, where land is at a premium.

CRITIQUES OF THE DISPERSED SUBURBAN MODEL

From the 1970s onwards, widening cracks began to show in the alignment of factors favorable to the dispersed suburb. The postwar period of

Creation and Perpetuation   181

sustained economic prosperity faltered with a succession of deep recessions from 1973–1974 onwards. The joint effects of unsteady economic performance, growing global competition resulting in massive outsourcing, and an ideological shift from Keynesianism to neoliberalism, shattered the prior harmony between the dispersed suburb and economic tendencies. With the shift from demand- to supply-side economics, brought on by the rise of neoliberalism and globalization, the suburb as an engine of consumption no longer resonated with economic policy priorities (Clarke 1988). An immediate consequence was the difficulty in funding the demanding infrastructure requirements of low-density, car-oriented development (Burchell et al. 2005). The resulting lag between highway provisioning and rising vehicle kilometers generated by ongoing suburban development, along with growing workforce participation rates and longer distances necessary to reach activities, was responsible for deteriorating traffic congestion and, therefore, more time spent travelling (Cervero 1986; Downs 2004). There was thus for households a worsening time penalty associated with the choice of a home in the suburbs, where the cost of land is generally lower than in more central parts.

One reason for the congruence between the dispersed suburb and demand-side economics was that the ample space availability provided by the suburbs not only made it possible to accumulate large amounts of goods, but encouraged this from of consumption. However, as the balance shifts towards the consumption of services, which require time rather than space, the abundance of space in the suburbs is no longer as much of an asset. These circumstances and the income polarization resulting from economic globalization and neoliberal policies have caused a reshuffling of the social ecology of the suburb (Daniels and Bryson 2002). It is easy to understand why, now that they account for most of the population of metropolitan regions, suburbs can no longer retain their middle-class composition as society-wide income distribution increasingly takes an hourglass shape. Sectors that enjoy the appeal of newness and are advantaged in terms of accessibility by good connections to downtown areas and/or nearby employment, maintain their middle- or high-income status. Meanwhile, suburban sectors that are older and poorly accessible increasingly host low-income households (Bunting, Walks, and Filion 2004; Hulchanski 2010).

The modification in the rapport between time and space was echoed in changes of preference regarding residential location. From the 1970s onwards, a growing segment of well-educated, middle-class individuals, a social category that would have previously readily opted for suburban living, chose to reside in the inner city. A taste for the cultural and recreational activities present in the inner city, as well as its diversity and animated streets, played a role in the choice of these gentrifiers (Lees, Slater, and Wyly 2008; Ley 1996; Zukin 1982). So did proximity to the downtown concentration of professional employment. A side effect of gentrification has been the settlement in older suburbs of low-income households that previously inhabited the inner city.

182   *Pierre Filion*

Changing values not only affected residential locations. They also altered the perception of suburbs. With the rise of environmentalism, the suburb and its reliance on the automobile were seen as a foremost source of environmental injury. The scope of environmental concerns expanded from a focus on local impacts of dispersed suburbanization, notably air and water pollution, along with the loss of rural and natural land, to an understanding of its global consequences, especially regarding the accumulation of greenhouse gases (Crenson 1971; Krooth 2009; Newman, Beatley, and Boyer 2009; Rees 2008). The influence of environmental arguments was felt in requests for a containment of urban sprawl (read dispersed suburbanization), the search for alternative development models, and the greening of the suburb promoted by Landscape Urbanism.

Another source of discontent towards dispersed suburbanization came from having to cope with problems emanating from its dynamics. Early planning proposals did not fully foresee the urban consequences of universal reliance on the car. We have seen that many central-city and downtown interests were misguided when requesting the construction of urban expressways to maintain centralized economic activity. Another lesson learned over time has been that as metropolitan regions expand, dispersed suburbanization is the source of an ever-growing number of automobile journeys, which tend to become longer (Boarnet and Crane 2001). Providing additional arterial and expressway capacity results in further outward growth and more per-capita space consumption, which, in turn, generate more car transportation (Noland 2000). Hence the popularity among opponents of new highway investments of the saying "We can't build ourselves out of congestion."

A further issue with dispersed suburbanism is its unsuitability to nonautomobile forms of transportation due to its low density and scattering of origins and destinations. Although the cost of land is lower in suburbs, especially towards the edge of urbanized areas and in older suburbs, combined expenses of housing and full automobile reliance are high, a source of financial stress for low-income households. It is especially difficult for individuals without cars to access activities present in the dispersed suburb (Deka 2004; Tomer et al. 2011). The suburban form and dynamics have also been held responsible for sedentary lifestyles and their adverse health effects (Frank, Engelke, and Schmid 2003; Frumkin, Frank, and Jackson 2004). Finally, some studies have linked long journeys and the clustering of activities in the home in the electronic age to anomie and lagging civic engagement in dispersed suburbs (Putman 2000).

In spite of these criticisms, the dispersed suburb remains by far the dominant form of urban development across North America (Flint 2006). It is important to note, however, that some core areas, such as those of Toronto, Chicago, and Vancouver, have experienced massive residential growth over the last decades (Birch 2009). The next section will address more fully the mechanisms responsible for the persistence of suburban dispersion, but two factors related to the present discussion are responsible for the ongoing spread of the dispersed suburban model.

First, until recently, the transformative impact of grievances about dispersed suburbanism was much reduced by the absence of a substitute development model. Second, when such a model took shape, it encountered obstacles to its implementation. Over the last two decades or so, an alternative model merging recentralization in downtowns, nodes, and corridors with the creation of high-quality public transit connections has achieved wide currency within planning circles. Indeed, a study of 331 metropolitan-scale plans in the 58 North American regions with population in excess of one million has revealed that virtually all of these regions have produced plans adhering to this model, albeit to different extents (Filion and Kramer 2012). The recentralization model is in direct opposition to the defining characteristics of dispersion. To counter the land-use specialization, scattering of activities, low density, and automobile dependence of the dispersed suburb, it proposes high-density multifunctional centers and corridors, as well as significant increases in reliance on public transit, walking, and cycling. Recentralization draws from the transit-oriented-development (TOD) perspective (Dittmar and Ohland 2004). But instead of limiting interventions to the surroundings of public transit stations, as is the case with most TOD initiatives, it aspires to redefine the way cities and suburbs develop. Presently, a wide-scale implementation of this alternative model is impeded by insufficient public knowledge of, and thus interest in, the model, in stark contrast with the broad public support that surrounded the adoption of the dispersed suburb in the postwar years. Moreover, as we will see, there are also daunting logistic problems confronting attempts at changing the form and dynamics of an urban model that has shaped North American cities for seventy years.

PATH DEPENDENCIES AND DISPERSED SUBURBANISM

The persistence of the dispersed suburb suggests the existence of path dependencies. The path-dependence approach addresses the disproportional influence some decisions enjoy over time. This perspective is concerned with why certain decisions leave a long-lasting trail of effects, whereas the consequences of other decisions do not extent beyond the present. The approach also explores circumstances where effects outlive conditions that motivated decisions. It points to the existence of different types of factors capable of perpetuating such influence. These include positive-feedback mechanisms, increasing returns, and self-reinforcement. Essentially, these factors refer to the rewards associated with the success of certain decisions, which encourage a continuation of the actions they set in motion. Additional instruments extending the effects of decisions include institutions and deterministic chains of events, where one decision leads to

184 *Pierre Filion*

a succession of events whose outcome is consistent with the purpose of the original decision (Pierson 2000).

To achieve its full explanatory potential, the path-dependence perspective must identify perpetuation mechanisms specific to objects of study under consideration. It needs to expose how these mechanisms operate in a path-dependent fashion. In the present case, it will explain the durability of dispersed suburbanism and difficulties in modifying this form of development (see Atkinson and Oleson 1996).

One of the perpetuation mechanisms at work here is the succession of macroscale decisions, depicted in Figure 11.1, creating a context for subsequent microscale decisions, which, in turn, become macroscale decisions for other microscale decisions by setting their trajectory. A fitting metaphor is that of Russian dolls, which are at once content and container. In this system, macroscale decisions perpetuate themselves through microscale decisions, and the more upstream macroscale decisions are in the sequence, the greater is their influence on dispersed suburbanization. The contexts created by macroscale decisions become vehicles for path-dependence effects. Launching the sequence were contexts set by Keynesian economic policies, which encouraged the adoption of programs supporting massive highway investments and the purchase of new single-family homes. Rapid suburban development and automobile accessibility patterns ensuing from these decisions then set the stage for forms of land-use planning and private development formulas that are adapted to car-defined accessibility patterns. These regulations and formulas, along with car accessibility potentials, then shaped the major decisions taken by households (e.g., location of the home and of the place of work). And these macroscale consumer decisions determined choices pertaining to the myriad of household behaviors taking place in the dispersed suburb.

Collectively, these decisions have fostered the piecing together and spread of dispersed suburbanism. But this model and its ongoing proliferation have outlived some of the conditions that prevailed in the sequence of macro-micro decisions. This is the case of the Keynesian policy environment and the strong performance of the economy, which prevailed over the postwar decades. A consequence has been the loss of momentum of highway investment in the subsequent neoliberal climate and slow-growth economy.

Attention now turns to path-dependence mechanisms assuring the persistence and ongoing spread of the dispersed suburb model. As will become apparent, although the first two boxes of the Figure 11.1 sequence have lost much of their explanatory value in present societal circumstances, the other ones maintain their role as factors perpetuating suburban dispersion. At the core of the enduring nature of dispersed suburbanism is the relation between transportation and land use. These two aspects of the dispersed suburb are tightly intertwined, and the difficulty of altering one without severely disrupting the other accounts largely for the absence of transformations affecting essential features of this model over its seventy-year existence. The main issue facing transformative efforts targeting the dispersed

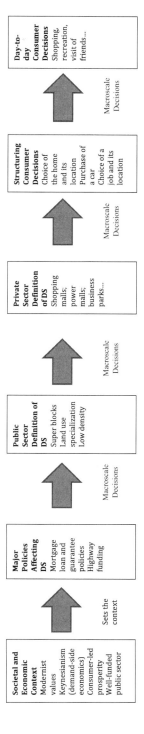

Figure 11.1 Circumstances and decisions associated with dispersed suburbanism (DS)

186 *Pierre Filion*

suburb, transportation, land-use interrelation is how and where to launch a strategy aimed at modifying this dynamic. For example, in the dispersed suburb, attempts at reducing surface parking in order to improve walkability will raise objections from drivers and nearby merchants. The presence of a high-quality public transit service, such as provided by a light rail or bus rapid-transit system, could attenuate car reliance and, thereby, the need for parking spaces. But to be viable in a dispersed suburban environment, such a system would need, as a prerequisite, a profound modification of land-use patterns so as to redistribute origins and destinations in a public transit–conducive fashion. Similar problems would ensue from important land-use changes. A massive rise in the density of a sector in a dispersed suburb will overload arterials and thus lend credence to NIMBY ("Not In My Back Yard") sentiments voiced against intensification (Inhaber 1998; Schively 2007). As in the prior example, such a transformation would need to be coordinated with improved public transit and a large-scale attendant reorganization of land use so as to make it conducive to public transit upgrading. Only seldom would such extensive chains of interventions be within the capacity of planning agencies.

One of the reasons for difficulties in transforming the land-use patterns of the dispersed suburb is that its land economics, derived from automobile-defined accessibility potentials, dictate possible urban forms. This is why a departure from prevailing, car-oriented morphologies requires major planning interventions capable of altering land value distributions. However, the present neoliberal policy context and depleted public-sector coffers do not lend themselves to the deployment of such ambitious measures (Filion and Kramer 2011; Hackworth 2006).

The endurance of the dispersed suburb model is also a function of interests vested in this urban form and its dynamics. For example, the suburb is the main, if not the only, market for the numerous developers who specialize in low-density projects. Likewise, property owners, who are concerned about the value of their home and/or are attached to their neighborhood, will often resist attempts at moving away from the dispersed suburbanism model. Many interests vested in this model owe their existence to the mutual expectations to which it gives shape. An illustration of these expectations is the bond between home purchasers, who know what to expect from a typical home in a suburban subdivision, and developers, who are aware of, and cater to, these expectations.

Not only are many suburban residents attached to aspects of the dispersed model, usually their home and neighborhood, but as they spend much of their life in dispersed environments they see this model as the norm regarding urban development. Dispersed suburbs influence the worldviews and political alignments of their residents (Walks 2006). It is then difficult for these suburbanites to acknowledge why this model should be modified or replaced. Attempts at achieving such changes can trigger movements, with the potential to ignite "culture wars," pitting residents, along with local businesspeople and politicians, against planners, external developers, and senior-level politicians. It is easy to depict these clashes as confronting average local residents against outside elites. Such a conflict erupted during the 2010 city of Toronto mayoral electoral campaign. Candidate Rob Ford was successful in tapping into a feeling of alienation on the part of residents of dispersed portions of the city. They were indeed resentful of plans aiming at transforming their suburban environment, with a particular focus on its transportation system. Plans included proposals for an extensive light rail–transit network running on rights-of-way occupying the central lanes of a number of suburban arterials. Candidate Ford captured the sentiments of many suburban residents when he lamented the obstruction to car circulation (which he perceived as part of a "war on the car") that these new systems would cause by removing existing lanes for automobile circulation and seriously limiting on-street parking and left-hand turns. He blamed proposals for such systems on "downtown elites." He handedly won the election with a large majority in all suburban districts (Filion 2011).

The main lesson to come out of this chapter is that path dependencies perpetuating dispersed suburbanism take many forms: economic policy, planning regulations, values and preferences, and vested interests. But all path dependencies bear the mark of the role generalized car use plays in shaping the morphology and dynamics that define dispersed suburbanism. In this sense, path dependencies identified here relate in large part to the durable dimensions of the urban phenomenon: its built environment and long-lasting patterns of behavior therein.

FUTURE SCENARIOS

To explore possible futures of dispersed suburbanism in light of the above discussion of path dependencies, the chapter proposes three contrasting scenarios. The first is a business-as-usual scenario whereby dispersed suburbs endure unaltered, and remain by far the preponderant form of urban development in North America. As a result, the proportion of urban residents living and carrying out their activities in this type of environment continues to increase over time.

In this scenario, shortcomings of this form of development accumulate. We can anticipate the presence of growing enclaves of poverty, the consequences of income polarization, and the settlement of large contingents of economic refugees from inner-city gentrification. Meanwhile, even if highway investments keep pace with development, with the ongoing expansion of the dispersed realm, journeys would inevitably become longer and consume more time. But with lagging highway expansion, and in most cases the absence of public-transit alternatives, traffic congestion is worsening with deleterious economic and quality-of-life downsides. In these circumstances, ever more expansive dispersed environments will make it difficult

188 *Pierre Filion*

for large metropolitan regions to function as one integrated market. For example, labor markets, interfirm linkages, retailing, and entertainment will operate increasingly at a submetropolitan scale. The main advantage of living in a large metropolitan region—potential access to a wide pool of opportunities—will therefore be lost. Economic possibilities, life chances, and cultural and recreational options will be scarcer than they could have been in a more integrated urban area. Finally, there is the plethora of environmental consequences brought on by dispersed suburbanism. Some of these can be mitigated through technological advancements and policy responses. For example, in the 1970s the fitting of catalytic converters on the exhaust systems of vehicles improved air quality substantially. In the future, reduced reliance on oil may further diminish air pollution. In a similar vein, tighter controls on development close to water and reliance on permeable surfaces will help protect water quality.

These environmental improvements will, however, be countered to some degree by the extension of the dispersed realm. The impacts of the dispersed suburb on the environment may be lessened, but there will be more of this type of development. One consequence of a further expansion of the dispersed realm will be an ongoing loss of rural and natural land and growing difficulties reaching the countryside.

But in this scenario, the powerful path dependencies discussed above maintain the dispersed suburbanism model in place despite these ill effects. Yet no path dependence is eternal. They are all eventually challenged by an exhaustion of their mechanisms, the rise of new path dependencies, or profound changes in the societal context in which they operate. Among possible disruptive forces looming on the horizon are a rise in public interest in other urban forms, as perhaps presaged by the present vogue of core and inner-city living in some metropolitan regions, and profound economic changes making the expenses associated with the dispersed suburban model unaffordable for a growing number of households, as well as for governments.

The second scenario assumes that dispersed suburbs are transformed along the lines of the recentralization model advanced within the planning community. Land-use and transportation patterns in suburbs are accordingly deeply modified. Henceforth, activities congregate in mixed-use centers and corridors, which are public-transit and pedestrian-friendly. Centers and corridors are aligned on public-transit spines, where service is rapid, frequent, and comfortable.

It is easy to identify obstacles to the implementation of such an alternative vision. There are many explanations for the gap between the enthusiasm of plans for the recentralization model and its relative absence on the ground (Downs 2005). Indeed, all the path dependencies responsible for the endurance of dispersed suburbanism also obstruct the emergence of alternative forms of development.

Its broad aspirations are a problem confronting recentralization. Unlike other transformative models, notably New Urbanism and TOD, which can exist in a sea of dispersion, the recentralization model seeks to alter the morphology and dynamics of metropolitan regions. Such a goal requires the presence of many centers and corridors interconnected by high-quality, public-transit services. Still, this model can exist side-by-side with dispersed suburbanism, in a fashion that would minimize zones of conflicts between the two formulas. This accommodation would lessen the effects of some of the obstacles to recentralization stemming from the path dependencies perpetuating dispersed suburbanism. More lifestyle options in areas where a walking and public-transit realm is juxtaposed with a car-oriented realm could be seen as an advantage of such a hybrid pattern (Filion 2000). There remains one lingering implementation difficulty, however. The present economic and political climate is not supportive of the important expenditures required to build and operate the public-transit networks, which are a prerequisite for recentralization.

Even in the best of circumstances, where recentralization would take place at a wide scale and appeal to residents, consumers, and businesses, this model could accentuate social inequity in the suburb. The appeal of lively multifunctional environments, which are hospitable to pedestrians and well served by public transit, could trigger gentrification. In consequence, low-income suburban households, which are most dependent on walking and public transit, would be denied access to sectors with superior transit services and where activities can be reached on foot.

The last scenario is about the possible impact of new technologies. One cannot escape noticing the contrast between deep transformations of many fields of human activity by technological innovation, and the relative inertia that characterizes the dispersed suburbanism model and overall urban development over the last seventy years. What if a wave of technological advancement, equivalent to the one that has revolutionized the information sector, were to alter suburban transportation? It is admittedly difficult to anticipate what future innovation would affect cities and how it would transform urban form and dynamics (Atkinson 2007). Despite much hype over past decades, the impact of rapid information technology advancements on cities has been relatively modest (Audirac 2005; Janelle 2004; Sohn, Tschangho and Hewings 2005). Although information technology has transformed work, social relations, and entertainment, it has had limited impact on the planning and building of cities and transportation systems. Yet, this may be about to change if the most radical urban transportation innovation presently on the horizon, the driverless Google car, were to be widely adopted. The Google car could function as a taxi, but would be far more convenient and much cheaper to use. For many, it could replace car ownership. And shorter reaction times of computerized vehicles relative to human-driven vehicles would make it possible to increase considerably the capacity of existing roads and highways. Such a solution would allow a perpetuation of dispersed suburbanism while abating some its most egregious sequels: air pollution (assuming Google cars would be electric),

190   *Pierre Filion*

transportation cost, and traffic congestion. If in high-density and central-ized areas, public transit would maintain an advantage over Google cars by virtue of reduced space requirement per passenger, these cars would enjoy considerable speed, frequency, flexibility, comfort, and possibly cost benefits over public transit in dispersed suburban sectors.

CONCLUSION

The chapter examined how a form of urban development, which marked a radical departure from the prior evolution of cites, came into being and then proliferated across North America. Explanations concentrated on the mutual reinforcement of automobile reliance and a dispersed morphology. First, a form of development that gives priority to the accommodation of the car was pieced together, and second, once in place, this pattern made the automobile indispensable and thus assured ever-growing reliance on this mode, as well as a further entrenchment of car-oriented development. The interpretive framework highlighted macroscale decisions, whose effects are perpetuated by long trails of microscale decisions. In the perspective devel-oped here, convergence between these different orders of decisions stems from the influence the interweaving between land-use configurations and near total reliance on the car exerts on them. The chapter has thus offered an interpretation that emphasizes the path dependencies linked to the land use–transportation interrelations of dispersed suburbanism.

NOTES

1. The chapter could have also included suburban developments in the northern part of Mexico, which largely adhere to the dispersed pattern discussed here.
2. Ironically, perhaps the fullest example of a highly planned, dispersed, car-oriented urban form is in the U.K.—the Milton Keynes new town.

WORKS CITED

Allan, Graham, and Graham Crow (eds.). *Home and Family: Creating the Domestic Sphere*. Basingstoke, Macmillan, 1989.
Atkinson, Adrian. "Cities after Oil: Sustainable Development and Energy Futures." *City* 11 (2007), p. 201–213.
Atkinson, Glen, and Ted Oleson. "Urban Sprawl as a Path Dependent Process." *Journal of Economic Issues* 30 (1996), p. 609–615.
Audirac, Ivonne. "Information Technology and Urban Form: Challenges to Smart Growth." *International Regional Science Review* 28 (2005), p. 119–145.
Boarnet, Marlon G., and Randall Crane. *Travel by Design: The Influence of Urban Form on Travel*. Oxford, Oxford University Press, 2001.
Bottles, Scott. *Los Angeles and the Automobile: The Making of a Modern City*. Berkeley, University of California Press, 1987.

Birch, Eugenie L. "Downtown in the 'New American City.'" *Annals of the American Academy of Political and Social Science* 626 (2009), p. 134–153.

Brown, Jeffrey R., Eric A. Morris, and Brian D. Taylor. "Planning for Cars in Cities: Planners, Engineers, and Freeways in the 20th Century." *Journal of the American Planning Association* 75 (2009), p. 161–178.

Bunting, Trudi, R. Alan Walks, and Pierre Filion. "The Uneven Geography of Housing Affordability Stress in Canadian Metropolitan Areas." *Housing Studies* 19 (2004), p. 361–394.

Burchell, Robert W., Anthony Downs, Barbara McCann, and Sahan Mukherj. *Sprawl Costs: Economic Impacts of Unchecked Development.* Washington DC, Island Press, 2005.

Cervero, Robert. *Suburban Gridlock.* New Brunswick NJ, Center for Urban Policy Research, 1986.

Clarke, Simon. *Keynesianism, Monetarism, and the Crisis of the State.* Aldershot, Hants, Edward Elgar, 1988.

Checkoway, Barry. "Large Builders, Federal Housing Programs, and Postwar Suburbanization." *International Journal of Urban and Regional Research* 4 (1980), p. 21–45.

Crenson, Matthew A. *The Un-politics of Air Pollution: A Study of Non-decision-making in the Cities.* Baltimore, Johns Hopkins University Press, 1971.

Daniels, Peter N., and John R. Bryson. "Manufacturing Services and Servicing Manufacturing: Knowledge-based Cities and Changing Forms of Production." *Urban Studies* 39 (2002), p. 977–991.

Dear, Michael J., and Steven Flusty. "Los Angeles as Postmodern Urbanism." In: Michael J. Dear and J. Dallas Dishman (eds.), *From Chicago to L.A.: Making Sense of Urban Theory.* Thousand Oaks CA, Sage, 2002, p. 55–84.

Deka, Devajyoti. "Social and Environmental Justice Issues in Urban Transportation." In: Susan Hanson and Genevieve Giuliano (eds.), *The Geography of Urban Transportation* (3rd ed). New York, The Guilford Press, 2004, p. 332–355.

Dittmar, Hank, and Gloria Ohland, eds. *The New Transit Town: Best Practices in Transit-Oriented-Development.* Washington DC, Island Press, 2004.

Downs, Anthony. *Still Stuck in Traffic: Coping with Peak-Hour Traffic Congestion.* Washington DC, Brookings Institution Press, 2004.

———. "Smart Growth: Why We Discuss It More than We Do It." *Journal of the American Planning Association* 71 (2005), p. 367–378.

Duany, Andres, Elizabeth Plater-Zyberk, and Jeff Speck. *Suburban Nation: The Rise of Sprawl and the Decline of the American Dream.* New York, North Point Press, 2000.

Filion, Pierre. "Balancing Concentration and Dispersion? Public Policy and Urban Structure in Toronto." *Environment and Planning C, Government and Policy* 18 (2000), p. 163–189.

Filion, Pierre. "Toronto's Tea Party: Right-wing Populism and Planning Agendas." *Planning Theory and Practice* 12 (2011), p. 464–469.

Filion, Pierre, Trudi Bunting, and Keith Warriner. "The Entrenchment of Urban Dispersion: Residential Location Patterns and Preferences in the Dispersed City." *Urban Studies* 36 (1999), p. 1317–1347.

Filion, Pierre, and Anna Kramer. "Metropolitan-scale Planning in Neo-liberal Times: Financial and Political Obstacles to Urban Form Transition." *Space and Polity* 15 (2011), p. 197–212.

———. "Transformative Metropolitan Development Models in Large Canadian Urban Areas: The Predominance of Nodes." *Urban Studies* 49 (2012), p. 2237–2264.

Flint, Anthony. *This Land: The Battle over Sprawl and the Future of America.* Baltimore, Johns Hopkins University Press, 2006.

192   Pierre Filion

Frank, Lawrence D., Peter O. Engelke, and Thomas L. Schmid. *Health and Community Design: The Impact of the Built Environment on Physical Activity*. Washington DC, Island Press, 2003.

Frumkin, Howard, Lawrence D. Frank, and Richard Jackson. *The Public Health Impacts of Sprawl*. Washington DC, Island Press, 2004.

Garreau, Joel. *Edge City: Life on New Frontier*. New York, Doubleday, 1991.

Grant, Jill L., and Stephanie Bohdanow. "New Urbanism Developments in Canada: A Survey." *Journal of Urbanism* 1 (2008), p. 109–127.

Grant, Jill L., and Katherine Perrott. "Where Is the Café? The Challenge of Making Retail Uses Viable in Mixed Use Suburban Developments." *Urban Studies* 48 (2011), p. 177–195.

Hackworth, Jason. *The Neoliberal City: Governance, Ideology, and Development in American Urbanism*. Ithaca NY, Cornell University Press, 2006.

Halberstam, David. *The Fifties*. New York, Random House, 1993.

Hardwick, M. Jeffrey. *Mall Maker: Victor Gruen, Architect of an American Dream*. Philadelphia, University of Pennsylvania Press, 2004.

Harris, Richard. *Creeping Conformity: How Canada Became Suburban, 1900–1960*. Toronto, University of Toronto Press, 2004.

Hayden, Dolores. *Building Suburbia: Green Fields and Urban Growth, 1820–2000*. New York, Pantheon Books, 2003.

———. "Building the American Way: Public Subsidy, Private Space." In: Becky Nocolaides and Andrew Wiese (eds.), *The Suburb Reader*. New York, Routledge, 2006, p. 273–280.

Hough, Michael. *Cities and Natural Processes: A Basis for Sustainability*. London, Routledge, 2004.

Hulchanski, David. *The Three Cities within Toronto: Income Polarization among Toronto's Neighbourhoods*. Toronto, University of Toronto, Cities Centre Press, 2010.

Inhaber, Herbert. *Slaying the NIMBY Dragon*. New Brunswick NJ, Transaction, 1998.

Jacobs, Jane. *The Death and Life of Great American Cities*. New York, Random House, 1961.

Janelle, Donald G. "Impact of Information Technologies." In: Susan Hanson and Genevieve Giuliano (eds.), *The Geography of Urban Transportation*. New York, Guilford, 2004, p. 86–114.

Jones, David W. *Mass Motorization + Mass Transit: An American History and Policy Analysis*. Bloomington, Indiana University Press, 2008.

Jones, Ken, and Michael Doucet. "Big-box Retailing and the Urban Retail Structure: The Case of the Toronto Area." *Journal of Retailing and Consumer Services* 7 (2000), p. 233–47.

Krooth, Richard. *Gaia and the Fate of Midas: Wrenching Planet Earth*. Lanham MD, University Press of America, 2009.

Kruse, Kevin M., and Thomas J. Sugrue, eds. *The New Suburban History*. Chicago IL, University of Chicago Press, 2006.

Lang, Robert E. *Edgeless Cities: Exploring the Elusive Metropolis*. Washington DC, Brookings Institution Press, 2003.

Lee, Shin, Jong Gook Seo, and Chris Webster. "The Decentralising Metropolis: Economic Diversity and Commuting in the US suburbs." *Urban Studies* 43 (2006), p. 2525–2549.

Lees, Loretta, Tom Slater, and Elvin K. Wyly. *Gentrification*. New York, Routledge, 2008.

Ley, David. *The New Middle Class and the Remaking of the Central City*. Oxford, Oxford University Press, 1996.

Lorch, Brian. "Auto-Dependent Induced Shopping: Exploring the Relationship between Power Centre Morphology and Consumer Spatial Behaviour." *Canadian Journal of Urban Research* 14 (2005), p. 364–383.

Lucy, William, and David L. Phillips. *Confronting Suburban Decline: Strategic Planning for Metropolitan Renewal*. Washington DC, Island Press, 2000.

———. *Tomorrow's Cities, Tomorrow's Suburbs*. Chicago, IL, American Planning Association, 2006.

Marglin, Stephen A., and Julian B. Schor. *The Golden Age of Capitalism: Reinterpreting the Postwar Experience*. Oxford, Oxford University Press, 1990.

Marshall, Alex. *How Cities Work: Suburbs, Sprawl, and the Roads Not Taken*. Austin, University of Texas Press, 2000.

McHarg, Ian L. *Design with Nature*. New York, John Wiley and Sons, 1969.

Miron, John. *Housing in Postwar Canada: Demographic Change, Household Formation and Housing Markets*. Montreal and Kingston, McGill-Queen's University Press, 1988.

Miron, John, ed. *House, Homes, and Community: Progress in Housing Canadians, 1945–1986*. Montreal and Kingston, McGill-Queen's University Press, 1993.

Moulaert, Frank, Erik Swyngedouw, and Patricia Wilson. "Spatial Responses to Fordist and post-Fordist Accumulation and Regulation." *Papers of the Regional Science Association* 64 (1988), p. 11–23.

Muller, Peter O. "Transportation and Urban Form: Stages in the Spatial Evolution of the American Metropolis." In: Susan Hanson and Genevieve Guiliano (eds.), *The Geography of Urban Transportation*. New York, Guilford, 2004, p. 59–85.

Mumford, Lewis. *The City in History: Its Origins, Its Transformations, Its Prospects*. New York, Harcourt, Brace and World, 1961.

Newman, Peter, Timothy Beatley, and Heather Boyer. *Resilient Cities: Responding to Peak Oil and Climate Change*. Washington DC, Island Press, 2009.

Noland, Robert B. "Relationship between Highway Capacity and Induced Vehicle Travel." *Transportation Research Part A, Policy and Practice* 35 (2000), p. 47–72.

Phelps, Nicholas A., and Andrew Wood. "The New Post-suburban Politics?" *Urban Studies* 48 (2011), p. 2591–2610.

Pierson, Paul. "Increasing Returns, Path Dependence, and the Study of Politics." *American Political Science Review* 94 (2000), p. 251–67.

Putman, Robert D. *Bowling Alone: The Collapse and Revival of American Community*. New York, Simon and Schuster, 2000.

Rees, William E. "Human Nature, Eco-footprints and Environmental Injustice." *Local Environment: The International Journal of Justice and Sustainability* 13 (2008): 685–701.

Rowe, Peter G. *Making a Middle Landscape*. Cambridge MA, MIT Press, 1991.

Rydell, Robert W., and Laura Burd Schiavo. *Designing Tomorrow: America's World's Fairs of the 1930s*. New Haven, Yale University Press, 2010.

Schively, Carissa. "Understanding the NIMBY and LULU Phenomena: Reassessing Our Knowledge Base and Informing Future Research." *Journal of Planning Literature* 21 (2007), p. 255–266.

Sewell, John. *The Shape of the Suburbs: Understanding Toronto's Sprawl*. Toronto, University of Toronto Press, 2009.

Sohn, Jungyul, John K. Tschangho, and Geoffrey D. Hewings. "Information Technology and Urban Spatial Structure: A Comparative Analysis of the Chicago and Seoul Regions." In: Harry W. Richardson and Cang-Hee Bae (eds.), *Globalization and Urban Development*. Berlin, Springer, 2005, p. 273–288.

Southworth, Michael, and Eran Ben-Joseph. "Street Standards and the Shaping of Suburbia." *Journal of the American Planning Association* 61 (1995), p. 65–81.

194 *Pierre Filion*

Talen, Emily. "New Urbanism and the Culture of Criticism." *Urban Geography* 21 (2000), p. 318–341.

Tomer, Adie, Elizabeth Kneebone, Robert Puentes, and Alan Berube. *Missed Opportunity: Transit and Jobs in Metropolitan America*. Washington DC, Brookings Institution (Metropolitan Policy Program), 2011.

Waldheim, Charles, ed. *The Landscape Urbanism Reader*. New York, Princeton Architectural Press, 2006.

Walks, R. Alan. "The Causes of City-Suburban Political Polarization? A Canadian Case Study." *Annals of the Association of American Geographers* 96 (2006), p. 390–414.

Zukin, Sharon. *Loft Living: Culture and Capital in Urban Change*. Baltimore, Johns Hopkins University Press, 1982.

———. *Point of Purchase: How Shopping Changed American Culture*. New York, Routledge, 2005.

12 Transportation Planning as Infrastructural Fix
Regulating Traffic Congestion in the Greater Toronto and Hamilton Area

John Saunders

INTRODUCTION

In many North American cities, the costs and challenges of traffic congestion have come under increasing scrutiny in recent years. Seen as the outcome of automobile-friendly, low-density, urban development, congestion is cast as a symptom of under-regulated expansion, as well as a significant hindrance to economic growth. In the Greater Toronto Area, renewed interest in regulating transportation and urban development is grounded in concerns over the costs of congestion. In this light, congestion serves as an entry point into questions of growth and regulation.

Transportation planning can be seen as a spatial and infrastructural fix—not only to the economic problems attributed to congestion, but also to more ingrained challenges posed by decades of loosely regulated, low-density, urban development. Attributing the loss of billions of dollars from the region's gross domestic product to congestion woes, organizations are seeking greater state intervention in coordinating policy and developing road and transit infrastructure. The condition of traffic congestion, itself linked to both market and policy-driven development for several decades, arises as a catalyst for further intervention and regulation by state and non-state agencies. The resulting shift in southern Ontario has seen the creation of a regional transit authority as one component in a mix of strategies to regulate growth, remediate problems of sprawl, and stabilize economic development.

A FRAMEWORK FOR RECONSIDERING REGIONS, MOBILITY, AND PLANNING

This chapter considers the emergence of transportation planning as a form of regional fix. It examines the prospects for managing urban growth through direct and indirect forms of governance that seek to resolve problems of transportation. The problem of traffic congestion is mobilized as an economic, political, and ecological concern requiring intervention. A closer

196   *John Saunders*

reading, however, opens up congestion for further analysis, namely how interventions to "fix" congestion reflect greater concerns for economic development and political stability through the scope and scale of the region. This analysis contributes to an emerging body of knowledge concerning the ways in which infrastructure intersects with the new politics of scale (Brenner 2004), supporting new assemblages of governance and means for stabilizing accumulation strategies.

This chapter also contributes to research focusing specifically on the regionalization of Canada's largest urban area (the Greater Toronto Area). This work considers a whole range of legislative interventions undertaken in recent years to regulate growth and stabilize development in southwestern Ontario. Transportation planning can be seen to fit within an increasingly complex network of laws, strategies, and plans initiated by public- and private-sector agencies that challenge previous planning efforts. Separately, these reflect very specific forms of regulation (sometimes at a distance, sometimes directly through the state). Taken together, however, they produce an urban region that is manifestly quite different from earlier in the twentieth century.

Faced with a history of automobile-driven development, contemporary actors must address earlier path dependencies while also grappling with a regulatory environment that is nearly always in flux. Competing and conflicting interests among different government agencies, private-sector actors, resident and nongovernmental groups become quite visible in this process. Although congestion at first glance appears to reflect a consensus on the need to act, various interpretations and reactions to this condition reveal deep divisions, tensions, and contradictions. Here, we may consider the irrationality of planning, or rather the ways in which particular forms of rationality submit to institutional or economic power (Flyvbjerg 1998).

With this analytical framework in mind, resolving the problem of congestion in the Greater Toronto Area entails the deployment of mobility as a means of governing. Indeed, it is the very concern for increasing mobility—of goods, people, and capital—that underpins the various interventions to be explored. What follows is a discussion of infrastructural and regional governance, with an emphasis on recent policy changes in Ontario, as well as emerging work on congestion. The emergence of Metrolinx, the provincially appointed transportation authority for the Greater Toronto and Hamilton Area (GTHA), will also be described, along with two major debates concerning regional and local conditions. The chapter will conclude with a discussion of the role of Metrolinx in relation to economic development and regional governance. To do this, the chapter will draw on a range of public and media accounts, decisions, and debates that reflect many of the path dependencies related to automobile-driven development. At the same time, municipal and provincial government policy decisions (and revisions) show a complex and unstable process at work.

INFRASTRUCTURAL FIXES AND THE POLITICS OF SCALE

Regulating congestion can be understood as a form of spatial fix. It mobilizes resources for sustaining the built environment for economic development and introduces prospects for financialization or commoditization of infrastructural networks (through road pricing, public–private partnerships, and other strategies). It is also an infrastructural fix, because it mobilizes state (and other) resources into resolving congestion to reduce economic losses and to stabilize longer-term economic development in a specific component of the built environment: transportation. It is also a regional fix, in that efforts to regulate congestion are territorial, extending beyond city boundaries and across legal jurisdictions.

Harvey (1989) outlines in great depth myriad tensions that arise regarding investment in the built environment as a means of resolving crises and enabling further accumulation of wealth. State investment serves as a means of stabilizing uncertainty and risk, while also providing for new opportunities for accumulation *through* the built environment itself (64). This institutional-infrastructural arrangement, however, has undergone significant rearrangement over the past forty years. The decentralization of the built environment, away from the metropolitan core and towards new sites of investment and development, has spawned a host of interpretative descriptions—"metropolis unbound" (Isin 1996), "postmetropolis" (Soja 2000), "the in-between city" (Sieverts 2003), and "edge" (Garreau 1991) or "edgeless" (Lang 2003) cities. These narratives describe a collapse of urban form, the end of a largely shared experience of western cities from intensive investment in the urban core, towards a fragmented landscape that contains a mix of residential, commercial, and industrial activities. For many, this splintering urbanism (Graham and Marvin 2001) is produced through the reterritorialization of both state and capital, expressed through the collapse of manufacturing in the west and the retreat of the state from redistributive strategies, further rendering planning as a largely deregulated, market-oriented activity, reducing (or redefining) the capacity for state intervention (Harvey 1996).

Infrastructural investment in this context is far more piecemeal, short term, and contingent on a range of demands for efficiency, cost-recovery, and risk minimization (Saunders 2009). The region emerges as a specific scale for marshalling resources and directing urban and economic development, albeit in a much different context that in the last century. Brenner (1998, 2002, 2004), for instance, contrasts early twentieth-century efforts to produce the region as a means of redistributing resources and supporting the development of the metropolis, with contemporary efforts that fall under the label "new regionalism."

Brenner challenges uncritical acceptance and reproduction of new forms of governance and development through the region. Instead of homogeneity and cohesion, he sees a divergent mix of strategies to navigate the

198 John Saunders

uncertainties of the contemporary global economy. These emerge as a regional fix, "a strategic political response to the deepening forms of uneven development and sociospatial polarization that have been induced during the last two decades of neoliberal state restructuring within major US urban regions" (Brenner 2002, 16). These strategies, which may create quasi-public agencies for infrastructural or economic development, claim a common vocabulary under the flag of new regionalism. They grapple with contradictory processes—the retreat (or redirection) of state investment across a broad spectrum of concerns, with the growing problems of market-driven urban development. Coming out of the realities of neoliberalization in Europe (MacLeod 1999; Tewdwr-Jones 2000) and North America (Young and Keil 2010), renewed efforts in governing through the region emphasize specific infrastructure systems (Priemus 2002) or customized network bundles (Graham 2000; Peck 1996) to attract investment and support economic growth.

REGIONAL GOVERNANCE AND INFRASTRUCTURAL DEVELOPMENT IN ONTARIO

In Ontario, the provincial government has enacted legislation and policy that, in effect, constitutes a regional framework for governing the Greater Toronto Area.[1] Faced with increasing infrastructural and ecological pressures from low-density, automobile-drive development, the government has attempted to coordinate growth across a number of municipal boundaries through specific pieces of legislation. The 2005 Places to Grow Act, for instance, designates specific areas for greater residential and commercial density, as well as transportation investment and expansion, requiring municipalities' official plans to conform to provincial goals. Ecological preservation is set out for specific areas in the GTA, establishing a regional green belt (the Green Belt Act of 2005), as well as protection for an important watershed (the Oak Ridges Moraine Conservation Act of 2001). A regional transportation authority was created in 2006 (the Greater Toronto Transportation Authority Act of 2006, subsequently renamed the Metrolinx Act), emphasizing a specific role for transportation in managing growth.

Following the enactment of these laws, a number of analyses have emerged, establishing a critique of the regionalization of governance in southwestern Ontario. Some point out the contradictions entailed with encouraging growth while protecting local and regional ecologies (Wekerle, Sandberg, Gilbert, and Binstock 2007; Wekerle and Abbruzzese 2010), whereas others note pressures to marketize regional and municipal resources (Young and Keil 2005). Analyses of contemporary regional transportation policy highlight the orientation of municipal interests towards continental and global scales—and markets—versus ecological and social justice (Keil and Young 2008; Courtney 2009; Addie 2013; Torrance 2008; Saunders 2011). Aimed at addressing rapid and uneven development in southwestern Ontario, these acts and plans adhere as a form of regional governance—without a single, specific governing body to administer (and interpret) them. Ultimately, debates over transportation planning reflect competing claims to rationality and authority. Congestion, ostensibly a universal condition of urban and suburban everyday life, allows for ways into discussing transportation and regional planning.

TOWARDS A CONSENSUS ON CONGESTION

At first glance, the emerging literature (including a range of scholarly and technical studies, policy analyses, industry briefs, and news reports) reflects a consensus on the growing costs of traffic congestion in North America. A number of accounts point to economic, health, social, and ecological harm posed by the seemingly unending growth of automobile use.

Metrolinx (2008) estimates traffic congestion in the GTHA costs $6 billion annually. This is split between commuters (who bear $3.3 billion) and the region's economy ($2.7 billion) (*Cost*, 13). Similarly, Mekky (2006) posts total congestion costs at $5.5 billion for the GTA in 2006. Transport Canada (2006), however, estimates the total cost to the Canadian economy from urban congestion is between $2.3 billion and $3.7 billion, attributing most of the amount to lost time for drivers and passengers (i).

Individual commuters and transportation-related businesses bear the brunt, but other effects are less immediately tangible, particularly those related to the environment and public health. Metrolinx (2008) posits four major areas of loss associated with traffic congestion: lower economic development (and job losses), costs of delays for commuters, higher vehicle operating costs (from longer and less predictable trips), and environmental costs (*Cost*, 2). Indirect effects on the regional economy include higher costs for business (including transportation and labor costs), which, in 2006, saw a reduction in business revenues of $4.7 billion, and a reduction of 25,962 jobs (21). Lost time is one of the most significant aspects of congestion costs. Transport Canada (2006) argues that time loss accounts for more than 90% of congestion costs, whereas Metrolinx (2007) estimates it accounts for about 67% of commuter costs (and about 38% of all related costs). Although most of these are currently borne by Toronto-based commuters, they will become more evenly shared over the next few decades, as road trips within and among other municipalities increase.

Industry-specific costs are another area of concern. Metrolinx (2008) outlines a litany of costs related to transportation and logistics, including higher fuel, maintenance, and labor expenses; missed deliveries; and the need to maintain higher inventories (*Cost*, 21). The Canadian trucking industry has also identified congestion as a serious concern (British Columbia Trucking Association 2011; Canadian Trucking Alliance 2010). Industry responses

200 John Saunders

have included reducing truck loads and implementing just-in-time inventory strategies, but these increase truck traffic on roadways and lead to higher prices for consumers (Lord 2011). There is also growing concern about traffic congestion in relation to the construction industry (Morsky 2011). Facing rising costs for road maintenance and repair, developers may also face additional charges (Harvey 2011).

For municipalities, unexpected infrastructure costs arise from congestion. The city of Mississauga, for instance, will need to build more fire halls as traffic delays have almost doubled response times, according to Mayor McCallion (Today'sTrucking.Com 2010). These concerns are echoed by the York Region, citing potential delays for fire, police, and emergency services not along major routes, but rather roads affected by "traffic infiltration" (4).

Contemporary discussions on the topic of congestion revolve around political and financial responsibility. These reflect a sense of urgency and frustration, as coordinating a long-term response among different governments (including lower- and upper-tier municipalities, as well as the provincial and federal governments), as well as in conjunction with resident and private-sector interests, has proven difficult. One response, the creation of a regional transportation authority for the Greater Toronto and Hamilton Area, exemplifies this conundrum. Charged with coordinating a long-term response to problems of traffic congestion and management, public transportation, and regional growth, the organization reflects a number of tensions in contemporary planning.

A REGIONAL TRANSPORTATION NETWORK EMERGES

In 2006, the Province of Ontario created a regional transportation body for the Greater Toronto and Hamilton Area. Charged with developing a regional plan to manage transportation, reduce congestion, and integrate public transit networks, the Greater Toronto Transportation Authority (since renamed Metrolinx) was closely tied to other provincial legislation and policy geared towards managing growth and protecting the environment (Province of Ontario 2009). The GTTA was also made responsible for operating GO Transit, a transit agency founded by the provincial ministry of transportation that operates throughout the Greater Toronto Area.

In 2007, the agency formally changed its name to Metrolinx, and announced its regional transportation plan (RTP) the following year, entitled, *The Big Move*. This laid out an interconnected network of existing and future transit systems, emphasizing supporting regional economic development (see Figure 12.1). Much of this will rely on expanding public transit networks, as well as more efficient management of roadways and the promotion of "active" transportation (including cycling and walking infrastructure).[2] The plan would span twenty-five years, with a capital budget of $50 billion.[3]

Infrastructural Fix 201

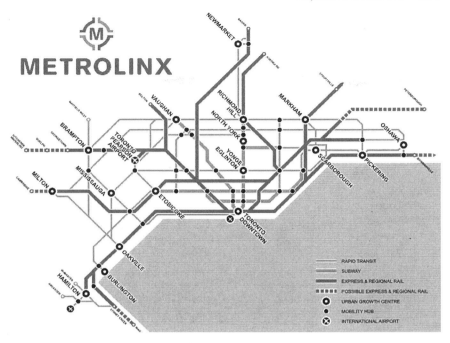

Figure 12.1 Map of proposed rapid transit network
Source: Metrolinx 2008, *Big Move*

In 2009, the province introduced numerous changes to Metrolinx's organization through the Greater Toronto and Hamilton Area Transit Implementation Act. The board of directors, who until that point had largely been mayors and councilors from municipalities in the region, was replaced with provincial appointees, many from the private sector, and others with experience in planning and nongovernmental organizations. Metrolinx was also merged with GO Transit, to provide "an integrated approach to planning, funding, implementing, operating and expanding all modes of transit in the regional transportation area" (Province of Ontario 2009).

The Metrolinx plan for transit development is oriented around provincially designated growth centers. The agency positions itself as a facilitator not only of traffic management and public transit, but also as a key support for greater residential and commercial density, under the provincial framework of smart growth—sustainable urban development that is regionally and globally oriented (see Keil and Young 2008, as well as Courtney 2009). Metrolinx (2008) has laid out nine specific projects as "priority actions" (dubbed "Big Moves") (*Big Move*, 20). These include an expanded regional transit network, improved connectivity to the Pearson Airport, expanding Toronto's Union Station, and developing a network of mobility "hubs" connecting commuters through different modes of transportation. Each prong of the strategy cites congestion as a regional problem, hindering economic development while posing health and environmental risks. Emphasizing greater efficiencies through integrating transportation networks, implementing traffic management systems, and deploying other technologies, Metrolinx asserts a regional and infrastructural fix to problems of growth and development. The term "integration" figures prominently here. By fostering a regional approach to transportation planning, Metrolinx seeks to improve efficiency in the use of roads and transit, with an eye to reducing congestion and related costs. The region that emerges complicates notions of political and economic scale. It is a provincially designated zone that incorporates municipal governments in coordination with legislation, but also seeks greater integration within networks at broader scales.

Another core strategy is closely aligned with regional economic growth—facilitating the movement of goods within the Greater Toronto and Hamilton Area. Again, the intent is to facilitate flows of goods not just across political boundaries and through areas of heavy congestion, but also to improve multimodal connections from a continent-wide perspective (*Big Move*, 55).[4] Similarly, the strategy to redevelop Union Station and improve transportation connections to Pearson Airport reflects Metrolinx's economic priorities. Indeed, these are the second and third items in the list of Big Moves. Union Station is considered to be the "heart" of the region's transportation system, linking up different modes and providers of transit across multiple jurisdictions—including plans to align rail-based transportation strategies with the province of Quebec and the federal government (*Big Move*, 25). The Big Move not only addresses internal issues of growth and development within the area, but projects them into continental and global networks.

In many ways, Metrolinx presents itself as a unique entity. Provincially deployed yet regionally focused, it serves as a point of focus for debates over congestion and transportation planning in the GTHA. It is charged with planning, developing, and funding a decades-long strategy, while also operating as a transit provider. As a public agency (a provincial crown corporation), it is directed by government-appointed experts (financial, organizational, technical). As a transportation authority, it must also align its goals and objectives with provincially designated growth strategies and ecological concerns (by law), while also negotiating with municipalities to develop and integrate their specific transportation plans.[5] Positioned as a regional transportation planning authority, Metrolinx straddles numerous tensions within and amongst municipal governments, residents, and nongovernmental organizations in the Greater Toronto and Hamilton Area.

TRANSIT CITY: ON-AGAIN-OFF-AGAIN PLANNING

Designated to operate as a regional authority, Metrolinx soon encountered tensions within specific municipalities and neighborhoods. These challenged

Infrastructural Fix   203

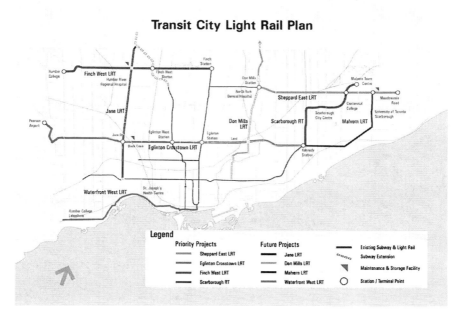

Figure 12.2 Toronto's Transit City plan
Source: City of Toronto 2010, 293

the cohesiveness of the agency's strategy, as well as its authority. Indeed, in areas where Metrolinx does not have strong jurisdiction or designated power, it may well concede transportation planning to municipal and provincial decision-makers. For instance, in 2007, Toronto city council and the Toronto Transit Commission announced plans for seven light rail transit (LRT) lines for the municipality, with initial support from the province of Ontario. Funding was to be provided through the province's Move Ontario 2020 program, which allocated $11.5 billion towards fifty-two transit projects in the GTHA (City of Toronto 2010). In all, eight LRT lines (including planned upgrades for the existing Scarborough RT line) were outlined, with four designated priorities for Transit City (see Figure 12.2).

In 2009, the province announced it would provide $8.5 billion for Transit City, and Metrolinx assumed control of the project. (The specific projects associated with Transit City were included in the 2008 report, *The Big Move*, but the strategy itself was not named in that document). Four lines were to be funded, including the Scarborough RT (to be renovated, not replaced), Finch West LRT, Eglinton Crosstown LRT, and Sheppard LRT. The latter also received $333 million in federal funding (City of Toronto 2010). At that time, Metrolinx was charged with planning, developing, owning, and operating the lines (City of Toronto 2010).

204 John Saunders

Yet by 2010, the provincial government asked for—and received—a delay providing Metrolinx $4 billion of funding for Transit City. The minister of finance cited economic conditions, a growing provincial deficit, and the need to allocate resources to other areas as reasons for the delay and funding cut, prompting anger from then-mayor David Miller (McDowell 2010, A6; Alcoba, March 27, 2010, A19). A revised plan was proposed and accepted, promising completion of the four projects within ten years, albeit with fewer stops and shorter lines (Wallace 2010, A10). Metrolinx and the TTC also disagreed over whether to postpone starting work on the Finch West LRT line. For one observer, this precipitated the end of the project, as the delay made it easier to cancel it later on (Bow 2011).

Transit City reflects a series of negotiations and conflicts between municipal and provincial representatives. Metrolinx, relatively removed from this process, became subject to greater scrutiny following municipal elections in late 2010. The victor in the mayoralty race, Rob Ford, campaigned on a fiscally conservative platform, promising to eliminate excess spending at city hall and to end "the war on the car"—policies and strategies that would expand the presence of public transit and cycling on city streets, and that might impede the flow of automobile traffic. This included cancelling the Transit City program and promoting underground subway development.

Among Ford's initial actions was a move to stop Transit City. Having previously declared his preference for subway development, he declared that LRT development in the city was dead. In its place, the city would promote the expansion of the Sheppard subway line, using funding originally earmarked for Transit City (Kalinowski and Rider 2010, A1). Tensions rose between the city and the province, with the latter threatening to withdraw all its funding. An agreement was reached in March 2011, however, seeing continued support for the Eglinton LRT, renamed the Eglinton-Scarborough Crosstown LRT, for $8.4 billion. The entire line would also be built underground. Up to $650 million in leftover funds would be repurposed for the Sheppard subway (assuming the Eglinton project came in under budget), to be matched by the original $333 million in federal funding—if the province contributed by 2014 (Dale 2011, A1). The city would assume responsibility for building the Sheppard subway line, and would be accountable for any costs related to cancelling Transit City contracts—an estimated $65 million (*Toronto Star*, February 9, 2012, GT3).

Throughout the process, Ford maintained that a subway could be built with no additional costs to residents. He proposed having a private-sector consortium plan, build, and manage the extension, as well as "tax increment financing" (borrowing against future increases in property values from lands near subway stations) or development charges to fund the project (Alcoba, April 1, 2011, A8). By the summer of 2011, however, few resources had been identified, and the mayor had requested an additional $1 billion from the provincial and federal governments (Dale 2011, A1). Over the following months, additional conflicts would arise, undermining the mayor's authority and the stability of transportation planning in the city. Ford, for instance, fought to have the Eglinton-Scarborough Crosstown LRT run completely underground (akin to a subway), arguing that this approach would prove less disruptive to surface (i.e., car) traffic. The province agreed to this in 2011, but councilors challenged the mayor on the issue. This conflict allows for a different understanding of congestion, inverting some of the other, contemporary narratives, which promote LRTs as more cost-effective and efficient ways of improving traffic. Indeed, public support for subways also appears to be strong, often couched in arguments against surface disruptions.[6]

In January 2012, a legal report commissioned by a councilor argued that the mayor did not have the authority to unilaterally cancel Transit City and renegotiate the previous arrangement with the province (Alcoba, January 31, 2012, A8). That same month, councilors (including the chair of the TTC) publically challenged the Eglinton-Scarborough decision. In early February, council voted to return to LRT systems (while establishing a committee to study the viability of new subways), as well as returning portions of the Eglinton-Scarborough line aboveground—redirecting savings from that project towards the Finch LRT (Kalinowski and Dale 2012, A1).

Throughout these debates, Metrolinx supported plans for LRTs over subways, albeit without directly confronting the mayor. The organization did not figure prominently in media accounts, but did occasionally intervene publicly. In February 2012, one board member expressed concern that the province would stop funding Toronto's transit expansion due to delays and changing plans. However, Metrolinx's chief executive officer downplayed the possibility, saying the province remained committed (CBC News, February 6, 2012). Another account of a Metrolinx board meeting cited the CEO as saying that the agency's role was to support council decisions and avoid siding with individual councilors (Munro 2012).

Metrolinx has been cited as a source of frustration. One newspaper columnist called the organization "spineless" for its role in Toronto's transit planning (James, January 6, 2012, GT2), although another questioned Metrolinx's ability to lead, arguing "it can only coordinate among rival transit silos" (Cohn, January 24, 2012, GT2). The chair of the Toronto Region Board of Trade has also argued for Metrolinx to be "freed to lead"—asking the province to bolster its planning authority (Wilding 2012). By late 2013, however, the shifting tides of transportation politics saw coordinated support for a subway extension into Scarborough—including support from Metrolinx. The proposed two- or three-stop extension requires the city to raise an additional $1 billion, largely through property tax increases, while also receiving provincial and federal support. Although plans have yet to coalesce, the mayor has proclaimed this a victory for his desire to transfer transit underground, and has announced he will renew his efforts to cancel LRT plans for Finch West and Sheppard East (Kalinowski and Powell 2013, GT1).

WESTON: LOCAL CONCERNS, REGIONAL GROWTH, AND GLOBAL CONNECTIVITY

With regards to Transit City and the debates over LRTs that followed, Metrolinx assumed a more passive role, with representatives expressing an interest in having the city commit to a plan, but not attempting to direct the process. The organization has taken a somewhat different approach in another Toronto-based project, however: the Union–Pearson rail link. In 2009, Metrolinx announced plans for a railway connection between Toronto's Union Station and the Pearson International Airport. The "air–rail link" would see upgrades to an existing stretch of track (the GO Transit Kitchener Corridor), as well as create a three-kilometer link connecting the line to the airport. Metrolinx estimates the link, to be completed by 2015 for the Pan Am Games, will transport about five thousand people a day and eliminate 1.2 million car trips during its first year (Metrolinx n.d.). The project faces opposition—largely from residents in the area adjacent to the railway line. The Weston Community Coalition countered Metrolinx's arguments in 2009 with a critique of the public consultation process and claims of ecological sensitivity. Residents expressed concerns over the increased number of diesel-powered trains (possibly from fifty to four hundred a day), as well as a fast-tracked environmental assessment, rising project costs, and a number of legal and jurisdictional conflicts with Metrolinx (Weston Community Coalition 2009).

Originally planned as a private–public partnership, the link was to be built by a group led by SNC Lavalin, which withdrew after receiving no promises of operating subsidies (Lorinc 2010, A1). In 2010, Metrolinx announced it would plan, build, own, and operate the line, estimating it would create ten thousand jobs in the process (Union–Pearson Express 2010). The provincial minister for transportation at the time stressed the need for transportation connectivity for the Pan Am Games, as well as regional interests. "The Air Rail Link will offer a quick and convenient transit option to reduce congestion, and as part of our Open Ontario plan it will create jobs and boost Ontario's economy" (Union–Pearson Express 2010). Total project costs are estimated to run $300 million to more than $400 million (O'Toole 2011, A11), although critics expect that number could rise (Sullivan 2011, A21). Additional costs to upgrade trains from diesel to electric are a source of debate, but Metrolinx estimates it would cost more than $450 million to upgrade the line, and take seven years to complete. As a result of public pressure, Metrolinx will be using so-called "clean diesel" trains (Tier 4) in the interim (CBC News, January 19, 2011). Residents have not directly opposed the project, but have called for greater public involvement in the planning process and have attempted to provide alternate approaches to environmentally informed transportation planning, such as through the creation of the Clean Train Coalition. They have also challenged Metrolinx's authority, with some success. In 2010, a federal court supported resident concerns over the use of heavy impact hammers along the line, limiting their use (*Toronto Star*, February 4, 2010, GT4). In 2011, an advertising industry body ruled that a Metrolinx flyer distributed to homes along the route was misleading (Kalinowski, August 20, 2011, GT10).

These debates reflect a further complication of the consensus on congestion. They point to the difficulty in managing localized concerns through regional planning, particularly as it is oriented towards global economic connectivity. They also reveal ways in which Metrolinx can assert authority more directly, because the organization owns and operates the lines and has federal and provincial government support for this initiative.

METROLINX AS A GROWTH MACHINE

Metrolinx has emerged as not only a transportation authority, but also as a form of growth machine. Charged with procuring equipment and expertise, as well as siting areas for transit development, Metrolinx supports economic development within the region and the province. For instance, Metrolinx ordered 182 LRT cars from Bombardier in 2010 to run on Toronto's proposed Transit City lines. The total cost of the purchase was $770 million, with an estimated two hundred jobs to be created at the company's Thunder Bay facility (Alcoba, January 15, 2010, A11; CAW 2010). However, the following year saw outrage over a decision to award a contract to refurbish GO Transit trains (owned by Metrolinx) to a Quebec-based firm. The firm, Canada Allied Diesel Railway Industries Ltd., submitted a bit of $122 million, $2 million less than that of an Ontario crown corporation, Ontario Northland Transportation Commission. Opposition party leaders in Ontario criticized the decision, as did the president of the Canadian Auto Workers' union (Talaga 2011, A6; CAW 2011).

Recent trade negotiations between Canada and the European Union (EU) may also affect Metrolinx's role in the regional and provincial economies. The Comprehensive Economic and Trade Agreement could, according to critics, allow for greater access to different markets in Canada and Europe, and potentially limit local procurement strategies. "Indeed, the EU's initial 'market access' request refers by name to Toronto transit, Metrolinx, the regional transit body, and Toronto water and emergency services as among the agencies whose contracts they want to ensure are open to European bidders" (Campion-Smith 2010, A19). Toronto city council called on the federal government to provide an exemption for the city (Walkom 2010, A14).[7] Although Metrolinx does not necessarily follow an "Ontario first" procurement strategy,[8] its ability to procure goods and services within the province could be limited by this sort of agreement. In October 2013, the Canadian government announced it had struck an agreement with the EU. Not all details have emerged, but initial accounts claim that the accord does contain protections for Canadian municipal and public-works contracts (Clark, Maldie, and Morrow 2010).

208 John Saunders

Metrolinx may pursue other growth-oriented strategies in partnership with the private sector. In 2009, for instance, Metrolinx announced it would consider working with private companies to build Transit City LRT lines. The Toronto Transit Commission, however, would still operate and maintain the lines (Hanes 2009, A15; Croome and Wallace 2009, A1). However, in 2011, TTC representatives said they would not take on a privately built line (Kalinowski 2011, A1). Metrolinx (2008) will also consider alternate financing and procurement (AFP) strategies, as directed by provincial and federal governments, "to expedite the delivery of transportation infrastructure and to ensure the most appropriate and cost-effective allocation of both private and public sector resources" (*Big Move*, 78–70). The agency has received support on AFP from the Toronto Board of Trade—specifically with the original contract with SNC Lavalin to build the Union–Pearson rail link, and the board has also raised the issue as a potential cost-saving strategy (Toronto Board of Trade 2009, 2011). However, uncertainty regarding provincial funding for Metrolinx itself may make it more difficult to attract private investors (Melnitzer 2010). Metrolinx's position as a transit planner is enmeshed with its position as an employer as well, complicating its relationship with labor groups, local residents, elected politicians, and business interests.[9]

METROLINX AS A GOVERNANCE MACHINE

Although its role and responsibilities are laid out through provincial legislation, Metrolinx nonetheless faces a good deal of uncertainty regarding its actual authority and involvement in long-term planning. This uncertainty can be read as productive in that it allows for administrative and political flexibility.[10] The deployment of transportation as a regional strategy, alongside other provincial legislation, bolsters efforts to stabilize risk through reterritorialization—in essence, producing a region through a new politics of scale.

In many ways, uncertainty does stymie the ability for Metrolinx to implement "The Big Move." Despite its existing mandate, for instance, there have been rumors of transferring responsibility for the TTC to Metrolinx (Howler, Mehler Paperny, and Radwanski 2010, A11; *Toronto Star*, January 27, 2011, A22). The current mayor of Toronto has also considered asking the province to upload municipal transit, an idea that has been officially rejected (Kalinowski and Benzie 2011, GT5; Jenkins 2012). Divisions within Toronto's city council have also slowed the rollout of Metrolinx's LRT plans for the city. Yet Metrolinx has continued its involvement in a number of projects. A unified fare system, linking the TTC with GO Transit, for instance, is expected to be in place by 2015 (Alcoba, January 26, 2011, A10). Outside Toronto, Metrolinx is working with the York Region to redevelop a major east–west thoroughfare, Highway 7, to make it more accessible to pedestrians and bicycles, and to spur high-rise development (Daubs 2011, GT3). Metrolinx—through GO Transit—has also partnered with the city of Mississauga to build an eighteen-kilometer Bus Rapid Transit (BRT) corridor (Chin 2010). These initiatives may reflect an incremental process of integration for regional transportation.

Integration remains a key component to Metrolinx's strategy for transportation management. The agency's vision of a seamless regional network of transit lines and hubs offers up a balanced, efficient, and stable plan for growth across the Greater Toronto and Hamilton Area. The lack of a specific funding strategy to achieve this vision is also productive, at least at this stage, because it avoids conflict over the prospect of road tolls and private-sector outsourcing.

The restructuring of the agency's board reflects a twofold transformation in governance. First, by removing political representatives, the province argued it had essentially depoliticized Metrolinx, leaving its overall direction in the hands of a more neutral leadership. Second, by mobilizing a language of business and organizational structure and leadership, the province also arguably *professionalized* the agency, bolstering claims to rationality, efficiency, and technical expertise. However, the organization is in many ways less directly accountable to area residents. Metrolinx arguably operates at arms-length from the province, and is not beholden to local interests, which also risks undermining popular support for its actions.[11]

Metrolinx's plans for regional integration not only address the challenges of traffic congestion, but also economic development. These align Metrolinx with other provincial strategies as a way of providing a stable, regional environment for longer-term investment.[12] Yet this vision of an integrated, efficient region also produces unevenness. At times, local consultation and participation are limited and contingent, and may be subordinate to greater global connectivity and economic development. Here, we may encounter what Flyvbjerg (1998) has observed through the urban planning process: how rationality and planning give way to political expediency and forms of institutional power.

A REGIONAL FIX, BUT NO FIXED REGION

Metrolinx can be seen as another plank in an emerging legislative approach to governing the Greater Toronto Area. Although no single regional governing authority exists, attempts to redirect growth to provincially designated zones, while also attempting to protect agricultural and environmental areas from development, in conjunction with a regionally oriented transit and transportation plan, reflect an institutional interest in designating the region as an infrastructural, economic, and ecological entity.

The region does not emerge as a stable, delimited, bounded entity provided with clear powers and responsibilities. It offers instead a flexible,

210 John Saunders

contingent, and indeterminate range of strategies for governing in both general and specific circumstances to bolster economic development while responding to various local and global contexts. It defies set boundaries (spatial and political) while opening up possibilities for coordinating investment and governance. Within this context, congestion provides an ostensibly consensus-building moment in terms of regional transportation policy. As an issue readily experienced throughout the expanding urban region, one that is increasingly identified as the source for greater economic, social, and health costs, it offers a shared point of entry into discussions of how to manage growth through transportation planning. Yet a closer analysis of regional transportation planning in the Greater Toronto Area reveals a number of tensions and inconsistencies, and, indeed, a lack of consensus on the definitions, causes, and responses to congestion in the region.

NOTES

1. The City of Toronto, with a population of about 2.5 million, was amalgamated from six separate municipalities in 1998 by the Ontario government. The Greater Toronto Area, although not a political or administrative entity, comprises Toronto as well as four surrounding regional municipalities, with a total population of about 5.5 million. The Greater Toronto and Hamilton Area comprises the GTA and the municipality of Hamilton, and is used specifically with reference to Metrolinx.
2. In early 2013, Metrolinx updated the "Big Move" to update elements of certain projects and to incorporate public and government input. Although certain items have been reworded or revised, the update "is not intended to change any of the foundational elements of the plan" (Metrolinx 2013, 1).
3. In the spring of 2013, Metrolinx outlined a proposed strategy to fund its various projects. These include raising the provincial sales tax, introducing a gas tax, deploying a parking levy, and increasing development charges. They have yet to receive formal, political support (Kallinowksy and Ferguson 2013).
4. Specifically, the "Big Move" refers to coordinating with the Continental Gateway Strategy, a federal initiative to develop comprehensive strategies for easing the flow of goods in and out of central North America.
5. Although Ontario legislation requires that municipal transportation planning adhere to provincial requirements and charges Metrolinx with coordinating municipal strategies, Courtney notes degrees of uncertainty concerning the agency's role and authority.
6. Indeed, Canada's prime minister also supports underground transportation as a way for drivers and transit users to commute "unimpeded" (Stone 2012, GT2).
7. More than twenty Canadian municipalities have asked to be exempted from the agreement (Peat 2012, 12).
8. A strategy that has been proposed by the Canadian Union of Public Employees' Ontario section.
9. More than 1,500 Go Transit workers nearly went on strike in fall of 2011, originally facing an offer of zero-percent wage increases, ultimately settling for a 6.3% raise over three years (*Toronto Star*, August 30, 2011; Amalgamated Transit Union, Local 1587 2011).

10. This has been noted by a number of journalists, who have argued that the province has used Metrolinx to deflect criticism (James 2012, GT2), or that the agency has had to remain flexible in the face of changing political direction (Cohn, February 28, 2012, A10).
11. Indeed, this was an argument made in December 2011 by the chair of the Toronto Transit Commission, as she called for reinstating municipal political representatives on the Metrolinx board (Kuitenbrouwer 2011, A11).
12. See, for instance, Wekerle, Sandberg, Gilbert, and Binstock (2007) who argue that provincial greenbelt legislation has not only preserved areas from development, but has also served as a "lubricant" for additional investment through regional growth management policies (33–34).

WORKS CITED

Addie, Jean-Paul. "Metropolitics in Motion: The Dynamics of Transportation and State Reterritorialization in the Chicago and Toronto City-Regions." *Urban Geography* 34 (2013), no. 20, p. 188–217.

Alcoba, Natalie. "$4B Transit Delay Leaves Miller Furious, Observers Perplexed." *National Post*, March 27, 2010, A19.

———. "Metrolinx Orders 182 LRT Cars." *National Post*, June 15, 2010, A11.

———. "Private Money to Build Subway." *National Post*, April 1, 2011, A8.

———. "Ford Tried to Upload Costly TTC to Metrolinx." *National Post*, January 26, 2011, A8.

———. "Transit Opponents Digging In." *National Post*, January 31, 2012, A8.

Amalgamated Transit Union, Local 1587. *GO Transit Workers Ratify Contract Settlement.* Web. 2011. http://www.newswire.ca/en/story/870635/go-transit-workers-ratify-contract-settlement.

Bow, James. *Toronto's Transit City LRT Plan.* Web. 2011. http://transit.toronto.on.ca/streetcar/4121.shtml.

Brenner, Neil. "Between Fixity and Motion: Accumulation, Territorial Organizations and the Historical Geography of Spatial Scales." *Environment and Planning D: Society and Space* 16 (1998), p. 459–481.

———. "Decoding the Newest 'Metropolitan Regionalism' in the USA: A Critical Overview." *Cities* 19 (2002), p. 3–21.

———. *New State Spaces: Urban Governance and the Rescaling of Statehood.* Oxford, Oxford University Press, 2004.

British Columbia Trucking Association. *About the Industry: Infrastructure.* Web. 2011. http://www.bctrucking.com/industry/infrastructure.php.

Campion-Smith, Bruce. "Negotiations Moving Canada Closer to Trade Pact with EU." *The Toronto Star*, May 1, 2010, A19.

Canadian Trucking Alliance. "Canadian Trucking Chief Calls for End to War on Truck in Urban Centres in DC Speech." Web. 2010. http://www.cantruck.ca/imispublic/news_releases1/AM/ContentManagerNet/ContentDisplay.aspx?Section=news_releases1&ContentID=8021.

Canadian Union of Public Employees. *McGuinty Plan an Economic Recovery Killer, Says CUPE Ontario.* Web. 2012. http://cupe.ca/government/mcguinty-plan-economic-recovery-killer.

CAW. *New Contract Means More Jobs in Thunder Bay, Ontario.* Web. 2010. http://www.caw.ca/en/9043.htm.

———. *North Bay Workers Frustrated, Angered by Metrolinx Contract Sign-off, CAW President Says.* Web. 2011. http://www.caw.ca/en/10452.htm.

212 John Saunders

CBC News. *Electrify Airport Rail Link Eventually: Metrolinx*. Web. January 19, 2011. http://www.cbc.ca/news/canada/toronto/story/2011/01/19/toronto-metrolinx-airport-rail-link352.htm.

———. *Toronto Risks Losing LRT Funds, Metrolinx Member Says*. Web. February 16, 2012. http://www.cbc.ca/news/canada/toronto/story/2012/02/16/toronto-metrolinx-subway-lrt.html.

Chin, Joseph. "City Breaks Ground on BRT Station." *Mississauga.com*. Web. November 19, 2010. http://www.mississauga.com/print/905575.

City of Toronto. *Council Briefing Book, 2010–2014, Volume 1*. Web. 2010. http://www1.toronto.ca/city_of_toronto/city_managers_office/civic_engagement/council_briefings/files/pdf/briefing-book.pdf.

Clark, Cambell, Paul Maldie, and Adrian Morrow. "EU-Canada Deal Will Include Access to Lucrative Public-Sector Contracts." *The Globe and Mail*, October 19, 2010, A10.

Cohn, Martin Regg. "Ford's Plan for Eglinton Seems Destined to Collapse." *The Toronto Star*, January 24, 2012, GT2.

———. "Premier Needs Bunker for Transit War." *The Toronto Star*, February 28, 2012, A10.

Courtney, Kevin. "Sustainable Urban Transportation and Ontario's New Planning Regime: The Provincial Policy Statement, 2005 and the Growth Plan for the Greater Golden Horseshoe." *Environmental Law and Practice* 19 (2009), p. 71–104.

Croome, Phillip, and Wallace Kenyan. "Metrolinx Touts Private Sector for Transit City." *National Post*, November 17, 2009, A1.

Dale, Daniel. " 'New Mayor, New Deal': Ford Seeks Public Cash for Subway." *The Toronto Star*, August 18, 2011, A1.

Daubs, Katie. "York Region's Boulevard of Dreams." *The Toronto Star*, October 5, 2011, GT3.

Flyvbjerg, B. *Rationality and Power: Democracy in Practice*. Chicago, University of Chicago Press, 1998.

Garreau, Joel. *Edge Cities: Life on the New Frontier*. New York, Doubleday, 1991.

Graham, Stephen. "Constructing Premium Network Spaces: Reflections on Infrastructure Networks and Contemporary Urban Development." *International Journal of Urban and Regional Research* 24 (2000), p. 183–200.

Graham, Stephen, and Simon Marvin. *Splintering Urbanism: Networked Infrastructures, Technological Mobilities and the Urban Condition*. New York, Routledge, 2001.

Hanes, Allison. "Private-Sector Cash Sought to Bankroll Major Projects." *National Post*, November 18, 2009, A15.

Harvey, David. "The Urban Process under Capitalism." In: *The Urban Experience*. Baltimore, Johns Hopkins University Press, 1989, p. 59–89.

———. "On Planning the Ideology of Planning." In: Scott Campbell and Susan Fainstein (eds.), *Readings in Planning Theory*. Cambridge, MA, Blackwell, 1996, p. 176–197.

———. "The Right to the City." *New Left Review* 53 (2008), p. 23–40.

Harvey, Ian. "Road-Repair Backlog a Challenge for Toronto: Urban Transportation Summit Speaker." Web. April 27, 2011. Daily Construction News. http://dcnonl.com/article/id44067.

Howler, Karen, Anna Mehler Papernay, and Adam Radwanski. "Queen's Park May Seek More Control over TTC." *The Globe and Mail*, February 17, 2010, A11.

Isin, Engin. "Metropolis Unbound: Legislators and Interpreters of Urban Form." In: John Caulfield and Linda Peake (eds.), *City Lives and City Forms: Critical*

Research and Canadian Urbanism. Toronto, University of Toronto Press, 1996, p. 98–127.

James, Royson. "Spineless Agency Fails City." *The Toronto Star*, January 26, 2012, GT2.

———. "Transit Circus Carries On." *The Toronto Star*, January 30, 2012, GT2.

Jenkins, Jonathan. "Metrolinx Logjam Remains." *Toronto Sun.* Web. February 25, 2012. http://m.torontosun.com/2012/02/25/metrolinx-logjam-remains.

Kalinowski, Tess "Metrolinx Criticized for Ad about Proposed Airport Train." *The Toronto Star*, August 20, 2011, GT10.

———. "TTC Derailed in Eglinton Light-rail Vision." *The Toronto Star.* November 30, 2011, A1.

Kalinowski, Tess, and Robert Benzie. "No Plans to Upload TTC, Says Province." *The Toronto Star.* January 26, 2011, GT5.

Kalinowski, Tess, and Daniel Dale. "Ford Trounced in Transit Vote." *The Toronto Star*, February 9, 2012, A1.

Kalinowski, Tess, and Rob Ferguson. "Metrolinx Funding Plan Gets Mixed Reaction." *The Toronto Star*, May 31, 2013, GT1.

Kalinowski, Tess, and Betsy Powell. "Scarborough Subway Confirmed." *The Toronto Star*, October 9, 2013, GT1.

Kalinowski, Tess, and David Rider. "'War on the Car Is over': Ford Moves Transit Underground." *The Toronto Star*, December 2, 2010, A1.

Keil, Roger, and Douglas Young. "Transportation: The Bottleneck of Regional Competitiveness in Toronto." *Environment and Planning C: Government and Policy* 26 (2008), p. 728–751.

Kuitenbrouwer, Peter. "Changing the Topic on TTC Crunch." *National Post*, December 13, 2011, A11.

Lang, Robert. *Edgeless Cities.* Washington DC, Brookings Institute, 2003.

Lorinc, John. "Metrolinx to Go It Alone on Union-Pearson Rail Link." *The Globe and Mail*, July 31, 2010, A1.

Lord, Simon. "Costs of Heavy Traffic Filter Down to Customers." Agence QMI. Web. April 20, 2011. http://www.canoe.com/cgi-bin/imprimer.cgi?langue=A&id=900534.

MacLeod, Gordon. "Space, Scale and State Strategy: Rethinking Urban and Regional Governance." *Progress in Human Geography* 23 (1999), p. 503–527.

McDowell, Adam. "Province Asks Metrolinx for $4B in Transit Savings." *National Post*, March 26, 2010, A6.

Mekky, Ali. "The Cost of Congestion in the Greater Toronto Area." Conference paper. Web. 2006. http://conf.tac-atc.ca/english/resourcecentre/readingroom/conference/conf2007/docs/s14/mekky.pdf.

Melnitzer, Julius. "The Pipeline of P3 Deals May Slow." *Financial Post*, December 1, 2010, FP6.

Metrolinx. *Transportation Trends and Outlooks for the Greater Toronto and Hamilton Area: Needs and Opportunities.* Toronto, Web. 2007.

———. *Cost of Road Congestion in the Greater Toronto and Hamilton Area: Impact and Cost Benefit Analysis of the Metrolinx Draft Regional Transportation Plan.* Prepared in conjunction with HDR Corporation. Web. 2008. http://www.metrolinx.com/en/regionalplanning/costsofcongestion/ISP_08–015_Cost_of_Congestion_report_1128081.pdf.

———. *The Big Move: Transforming Transportation in the Greater Toronto and Hamilton Area.* Web. 2008. http://www.metrolinx.com/en/docs/pdf/board_agenda/20080926/PP08–013DraftRTP-AppendixA.pdf.

———. *The Air Rail Link Fact Sheet.* Web. n.d. http://www.metrolinx.com/en/projectsandprograms/airraillink/air_rail_link.aspx.

214 John Saunders

———. *Board Report: The Big Move Update—Recommended Changes*. Web. February 13, 2013. http://www.metrolinx.com/en/docs/pdf/board_agenda/2013 0214/20130214_BoardMtg_The_Big_Move_Update_EN.pdf.

Morsky, Wayne. *Speech Given to National Infrastructure Summit*. Web. January 28, 2011. http://www.cca-acc.com/news/ccanews/WayneNISReginaSpeech2011.pdf.

Munro, Steve. *Metrolinx and the Toronto Council LRT Decision*. Web. February 16, 2012. http://stevemunro.ca/?p=6024.

O'Toole, Megan. "Construction on Rail Line to Pearson to Start in Spring." *National Post*. December 20, 2011, A11.

Peat, Don. "Councillors Warn of Perils from European Union Trade Agreement." *Toronto* Sun. Web. January 23, 2012. http://www.torontosun.com/2012/01/23/councillors-warn-of-perils-from-european-union-trade-agreement.

Peck, F. W. "Regional Development and the Production of Space: The Role of Infrastructure in the Attraction of New Inward Investment." *Environment and Planning A* 28 (1996), p. 327–339.

Priemus, Hugo. "Spatial-Economic Investment Policy and Urban Regeneration in the Netherlands." *Environment & Planning C: Government & Policy* 20 (2002), p. 775–791.

Province of Ontario. *Bill 163: An Act to Amend the Greater Toronto Transportation Authority Act, 2006 and to Make Consequential Amendments to Another Act*. Web. May 14, 2009. http://www.e-laws.gov.on.ca/html/source/statutes/english/2009/elaws_src_s09014_e.htm.

Saunders, John. "Recreational Space and the Politics of Infrastructure in the In-between City: A Study of Parc Downsview Park, Canada's First National Urban Park." In: Roger Keil, Patricia Wood, and Douglas Young (eds.), *In-Between Infrastructure: Urban Connectivity in an Age of Vulnerability*. Kelowna, Praxis (e) Press, 2011.

———. "Of Strikes, Subways, and the Big-Box University: Reconsidering the Spatial Fixations of Infrastructure." *Problématique: Journal of Political Studies* 12 (2009). Web. http://www.yorku.ca/problema/Issues/Problematique1201.pdf.

Sieverts, Thomas. *Cities without Cities: An Interpretation of the Zwischenstadt*. London, Routledge, 2003.

Soja, Edward. *Postmetropolis: Critical Studies of Cities and Regions*. Oxford, Blackwell Publishers, 2000.

Stone, Laura. "Subways Are the Better Way to Go for Transit, Prime Minister Says." *The Toronto Star*, March 10, 2012, GT2.

Sullivan, Mike. "The Ever-changing but always Inadequate Pearson Rail Link." *The Toronto Star*, December 19, 2011, A21.

Talaga, Tanya. "Hudak Vows to 'Suspend' $122M Deal to Quebec." *The Toronto Star*, August 18, 2011, A6.

Tewdwr-Jones, Mark. "The Politics of City-Region Planning and Governance: Reconciling the National, Regional and Urban in the Competing Voices of Institutional Restructuring." *European Urban and Regional Studies* 7 (2000), p. 119–134.

Today'sTrucking.com. *Hurricane Hazel to Keep on Trucking*. Web. July 14, 2010. http://www.topdaystrucking.com/news.cfm?intDocID=24309.

Toronto Board of Trade. *Progress on Union-Pearson Link Long Overdue: Toronto Board of Trade*. Web. January 21, 2009. http://www.marketwired.com/press-release/progress-on-union-pearson-link-long-overdue-toronto-board-of-trade-940191.htm.

———. *The Move Ahead: Funding "The Big Move."* Web. 2010. http://www.bot.com/advocacy/Documents/VoteToronto2010/The_Move_Ahead.pdf.

Toronto Star. "Piledriving Order Upheld." February 4, 2010, GT04.

———. "Strike Deadline Looms for GO Transit Workers." Web. August 30, 2011. http://www.thestar.com/news/city_hall/2011/08/30/strike_deadline_looms_for_go_transit_workers.html.

———. "Unified Transit Makes Sense." January 27, 2011, A22.

———. "Ford Tough Lame Duck." February 9, 2012, GT3.

Torrance, Morag. "Forging Glocal Governance? Urban Infrastructures as Networked Financial Products." *International Journal of Urban and Regional Research* 32 (2008), p. 1–21.

Transport Canada. *The Cost of Urban Congestion in Canada*. Web. 2006. http://www.adec-inc.ca/pdf/02-rapport/cong-canada-ang.pdf.

Union–Pearson Express. *Metrolinx to Build, Own and Operate Air Rail Link*. Web. July 30, 2010. http://www.upexpress.com/en/news/news_MetrolinxToBuildARL.aspx.

Walkom, Thomas. "Toronto's Late Attempt to Soften EU Trade Deal." *The Toronto Star*, March 8, 2012, A14.

Wallace, Kenyan. "Province Commits to Transit City." *National Post*, April 30, 2010, A10.

Wekerle, Gerda, and Teresa Abbruzzese. "Producing Regionalism: Regional Movements, Ecosystems and Equity in a Fast and Slow Growth Region." *GeoJournal* 75 (2010), p. 581–594.

Wekerle, Gerda, Anders Sandberg, Liette Gilbert, and Matthew Binstock. "Nature as the Cornerstone of Growth: Regional and Ecosystems Planning in the Greater Golden Horseshoe." *Canadian Journal of Urban Research* 16 (2007), supplement, p. 20–38.

Weston Community Coalition. *Open Report from the WCC to Environment Minister John Gerretsen*. Web. 2009. http://www.westoncommunitycoalition.ca/node/10.

Wilding, Carol. "Metrolinx Should Be Freed to Lead." *The Globe and Mail*. Web. February 16, 2012. http://www.theglobeandmail.com/news/opinions/opinion/metrolinx-should-be-freed-to-lead/article2340989.

Young, Douglas, and Roger Keil. "Urinetown or Morainetown? Debates on the Deregulation of the Urban Water Regime in Toronto." *Capitalism, Nature, Socialism* 16 (2005), p. 62–84.

———. "Reconnecting the Disconnected: The Politics of Infrastructure in the In-between City." *Cities* 27 (2010), p. 87–105.

13 Move and Maintain
Mapping Multilocal Lifestyles in Hyderabad, India

Angela Jain and Gowkanapalli Lakshmi Narasimha Reddy

BETWEEN RURAL AND URBAN: "SUSTAINABLE HYDERABAD" PROJECT

This chapter is one of the outcomes of field research conducted in Hyderabad, India, in the 2011–2012 period as part of the Indo-German research project entitled, "Climate and Energy in a complex Transition Process towards Sustainable Hyderabad." Its purpose was to employ an interdisciplinary perspective to assess crucial issues, including both dangers and potentials, for the future of the fast growing megacity. Through the combined work of German and Indian partners, various fields such as transport, energy, water, and climate change were scientifically assessed and vulnerabilities identified. The underlying question was the following: How should governance structures, institutions, and lifestyles in the Hyderabad region be arranged in order to foster sustainable development and respond to increasing resource and energy consumption and rising greenhouse gas emissions?

Such an approach includes the rural–urban relationship as an influential factor for transport, production, consumption, employment, social relations, and more. Migration of families or family members and resulting domestic, "translocal" linkages not only have environmental effects, but also comprise social and economic processes that hold the potential for more sustainable development.

The research used, among other tools, interviews with rural–urban migrants and experts in the field. The outcomes of the research includes two theses. In her master's thesis, "Between Village and City: Rural–Urban Linkages in the Broader Region of Hyderabad," Alva Bonaker highlighted rural–urban linkages in Hyderabad and the role of technology in bridging the divide. Her work contributed significantly to this chapter (Bonaker 2012). Manuel Benteler examined the multilocal lives of middle- and upper-class city residents in his dissertation, "Translocal?—Migrants in Hyderabad, India" (Benteler 2011), which will be referred to throughout this chapter.

This chapter focuses on Hyderabad's rural migrants and their linkages to their home villages. It analyzes the practical, symbolic, and emotional links between those two poles. Among the outcomes of these links, the fieldwork showed a robust flow of people, goods, and information, which are physical representations of the multiple identities embraced by emigrants. Although the case study of Hyderabad largely confirms the classical patterns of migration, these elements should be analyzed in an innovative way, and the focus should be moved to an investigation of new flows as generated by migrants. In this vein, the field research shows how rural migrants largely use transport and communication facilities to maintain their bonds to their home villages, and how those flows of people, goods, and information are more entangled than usually assessed. Thus, this chapter will illustrate that a study on transport regimes and systems must be connected to an analysis of communication facilities. Likewise, passenger and goods mobility must be regarded as two sides of the same coin. These elements point to the need for a closer connection between transport and communication research, not to mention the need to link—to some extent—migration and transport studies.

THE CASE OF HYDERABAD: CONTEXT OF A MIGRANT CITY

The city of Hyderabad is located in the southern Indian state of Andhra Pradesh. Hyderabad is the state capital and the biggest urban agglomeration in the state. It is also currently ranked as the sixth largest urban agglomeration in the country of India. The population of the Hyderabad Urban Agglomeration (HUA) increased from 4.3 million in 1991 to 5.7 million in 2001 and 7.7 million in 2011; it is estimated that the population will reach 10.9 million by 2021 (*Ibid.*). With the exception of the highly urbanized capital region of Hyderabad, Andhra Pradesh is mostly rural, as approximately 60% of the population works in agriculture (*Ibid.*).

Hyderabad was founded by Muhammad Quli in 1591 and for centuries Islamic influences shaped the city's landscape, although this dominant culture amalgamated with native Telugu culture. The city was originally sited on the south side of the Musi River, today referred to as the "Old City." Its nucleus is the Charminar monument, where the first influx of migrants, mostly Hindu and Muslim traders from Rajasthan and Gujarati in the northwest of India, settled.

Although Hyderabad has its own, unique history, the city's development shares some common elements with that of its parent nation, India, particularly with respect to migration, the complexity of which cannot be captured here. Generally speaking, India is still conceived as a "country of villages" with a relatively small proportion of the population living in urban areas. However, it is currently facing processes of rapid urbanization comparable only to that which is taking place in China, as the share of urban residents in India is predicted to increase from 30% in 2008 to 40% by 2030 (McKinsey Global Institute 2010). Contributing to one-third of the urban population growth, the rural exodus is gaining speed, which makes mobility and the increasing relevance of rural–urban linkages particularly important.

218   *Angela Jain and G.L.N. Reddy*

Therefore, a high level of mobility is not uncommon in the subcontinent. As of 2001 the overall number of internal migrants in India is estimated to be 307 million—or 30% of the population (Government of India, Ministry of Home Affairs 2011). The data on migration determined by "last residence" as per Census 2001 shows that the total number of migrants in India is 314 million. Out of these, 268 million (85%) have been intrastate migrants, those who migrated from one state to another, whereas an additional 41 million (13%) were interstate migrants and 5.1 million (1.6%) migrated to India from outside the country (*Ibid.*).

Among those who moved or resettled within India, rural-to-rural migration is still the predominant form of migration (55% of all migrants between 1991 and 2001), and mostly comprised of moves over short distances and recently married women joining their husbands' households (Sivaramakrishnan et al. 2007). Nonetheless, rural–urban migration rates are growing, especially after the economic liberalization of the early 1990s that shook the peasant society. The latest available calculations of the 2011 census show that in the preceding decade around 20.5 million Indians migrated from rural to urban areas (Government of India, Ministry of Home Affairs 2011). Indeed, those numbers are significant, but may not tell the whole story.

Statistically, migration processes are still hard to assess for social scientists and demographers due to difficulties in registration and reporting, especially in developing countries. Conventional censuses are likely to underestimate real migration rates, as insights gained from village studies indicate a much higher prevalence of mobility (Bird and Deshingkar 2009). However, not only statistics, but also politics is tuned to the well-defined matching of people and places, with the result that government policies address and reach primarily registered and settled citizens, while neglecting mobile, and often deprived, individuals who lack formal status (*Ibid.*). In this regard, the idea of relatively static populations and "monolocal" lives is increasingly challenged by "multilocal" realities.

RURAL–URBAN LINKAGES: THE NEED FOR MOBILITY

Social networks that play an important role among short-distance migrants tend to lose their significance as the distance between place of origin and destination increases, though there are some exceptions to this principle (migrants from Bihar to Delhi, Maharashtra, or West Bengal, for example). As noted in the case of intrastate, rural, male migrants, southern Indian states do not show a higher interstate male migration rate than other Indian states (Keshri and Bhagat 2012: 12).

However, in opportune economic situations, the search for new opportunities has led to patterns of temporary and circular migration. Recent studies show that migration rates differ across caste groups and villages, with the highest incidence among chronically poor people living in remote villages. According to Deshingkar (2010), overall mobility levels have grown: in Andhra Pradesh the number of households with at least one person working outside the village has increased from 41% in 2003–2004 to 54% in 2006–2007. Comparing figures on circular migration, commuting, and permanent migration shows that commuting has emerged as the main form of mobility as growing prosperity and small-town development become more apparent in the state. "In remote villages, migration involved all but the poorest (disabled, old and sick) and the richest" (Deshigkar 2010: vii). This picture is "challenging the notion that migration benefits only a privileged few with the right contacts, assets, and education" and reveals that migration is crucial to managing risks for a majority of chronically poor households in remote rural areas. Moreover, "migration has improved the creditworthiness of the families left behind in the village who can now obtain large loans easily" (*Ibid.*).

Temporary and seasonal migration has been an important income diversification and risk-coping strategy in agricultural areas, not just in developing countries. "In places where access to non-agricultural employment is limited, or climate (or technology) prevents continuous cultivation, seasonal migration is often the key to a household's income during the agricultural lean season" (Keshri and Bhagat 2012: 87). It is not only an important form of labor mobility in a country like India with an increasing shift from agriculture to industry and the tertiary sector, but also fundamental to the livelihoods of socially deprived groups, especially tribal people and those from rural areas who lack employment at their place of origin (*Ibid.*).

How do people actually move from one place to another? The Indian transport system has developed rapidly in recent years. However, the traditional forms of transport in the villages, such as bullock carts and horse carriages, are still seen quite often. Bicycles and cycle-rickshaws have been an integral mode of transport in rural India, too, recently aided by scooters and mopeds as faster means of transport. As for public transport, in some places auto rickshaws run on fixed routes and on fixed fares. For commuter and goods transport, vans or minibuses have become a prevalent form of transportation, especially in remote areas of India; these vans run along the common route and fulfil consistent, yet small, transportation needs.

With the construction of village roads, rural India is rapidly transforming. "Wherever the roads network has come up the rural economy and quality of life has improved." (The World Bank n.d.). Still, only 60% of the rural population has access to an "all season road," which means that they live within two kilometers of a "motorable road" (Government of India, Ministry of Rural Development, 2002).

Unfortunately, more up-to-date statistics on modes and distances of rural (to urban) transport, which would allow for quantitative reflection on mobility patterns, cannot be found. However, as is usually the case in many developing nations, India's communication sector grows faster than its road network: around 70 out of 100 people subscribe to a public mobile telephone

220 *Angela Jain and G.L.N. Reddy*

service using cellular technology (in Germany and the U.K. around 130; in the United States around 100) (The World Bank 2013).

Although the transport and communication situation in rural areas has been improving rapidly and helping to bring about greater connectivity, major Indian cities like Hyderabad face huge challenges in their urban transport regimes. The lion's share of Hyderabad's population used to travel by foot because a large proportion of the population was too poor to afford public transport, let alone other kinds of motorized or wheeled transport. Moreover, the city's urban structure made walking feasible.

In addition, Hyderabad used to have a large proportion of public transport users, due to the city having a bus system with good coverage. But this statistic is on the decline, as is the share of resident pedestrians. In 2003, the modal spilt consisted of pedestrians (30%), bicycles (3%), public transport (28%), motorcycles (31%), cars (2%), and other forms of transport like ox-carts or three-wheelers (5%). However, these shares are changing rapidly as private motorized transport increases exponentially. On the one hand, this is caused by the massive urban sprawl of Hyderabad, which has resulted in increased trip lengths for most urban residents, deterioration of public-transport coverage, and, simultaneously, a decrease in pedestrian and bicycle traffic. The latter modes of transport are especially affected as appropriate infrastructure is missing and growing traffic volumes make walking or cycling on the roads unattractive and even dangerous. On the other hand, rapidly growing incomes and the rise of the middle class makes private motorized transport affordable to a growing number of Hyderabad residents: thus creating a vicious circle with respect to sustainable transport systems. Hence, in 2007, around 2.3 million motorized vehicles were registered. A study of registered vehicles reveals that Hyderabad's vehicle fleet almost doubled between 2002 and 2007 and contains a high proportion of two-wheel vehicles (see Table 13.1) (HMDA, 2011).

Firsthand accounts of rural and urban mobility provide an idea of how villagers attempt to realize their transport demands and how urban citizens put their personal rural–urban linkages into practice. With accessibility, distances get shortened and visits between family members become more frequent. Shakuntala Verma said, "Our pace of life has suddenly changed, people are earning better and travel is less time consuming. Even our sons, working in big cities, are visiting us for festivals as just three days leave is enough for a home visit" (The World Bank n.d.: 20). In the dusty, dry landscape of Rajasthan, young Kalyani Devi is happy having access to a road. Busy working in her fields, she said smilingly that she could slip away to the next village every second day to chat with her mother. For the villagers of Thooni Ahiran, rural roads have meant better marriage offers for their sons and daughters. "Few people were willing to give their daughter in marriage into a village where access was difficult and time consuming. With the road connecting the village to the nearest town, Fagu, multiple educational choices have opened up for the villagers. Some farmers have started a car

Table 13.1 Growth trend of motor vehicles in Hyderabad

Mode	January 2007	March 2002	March 1993	Percent Increase from 2002	Percent of Total Vehicles for 2007
Buses and private service vehicles	15,299	13,817	3,836	10%	0.7%
Auto rickshaws	99,105	71,069	23,874	39%	4.3%
Cars and jeeps	324,347	184,715	66,793	75%	14.2%
Two-wheelers	1,738,640	1,124,508	467,225	54%	76.2%
Goods vehicles	82,534	48,292	16,473	71%	3.6%
Taxi cabs	21,434	5,531	5,333	288%	0.9%
Total	2,281,359	1,447,932	583,534		100%

pool to take their children to an English medium private school in the town four kilometers away" (*Ibid.*).

A "SENTIMENTAL LINK"

In order to analyze the qualities of rural–urban linkages more deeply and assess their dimensions and their intensity, fieldwork and interviews were conducted in and around Hyderabad during 2010 and 2011. The studies addressed factors such as the extent of migration, the nature and frequency of contact, and the exchange of goods between the two areas, as well as the duration of migrants' stays in the city.

Many of our interviewees state that rural–urban migrants maintained a "sentimental link" between Hyderabad and their home villages. Because it is common for family members or relatives to stay behind in a village when migrants move to the city, most informants go to great lengths to maintain close contact with those left behind, because family ties are very important in Indian society. With regard to middle- and upper-class migrants, Benteler corroborates the hypothesis that linkages to the place of origin are primarily based on family ties. If parents or other close relatives leave the village, the rural–urban connections often decline or even disappear. Hence, caste, and community as binding factors are only secondary to maintaining rural ties (Benteler 2011). However, besides the important role played by kinship bonds, other factors influence linkages to home regions. As many first-generation migrants in India desire to maintain relationships with their native regions, they often prefer that their children marry a girl or boy from their native region. This custom is not limited to internal-migrant families, but also applies to the vast majority of international migrants. It can also be assumed that the patterns are roughly comparable in all parts of India, because tradition and the relevance of family and religious events are high. Habits and customs such as festivals, dress, and notably food and dietary practices represent soft ties to rural communities and cultures, but are an essential part of the translocal social space.

The social aspect of property as an anchor to villages is connected with the interactions that take place between rural and urban spheres. Visits during religious festivals ("City kitata" Saakshi: telugudialy" [Hyderabad, January 14, 2011, second city edition]) play a crucial role in reinforcing strong ties within communities even if celebrants live in different places. Hyderabad's character as a modern, technology-centered, globalized mega-city is often turned inside out during festival times when the city reveals its more traditional heart and mind. During Sankranti in January, which celebrates the harvest season, especially in the coastal area, Ugadi in April, and Dushera in October, a substantial increase in demand for travel means typically occurs as city residents return to their "native place." Bus and train operators run additional services at higher fares. Some estimates indicate that around one-fourth of the population (or around two million people) leave Hyderabad during Sankranti, giving the appearance of an undeclared city holiday (Committee for Consultations on the Situation in Andhra Pradesh 2011). In all, our informants estimated that migrants return to their villages between two and six or eight times per year for festivals. It makes sense for them to return home for festivals and functions, because during interim times few acquaintances will be in Hyderabad. At festival times, however, many old friends return and gather in home villages, which makes interaction and maintaining social relations much easier.

Weddings are mentioned most often as a further reason for visiting home villages. They allow whole families to reunite, thus strengthening integration of the village. Therefore wedding attendance by family and friends is expected and considered to be a social obligation. Yet, unless migrants strongly identify with the whole village, which seems to be rare among middle- and upper-class migrants, visits are confined to the marriages of close family members, not simply any community member. Benteler's study (2011) further indicates that there is no difference between visiting the husband's or the wife's family. However, the number of visits to the home village seems to decrease significantly when first-generation migrants establish their own families. Consequently, the frequency of visits declines significantly in the second generation, who spend little time in country villages during their youth.

The duration of home visits may span from several hours to several weeks depending on the distances traveled, but also the status and resources of migrants, because many cannot afford to leave their urban workplaces for long unless they "circulate" and return for work purposes. Interestingly, interviewees mention returning home for agricultural work much less often than returning for cultural functions. Instead, other important reasons for returning to the village include instances of illness among migrants, if the illness is not too serious, and to participate in elections. Urbanized migrants also receive visits from their village relatives. However, visitation patterns and reasons probably vary greatly according to status and resources, as will become clearer later in the chapter.

Although estimates about the frequency of contact vary, most of the informants approached in our fieldwork mention mobile phones as the most important medium used in both city and villages for staying in contact. One interviewee even claimed that interaction is increasing as the spread of mobile phones makes it easier to keep in touch without spending much money or time on travelling. Although there might have been telephone connections previously, the propagation of cheap mobile phone tariffs means that even poor migrants can afford to stay in touch with relatives by placing a few calls per month. However, there is some indication that communication, too, is mostly limited to the family circle. Contacts with friends exist, but are less frequent, which also applies to the use of the Internet as medium of communication. It can be assumed that online communication is more and increasingly relevant among young peers, rather than within families.

Other members of the village community were hardly ever contacted before mobile phones appeared because there was no way to stay in touch across large distances. Interviewees state that it is much easier nowadays to keep connected, which is a good example of the way that communication regimes shape and foster the development of rural–urban linkages. This even applies to poor migrants who can afford mobile phone calls, which, in turn, enable them to reduce spending for sometimes distant and costly trips to their villages. As a consequence, return visits may significantly decrease, because contact can be maintained via new communication media. This, of course, may also affect the transfer of in-kind or financial resources (depending on the availability of other transfer possibilities).

SYMBOLIC VALUE AND MATERIAL EVIDENCE

As studies of migration show, networks between urban residents and villagers are crucial for supporting the latter with information and concrete employment opportunities, thus facilitating or at times even initiating resettlement or circular migration schemes. As one interviewee states: "They come normally through family links, somebody who stays already here will accommodate them. So they don't come as an unknown individual, but they come through reference, caste reference or community reference, some kind of link. And in fact people who are here, they go and then get others. You can say they are collected from the villages" (Jain et al. 2012).

This, in turn, increases pressure on city residents to provide employment for many interested potential migrants, even though their ability to provide jobs or helpful resources is limited. Furthermore, this manner of recruitment can also harm the reputations of migrants if those that they referred are not qualified or perform badly. This observations made in Hyderabad may be in line with Banerjee's study on migrants in Delhi, which revealed that networks used for job searches are less important for skilled and highly qualified migrants, because their employment is based also on qualifications that are assessed through interviews and tests (Banerjee 1998). However, class and caste differences may also be significant, as people from disadvantaged segments may use (and rely more on) their support networks (Benteler 2011).

In most cases, close contact between migrants in the city and their relatives in villages also facilitates an exchange of goods between these areas. According to most of the informants, money is the main resource being transferred, because people send it to their families or bring it back to their villages depending on their income. Rough estimates suggest that migrants in Hyderabad send up to 50% of their savings home. In terms of money transfers, some of those interviewed mention the "money order" system that is offered by post offices. In any case, the importance of remittances should not be overstated, though it is hard to assess precisely. A study by Deshingkar et al. indicates that remittances account for only 5–10% of rural income, which is, of course, still a substantial amount (Deshingkar et al. 2009).

Apart from a general need or desire to migrate in order to increase general income, some informants point out that there might also be concrete reasons why people want to earn money in the city. Those earnings flow back to home villages, where they are spent to build or renovate houses, buy land in the village, or pay back debts (Bonaker 2012). Such activities indicate that many migrants wish to maintain a presence in their home villages or even to invest in them—be it for themselves or their relatives. This aspect of the village–city link fits into the previously mentioned paradigm of migrants maintaining strong ties to their villages, a situation that is very much emphasized by the informants.

In terms of nonfinancial exchanges, there are informal flows of goods between rural and urban areas, which are mainly directed from the village to the city and primarily consist of food supplies. Migrants visiting their places of origin may return to the city with local specialties or food that is cheaper in the village such as rice, daal (pulse), spices, nonvegetarian items, pickles, vegetables, grains, and sweets. Our interviewees point out that there are even well-established courier services and agencies that deliver goods and food items from villages to the city via normal buses, as well as informal networks of friends and relatives who transport things in both directions.

Food, in particular, is of great relevance in Indian culture, and local and regional habits and preferences are most likely to remain long after migration. This explains for instance, why an exceptional phenomenon like the "dabbawallah-system" in cities like Mumbai can exist. The dabbawallah is a serviceman who works as part of a delivery system that collects hot food items from workers' residences in the late morning and delivers them to the workplace utilizing various modes of transport, predominantly bicycles and trains, and returns the empty boxes to the customers' residences that afternoon. Because it is so important to eat homemade food, preferably cooked with village-grown items, such services find their market.

However, our interviewees stated that there is little need to bring items to their home villages because most things are available in these locations, too.

Nonetheless, some luxury items among upper-caste migrants or electronic articles, fruits, and dresses might be brought from the city if they are hard to get or more expensive in the village, particularly for poor groups.

As interactions between village and city are especially strong if they are based on kinship ties, the spatial distribution of family members and multilocal patterns are crucial for the development of rural–urban linkages. There are various mechanisms at play, which either foster or hamper reunification and chain migration. Whether parents follow their children to the city or children follow their parents often determines the length of rural ties and how such ties are maintained.

Very few rural people who migrate to the city in search of better livelihoods allow their parents to live with them after resettlement. There are many reasons for this: Farmers wedded to agricultural hinterlands never show much interest in permanently resettling in urban areas as these are unfamiliar environments to them. In Indian tradition, sons typically live with their families in their parents' homes. Daughters usually leave their families to live with their husbands' families. If their children settle in cities, parents visit them as guests, or for care in the case of severe illness, but prefer not to stay permanently. Even if they have only one son and no other children live with them, many of them remain in their village, because they feel comfortable in the company of other villagers and relatives. The only request they have for their son is to visit them frequently. In most cases, parents do not stay with their daughters, even if they have only one daughter.

Nowadays, many couples work, unlike in the past where wives were confined to the house while husbands worked. As a result, the present generation often "employs" their retired parents to take care of grandchildren at home.

On the other hand, older urban migrants with connections to their rural villages of origin face the question of whether to go back to their village or stay in the city. Although some of the interviewees argued that the hard work in which they engage can only be done up to a certain age and that they want to go back to the village soon after retirement, others assume that the trend of return migration for retirees will start at a later time. However, many farmers who migrated from villages to urban centers have strong sentimental attachments to their places of origin and wish to be cremated on their lands. In many villages, one therefore finds graves of dead landlords in the midst of the farmland.

TWO TYPES OF MIGRANTS

"The Successful and the Aspirants: Educated and Better-off"

Most of the informants emphasize that education has become more and more important, even among very poor people. The lack of educational facilities drives many children of villagers to the city. Education was traditionally a domain of Brahmins and a way to shift their dominance to the

226   Angela Jain and G.L.N. Reddy

urban centers. Today, people with various backgrounds come to the city in order to upgrade their skills and seek out better job opportunities. Among these professional aspirants, two groups can be identified: those looking for traditional, government-related jobs and those looking for training courses and employment in the information and communication technologies (ICT) sector. As the number of government jobs dwindled, there was an employment boom in the private sector. This has changed the employment situation in Andhra Pradesh. Jobs with multinational companies are so enticing that many graduates have rejected coveted jobs in government departments for lucrative software positions. Because major software companies have started to prefer engineering graduates, many rural, middle-class families enrolled their children in engineering courses, even though it meant facing financial hardships. However, their sacrifices seem to have paid off, as many young Indians have realized their dreams.

After completing courses of study, some graduates shift their residences repeatedly between Hyderabad, Bangalore, and Pune, the major software hubs in India. Although in other areas rural people are the most common migrants, in Hyderabad the number of semiurbanites and rural aspirants is roughly even. Similar to government aspirants, those coming from rural areas commonly share a room with two or three other people and consume self-cooked food because their parents' incomes are very meager. They make short trips to home villages perhaps once every two months for approximately two days in order to receive money or for other occasions.

Although most of the financial transfers among lower-status, multilocal migrants are usually confined to the family unit, the case of upper-caste, urban dwellers is different. As some have or had special positions in the village, monetary gifts to remote relatives or former servants are at times considered mandatory and seen as a good habit (Benteler 2011). During visits by former village chiefs or other elite families, small donations are expected. Also, they are approached by urban migrants from their home villages to provide financial support to unlucky migrants who came to the city and ran out of money or on behalf of those unable to migrate due to lack of financial means. Yet, this scenario is likely to apply only to a small portion of privileged urban migrants.

Similarly, according to our experts, high-status migrants display no discernable pattern with respect to moving back to home villages for retirement. On the one hand, they assert that as the city becomes increasingly noisy and polluted, people wish to spend their postretirement life in a calm village. On the other hand, issues such as insufficient health care and lack of other modern facilities prevent people from moving back to their villages.

"The Struggling and Deprived: Low Skill and Low Income"

Apart from jobs directly related to the ICT sector, the sector's boom has also had some influence on the job situation of less-skilled migrants from the villages. Observers have noted that growth in this particular industry also creates a lot of jobs in the unskilled labor and service sector. In addition to the most apparent need for labor in the construction of new offices and residences, people in ICT jobs develop a need for service workers, such as drivers, gardeners, shopkeepers, nannies, and nurses.

The study shows, on the one hand, that low-skilled migrants do not want to stay for long because "people do not sacrifice their family for earning money"—as one interviewee stated—and therefore prefer seasonal jobs. On the other hand, studies show that migrants normally do not go back to stay in villages, but try to become permanent residents in the city. Both observations are true, as there is a lot of diversity among the unskilled and poor in using migration and urban ties to improve their situation and diversify their often threatened livelihoods.

A common pattern that can also be found in Hyderabad is that parcels of village land purchased by migrants are not disposed of and income from migration is used for investments. Also it has been shown for Andhra Pradesh that circular migration is to some extent negatively correlated with the level of monsoon rainfall (Badiani and Safir 2009). A pattern of seasonal migration seems to be increasingly common among people in agricultural occupations. As one expert notes: "They live in two places many times, they come to the city when the crops are growing, but when the crops have to be harvested or sown they go back to their villages. . . . Probably they spend three month in the villages and the rest of the time in the city" (see Jain et al. 2012).

In the city, many rural migrants stay in roadside huts near construction sites or even in the same buildings on which they are working with people from their native villages. When work is completed on one site, they move to the next. Initially they often leave their families behind in the village. Once they gain some confidence that they can provide food and living accommodations for others, they try to get their families to migrate, too. The wives, then, often work similarly in low-income, contract work, typically as maids and servants. As a result, return visits to villages largely depend on whether migrants' families are with them or remain in the villages. If their spouses are with them, their trips are usually limited to only one or two visits per year. For this type of more permanent urban migrant, visits are closely related to functions and festivals.

CONCLUSION: MULTILOCAL LIFESTYLES TURN TO NORMALITY

As has been described, rural–urban linkages of a personal dimension are largely dependent on kinship and family still residing in the villages. With the reunification of families in the cities, either parents and/or children, those links are likely to decline. As a result of this and also because of weaker emotional ties, rural ties are predominantly confined to first-generation

228 *Angela Jain and G.L.N. Reddy*

migrants and are likely to decline or disappear in the second generation (Benteler 2011). Once the nuclear family has moved to the city, children of the next generation rarely visit the village, which makes the establishment of emotional and social links unlikely. However, this long-term tendency might involve much variation due to socioeconomic or other factors and needs to be further examined.

Indeed, the vast variation of relevant background variables like caste, socioeconomic status, gender, and age correlate with motives, interaction forms, and mobility patterns. The complexity of characteristics can hardly be delineated within the limited scope of this study. That is why the chapter has tried to construe different types of migrants with their various mobility patterns. This allows for the generation of crucial insights into various forms of migration and the relationship between political and economic contexts, individual socioeconomic backgrounds, migration motives, distance, and so forth. Although some classification can be attempted that match individual characteristics and mobility patterns (high-skilled professionals settle predominately in the city and maintain some village connections, whereas low-skilled workers are mostly seasonal migrants linked to villages by regular farm activity), there is a lot of overlap and uncaptured variations.

As has been shown, the realm of rural–urban linkages in the Hyderabad region is utterly diverse, as are the impact of these linkages on developmental trajectories of the megacity and its surroundings. In the past, rural–urban migration, and the links between these two sectors instigated by political and economic transformations, played a major role in Hyderabad's development. In order to shape its future in a way that favors sustainability, insights from past and present processes concerning the city–village nexus have to be taken seriously. First and foremost, it has to be acknowledged that rural–urban linkages exist and that they are strong and relevant. This not only has theoretical implications in the sense of a new heuristic that breaks up the urban–rural dichotomy and the assumption of unambiguously localizable households and populations. It is at least equally important from a policy perspective that for much too long has been shaped by a strong distinction between city and village. The old view is to blame for policy measures that attempted to inhibit migration to the cities, which led to negative side effects such the neglect of rural–urban connections. It is quite evident that migration impulses and migration streams are very hard, if not impossible, to stop.

Instead of depending on ineffective measures to stem migration or simply turning a blind eye to the process, the importance of rural–urban migration for promoting development, as this chapter has documented, must be acknowledged. Partly, positive effects result from the systemic links and the strategic actions of people striving for survival, decent livelihoods, and upward mobility without government assistance or even in spite of political policies. However, it is out of the question that legal frameworks, labor regulation, social programs and schemes, and other factors can shape those outcomes to a large extent—for better or worse. This is particularly true when it comes to sustainability. People move and live "between" the city and the village, a way of life with a significant, long-term environmental, social, and economic impact. India is facing impressive growth of its urban agglomerations, structural change in the countryside, increasing demand for goods, and the expansion of consumption patterns. Still, the impacts on mobility and of mobility have not been explored sufficiently. These trends will likely lead to growing use of resources, mounting emissions, strains on urban infrastructure, shortage of housing, and lack of space, not to mention the possibility of growing social tensions between various subgroups. Rural–urban migration and the manifold links between city and village may be a part of the problem, but they can also be part of the solution for coping with these challenges.

WORKS CITED

Badiani, R., and Safir, A. "Circular Migration and Labour Supply: Responses to Climate Shocks." In: P. Deshingkar and J. Farrington (eds.), *Circular Migration and Multilocational Livelihood Strategies in Rural India*. New Delhi, Oxford University Press, 2009.

Banerjee, B. "Migration Motivation, Family Links, and Job Search Methods of Rural-to-Urban Migrants in India." In: R. E. Bilsborrow (ed.), *Migration, Urbanization, and Development: New Directions and Issues*. Proceedings of the Symposium on Internal Migration and Urbanization in Developing Countries, January 22–24, 1996. New York. Norwell, Kluwer, 1998, p. 187–220.

Benteler, M. *Translokal? MigrantInnen in Hyderabad (Indien)* [Translocal—Migrants in Hyderabad, India]. Akademische Verlagsgemeinschaft, München, 2011.

Bird, K., and Deshingkar, P. *Circular Migration in India*. Policy briefing N. 4, prepared for World Development Report. London, Overseas Development Institute, 2009.

Bonaker, A. *Between Village and City: Rural–Urban Linkages in the Broader Region of Hyderabad*. Europäischer Hochschulverlag, 2012.

Deshingkar, P. *Migration, Remote Rural Areas and Chronic Poverty in India*. ODI Working Paper 323, London, 2010.

Deshingkar, P., S. L. Rao, and S. Akter. "The Evolving Pattern of Circular Migration and Commuting: Household Surveys in Andhra Pradesh." In: P. Deshingkar and J. Farrington (eds), *Circular Migration and Multilocational Livelihood Strategies in Rural India*. New Delhi, Oxford University Press, 2009, p. 58–87.

Government of India, Ministry of Home Affairs, Rural Urban Distribution of Population. *Census of India 2011*. Web. http://censusindia.gov.in/2011-prov-results/paper2/data_files/india/Rural_Urban_2011.pdf (22.4.2014).

Hyderabad Metropolitan Development Authority (HMDA). *Inception Report*. In: Comprehensive Transportation Study (CTS) for Hyderabad Metropolitan Area (HMA), Volume I/2011. LEA Associates South Asia Pvt., Ltd., New Delhi, India, 2011.

Jain, A., G. L. N. Reddy, Alva Bonaker, and Marc Holland-Cruz. *Move and Maintain: Rural-Urban Linkages and Sustainable Development in the Indian Megacity of Hyderabad*. nexus Discussion Paper, 2012. Web. http://www.nexusin stitut.de/de/arbeits-forschungsbereiche/mobilitaet-raum-demografie/44-kuerz lich-abgeschlossene-projekte/7-megacity-hyderabad.

Keshri, K., and R. B. Bhagat. "Temporary and Seasonal Migration: Regional Pattern, Characteristics and Associated Factors." *Economic & Political Weekly*, January 28, 2012.

McKinsey Global Institute. *India's Urban Awakening: Building Inclusive Cities, Sustaining Economic Growth*. Web. 2010. http://www.mckinsey.com/~/media/McKinsey/dotcom/Insights%20and%20pubs/MGI/Research/Urbanization/Indias%20urban%20awakening%20Building%20inclusive%20cities/MGI_Indias_urban_awakening_full_report.ashx.

Sivaramakrishnan, K. C., A. Kundu, and B. N. Singh. *Handbook of Urbanization in India: An Analysis of Trends and Processes*. Oxford India Handbooks, 2nd ed. New Delhi, Oxford University Press, 2007.

The World Bank (n.d.). *Rural Roads—A Lifeline for Villages in India*. Web. http://web.worldbank.org/wbsite/external/countries/southasiaext/extsarregtoptransport/0,,contentmdk:21755700~pagepk:34004173~pipk:34003707~thesitepk:579598,00.html.

———. *Data—Mobile Cellular Subscriptions 2013*. Web. http://data.worldbank.org/indicator/IT.CEL.SETS.P2.

14 Dwelling in between? Multilocation between History and New Sociotechnical Systems

Hans-Liudger Dienel and Massimo Moraglio

"Multilocation," as used in this chapter, refers to a lifestyle in which subjects dwell in more than one living place, and thus travel (with a certain degree of regularity) between those locations. This concept has been explored as "multiresidentiality" (Kaufmann 2002), as multiple dwelling (Stock 2006), and as multilocal living, namely, "the existence and use of more than one place of residence" (Hilti 2009: 148). We can also speak of multilocation as an "extreme" form of *migration pendulaires* (commuting migration), to use Meissoner's (2001) words. To give some anecdotal examples, multilocal living can refer to the businessperson who works in Frankfurt but has family in Bordeaux; the miner returning home every two weeks; the academic researcher with a fellowship in Madrid but returning every week to Vienna, the city where her or his family lives; or the Dutch retired couple travelling every two months to a little house they purchased in Greece.

Multilocation is depicted as a rapidly growing phenomenon, although it is largely neither recognized in official statistics nor in political discussions, whose consequences in the social fabric remain largely unexplored. Considering multilocation participants' extensive use of transport facilities, however, dwelling "in-between" heavily affects transport systems, energy consumption, and infrastructures; it also influences real estate markets, welfare requests, and especially labor markets.

The chapter will raise some issues with this multilocational lifestyle. Namely, it will first address the long history of the phenomenon, and thus illustrate that it is not a prerogative of modern times. In reality, multilocation has been performed extensively in the past by very different social groups with very different purposes and outcomes.

Secondly, based on the rich debate that arose in the late 1990s (Urry 1999), the chapter will examine the relationship between transport networks, communication facilities, and multilocational lifestyles, stressing how these three aspects together are forming a new sociotechnical mixture—while acknowledging historical precedents, which thus requires a different theoretical approach to investigate questions of mobility. In particular, the role that innovative transport systems played during the past thirty years and—even more—the massive use of information and communication

232 Hans-Liudger Dienel and Massimo Moraglio

technologies (ICT) are major topics of investigation, as they play a central part in the spread of multilocational lifestyles. Much of the literature on the topic has also stressed the importance of societal changes and labor market shifts in promoting multilocation, though scholarly consensus is far from unanimous regarding the causes of multilocation and mobility growth. In particular, the role of ICTs has been investigated in depth, which has revealed new outcomes regarding their role in fuelling high-mobility and multilocation.

To summarize the scholarly debate, the chapter considers a set of entangled questions, namely: *Why* do people engage in multilocational lifestyles? *What* is the main driving force of this trend? *What* role do new sociotechnical regimes in transport and ICT play in the process? *What* role does the compression of time and space generated by those new settings play? *Do* familiar and occupational settings promote or limit multilocation? And, finally, as noted above, is multilocation a truly innovative trend, or has it, *mutatis mutandis*, a long history?

It is not easy to address all these questions because the concept of multilocation still is awaiting a clear definition (Hilti 2009). Multilocation is indeed a blurry concept, which often falls outside the classical approach employed by scholars of migration studies. Is a multilocational person a migrant? Or is she or he a commuter who has pushed the concept of splitting the proximity of home and work to the extreme? Based on the 1990s debate, it appears that multilocation defies both the traditional concept of the migrant and the commuter: multilocation indeed requires a new means of conceptualization (Kaufmann 2002).

Additionally, multilocation is difficult to assess and scrutinize because the magnitude of the phenomenon simply does not appear formally (or may appear only marginally) in official statistics. Formal recognition of multilocation is often not requested by states, namely because official changes of residency may be avoided, nor is working in a location far from home noted in official surveys. Travel between the residencies is not recorded, *in se*, whereas information about travel behaviors is collected in a general scale, providing no evidence to disaggregate important elements. These details provide little, if any, information with which to assess the quantitative side of multilocational lifestyles. A better way to assess the phenomenon is to consider the impressive increase in transport performed—as an average—by so-called western-world inhabitants, which can give us a rough but powerful estimation of a society on the move, including multilocation performances. The same can be said about the dramatic expansion in the volume of civil aviation, especially the passenger market, which inevitably corresponds to a faster and more mobile society connected (as aviation is) by long-distance trips. Data about the increasing use of ICT appears to be even more convincing.

The other way to grasp the topic is through fieldwork, as has been done during the past years. The outcomes are really quite interesting and document relationship networks in which geographical proximity is not a relevant factor in keeping the network alive and vibrant (Larsen et al. 2006), but studies also display how personal targets, familiar issues, and professional choices are more relevant than the potential use of ICT when the time comes for subjects to make choices about engaging in multilocational lifestyles (Nobis and Lenz 2009).

HISTORICAL ROOTS

Although it may be difficult to assess the current scale of multilocation, it seems as though it may be downright impossible to frame its historical trends. In order to reduce complexity and map the problem, it is important to recognize that as "World War II ended, geographical approaches to mobility structured around four categories of spatial mobility were developed in both fields. Daily mobility, travel [tourism], residential mobility and migration, the principal forms, were distinctive in terms of temporality (long or short) and the space in which they took place (in or outside a population basin)" (Kaufmann 2011: 25). Sheller and Urry (2006: 207) further note that "social science has largely ignored or trivialized the importance of the systematic movements of people for work and family life, for leisure and pleasure, and for politics and protest. The paradigm challenges the ways in which much social science research has been 'a-mobile.' " Naturally, multilocation and all the other forms "of long distance commuting and weekly commuting fit poorly into the already-established models of spatial mobility" (Kaufmann 2011: 34).

We have anecdotal evidence pointing to the fact that multilocation was quite common in the past century. The superrich and aristocrats have typically dwelled "in between" residencies, namely sharing their time and living patterns between winter residences in the city and summer homes (usually) in the countryside. Some cities became poles of attraction for diplomats, politicians, and lobbyists (e.g., Geneva, Brussels, Washington, D.C., but also New Delhi and Canberra), and these politically connected individuals often "commuted" between these locations. Academics often "visited" other university faculties as well, and/or held chairs in cities different from those in which they lived.

However, historically, the concept of multilocation and high mobility can be quite easily traced in other classes, too. In the early modern and modern eras, residents of Europe were hardly rooted to their birthplaces. Lucassen and Lucassen worked on migration in early modern and modern Europe, collecting estimates about different population flows, including emigration, immigration, colonization, and seasonal migration. Their findings (which focus on the period from 1500 to 1900) show a continent on the move, with increasing rates of mobility, challenging "Zelinsky's conjecture . . . that Europeans were rather sedentary and immobile until the industrial

234 *Hans-Liudger Dienel and Massimo Moraglio*

revolution . . . unchained the population and led to unprecedented mobility" (Lucassen and Lucassen 2010: 7). In their calculation, they find that mobility was a rather normal trend in modern Europe before industrialization and "modern" transport networks, although the European migration rate, as a whole, increased between the sixteenth and nineteenth centuries. The findings regarding *seasonal* migrants show increasing numbers during these centuries, from an estimated half-million migrants annually in the period from 1601 to 1650 to more than twelve million annually during the second half of nineteenth century.

These figures do not include nomadic peoples, shepherds who traveled seasonally between different pasture areas, seamen, or soldiers and their *impedimenta* (which usually included their kin until the seventeenth century). These categories of migrants had different "homes," which could be ships, barracks, or shelters, and although they were constantly on the move, they also had fixed homes, somewhere to which they could return. However we define them, though, they repeatedly spent weeks, months, or even years dwelling in different places.

These occupational migrants were not the focus of this chapter's investigation, *in se*, and are most similar to seasonal migrants in nature, which, according to Lucassen and Lucassen (2010: 33), are "one of the most neglected topics in migration history." However, the core concept of seasonal migrants (e.g., someone travelling based on seasonal rhythms) does not grasp as a whole the idea of multilocation. As previously noted, multilocational living refers to people who have two or more homes, in which they spend—on a weekly or monthly basis—a relevant portion of their time. They have, in other words, two (or more) places with which they are not just familiar but also fully invested and experienced, and that they call "home."

It is important to note that Lucassen and Lucassen openly discharged some categories of seasonal workers because "they were rarely away from home for more than a week at the most" (2010, 41). Such a statement is truly interesting, because while it discounts the relevance of these multi-locational individuals, it illustrates how such a phenomenon was experienced in the past, and shows how the research regarding (high-rate) physical mobility before the Industrial Revolution and modern transport networks should be further delineated. In other words, their statements show that there were workers retuning home on a weekly basis, thus boosting further the estimated number of atypical migrants in the past (whose magnitude is still unresearched).

Even more convincing is the "study of Colin Pooley and Jean Turnbull (1998) on the history of social mobility in Britain, one of the few to deal with this subject from a detached historical perspective" (Kaufmann and Montulet 2008: 48). In their data, they show how "substitution of migrations by residential mobility . . . was perceptible from the 1880s and intensified as of the 1920s" (Kaufmann and Montulet 2008: 48). As summarized by Hilti (2009, 149), "multilocal living as such is not a product of modernity or late-modernity, but has changed remarkably in the light of a number of, historically speaking, relatively recent social, political and economic developments."

SPLITTING SPACE, MENDING DISTANCE

Although ignored in the past by scholars, today multilocation is considered to be the core of a new perspective in which "the particularity of the contemporary ideology of spatial mobility is that it equates spatial mobility with social fluidity" (Kaufmann and Montulet 2008: 53). The current "critique of 'static' social science also departs from those that concentrate on postnational deterritorialization processes and the end of states as containers for societies. Theories of a 'liquid modernity' (Bauman 2000) usefully redirect research away from static structures of the modern world to see how social entities comprise people, machines, and information/images in systems of movement" (Sheller and Urry 2006, 210). Based on this critique, scholars have focused on two elements that are particularly relevant here: first, the lower cost of transport as experienced in the recent decades, and its extreme flexibility and self-management; second, the growing fluidity of society, which is to say—in brief—the end of the "Fordist" era and the supposed stability of occupation, residence, and lifestyle.

It is possible, therefore, to assume, with some risks, that today's "multilocaters" are experiencing conditions similar to those that encouraged migration in the past, although they are definitely exploiting different sociotechnical systems (namely faster and cheaper transport networks and ICT in a scale unimaginable only twenty years ago). Those new regimes allow them to use faster transport systems and—compared to the past—it is very tempting to claim that the scale of these events is multiplied. Low-cost airfares (and high-speed trains) support multilocation, allowing a hypermobility that otherwise would be a prerogative of a few super-rich and super-powerful people. Time budgets and financial budgets are still major concerns, but the whole transport system is, through the Internet, immensely easier to manage individually, therefore allowing personally shaped journeys, which, consequently, boost mobility to the point that multilocation could be a concrete and routine lifestyle choice (Mokhtarian 2003). But ICT enters the scene in a more formidable way when it is time to be connected to distant locations: ICT has been presented as a form of annihilation of distance and geographies (Cairncross 1997), in which the space-time compression is made possible through communication, thus making personal networks indifferent to remoteness,. Physical connectivity can be replaced by virtual connections, making—for the purposes of this chapter—multilocaters always reachable. As noted by researchers, thanks to ICT, multilocaters do not move just themselves, but their entire networks, at least virtually (Urry 2007).

236 Hans-Liudger Dienel and Massimo Moraglio

But, and it is appropriate to repeat the concept, it has also been pointed out that "that individual characteristics (especially age and education) seem to be more important factors influencing the choice between working at home and out-of-home than ICT availability or commuting time. Hubers and colleagues (2008a), for instance, found that age, the presence of children, and education levels have stronger relationships with fragmentation than ICTs do." (Alexander et al. 2010: 58)

What is less disputable and surely central to multilocational lifestyles is the end of the clear (spatial) division between different spheres of life. In the classical approach, workplaces, venues for pleasurable activities, and venues for family activities (e.g., "homes") had a spatial diversity (the office for work, the pub for social activities, home for the family routine, just to follow a classical, male-focused stereotype) rooted in a geographical coherency, namely spatial proximity such as that found in a village. So the distance among those poles was limited to a walkable gap, glued by personal movements, and eventually by transport systems or devices (bicycles, tramways, commuter buses, and train lines) linking those different environments, which lay close enough to be reachable in the one-hour daily commuting period.

Multilocation shatters geographical proximity and interrupts the clear division of life-spheres. In other words, multilocation splits away life activities from each other by hundreds or even thousands of kilometers, making impossible a daily connection. The above forces multilocaters, who find themselves having two (or more) houses and performing in two (or more) places where they practice social encounters, to recreate the minimum condition for their social reproduction. According to familiar and social backgrounds and to personal preferences, this tension can be seen as a positive experience, or an unbearable and schizophrenic burden.

These factors raise three questions:

1. What are the reasons behind multilocational lifestyles?
2. Why avoid (traditional) migration and opt for multilocation?
3. Do multilocational people care to mend the tears in their life-spheres? If yes, how?

WHAT ARE THE REASONS BEHIND MULTILOCATIONAL CHOICE?

Social science has claimed, with formidable arguments and a vast array of evidence, how in the past decades there has been a shift from a fixed and lasting form of social fabric to "liquid life," in which mobility (both geographical and social) emerged as a key factor. Those elements have been—generally speaking—described as "globalization," in which political shifts, societal changes, and new technologies resulted in the creation of a radical new framework. The role of ICT has been particularly relevant

Dwelling in between? 237

here, and communication flow has been assessed to be a revolutionary factor, allowing people to be always on the move (Makimoto and Manners 1997), or—more extremely—letting ICT simply annihilate space (Cairncross 1997). Regardless of these points, the crux of the debate is the deformation of time and space in contemporary society compared to that of the past. This deformation has led to a compression of time and space, as they are more and more linked together:

> While 'time-space compression' (Harvey 1989) is characteristics of modern societies, it seems that we are living through an extraordinary period involving significant further changes to how not only business networks but also many social networks are spatially distributed at any time and over people's life-course. 'Time-space compression' also involves 'time-space distanciation' or the spatial stretching of social networks.
>
> (Larsen et al. 2006: 261)

The notion of time and space compression should be associated with the correlated concept of activity fragmentation. As Couclelis (2000) suggested, the concept of fragmentation of activity,

> refers to the tendency that "activities that used to be associated with a single location (e.g., my workplace) are now increasingly scattered among geographically distant locations (e.g., my office, home, associate's home, hotel room, car, train, or plane)." Fragmentation therefore may lead to an increase in travel as activities are no longer tied to particular places and/or times.
>
> (Kwan et al. 2007: 23)

More precisely,

> It is a common belief that the advancement of modern information and communication technologies (ICTs) such as broadband and mobile internet connection, phone, and laptop has brought changes in the way business is conducted and work is done. . . . A potential effect of ICTs is that they alleviate the traditional space-time constraints of paid work activities and increase the range of locations and times available for conducting these activities. . . . This relaxation of spatial and temporal constraints allows for the decomposition of work into multiple segments of subtasks that can be performed at different times and/or locations. Such separation of activities into discrete pieces is commonly termed the fragmentation of activity.
>
> (Alexander et al. 2010: 55)

We have, in other words, a disintegration of activities on the geographical scale: professional activities can be performed in very different locations

238 *Hans-Liudger Dienel and Massimo Moraglio*

(office A, airplane, home, office B), as well as leisure activities (a short holiday or weekend spent away, social encounters performed out of the regular tracks). But, naturally, time is also fragmented: instead of eight-hour stretches, work could be performed in shorter legs, distanciated during the day, and this can also "invade" the weekends or the evenings (or the nights), breaking down clear distinctions between professional and nonprofessional times. The trend favors splitting activities in time and space, but also the other way around, concentrating spatially activities that were previously split (such as working at home). The resulting outcome is a mishmash of deconstruction and reconstruction. Work and family spheres can be traced, today as well as in the past, in the very same manner: "housing is increasingly seen not only as a domestic and family space, but as a leisure space (video, TV, Internet) or a workplace (notably due to the computer and internet hookup)." This "leads to the mix-up of public and private spheres and the interlocking of leisure and captive time" (Kaufmann and Montulet 2008: 47).

This mix-up makes borders and divisions blurrier than in the recent past. The central question becomes, as Lenz and Nobis (2007) have clearly pointed out: Why does fragmentation happen? They also concluded that the "fragmentation concept concentrates on ICT as an instrument to expand action spaces and action times. The question *why* people fragment activities at all remains beyond the conceptual framework thus giving the concept a deterministic character" (Lenz and Nobis 2007: 192, italics in the original). Even more remarkable is how for them, "the casual relationship between the fragmentation of activities and the effects on travel demand are still not clear" (Lenz and Nobis 2007: 203), leaving room for further research on that (central) issue.

Although scholarly research is still ongoing, there is no lack of information regarding the fragmentation of activities in contemporary society. Though their research focused primarily on long-distance commuters and multidwellers, Schneider and Limmer (2008) stressed the social aspects of such a choice, pointing out the variety of factors, mainly related to family stability and professional anxiety, that led to fragmentation:

> Mobility decisions are influenced by family circumstances and job-related factors as well as individual dispositions. In particular, family criteria and ensuring the occupational career of a partner and consideration for children, who ought to be spared the burdens of mobility, have the largest influence on the mobility decision. Next in line are job-related considerations, most notably better career and salary opportunities as well as avoiding unemployment. An evaluation of individual dispositions and attitudes reveals three particularly influential areas: the most important is the image of an ideal partnership or family life. This ideal could include aspects of proximity, distance, togetherness and autonomy. A second factor is something like local solidarity and individual

Dwelling in between? 239

attachment to the home area. A third, mainly psychological, criterion is the individual desire for security.

(Schneider and Limmer 2008: 126–127)

Two elements are definitely clear in their assessment: First, multilocation as a gendered phenomenon, in which there is an imbalance of women's duties whether they stay at home or travel (and the imbalance is definitely greater once children are involved); second, the perception of familiar stability against an uncertain labor market:

> the "rhythm of job life is characterized by flexibility; it is short-lived and competitive. The family, however, is characterized by steadiness and solidarity. The idea that mobility is necessarily connected to negative consequences is as unfounded as the idea that spatial flexibility per se opens new options. Job mobility is manifold not only in terms of its forms but also in terms of its importance in the lives of people.
>
> (Schneider and Limmer 2008: 136)

WHY AVOID MIGRATION AND OPT FOR MULTILOCATION?

Focusing mainly on the contradictory role of mobility, Kaufmann and Montulet assessed how "the effects of communication and motorized transport do not boil down to only the spatial and temporal transportation of integration modalities," but "they also lead to the *reversibility* of mobility and space" (Kaufmann and Montulet 2008: 48, italics in the original). This means that the individuals can be supported by incremented transport systems' functions and by communication networks to avoid *irreversible* shifts. The facilities developed in the past decades, both in term of widespread communication facilities and transport access, open a choice, that was not fully available before (or that was too expensive, which often produces the same outcome). So, more powerful sociotechnical systems—such as the contemporary transport network and ICT system—make it possible for individuals to avoid migration, creating an innovative type of migrant that compress time and space by being able to commute on a weekly basis and no longer having to return home only seasonally or once a year. Additionally, a reversible shift is made possible *en masse*.

In this vein, the multilocational lifestyle seems to be a valid substitute for seasonal migration, or for migration *tout court*, although beyond the substitution effects there is also a likely catalyzing effect, which means that changes in working (or pleasure) locations are now available at affordable prices, making multilocational lifestyles an option that earlier was not envisioned, and thus increasing the volume of location changes amongst individuals. In other words, new societal and professional pressures, as well as new infrastructural networks, unleash potential mobility that was not available

240   *Hans-Liudger Dienel and Massimo Moraglio*

in an earlier era or was out of reach due to time and budgetary constraints. It is also important to understand better if and how multilocation can be appealing exactly because it allows potential migrants new experiences and job opportunities, and *at the same time*, maintains original social networks. If this is the case, unexpectedly, multilocation is often experienced *in order to keep and to save previous social and familiar arrangements, routines, and obligations*. Multilocational lifestyles and the high mobility associated with them are not, therefore, simply adopted to provide freedom from immobility or made in order to experience novel environments. Having a home in two different places can be a necessary and socially legitimated way of having a job somewhere else, while maintaining an identity at a location of origin. Even more, as noted earlier, professional instability and anxiety, as well as short-term employment situations, can be factors that need to be compensated for through familiar stability in the place of origin.

In this respect, multilocation is indeed conceptually different from migration, but also from its closer kin, as defined in social science, namely, seasonal migration. The difference lies mainly in the lack of a breaking moment, a complete radical shift in the life of the individual, as is often seen in the case of migration.

HOW TO MEND THE SPATIAL GAP?

The aforementioned analysis shows how multilocation can both compromise and unite different needs, such as personal identity, familiar stability, and professional income. Multilocational lifestyles thus are accomplished in order to allow participants to benefit from the best of both worlds, original residency and a new professional destination(s). Considering how multilocation is often employed to keep participants connected to original and the new life-spheres, multilocation has to mend the spatial gap: if this gap remains torn, the whole concept of the multilocational lifestyle collapses, and eventually one cannot speak of multidwellers, but rather of migrants or seasonal migrants.

So, the issue is to better understand which strategies are implemented in order to bridge distances, in order to permit multidwellers to exploit and/or enjoy both locations. Three paths are possible here: first, constant (and chronologically regular) travel between the places, which helps to mend geographical divides with physical travel, and thus face-to-face social and familiar encounters; second, greater use of ICT in order to maintain the network owned in the other location (i.e., mending the geographical distance with communication exchanges); and third, renouncing multilocation and moving to traditional migration (i.e., reducing geographical fragmentation).

Kaufmann and Montulet (2008: 46) write, the "generalized use of IT and motorized transport has given rise to the development of social insertion via connectivity; that is, overcoming spatial distance by technical mediation."

Dwelling in between? 241

For Larsen et al. (2006: 262), a fragmented lifestyle relies on easy access to networks that help to keep alive ties otherwise impeded by geographical distance. Thus,

> as easy availability of cars, trains, planes and communication technologies seem to spread social networks beyond cities, regions and nations, so they reconnect them by helping to afford intermittent visits, meetings and frequent communication at-a-distance. People can travel, relocate and migrate and yet still be connected with friends and family members 'back home' and elsewhere. So increasingly people near emotionally may be geographically far away; yet they are only a journey, email or a phone call away.
>
> (Larsen et al. 2006: 262)

Larsen et al. (2006: 265) go further, claiming that "scholars of migration have long known that presence and absence—or proximity and distance—do not necessarily conflict and that caring and indeed presence do not necessarily imply face-to-face co-presence." There is a major discussion about the role of telecommunication in replacing physical travel, and how "'telepresence' is not a substitute for physical copresence. But it enlarges the motilities of actors and opens up new configurations and accesses to networks of cooperation, sharing of knowledge and solidarity" (Kesserling 2008: 79).

Nobis and Lenz (2009: 93) have remarked how the "parallel increase of both travel and telecommunication could be registered for many countries of the industrialized world, the scientific discussion about the interaction between telecommunication and travel is far from asserting an 'automatism' between them." They also have noticed that "most analysis have tended to presume that the direction of influence is above all from telecommunication to travel thus neglecting or at least underestimating the likely impact of travel on telecommunications." If there is a general agreement to conclude that "the use of and experience with ICT contributes to more fragmented work patterns," it can also "be noted, however, that the causality of this effect is unclear. It is likely that those whose work organization allows for fragmentation of the work activity will have used ICTs more in order to effectuate working from home and other places" (Alexander et al. 2010: 62).

This brief overview of the current debate on the role of ICT in bridging physical and conceptual distances should be completed with an addition quote from Alexander et al. (2010) in which the role of ICT as a variable seems less relevant than other factors:

> Work, personal, and house-hold-related variables are associated with fragmentation patterns more strongly than ICT variables are. Professionals and people with a high educational level, for instance, have a strong positive association with temporally and spatially fragmented

242 *Hans-Liudger Dienel and Massimo Moraglio*

work patterns. The occurrence of the fragmentation of paid work is also increasing for people with a long commute distance. With respect to the personal-household attributes, gender has a strong association with more fragmented work patterns, a result consistent with previous studies.

(Alexander 2010: 623)

So, in summary, the availability of ICT connections (in order to keep social ties alive despite the lack of proximity) seems to provide a means to correct for the reduced availability of proximal social connections, but the literature gives conflicting evidence about ICT as driving factor for multilocation.

This conclusion hints at a second action that can be implemented to mend the gap, which involves frequent trips among the different residences. The multidwellers experience two constraints in their annihilation of space through frequent trips. Geography can be less relevant, but it does not disappear: space still matters and the "tyranny of distance" (Blainey 1966) can make the broad use of multilocation difficult or impossible once the spatial gap between the residency poles reaches a critical point. But, in some dense regions, like Europe, the diffusion of low-cost airlines companies and high-speed trains, and the ease of use of those services (and self-management of travel via the Internet), provides for frequent and regular trips, which are achievable en mass from both a time and budgetary standpoint.

CONCLUSION

Multilocation, often conceived as a "happy-few" opportunity, is indeed experienced as a way to increase professional and personal prospects. Multidwellers wish to gain additional opportunities, but they want, for several reasons, to maintain their roots in their original place. This can be seen as an additional enriching experience, but can also be a burden, not a joy, once practiced as a way to cope with the uncertainty of life.

In other words, multilocation is definitely an ambivalent experience for participants, in which "increases in travel and commuting are as much a factor of inequality as of equality, as the skills needed to move are uneven—and unequally—distributed resources" (Kaufmann 2011: 43). Therefore, "changes due to new speed potentials are therefore not socially neutral, since they foster modes of appropriation that are not distributed haphazardly within the social space" (Kaufmann and Montulet 2008: 47).

Another ambiguous point is the role of new transport and ICT in speeding and increasing the prospects for multilocation. There is a vast literature on the catalyzing effects of new technological devices and transport regimes, and how those are feeding a hidden demand for higher mobility. The role of ICT is additionally depicted as central in favoring multilocational lifestyles, because it helps to mend the spatial tear among the different personal spheres, namely keeping ties with the different networks otherwise dispersed in different locations (Lyon and Urry 2005).

Against these arguments, Lenz and Nobis questioned "the causality between ICT use and travel behavior, arguing that high travel frequency induces demand for ICT rather than the other way around," (Kwan et al. 2007: 123), which means that the correlation between these two poles is far more complex than it appears. Beside Lenz and Nobis' work, ICT's role as a prime mover of multilocation is open to question, because family and personal constrains and aspirations play, apparently, a greater role than technologically innovative opportunities.

The role of new technological regimes in spreading multilocation and hypermobility provided the main focus of this chapter, namely, questioning multilocation as a new phenomenon. The attention devoted to these novel apparatuses can, to some extent, hide multilocation as a long-term experience, which can (and has) been practiced with means other than aviation, and which can be realized without the Internet and personal computing devices. Multilocation has a hidden history, and the broader topic remains to be properly investigated.

WORKS CITED

Alexander, B., D. Ettema, and M. Dijst. "Fragmentation of Work Activity as a Multi-dimensional Construct and Its Association with ICT, Employment and Sociodemographic characteristics." *Journal of Transport Geography* 18 (2010), p. 55–64.

Bauman, Z. *Liquid Society*. Cambridge, Polity Press, 2000.

Blainey, G. *The Tyranny of Distance*. Sydney, Allen and Unwin, 1966.

Cairncross, F. *The Death of Distance: How the Communications Revolution Will Change Our Lives*. Boston, Harvard Business School Press, 1997.

Couclelis, H. "From Sustainable Transportation to Sustainable Accessibility: Can We Avoid a New Tragedy of Commons?" In: D. G. Janelle and D. C. Hodge (eds.), *Information, Place and Cyberspace*. Berlin, Springer, 2000, p. 341–356.

Harvey, D. *The Condition of Postmodernity: An Enquiry into the Origins of Cultural Change*. Cambridge, MA, Blackwell, 1989.

Hilti, N. "Here, There and In-between. On the interplay of Multilocal Living, Space and Inequality." In: T. Ohnmacht, H. Maksim, and M. M. Bergman (eds.), *Mobiltiy and Inequality*. Farnham, Ashgate, 2009, p. 145–165.

Hubers, C., T. Schwanen, M. Dijst. "ICT and Temporal Fragmentation of Activities: An Analytical Framework and Initial Empirical Findings." *Tijdschrift voor economische en sociale geografie* 99 (2008), no. 5, p. 528–546.

Kaufmann, V. *Re-thinking mobility. Contemporary Sociology*. Farnham, Ashgate, 2002.

———. *Rethinking the City. Urban dynamics and motility*. Lausanne, EPFL Press, 2011.

Kaufmann, V., and B. Montulet. "Between Social and Spatial Mobilities: The Issue of Social Fluidity." In: W. Canzler, V. Kaufmann, and S. Kesselring (eds.), *Tracing Mobilities. Towards a Cosmopolitan Perspective*. Adlershot, Ashgate, 2008, p. 37–55.

244 *Hans-Liudger Dienel and Massimo Moraglio*

Kesserling, S. "The Mobile Risk Society." In: W. Canzler, V. Kaufmann, and S. Kesselring (eds.), *Tracing Mobilities. Towards a Cosmopolitan Perspective*. Adlershot, Ashgate, 2008, p. 77–102.

Larsen, J., K. W. Axhausen, and J. Urry. "Geographies of Social Networks: Meetings, Travel and Communications." *Mobilities* 1 (2006), p. 261–283.

Lenz, B., and C. Nobis. "The Changing Allocation of Activities in Space and Time by the Use of ICT—'Fragmentation' as a New Concept and Empirical Results." *Transportation Research A* (2007), p. 190–204.

Lucassen J., and L. Lucassen. *The Mobility Transition in Europe Revisited, 1500–1900. Sources and Methods*. IISH Research Paper 44. Amsterdam, International Institute of Social History, 2010.

Lyons, G., and J. Urry. "Travel Time Use in the Information Age." *Transportation Research Part A: Policy and Practice* 39 (2005), p. 257–276.

Kwan, M.-P., M. K. Dijst, and T. Schwanen. "Guest Editorial. The Interaction between ICT and Human Activity-Travel Behavior." *Transportation Research Part A* 41 (2007), p. 121–124.

Meissonnier, J. *Provinciliens: les voyageurs du quotidian*. Paris, L'Harmattan, 2001.

Mokhtarian, P. L. "Telecommunications and Travel: The Case for Complementarity." *Journal of Industrial Ecology* 6 (2003), p. 43–57.

Makimoto, T., and D. Manners. *Digital Nomad*. Chichester, Wiley, 1997.

Nobis, C., and B. Lenz. "Communication and Mobility Behavior—A Trend and Panel Analysis of the Correlation between Mobile Phone Use and Mobility." *Journal of Transport Geography* 17 (2009), p. 93–103.

Pooley, C., and J. Turnbull. *Migration and Mobility in Britain since the 18th Century*. London, UCL Press, 1998.

Schneider, N. F., and R. Limmer. "Job Mobility and Living Arrangements." In: W. Canzler, V. Kaufmann, and S. Kesselring (eds.), *Tracing Mobilities. Towards a Cosmopolitan Perspective*. Adlershot, Ashgate, 2008, p. 119–139.

Sheller, M., and J. Urry. "The New Mobilities Paradigm." *Environment and Planning A* 38 (2006), p. 207–226.

Stock, M. "L'hypothèse de l'habiter poly-topique : pratiquer les lieux géographiques dans les sociétés à individus mobiles." *EspacesTemps.net*. Web. February 26, 2006. http://www.espacestemps.net/en/articles/lrsquohypothese-de-lrsquohabiter-poly-topique-pratiquer-les-lieux-geographiques-dans-les-societes-a-individus-mobiles-en/.

Urry, J. *Sociology beyond Societies. Mobilities for the Next Century*. London, Routledge, 1999.

———. *Mobilities*, Malden, Polity Press, 2007.

Contributors

Jim Conley is an Associate Professor of Sociology at Trent University in Peterborough, Canada. His current research concerns the contributions of the work of the Groupe de sociologie politique and morale to contemporary sociology and the sociology of urban mobilities.

Peter Cox is a Senior Lecturer in Sociology at the University of Chester in the U.K. His current research investigates multidisciplinary approaches to understanding cycling and is the subject of a Leverhulme International Academic Fellowship.

Hans-Liudger Dienel is professor for work and technology at the Berlin University of Technology (Technische Universität Berlin). He studied history, philosophy, sociology and mechanical engineering in Hannover, Munich, and Washington. Dienel has been publishing for fifteen years on historical and social science mobility studies, and currently serves as president of the International Association for the History of Transport, Traffic and Mobility (www.t2m.org).

Jill Ebrey is currently working at CRESC, University of Manchester, on the "Understanding Everyday Participation—Articulating Cultural Values" research project, funded jointly by the Arts and Humanities Research Council and Creative Scotland. This work explores social and cultural participation across a number of different locations across Britain. Jill has also been working for some time on a sociology of the weekend.

Pierre Filion is a professor at the School of Planning of the University of Waterloo. His research interests include metropolitan scale planning, the relation between transportation and land use, suburban planning, and downtown redevelopment policies.

Angela Jain is director "infrastructure and society" at nexus Institute for Cooperation Management and Interdisciplinary Research, Berlin. Her

246 *Contributors*

research includes governance and sustainable development in emerging economies, new mobility concepts in peri-urban and rural areas, and public participation.

Christopher Kopper is Professor of Economic and Social History at the Universität Bielefeld (Germany). He has published several books and numerous articles about the history of transport and the history of banking and insurance.

Steven Logan is a doctoral candidate in the Graduate Programme in Communication and Culture at York University. His dissertation is a cultural history of suburbs and automobility in twentieth-century Toronto and Prague.

Alberte Martínez is a Professor of Economic History at University of A Coruña, Spain. His current research concerns the role played by foreign companies in the Spanish utilities.

Jesús Mirás is a Lecturer of Economic History at University of A Coruña, Spain. His research deals with Spanish urban history and public utilities.

Gijs Mom teaches at Eindhoven University of Technology. He is editor of *Transfers*. This year a monograph on the history of Atlantic Automobilism will appear at Berghahn Books, as well as a book on the history of car technology, to be published by SAE International. He is currently working on a monograph on World Mobility History.

Massimo Moraglio is a senior researcher at the Technische Universitaet Berlin, working on mobility and its wide effects on economic, social, and cultural fields. Currently he is working on the genealogy of the future in the mobility realm, with a special look on the twentieth-century prophecies about transport and transport systems.

Gowkanapalli Lakshmi Narasimha Reddy is an independent researcher and freelance journalist based in Hyderabad, India. His current research area is sociocultural and political history of Telugu cinema.

John Saunders is a contract faculty member with York University's Department of Geography and Faculty of Environmental Studies. His current research examines how infrastructure planning incorporates and reflects acts of citizenship.

Takeshi Yuzawa is a Professor Emeritus of Faculty of Economic at Gakushuin University in Tokyo, Japan. His current interest is the globalization of railway industry, which includes transfer of technologies, foreign investments, and attitudes of recipient countries.

Index

Belgium 11, 13, 99, 137, 159
bicycle 9, 13, 36, 38, 42, 45, 49–64, 69, 76–7, 79–80, 99, 160, 164, 209, 219–220, 224, 236
bus (also trolleybus) 8–14, 18, 22, 32, 37–9, 51, 54, 62, 86–91, 92–3, 103, 113–114, 127, 135, 139, 141–2, 144–50, 157–8, 160, 162, 165, 169, 186, 209, 219–220, 224, 236

Canada 54, 69–70, 72–8, 174, 176, 179–180, 182, 187, 195–6, 198–211
city planning *see* urban planning
commuter 112, 147, 149, 199, 201, 219, 232, 236, 238
congestion 21, 86–87, 97, 99, 101, 103–104, 111, 113, 147–9, 158, 161–2, 168, 181–2, 187, 190, 195–7, 199–200, 202, 205, 209
Czechoslovakia 122, 125, 127

demand 1, 3, 17, 34–5, 106, 110, 115–6, 136, 138, 141–2, 144–6, 148–51, 161–162, 175–6, 181, 197, 202, 220, 222, 229, 238, 243

fare 63, 100–1, 114, 136, 138–9, 141–2, 145, 208, 219, 222, 231, 235
France 11, 13, 18–20, 42, 45, 54, 62–3., 71, 137, 163–6

Germany 5–6, 14–16, 18, 23–4, 45, 50, 54, 58–9, 62–3, 87, 96, 99, 102, 104, 107–12, 115, 135–7, 148, 159, 220
Great Britain 18, 43, 59, 62, 86–97, 137

ICT 226–7, 232–3, 235–243
India 56, 60, 216–28
infrastructure 2–5, 9–10, 61, 81, 89, 99, 103, 113–16, 132, 138, 143–4, 148–50, 157, 164, 166–7, 181, 195–6, 198, 200, 220, 229, 231
innovation 1, 51, 62, 145, 150, 165, 180
intermodal 21, 23, 148–9, 151
Italy 62–3, 120, 137, 162–3

Japan 13, 51, 53, 59–60, 86, 97–104

modal split 12, 14, 20, 24, 62, 114

Netherlands 9–11, 13–14, 58–9, 231

parking 107, 110–111, 114, 161, 167, 178, 186–7.
pedestrian 5–6, 68–9, 70, 75, 78–80, 109, 122, 127, 143, 149, 178–9, 188–9, 209, 220

railroad/railway 8–9, 10–25, 32, 35–7, 41, 46, 86–94, 97, 99–100, 103, 115, 127, 140, 147, 206–7
regulation 3, 9–12, 14, 17–23, 60, 71, 93–4, 104, 114, 179, 184, 187, 195–6, 228

248   *Index*

Spain 45, 135–51
sprawl, urban 6, 110–12, 129, 148,
    182, 195, 220
streetcar 113–4, 126, 155–7
suburbanization 174–7, 182–90
subway (also underground) 87, 89–93,
    102–4, 113–15, 127, 140–1,
    147, 149, 159, 163–6, 204–5
supply 1, 3, 61, 101, 108, 142

tariffs 16, 18, 23–4, 100, 139, 142,
    146, 148, 223
trains 12–3, 18, 32, 36–7, 103, 121,
    148, 206–7, 224, 235, 241–2
tram/tramway 6, 9–11, 17, 53–4, 57,
    86, 87–94, 96, 99–104, 113–4,

    120, 127, 135–45, 147–50,
    156–9, 162–9, 236
trolleybus *see* bus
truck 8–9, 11, 13–20, 22–5, 74, 78,
    99, 158, 199–200, 207

underground *see* subway
United States 5, 11–13, 15, 17, 20–1,
    23, 49, 51–2, 54–5, 59, 65, 91,
    96, 110–14, 135–6, 142, 148,
    157–8, 162, 164, 174, 176
urban planning (also city planning) 5,
    99, 106–11, 113, 120, 125,
    129, 131, 168, 175, 177–9,
    183–4, 186–9, 195–7, 199,
    201, 210